LEGAL AND ILLEGAL IMMIGRATION

ISSN 2327-9168

71

LEGAL AND ILLEGAL IMMIGRATION

Mark Lane

INFORMATION PLUS® REFERENCE SERIES
Formerly Published by Information Plus, Wylie, Texas

GALE
CENGAGE Learning·

Farmington Hills, Mich • San Francisco • New York • Waterville, Maine
Meriden, Conn • Mason, Ohio • Chicago

GALE
CENGAGE Learning®

Legal and Illegal Immigration

Mark Lane

Kepos Media, Inc.: Steven Long and Janice Jorgensen, Series Editors

Project Editors: Tracie Moy, Laura Avery

Rights Acquisition and Management: Ashley Maynard, Amanda Kopczynski

Composition: Evi Abou-El-Seoud, Mary Beth Trimper

Manufacturing: Rita Wimberley

Product Design: Kristine Julien

For product information and technology assistance, contact us at **Gale Customer Support, 1-800-877-4253.** For permission to use material from this text or product, submit all requests online at **www.cengage.com/permissions.** Further permissions questions can be e-mailed to **permissionrequest@cengage.com**

Cover photograph: © Konstantin L/Shutterstock.com.

Gale
27500 Drake Rd.
Farmington Hills, MI 48331-3535

ISBN-13: 978-0-7876-5103-9 (set)
ISBN-13: 978-1-57302-647-5

ISSN 2327-9168

This title is also available as an e-book.
ISBN-13: 978-1-57302-675-8 (set)
Contact your Gale sales representative for ordering information.

Printed in the United States of America
1 2 3 4 5   19 18 17 16 15

TABLE OF CONTENTS

PREFACE

Legal and Illegal Immigration is part of the *Information Plus Reference Series*. The purpose of each volume of the series is to present the latest facts on a topic of pressing concern in modern American life. These topics include the most controversial and studied social issues of the 21st century: abortion, animal rights, capital punishment, crime, the environment, health care, national security, race and ethnicity, social welfare, water, women, youth, and many more. Although this series is written especially for high school and undergraduate students, it is an excellent resource for anyone in need of factual information on current affairs.

By presenting the facts, it is the intention of Gale, Cengage Learning, to provide its readers with everything they need to reach an informed opinion on current issues. To that end, there is a particular emphasis in this series on the presentation of scientific studies, surveys, and statistics. These data are generally presented in the form of tables, charts, and other graphics placed within the text of each book. Every graphic is directly referred to and carefully explained in the text. The source of each graphic is presented within the graphic itself. The data used in these graphics are drawn from the most reputable and reliable sources, such as from the various branches of the U.S. government and from private organizations and associations. Every effort has been made to secure the most recent information available. Readers should bear in mind that many major studies take years to conduct and that additional years often pass before the data from these studies are made available to the public. Therefore, in many cases the most recent information available in 2015 is dated from 2012 or 2013. Older statistics are sometimes presented as well, if they are landmark studies or of particular interest and no more-recent information exists.

Although statistics are a major focus of the *Information Plus Reference Series*, they are by no means its only content. Each book also presents the widely held positions and important ideas that shape how the book's subject is discussed in the United States. These positions are explained in detail and, where possible, in the words of their proponents. Some of the other material to be found in these books includes historical background, descriptions of major events related to the subject, relevant laws and court cases, and examples of how these issues play out in American life. Some books also feature primary documents or have pro and con debate sections that provide the words and opinions of prominent Americans on both sides of a controversial topic. All material is presented in an evenhanded and unbiased manner; readers will never be encouraged to accept one view of an issue over another.

HOW TO USE THIS BOOK

The United States is known as a melting pot, a place where people of different nationalities, cultures, ethnicities, and races have come together to form one nation. This process has been shaped by both legal and illegal immigration, and American attitudes toward immigrants have varied over time. Whether in the country legally or not, immigrants have faced discrimination based on prevailing social and political trends. For example, unprecedented immigration from Mexico, much of it illegal, began dramatically reshaping the United States in the latter decades of the 20th century. The resulting anxieties and cultural tensions not only shaped the lives of immigrants but also had major policy implications well into the 21st century. This book discusses these and other legal, social, and political aspects of immigration.

Legal and Illegal Immigration consists of nine chapters and five appendixes. Each chapter is devoted to a particular aspect of immigration in the United States. For a summary of the information that is covered in each chapter, please see the synopses that are provided in the Table of Contents. Chapters generally begin with an overview of the basic facts and background information on the chapter's topic, then proceed to examine subtopics of particular interest. For example, Chapter 5, Illegal Immigration, begins with a discussion of the constraints on legal immigration to the United States that contribute to the phenomenon of illegal immigration, and then it presents estimates of the size and characteristics of the unauthorized immigrant population. The chapter then details the responses of the federal and state governments to the many security and humanitarian issues that arise as a result of illegal immigration. Readers can find their way through a chapter by looking for the section and subsection headings, which are clearly set off from the text. They can also refer to the book's extensive Index, if they already know what they are looking for.

Statistical Information

The tables and figures featured throughout *Legal and Illegal Immigration* will be of particular use to readers in learning about this topic. These tables and figures represent an extensive collection of the most recent and valuable statistics on the subject—for example, graphics cover the number of immigrant children adopted by U.S. citizens, the percentage of native-born and foreign-born workers employed in various industries, population projections by nativity, and the costs of maintaining the immigration status quo versus the benefits of comprehensive immigration reform. Gale, Cengage Learning, believes that making this information available to readers is the most important way to fulfill the goal of this book: to help readers understand the issues and controversies surrounding immigration and unauthorized immigrants in the United States and to reach their own conclusions.

Each table or figure has a unique identifier appearing above it for ease of identification and reference. Titles for the tables and figures explain their purpose. At the end of each table or figure, the original source of the data is provided.

To help readers understand these often complicated statistics, all tables and figures are explained in the text. References in the text direct readers to the relevant statistics. Furthermore, the contents of all tables and figures are fully indexed. Please see the opening section of the Index at the back of this volume for a description of how to find tables and figures within it.

Appendixes

Besides the main body text and images, *Legal and Illegal Immigration* has five appendixes. The first is a reproduction of a pamphlet published by the U.S. Department of Justice titled "Federal Protections against National Origin Discrimination—U.S. Department of Justice: Potential Discrimination against Immigrants Based on National Origin." The second appendix features maps of the world to assist readers in pinpointing the places of birth of the United States' immigrant population. The third is the Important Names and Addresses directory. Here, readers will find contact information for a number of government and private organizations that can provide further information on aspects of immigration and unauthorized immigrants. The fourth appendix is the Resources section, which can also assist readers in conducting their own research. In this section the author and editors of *Legal and Illegal Immigration* describe some of the sources that were most useful during the compilation of this book. The final appendix is the Index. It has been greatly expanded from previous editions and should make it even easier to find specific topics in this book.

COMMENTS AND SUGGESTIONS

The editors of the *Information Plus Reference Series* welcome your feedback on *Legal and Illegal Immigration*. Please direct all correspondence to:

Editors
Information Plus Reference Series
27500 Drake Rd.
Farmington Hills, MI 48331-3535

CHAPTER 1
IMMIGRATION IN THE UNITED STATES FROM THE COLONIAL PERIOD TO 1980

The United States has always been a land of immigrants. The nation was founded by people from other countries seeking free choice of worship and new opportunities, and as it grew it was populated to a large degree by those escaping from cruel governments elsewhere or seeking relief from war, famine, or poverty. All came with dreams of a better life for themselves and their families. In spite of the diverse backgrounds, customs, and beliefs of its many immigrant peoples, the United States has accommodated them all, although not without considerable friction along the way.

On the eastern shore of the peninsula that is now Florida, Spanish conquistadors established a settlement in 1565. The city of St. Augustine survived to become the oldest continuously occupied settlement of European origin in North America. It was the northern colonies, however, that expanded rapidly and became central to the development of the nation. In *Immigration: From the Founding of Virginia to the Closing of Ellis Island* (2002), Dennis Wepman chronicles the immigrants who shaped the United States. Not long after English settlers established the first permanent colony on the James River in Virginia in 1607, the French developed a settlement on the St. Lawrence River at what is now Quebec, Canada. Dutch explorers soon built a fur trading post, Fort Nassau, on the Hudson River at what is now Albany, New York. Swedes settled on the Delaware River near present-day Wilmington, Delaware. German Quakers and Mennonites joined William Penn's (1644–1718) experimental Pennsylvania colony. Jewish settlers from Brazil, Protestant Huguenots from France, and Puritans and Catholics from England all came to escape persecution based on their religious beliefs and practices.

During the colonial period many immigrants came as indentured servants bound by contracts requiring them to work for four to seven years to earn back the cost of their passage. To the great aggravation of the colonists, some

were convicts who accepted being shipped across the ocean as an alternative to imprisonment or death. Wepman estimates that as many as 50,000 British felons were sent to the colonies as indentured servants. The first Africans arrived in Jamestown in 1619 as indentured servants, but other Africans were soon brought in chains and sold as slaves.

A continual flow of immigrants provided settlers to develop communities along the Atlantic coast, pioneers to push the United States westward, builders for the Erie Canal and the transcontinental railways, pickers for cotton in the South and vegetables in the Southwest, laborers for U.S. industrialization, and intellectuals in all fields. Together, these immigrants built what is widely considered the most diverse nation in the world.

According to Campbell Gibson and Kay Jung of the U.S. Census Bureau, in *Historical Census Statistics on Population Totals by Race, 1790 to 1990, and by Hispanic Origin, 1970 to 1990, for Large Cities and Other Urban Places in the United States* (February 2005, http://www.census.gov/population/www/documentation/twps0076/twps0076.html), the 1790 census in the United States showed a population of 3.2 million white people and 757,000 black people, of whom about 60,000 were free and the rest slaves. (See Table 1.1.) The white U.S. population was predominantly of English heritage, but also included people of Dutch, French, German, Irish, Scottish, and Spanish descent. Native Americans were not counted.

EARLY ATTITUDES TOWARD IMMIGRANTS

Although immigration was the way of life in the country's first century, negative attitudes began to appear among the already settled English-heritage population. Officially, with the major exception of the Alien and Sedition Acts of 1798, the United States encouraged immigration. The Articles of Confederation, drafted in

TABLE 1.1

Race and Hispanic origin of the U.S. population, 1790–1990

Census year	Total Population	Race White	Race Black	Race American Indian, Eskimo, and Aleut	Race Asian and Pacific Islander	Other race	Hispanic origin (of any race)	White, not of Hispanic origin
Number								
1990	248,709,873	199,686,070.0	29,986,060	1,959,234	7,273,662	9,804,847	22,354,059	188,128,296
Sample	248,709,873	199,827,064.0	29,930,524	2,015,143	7,226,986	9,710,156	21,900,089	188,424,773
1980	226,545,805	188,371,622.0	26,495,025	1,420,400	3,500,439	6,758,319	14,608,673	180,256,366
Sample	226,545,805	189,035,012.0	26,482,349	1,534,336	3,726,440	5,767,668	14,603,683	180,602,838
1970	203,211,926	177,748,975.0	22,580,289	792,730	1,369,412	720,520	(NA)	(NA)
15% sample[a]	203,210,158	178,119,221.0	22,539,362	760,572	1,356,967	434,036	9,589,216	169,023,068
5% sample	203,193,774	178,081,520.0	22,565,377	(NA)	(NA)	(NA)	9,072,602	169,615,394
1960[b]	179,323,175	158,831,732.0	18,871,831	523,591	877,934	218,087	(NA)	(NA)
1960[c]	178,464,236	158,454,956.0	18,860,117	508,675	565,443	75,045	(NA)	(NA)
1950	150,697,361	134,942,028.0	15,042,286	343,410	259,397	110,240	(NA)	(NA)
1940[d]	131,669,275	118,214,870.0	12,865,518	333,969	254,918	(X)	1,858,027	116,356,846
5% sample[d]	(NA)	118,392,040.0	(NA)	(NA)	(NA)	(X)	1,861,400	116,530,640
1930	122,775,046	110,286,740.0	11,891,143	332,397	264,766	(X)	(NA)	(NA)
1920	105,710,620	94,820,915.0	10,463,131	244,437	182,137	(X)	(NA)	(NA)
1910	91,972,266	81,731,957.0	9,827,763	265,683	146,863	(X)	(NA)	(NA)
1900	75,994,575	66,809,196.0	8,833,994	237,196	114,189	(X)	(NA)	(NA)
1890[e]	62,947,714	55,101,258.0	7,488,676	248,253	109,527	(X)	(NA)	(NA)
1890[f]	62,622,250	54,983,890.0	7,470,040	58,806	109,514	(X)	(NA)	(NA)

Census year	Total Population	White	Black	American Indian, Eskimo, and Aleut	Other race	Black Total	Black Free	Black Slave
1880	50,155,783	43,402,970.0	6,580,793	66,407	105,613			
1870	38,558,371	33,589,377.0	4,880,009	25,731	63,254	Total	Free	Slave
1860	31,443,321	26,922,537.0	4,441,830	44,021	34,933	4,441,830	488,070	3,953,760
1850	23,191,876	19,553,068.0	3,638,808	(NA)	(NA)	3,638,808	434,495	3,204,313
1840	17,063,353	14,189,705.0	2,873,648	(NA)	(NA)	2,873,648	386,293	2,487,355
1830	12,860,702	10,532,060.0	2,328,642	(NA)	(NA)	2,328,642	319,599	2,009,043
1820	9,638,453	7,866,797.0	1,771,656	(NA)	(NA)	1,771,656	233,634	1,538,022
1810	7,239,881	5,862,073.0	1,377,808	(NA)	(NA)	1,377,808	186,446	1,191,362
1800	5,308,483	4,306,446.0	1,002,037	(NA)	(NA)	1,002,037	108,435	893,602
1790	3,929,214	3,172,006.0	757,208	(NA)	(NA)	757,208	59,527	697,681

Census year	Total Population	White	Black	American Indian, Eskimo, and Aleut	Asian and Pacific Islander	Other race	Hispanic origin (of any race)	White, not of Hispanic origin
Percent								
1990	100.0	80.3	12.1	0.8	2.9	3.9	9.0	75.6
Sample	100.0	80.3	12.0	0.8	2.9	3.9	8.8	75.8
1980	100.0	83.1	11.7	0.6	1.5	3.0	6.4	79.6
Sample	100.0	83.4	11.7	0.7	1.6	2.5	6.4	79.7
1970	100.0	87.5	11.1	0.4	0.7	0.4	(NA)	(NA)
15% sample[a]	100.0	87.7	11.1	0.4	0.7	0.2	4.7	83.2
5% sample	100.0	87.6	11.1	(NA)	(NA)	(NA)	4.5	83.5
1960[b]	100.0	88.6	10.5	0.3	0.5	0.1	(NA)	(NA)
1960[c]	100.0	88.8	10.6	0.3	0.3	—	(NA)	(NA)
1950	100.0	89.5	10.0	0.2	0.2	0.1	(NA)	(NA)
1940[d]	100.0	89.8	9.8	0.3	0.2	(X)	1.4	88.4
5% sample[d]	(NA)	100.0	(NA)	(NA)	(NA)	(X)	1.4	88.5
1930	100.0	89.8	9.7	0.3	0.2	(X)	(NA)	(NA)
1920	100.0	89.7	9.9	0.2	0.2	(X)	(NA)	(NA)
1910	100.0	88.9	10.7	0.3	0.2	(X)	(NA)	(NA)
1900	100.0	87.9	11.6	0.3	0.2	(X)	(NA)	(NA)
1890[e]	100.0	87.5	11.9	0.4	0.2	(X)	(NA)	(NA)
1890[f]	100.0	87.8	11.9	0.1	0.2	(X)	(NA)	(NA)

Census year	Total Population	White	Black	American Indian, Eskimo, and Aleut	Asian and Pacific Islander	Black Total	Black Free	Black Slave
1880	100.0	86.5	13.1	0.1	0.2			
1870	100.0	87.1	12.7	0.1	0.2	Total	Free	Slave
1860	100.0	85.6	14.1	0.1	0.1	100.0	11.0	89.0
1850	100.0	84.3	15.7	(NA)	(NA)	100.0	11.9	88.1
1840	100.0	83.2	16.8	(NA)	(NA)	100.0	13.4	86.6
1830	100.0	81.9	18.1	(NA)	(NA)	100.0	13.7	86.3
1820	100.0	81.6	18.4	(NA)	(NA)	100.0	13.2	86.8
1810	100.0	81.0	19.0	(NA)	(NA)	100.0	13.5	86.5
1800	100.0	81.1	18.9	(NA)	(NA)	100.0	10.8	89.2
1790	100.0	80.7	19.3	(NA)	(NA)	100.0	7.9	92.1

1777, made anyone who was a citizen of one state a citizen of every other state. The U.S. Constitution, adopted in 1787, made only one direct reference to immigration. Article 1, Section 9, Clause 1 provided that the "Migration or Importation of such Persons as any of the States now existing shall think proper to admit, shall not be prohibited by the Congress prior to the Year one thousand eight hundred and eight, but a Tax or duty may be imposed on such importation, not exceeding ten dollars for each Person." Article 1 also gave Congress power to establish "a uniform rule of naturalization" to grant U.S. citizenship.

(X) = Not applicable.
(NA) = Not available.
^aHispanic origin based on Spanish language.
^bIncludes Alaska and Hawaii.
^cExcludes Alaska and Hawaii.
^dHispanic origin based on the white population of Spanish mother tongue. Percentages shown based on sample data prorated to the 100-percent count of the white population and on the 100-percent count of the total population. These estimates are in italics.
^eIncludes Indian territory and Indian reservations.
^fExcludes Indian territory and Indian reservations.

SOURCE: Campbell Gibson and Kay Jung, "Table A-1. Race and Hispanic Origin for the United States: 1790 to 1990," in *Historical Census Statistics on Population Totals by Race, 1790 to 1990, and by Hispanic Origin, 1970 to 1990, for Large Cities and Other Urban Places in the United States*, U.S. Census Bureau, Population Division, February 2005, http://www.census.gov/population/www/documentation/twps0076/twps0076.pdf (accessed January 6, 2015)

Alien and Sedition Acts

Early federal legislation established basic criteria for naturalization: five years' residence in the United States, good moral character, and loyalty to the U.S. Constitution. These requirements were based on state naturalization laws. In 1798 the Federalist-controlled Congress proposed four laws, collectively called the Alien and Sedition Acts:

- The Naturalization Act lengthened the residence requirement for naturalization from five to 14 years.

- The Alien Act authorized the president to arrest and/or expel allegedly dangerous aliens (noncitizens).

- The Alien Enemies Act allowed the imprisonment or deportation of aliens who were subjects of an enemy nation during wartime.

- The Sedition Act authorized fines and imprisonment for acts of treason, by immigrants or citizens, including "any false, scandalous and malicious writing."

The Sedition Act was used by the Federalist administration of President John Adams (1735–1826) to arrest and silence a number of newspaper editors who publicly opposed the new laws. The strong public outcry against the Alien and Sedition Acts was partly responsible for the election of Thomas Jefferson (1743–1826), the Democratic-Republican presidential candidate, in 1800. Jefferson pardoned the individuals who had been convicted under the Sedition Act. The Naturalization Act was repealed by Congress in 1802, and the other three laws were allowed to lapse.

THE FIRST CENTURY OF IMMIGRATION

During the early 1800s U.S. territory more than doubled in size with the addition of 828,000 square miles (2.1 million square kilometers) of land with the Louisiana Purchase. Reports of rich farmland and virgin forests provided by explorers such as Meriwether Lewis (1774–1809) and William Clark (1770–1838) enticed Europeans

from all walks of life—farmers, craftsmen, merchants, miners, laborers, and wealthy investors—to leave Europe for the land of opportunity. The U.S. Department of Homeland Security's Office of Immigration Statistics reports in *2013 Yearbook of Immigration Statistics* (2014, http://www.dhs.gov/yearbook-immigration-statistics) that in 1820, the first year immigration records were kept, only 8,385 immigrants were granted legal permanent residence in the United States. (See Table 1.2.) The number rose slowly at first and then more rapidly, with substantial year-to-year variations. In 1828, for example, 27,382 immigrants were granted legal permanent residence, and then between 1829 and 1831 the totals fluctuated between 22,000 and 23,500 annually, before jumping to 60,482 in 1832.

Wave of Irish and German Immigration

Europe experienced a population explosion during the 1800s. As land in Europe became more and more scarce, tenant farmers were pushed off their farms and forced into poverty. Some of these farmers immigrated to the United States to start a new life. This situation was made worse in Ireland when a fungus that caused potato crops to rot struck in 1845. Many poor Irish farmers depended on potatoes for food. They suffered greatly from famine, and epidemics of cholera and typhoid spread among the malnourished populace from village to village. The potato famine forced people to choose between starving to death and leaving their country. In the 10-year period between 1830 and 1839, 170,672 Irish immigrants arrived in the United States. (See Table 1.3.) Driven by the potato famine, the number of Irish immigrants rose to 656,145 between 1840 and 1849, an increase of 284%. The flow of emigrants from Ireland to the United States peaked at a little over 1 million during the 1850s.

Increasing numbers of German immigrants, who were affected by a potato famine as well as by failed political revolutions, also came to the United States in

TABLE 1.2

Immigrants granted lawful permanent resident status, fiscal years 1820–2013

Year	Number	Year	Number	Year	Number	Year	Number
1820	8,385	1869	352,768	1918	110,618	1967	361,972
1821	9,127	1870	387,203	1919	141,132	1968	454,448
1822	6,911	1871	321,350	1920	430,001	1969	358,579
1823	6,354	1872	404,806	1921	805,228	1970	373,326
1824	7,912	1873	459,803	1922	309,556	1971	370,478
1825	10,199	1874	313,339	1923	522,919	1972	384,685
1826	10,837	1875	227,498	1924	706,896	1973	398,515
1827	18,875	1876	169,986	1925	294,314	1974	393,919
1828	27,382	1877	141,857	1926	304,488	1975	385,378
1829	22,520	1878	138,469	1927	335,175	1976*	499,093
1830	23,322	1879	177,826	1928	307,255	1977	458,755
1831	22,633	1880	457,257	1929	279,678	1978	589,810
1832	60,482	1881	669,431	1930	241,700	1979	394,244
1833	58,640	1882	788,992	1931	97,139	1980	524,295
1834	65,365	1883	603,322	1932	35,576	1981	595,014
1835	45,374	1884	518,592	1933	23,068	1982	533,624
1836	76,242	1885	395,346	1934	29,470	1983	550,052
1837	79,340	1886	334,203	1935	34,956	1984	541,811
1838	38,914	1887	490,109	1936	36,329	1985	568,149
1839	68,069	1888	546,889	1937	50,244	1986	600,027
1840	84,066	1889	444,427	1938	67,895	1987	599,889
1841	80,289	1890	455,302	1939	82,998	1988	641,346
1842	104,565	1891	560,319	1940	70,756	1989	1,090,172
1843	52,496	1892	579,663	1941	51,776	1990	1,535,872
1844	78,615	1893	439,730	1942	28,781	1991	1,826,595
1845	114,371	1894	285,631	1943	23,725	1992	973,445
1846	154,416	1895	258,536	1944	28,551	1993	903,916
1847	234,968	1896	343,267	1945	38,119	1994	803,993
1848	226,527	1897	230,832	1946	108,721	1995	720,177
1849	297,024	1898	229,299	1947	147,292	1996	915,560
1850	369,980	1899	311,715	1948	170,570	1997	797,847
1851	379,466	1900	448,572	1949	188,317	1998	653,206
1852	371,603	1901	487,918	1950	249,187	1999	644,787
1853	368,645	1902	648,743	1951	205,717	2000	841,002
1854	427,833	1903	857,046	1952	265,520	2001	1,058,902
1855	200,877	1904	812,870	1953	170,434	2002	1,059,356
1856	200,436	1905	1,026,499	1954	208,177	2003	703,542
1857	251,306	1906	1,100,735	1955	237,790	2004	957,883
1858	123,126	1907	1,285,349	1956	321,625	2005	1,122,257
1859	121,282	1908	782,870	1957	326,867	2006	1,266,129
1860	153,640	1909	751,786	1958	253,265	2007	1,052,415
1861	91,918	1910	1,041,570	1959	260,686	2008	1,107,126
1862	91,985	1911	878,587	1960	265,398	2009	1,130,818
1863	176,282	1912	838,172	1961	271,344	2010	1,042,625
1864	193,418	1913	1,197,892	1962	283,763	2011	1,062,040
1865	248,120	1914	1,218,480	1963	306,260	2012	1,031,631
1866	318,568	1915	326,700	1964	292,248	2013	990,553
1867	315,722	1916	298,826	1965	296,697		
1868	138,840	1917	295,403	1966	323,040		

*Includes the 15 months from July 1, 1975 to September 30, 1976 because the end date of fiscal years was changed from June 30 to September 30.

SOURCE: "Table 1. Persons Obtaining Lawful Permanent Resident Status: Fiscal Years 1820 to 2013," in *Yearbook of Immigration Statistics: 2013*, U.S. Department of Homeland Security, Office of Immigration Statistics, October 2014, http://www.dhs.gov/sites/default/files/publications/immigration-statistics/yearbook/2013/LPR/table1.xls (accessed January 6, 2015)

large numbers. Between 1850 and 1859 the number of German immigrants (976,072) approached that of Irish immigrants. (See Table 1.3.) The influx of Germans peaked at 1.4 million immigrants between 1880 and 1889.

Immigration, Politics, and the Civil War

This new wave of immigration led to intense anti-Irish, anti-German, and anti-Catholic sentiments among Americans, even among those whose families had been in the United States for only a few generations. It also triggered the creation of secret nativist societies (groups professing to protect the interests of the native born

against immigrants). Out of these groups grew a new political party, the Know Nothing movement (later known as the American Party), which claimed to support the rights of Protestant, U.S.-born voters. The American Party won 75 seats in Congress and six governorships in 1855 before it dissolved.

In contrast to the nativists, the Republican Party was welcoming to immigrants. The "Republican Party Platform of 1864" (http://www.presidency.ucsb.edu/ws/index.php?pid=29621), which was written in part by Abraham Lincoln (1809–1865), stated, "Resolved, That

TABLE 1.3

Immigrants granted lawful permanent resident status, by region and selected country of last residence, fiscal years 1820–2013

Region and country of last residence[a]	1820 to 1829	1830 to 1839	1840 to 1849	1850 to 1859	1860 to 1869	1870 to 1879	1880 to 1889	1890 to 1899	1900 to 1909	1910 to 1919	1920 to 1929	1930 to 1939
Total	128,502	538,381	1,427,337	2,814,554	2,081,261	2,742,137	5,248,558	3,694,294	8,202,388	6,347,380	4,295,510	699,375
Europe	99,618	422,853	1,369,423	2,622,617	1,880,389	2,252,050	4,638,684	3,576,411	7,572,569	4,985,411	2,560,340	444,404
Austria-Hungary[b, c]	—	—	—	—	3,375	60,127	314,787	534,059	2,001,376	1,154,727	60,891	13,902
Austria[b, c]	—	—	—	—	2,700	54,529	204,805	268,218	532,416	589,174	31,392	6,678
Hungary[b, c]	—	—	—	—	483	5,598	109,982	203,350	685,567	565,553	29,499	7,224
Belgium	28	20	3,996	5,765	5,785	6,991	18,738	19,642	37,429	32,574	21,511	4,013
Bulgaria[d]	—	—	—	—	—	—	—	52	34,651	27,180	2,824	1,062
Czechoslovakia[e]	—	—	—	—	—	—	—	—	—	—	101,182	17,757
Denmark	173	927	671	3,227	13,553	29,278	85,342	56,671	61,227	45,830	34,406	3,470
Finland[f]	—	—	—	—	3	286	9,617	36,719	—	—	16,922	2,438
France	7,694	39,330	75,300	81,778	35,938	71,901	48,193	35,616	67,735	60,335	54,842	13,761
Germany[c]	5,753	124,726	385,434	976,072	723,734	751,769	1,445,181	579,072	328,722	174,227	386,634	117,736
Greece	17	49	17	32	51	209	1,807	12,732	145,402	198,108	60,774	10,599
Ireland[g]	51,617	170,672	656,145	1,029,486	427,419	422,264	674,061	405,710	344,940	166,445	201,644	28,195
Italy	430	2,225	1,476	8,643	9,853	46,296	267,660	603,761	1,930,475	1,229,916	528,133	85,053
Netherlands	1,105	1,377	7,624	11,122	8,387	14,267	52,715	29,349	42,463	46,065	29,397	7,791
Norway-Sweden[h]	91	1,149	12,389	22,202	82,937	178,823	586,441	334,058	426,981	192,445	170,329	13,452
Norway[h]	—	—	—	—	—	88,644	185,111	96,810	182,542	79,488	70,327	6,901
Sweden[h]	—	—	—	—	—	90,179	401,330	237,248	244,439	112,957	100,002	6,551
Poland[c]	19	366	105	1,087	1,886	11,016	42,910	107,793	—	—	224,420	26,460
Portugal[i]	252	896	359	4,218	4,741	13,990	15,189	25,874	65,154	82,489	44,829	3,518
Romania	—	—	—	—	—	—	5,842	6,808	57,322	13,566	67,810	5,264
Russia[c, f, j]	86	280	520	423	1,667	34,977	173,081	413,382	1,501,301	1,106,998	61,604	2,473
Spain	2,866	2,016	1,917	8,803	6,970	5,571	3,999	9,189	24,818	53,262	47,109	3,669
Switzerland	3,148	4,430	4,819	24,423	21,124	25,212	81,151	37,020	32,541	22,839	31,772	5,990
United Kingdom[k]	26,336	74,350	218,572	445,322	532,956	578,447	810,900	328,759	469,518	371,878	342,762	61,813
Yugoslavia[l]	—	—	—	—	—	—	—	—	—	—	49,215	6,920
Other Europe	3	40	79	14	10	626	1,070	145	514	6,527	21,330	9,068
Asia	34	55	121	36,080	54,408	134,071	71,152	61,304	300,441	269,736	126,740	19,292
China	3	8	32	35,933	54,028	133,139	65,797	15,268	19,884	20,916	30,648	5,874
Hong Kong	—	—	—	—	—	—	—	—	—	—	—	—
India	9	38	33	42	50	166	247	102	3,026	3,478	2,076	554
Iran	—	—	7	—	4	17	18	26	—	—	208	198
Israel	—	—	—	—	—	—	—	—	—	—	—	—
Japan	—	—	—	—	138	193	1,583	13,998	139,712	77,125	42,057	2,683
Jordan	—	—	—	—	—	—	—	—	—	—	—	—
Korea[m]	—	—	—	—	—	—	—	—	—	—	—	—
Philippines	—	—	—	—	—	4	1	19	605	—	—	457
Syria[n]	—	—	—	—	2	7	140	—	—	—	5,307	—
Taiwan	—	—	—	—	—	—	—	—	—	—	—	2,188
Turkey	19	8	45	94	129	382	2,478	27,510	127,999	160,717	40,374	1,314
Vietnam	—	—	—	—	—	—	—	—	—	—	—	—
Other Asia	3	1	4	11	57	163	888	4,381	9,215	7,500	6,070	6,024
America	9,656	31,911	50,527	84,201	130,427	345,889	529,845	38,756	277,882	1,070,539	1,591,278	230,319
Canada and Newfoundland[o, p, q]	2,297	11,875	34,285	64,171	117,975	323,974	492,508	2,668	123,067	708,715	949,286	162,703
Mexico[p, q]	3,835	7,187	3,069	3,446	1,957	5,133	2,405	734	31,188	185,334	498,945	32,709
Caribbean	3,061	11,792	11,803	12,447	8,809	14,592	27,600	31,885	100,960	120,860	83,482	18,052
Cuba	—	—	—	—	3,420	8,705	20,134	23,669	—	—	12,769	10,641
Dominican Republic	—	—	—	—	78	149	124	101	—	—	—	1,165
Haiti	—	—	—	—	61	257	355	223	—	—	—	207
Jamaica[i]	—	—	—	—	—	—	—	—	—	—	—	—
Other Caribbean[f]	3,061	11,792	11,803	12,447	5,250	5,481	6,987	7,892	100,960	120,860	70,713	6,039

TABLE 1.3

Immigrants granted lawful permanent resident status, by region and selected country of last residence, fiscal years 1820–2013 [CONTINUED]

Region and country of last residence[a]	1820 to 1829	1830 to 1839	1840 to 1849	1850 to 1859	1860 to 1869	1870 to 1879	1880 to 1889	1890 to 1899	1900 to 1909	1910 to 1919	1920 to 1929	1930 to 1939
Central America	57	94	297	512	70	202	359	674	7,341	15,692	16,511	6,840
Belize	—	—	—	—	9	26	80	25	583	40	285	193
Costa Rica	—	—	—	—	2	4	1	4	—	—	—	580
El Salvador	—	—	—	—	—	3	—	7	—	—	—	712
Guatemala	—	—	—	—	1	10	3	9	—	—	—	632
Honduras	—	—	—	—	—	11	4	4	—	—	—	809
Nicaragua	—	—	—	—	—	1	1	3	—	—	—	564
Panama[g]	—	—	—	—	—	—	—	—	—	—	—	1,774
Other Central America	57	94	297	512	58	147	270	622	6,758	15,652	16,226	1,576
South America	405	957	1,062	3,569	1,536	1,109	1,954	1,389	15,253	39,938	43,025	9,990
Argentina	—	—	—	—	7	58	64	36	—	—	—	1,397
Bolivia	—	—	—	—	—	5	—	—	—	—	—	77
Brazil	—	—	—	—	32	219	199	92	—	—	4,627	1,468
Chile	—	—	—	—	25	92	44	66	—	—	—	568
Colombia	—	—	—	—	2	196	1,210	607	—	—	—	1,278
Ecuador	—	—	—	—	—	7	14	33	—	—	—	320
Guyana	—	—	—	—	41	95	68	27	—	—	—	193
Paraguay	—	—	—	—	—	2	—	—	—	—	—	36
Peru	—	—	—	—	35	127	25	79	—	—	—	460
Suriname	—	—	—	—	—	2	—	—	—	—	—	33
Uruguay	—	—	—	—	—	22	4	144	—	—	—	153
Venezuela	—	—	—	—	36	190	248	—	—	—	—	1,360
Other South America	405	957	1,062	3,569	1,358	96	78	305	15,253	39,938	38,398	2,647
Other America	1	6	11	56	80	879	5,019	1,406	73	—	29	25
Africa	19	66	67	104	458	441	768	432	6,326	8,867	6,362	2,120
Egypt	—	—	—	5	8	29	145	51	—	—	1,063	781
Ethiopia	—	—	—	—	—	—	—	—	—	—	—	10
Liberia	1	8	5	7	43	52	21	9	—	—	—	35
Morocco	—	4	1	—	—	15	12	9	—	—	—	110
South Africa	—	—	—	—	79	48	23	9	—	—	—	312
Other Africa	18	54	61	92	328	297	567	354	6,326	8,867	5,299	872
Oceania	2	1	3	110	107	9,094	7,341	3,279	11,677	12,339	9,860	3,240
Australia	2	1	2	104	96	8,933	7,250	3,098	11,191	11,280	8,404	2,260
New Zealand[f]	—	—	—	—	6	39	21	12	—	—	935	790
Other Oceania	—	—	1	4	5	122	70	169	486	1,059	521	190
Not Specified[h]	19,173	83,495	7,196	71,442	15,472	592	778	14,112	33,493	488	930	—

Region and country of last residence[a]	1940 to 1949	1950 to 1959	1960 to 1969	1970 to 1979	1980 to 1989	1990 to 1999	2000 to 2009	2010	2011	2012	2013
Total	856,608	2,499,268	3,213,749	4,248,203	6,244,379	9,775,398	10,299,430	1,042,625	1,062,040	1,031,631	990,553
Europe	472,524	1,404,973	1,133,443	826,327	669,694	1,349,219	1,349,609	95,429	90,712	86,956	91,095
Austria-Hungary[b,c]	13,677	113,015	27,590	20,387	20,437	27,529	33,929	4,325	4,703	3,208	2,061
Austria[b,c]	8,496	81,354	17,571	14,239	15,374	18,234	21,151	3,319	3,654	2,199	1,053
Hungary[b,c]	5,181	31,661	10,019	6,148	5,063	9,295	12,778	1,006	1,049	1,009	1,008
Belgium	12,473	18,885	9,647	5,413	7,028	7,077	8,157	732	700	698	803
Bulgaria[d]	449	97	598	1,011	1,124	16,948	40,003	2,465	2,549	2,322	2,720
Czechoslovakia[e]	8,475	1,624	2,758	5,654	5,678	8,970	18,691	1,510	1,374	1,316	1,258
Denmark	4,549	10,918	9,797	4,405	4,847	6,189	6,049	545	473	492	546
Finland[f]	2,230	4,923	4,310	2,829	2,569	3,970	3,970	414	398	373	360
France[f]	36,954	50,113	46,975	27,018	32,894	36,552	45,637	4,339	3,967	4,201	4,668
Germany[c]	119,403	576,905	209,616	77,142	85,752	92,207	122,373	7,929	7,072	6,732	6,880

TABLE 1.3

Immigrants granted lawful permanent resident status, by region and selected country of last residence, fiscal years 1820–2013 [CONTINUED]

Region and country of last residence[a]	1940 to 1949	1950 to 1959	1960 to 1969	1970 to 1979	1980 to 1989	1990 to 1999	2000 to 2009	2010	2011	2012	2013
Greece	8,605	45,153	74,173	102,370	37,729	25,403	16,841	966	1,196	1,264	1,526
Ireland[b]	15,701	47,189	37,788	11,461	22,210	65,384	15,642	1,610	1,533	1,694	1,765
Italy	50,509	189,061	200,111	150,031	55,562	75,992	28,329	2,956	2,670	2,946	3,233
Netherlands	13,877	46,703	37,918	10,373	11,234	13,345	17,351	1,520	1,258	1,294	1,376
Norway-Sweden[h]	17,326	44,231	36,150	10,298	13,941	17,825	19,382	1,662	1,530	1,441	1,665
Norway[h]	8,326	22,813	17,371	3,927	3,835	5,211	4,599	363	405	314	389
Sweden[h]	9,000	21,418	18,779	6,371	10,106	12,614	14,783	1,299	1,125	1,127	1,276
Poland[c]	7,774	6,498	55,773	33,699	63,483	172,249	117,921	7,391	6,634	6,024	6,073
Portugal[i]	6,765	13,928	70,568	104,754	42,685	25,497	11,479	759	878	837	917
Romania	1,254	914	2,339	10,774	24,753	48,136	52,154	3,735	3,679	3,477	3,475
Russia[c,f,j]	605	453	2,329	28,132	33,311	433,427	167,152	7,502	8,548	10,114	10,154
Spain	2,774	6,880	40,793	41,718	22,783	18,443	17,695	2,040	2,319	2,316	2,970
Switzerland	9,904	17,577	19,193	8,536	8,316	11,768	12,173	868	861	916	1,040
United Kingdom[k]	131,794	195,709	220,213	133,218	153,644	156,182	171,979	14,781	13,443	13,938	15,321
Yugoslavia[l]	2,039	6,966	17,990	31,862	16,267	57,039	131,831	4,772	4,611	4,488	4,445
Other Europe	5,387	7,231	6,814	5,242	3,447	29,087	290,871	22,608	20,316	16,865	17,839
Asia	34,532	135,844	358,563	1,406,526	2,391,356	2,859,899	3,470,835	410,209	438,580	416,488	389,301
China	16,072	8,836	14,060	17,627	170,897	342,058	591,711	67,634	83,603	78,184	68,410
Hong Kong	—	13,781	67,047	117,350	112,132	116,894	57,583	3,263	3,149	2,642	2,614
India	1,692	1,922	18,638	148,018	231,649	352,528	590,464	66,185	66,331	63,320	65,506
Iran	1,144	3,195	9,059	33,763	98,141	76,899	76,755	9,078	9,015	8,955	9,658
Israel	98	21,376	30,911	36,306	43,669	41,340	54,081	5,172	4,389	4,640	4,555
Japan	1,557	41,968	40,956	52,812	44,150	66,582	84,552	7,100	6,751	6,581	6,383
Jordan	3	4,919	9,230	25,541	28,928	42,755	53,550	9,327	8,211	7,014	5,949
Korea[m]	83	4,845	27,048	241,192	322,708	179,770	209,758	22,022	22,748	20,802	22,937
Philippines	4,099	17,245	70,660	337,726	502,056	534,338	545,463	56,399	55,251	55,441	52,955
Syria[n]	1,179	1,091	2,432	8,086	14,534	22,906	30,807	7,424	7,983	6,674	3,999
Taiwan	—	721	15,657	83,155	119,051	132,647	92,657	6,785	6,206	5,295	5,336
Turkey	754	2,980	9,464	12,209	19,208	38,687	48,394	7,435	9,040	7,362	7,189
Vietnam	—	290	2,949	121,716	200,632	275,379	289,616	30,065	33,486	27,578	26,578
Other Asia	7,851	12,675	40,452	171,025	483,601	637,116	745,444	112,320	122,417	122,000	107,232
America	328,435	921,644	1,674,185	1,903,636	2,694,504	5,137,142	4,441,529	426,981	423,277	409,664	399,380
Canada and Newfoundland[b,p,q]	160,911	353,169	433,128	179,267	156,313	194,788	236,349	19,491	19,506	20,138	20,489
Mexico[o,q]	56,158	273,847	441,824	621,218	1,009,586	2,757,418	1,704,166	138,717	142,823	145,326	134,198
Caribbean	46,285	115,869	427,843	708,643	789,343	1,004,114	1,053,357	139,389	133,012	126,615	121,349
Cuba	25,976	73,221	202,030	256,497	132,552	159,037	271,742	33,372	36,261	32,551	31,343
Dominican Republic	4,802	10,219	83,552	139,249	221,552	359,818	291,492	53,890	46,036	41,535	41,487
Haiti	823	3,787	28,992	55,166	121,406	177,446	203,827	22,336	21,802	22,446	20,083
Jamaica[i]	—	7,397	62,218	130,226	193,874	177,143	172,523	19,439	19,298	20,300	19,052
Other Caribbean[i]	14,684	21,245	51,051	127,505	119,959	130,670	113,773	10,352	9,615	9,783	9,384
Central America	20,135	40,201	98,569	120,376	339,376	610,189	591,130	43,597	43,249	39,837	44,056
Belize	433	1,133	4,185	6,747	14,964	12,600	9,682	997	933	875	969
Costa Rica	1,965	4,044	17,975	12,405	25,017	17,054	21,571	2,306	2,230	2,152	2,232
El Salvador	4,885	5,094	14,405	29,428	137,418	273,017	251,237	18,547	18,477	15,874	18,015
Guatemala	1,303	4,197	14,357	23,837	58,847	126,043	156,992	10,263	10,795	9,857	9,829
Honduras	1,874	5,320	15,087	15,653	39,071	72,880	63,513	6,381	6,053	6,773	8,795
Nicaragua	4,393	7,812	10,383	10,911	31,102	80,446	70,015	3,476	3,314	2,943	2,940
Panama[s]	5,282	12,601	22,177	21,395	32,957	28,149	18,120	1,627	1,447	1,363	1,276
Other Central America	—	—	—	—	—	—	—	—	—	—	—
South America	19,662	78,418	250,754	273,529	399,803	570,596	856,508	85,783	84,687	77,748	79,287
Argentina	3,108	16,346	49,384	30,303	23,442	30,065	47,955	4,312	4,335	4,218	4,227
Bolivia	893	2,759	6,205	5,635	9,798	18,111	21,921	2,211	2,113	1,920	2,005
Brazil	3,653	11,547	29,238	18,600	22,944	50,744	115,404	12,057	11,643	11,248	10,772

TABLE 1.3

Immigrants granted lawful permanent resident status, by region and selected country of last residence, fiscal years 1820–2013 [CONTINUED]

Region and country of last residence[a]	1940 to 1949	1950 to 1959	1960 to 1969	1970 to 1979	1980 to 1989	1990 to 1999	2000 to 2009	2010	2011	2012	2013
Chile	1,320	4,669	12,384	15,032	19,749	18,200	19,792	1,940	1,854	1,628	1,751
Colombia	3,454	15,567	68,371	71,265	105,494	137,985	236,570	21,861	22,130	20,272	20,611
Ecuador	2,207	8,574	34,107	47,464	48,015	81,358	107,977	11,463	11,068	9,284	10,553
Guyana	596	1,131	4,546	38,278	85,886	74,407	70,373	6,441	6,288	5,282	5,564
Paraguay	85	576	1,249	1,486	3,518	6,082	4,623	449	501	454	437
Peru	1,273	5,980	19,783	25,311	49,958	110,117	137,614	14,063	13,836	12,414	12,370
Suriname	130	299	612	714	1,357	2,285	2,363	202	167	216	170
Uruguay	754	1,026	4,089	8,416	7,235	6,062	9,827	1,286	1,521	1,348	1,314
Venezuela	2,182	9,927	20,758	11,007	22,405	35,180	82,087	9,497	9,229	9,464	9,512
Other South America	7	17	28	18	2	—	2	1	2	—	1
Other America	25,284	60,140	22,076	603	83	37	19	4	—	—	1
Africa	6,720	13,016	23,780	71,405	141,987	346,410	759,734	98,246	97,429	103,685	94,589
Egypt	1,613	1,996	5,581	23,543	26,744	44,604	81,564	9,822	9,096	10,172	10,719
Ethiopia	28	302	804	2,588	12,927	40,097	87,207	13,853	13,985	15,400	13,484
Liberia	37	289	841	2,391	6,420	13,587	23,316	2,924	3,117	3,451	3,036
Morocco	1,463	3,293	2,880	1,967	3,471	15,768	40,844	4,847	4,249	3,534	3,202
South Africa	1,022	2,278	4,360	10,002	15,505	21,964	32,221	2,705	2,754	2,960	2,693
Other Africa	2,557	4,858	9,314	30,914	76,920	210,390	494,582	64,095	64,228	68,168	61,455
Oceania	14,262	11,319	23,659	39,983	41,432	56,800	65,793	5,946	5,825	5,573	6,061
Australia	11,201	8,275	14,986	18,708	16,901	24,288	32,728	3,077	3,062	3,146	3,529
New Zealand[t]	2,351	1,799	3,775	5,018	6,129	8,600	12,495	1,046	1,006	980	1,027
Other Oceania	710	1,245	4,898	16,257	18,402	23,912	20,570	1,823	1,757	1,447	1,505
Not Specified[u]	135	12,472	119	326	305,406	25,928	211,930	5,814	6,217	9,265	10,127

—Represents zero or not available.

[a]Prior to 1906 refers to country of origin; from 1906 to 2013 refers to country of last residence. Because of changes in country boundaries, data for a particular country may not necessarily refer to the same geographic area over time.

[b]Austria and Hungary not reported separately for all years during 1860 to 1869, 1890 to 1899, and 1900 to 1909.

[c]Poland included in Austria, Germany, Hungary, and Russia from 1899 to 1919.

[d]Bulgaria included Serbia and Montenegro from 1899 to 1919.

[e]Includes Czech Republic, Czechoslovakia (former), and Slovakia.

[f]Finland included in Russia from 1899 to 1919.

[g]Northern Ireland included in Ireland prior to 1925.

[h]Norway and Sweden not reported separately until 1861.

[i]Cape Verde included in Portugal from 1892 to 1952.

[j]Refers to the Russian Empire from 1820 to 1920. Between 1920 and 1990 refers to the Soviet Union. From 1991 to 1999, refers to Russia, Armenia, Azerbaijan, Belarus, Georgia, Kazakhstan, Kyrgyzstan, Moldova, Tajikistan, Turkmenistan, Ukraine, and Uzbekistan. Beginning in 2000, refers to Russia only.

[k]United Kingdom refers to England, Scotland, Wales and Northern Ireland since 1925.

[l]Includes Bosnia-Herzegovina, Croatia, Kosovo, Macedonia, Montenegro, Serbia, Serbia and Montenegro, and Slovenia.

[m]Includes both North and South Korea.

[n]Syria included in Turkey from 1886 to 1923.

[o]Includes British North America and Canadian provinces.

[p]Land arrivals not completely enumerated until 1908.

[q]No data available for Canada or Mexico from 1886 to 1893.

[r]Jamaica included in British West Indies from 1892 to 1952.

[s]Panama Canal Zone included in Panama from 1932 to 1972.

[t]New Zealand included in Australia from 1892 to 1924.

[u]Includes 32,897 persons returning in 1906 to their homes in the United States.

Note: Official recording of immigration to the United States began in 1820 after the passage of the Act of March 2, 1819. From 1820 to 1867, figures represent alien passenger arrivals at seaports; from 1868 to 1891 and 1895 to 1897, immigrant alien arrivals; from 1892 to 1894 and 1898 to 2013, immigrant aliens admitted for permanent residence; from 1892 to 1903, aliens entering by cabin class were not counted as immigrants. Land arrivals were not completely enumerated until 1908. For this table, Fiscal Year 1843 covers 9 months ending September 30, 1843; Fiscal Years 1832 and 1850 cover 15 months ending December 31 of the respective years; and Fiscal Year 1868 covers 6 months ending June 30, 1868; and Fiscal Year 1976 covers 15 months ending September 30, 1976.

SOURCE: "Table 2. Persons Obtaining Lawful Permanent Resident Status by Region and Selected Country of Last Residence: Fiscal Years 1820 to 2013," in Yearbook of Immigration Statistics: 2013, U.S. Department of Homeland Security, Office of Immigration Statistics, October 2014, http://www.dhs.gov/sites/default/files/publications/immigration-statistics/yearbook/2013/LPR/table2.xls (accessed January 6, 2015) foreign immigration, which in the past has added so much to the wealth, development of resources and increase of power to the nation, the asylum of the oppressed of all nations, should be fostered and encouraged by a liberal and just policy."

In 1862 Lincoln signed the Homestead Law, which offered 160 acres (65 hectares) of free land to any adult citizen or prospective citizen who agreed to occupy and improve the land for five years. Wepman notes that between 1862 and 1904 more than 147 million acres (59.5 million hectares) of land were claimed by adventurous citizens and eager new immigrants. Most homestead claims were for land in the West, but homesteaders also took possession of lands in states east of the Mississippi River, including Alabama, Florida, and Wisconsin. In addition, efforts to complete a transcontinental railroad during the 1860s provided work for predominantly Irish and Chinese laborers.

The Civil War (1861–1865) initially restricted the flow of immigrants to the United States, but then growth of the immigrant population returned to prewar levels. As Table 1.2 shows, the number of immigrants granted legal permanent resident status dropped from 153,640 in 1860 to just under 92,000 in both 1861 and 1862, before rising to 176,282 in 1863, 193,418 in 1864, and 248,120 in 1865.

Post–Civil War Growth in Immigration

During the Industrial Revolution, which began in the United States in the early 1800s, factory machines and large-scale manufacturing replaced hand tools and small craft shops. These changes accelerated after the Civil War, fueling the need for workers in the nation's flourishing factories. The number of arriving immigrants averaged about 335,000 annually between 1866 and 1874. (See Table 1.2.) After a short falloff in immigration between 1875 and 1879, the numbers continued their climb during the 1880s. Throughout this period the bulk of the immigrant population came from Germany, Ireland, and the United Kingdom, and the numbers of Canadians immigrating to the United States began to rival these other groups. (See Table 1.3.) Opposition to immigration continued among some factions of established citizens. Secret societies of white supremacists, such as the Ku Klux Klan, formed throughout the South to oppose not only African American suffrage but also the influence of the Roman Catholic Church and rapid naturalization of foreign immigrants.

East European Influx during the 1880s

The decade from 1880 to 1889 marked a new era in immigration to the United States. The volume of immigrants nearly doubled, from 2.7 million in the 1870s to 5.2 million in the 1880s. (See Table 1.3.) German arrivals

peaked, and the numbers arriving from Norway, Sweden, and the United Kingdom also reached their highest levels. At the same time, a new wave of immigrants began to arrive from Russia (including a significant Jewish population fleeing massacres called pogroms), Poland, Austria-Hungary, and Italy. The mass exodus from eastern Europe foretold of events that would result in World War I (1914–1918). These newcomers came from countries with limited public education and, in some cases, less sense of social equality than previous immigrants' countries of origin. They were often unskilled and illiterate. They tended to form tight ethnic communities within large cities, where they maintained their own language and customs, which further limited their ability to assimilate into U.S. culture.

A Developing Federal Role in Immigration

The increasing numbers of immigrants prompted a belief that there should be some type of administrative order to the ever-growing influx. In 1864 Congress created the Commission of Immigration under the U.S. Department of State. A one-person office was set up in New York City to oversee immigration.

The 1870s witnessed a national debate over the importation of contract labor and limiting immigration for such purposes. In 1875, after considerable debate, Congress passed the Page Law. As the first major piece of restrictive immigration legislation, it prohibited alien convicts and prostitutes from entering the country.

With the creation of the Commission of Immigration, the federal government began to play a central role in immigration, which had previously been handled by the individual states. Beginning in 1849 court decisions had strengthened the federal government's role and limited the states' role in regulating immigration. In 1875 the U.S. Supreme Court ultimately ruled in *Henderson v. Mayor of the City of New York* (92 U.S. 259) and *Chy Lung v. Freeman* (92 U.S. 275) that the immigration laws of New York, Louisiana, and California were unconstitutional. This ended the rights of states to regulate immigration and exclude undesirable aliens. Thereafter, the federal government had complete responsibility for immigration.

In 1882 Congress passed the first general immigration law. The Immigration Act of 1882 established a centralized immigration administration under the U.S. secretary of the treasury. The law also allowed the exclusion of "undesirables," such as paupers, criminals, and the insane. A head tax was added at $0.50 per arriving immigrant to defray the expenses of immigration regulation and caring for the immigrants after their arrival in the United States.

Influx of Immigrants from Asia

Before the discovery of gold in California in 1848, few Asians (only 121 between 1840 and 1849) came to the United States. (See Table 1.3.) Between 1849 and 1852 large numbers of Asian immigrants began arriving in the United States. These early arrivals came mostly from southern China, spurred on by economic depression, famine, war, and flooding. Thousands of Chinese immigrants were recruited to build railroads and work in mines, construction, and manufacturing. Many became domestic servants. Former mining-camp cooks who had saved some of their income opened restaurants. Others invested small amounts in equipment to operate laundries, performing a service few other people wanted to tackle. Between 1850 and 1879, 223,100 immigrants from China arrived in the United States, whereas only a few thousand arrived from other Asian countries.

Some people became alarmed by this increase in Chinese immigration. Their fears were fueled by a combination of racism and concerns among U.S.-born workers that employers were bringing over foreign workers to replace them and keep unskilled wages low. The public began to call for restrictions on Chinese immigration.

Chinese Exclusion Act

In 1882 Congress passed the Chinese Exclusion Act, which prohibited further immigration of Chinese laborers to the United States for 10 years. Exceptions included teachers, diplomats, students, merchants, and tourists. This act marked the first time the United States barred immigration of a national group. The law also prohibited Chinese immigrants in the United States from becoming naturalized U.S. citizens. As a result, the law dramatically reduced Chinese immigration. Between 1890 and 1899 only 15,268 Chinese immigrants arrived, compared with the 133,139 Chinese immigrants who had arrived in the decade before the act was passed. (See Table 1.3.)

Four other laws that prohibited the immigration of Chinese laborers followed the Chinese Exclusion Act. The Geary Act of 1892 extended the Chinese Exclusion Act for 10 more years. In cases brought before the U.S. Supreme Court, the court upheld the constitutionality of these two laws. The Immigration Act of 1904 made the Chinese exclusion laws permanent. Under the Immigration Act of 1917 the United States suspended the immigration of laborers from almost all Asian countries.

During World War II (1939–1945) the United States and China became allies against the Japanese in Asia. As a gesture of goodwill, President Franklin D. Roosevelt (1882–1945) signed in December 1943 the Act to Repeal the Chinese Exclusion Acts, to Establish Quotas, and for Other Purposes. The new law lifted the ban on the naturalization of Chinese nationals but established a quota (a prescribed number) of 105 Chinese immigrants to be admitted per year.

Beginning of Japanese Immigration

Until the passage of the Chinese Exclusion Act, Japanese immigration was hardly noticeable, with the total flow at 331 between 1860 and 1879. (See Table 1.3.) Because Japanese immigrants were not covered by the Chinese Exclusion Act, Japanese laborers were brought in to replace Chinese workers. Consequently, Japanese immigration increased from 1,583 during the 1880s to 139,712 during the first decade of the 20th century.

The same anti-Asian attitudes that led to the Chinese Exclusion Act of 1882 culminated in President Theodore Roosevelt's (1858–1919) Gentlemen's Agreement of 1907, an informal arrangement between the United States and Japan that cut the flow of Japanese immigration to a trickle. This anti-Asian attitude resurfaced a generation later in the National Origins Act of 1924. The immigration quota for any nationality group had been based on the number of people of that nationality that were residents in the United States during the 1910 census. The new law reduced quotas from 3% to 2% and shifted the base for quota calculations from 1910 to 1890. Because few Asians lived in the United States in 1890, the 1924 reduction in Asian immigration was particularly dramatic. Asian immigration was not permitted to increase until after World War II.

Greater Federal Control

In "Overview of INS History" (2012, http://www.uscis.gov/sites/default/files/USCIS/History%20and%20Genealogy/Our%20History/INS%20History/INSHistory.pdf), the U.S. Citizenship and Immigration Services (USCIS), one of the three main immigration agencies within the Department of Homeland Security (along with U.S. Customs and Border Protection and U.S. Immigration and Customs Enforcement), notes that in 1891 the federal government assumed full control over immigration issues. The Immigration Act of 1891 authorized the establishment of the U.S. Office of Immigration under the U.S. Department of the Treasury. This first comprehensive immigration law added to the list of inadmissible people those suffering from certain contagious diseases, polygamists (married people who have more than one spouse at the same time), and aliens convicted of minor crimes. The law also prohibited using advertisements to encourage immigration.

On January 1, 1892, a new federal immigration station began operating on Ellis Island in New York City. In 1893, 119 of the total 180 staff members of the U.S. Office of Immigration were employed at Ellis Island, which remained the country's largest port of entry for immigrants for decades. Between 1892 and 1924, more than 12 million immigrants were processed through Ellis Island, according to the National Parks Service in "Ellis Island: History & Culture" (April 3, 2015, http://www.nps.gov/elis/historyculture/index.htm). This figure represents nearly half of the more than 23 million total immigrants who arrived during that period.

In 1895, as USCIS notes, the Office of Immigration became the Bureau of Immigration under the commissioner-general of immigration. In 1903 the Bureau of Immigration was transferred to the U.S. Department of Commerce and Labor. The Basic Naturalization Act of 1906 consolidated the immigration and naturalization functions of the federal government under the Bureau of Immigration and Naturalization. When the Department of Commerce and Labor was separated into two cabinet departments in 1913, two bureaus were formed: the Bureau of Immigration and the Bureau of Naturalization. In 1933 the two bureaus were reunited as the U.S. Immigration and Naturalization Service (INS).

A MILLION IMMIGRANTS PER YEAR BY 1905

By the 1890s the origins of those arriving in the United States had changed. Fewer immigrants came from northern Europe, whereas immigrants from southern, central, and eastern Europe increased every year. Of the 7.6 million European immigrants who arrived between 1900 and 1909, 5.4 million (71%) came from Austria-Hungary, Italy, and Russia. (See Table 1.3.) The exodus of Jews from eastern Europe was particularly significant. The number of European Jewish immigrants had been growing since the 1880s, as a result of religious persecution and a lack of economic opportunity. As the Library of Congress notes in online materials related to its exhibit "From Haven to Home: 350 Years of Jewish Life in America" (http://www.loc.gov/exhibits/haventohome), most of the Jewish immigrants who arrived during this period "settled in cities where they clustered in districts close to downtowns, joined the working class, spoke Yiddish, and built strong networks of cultural, spiritual, voluntary, and social organizations."

As Table 1.2 shows, the nation's already high immigration rate at the turn of the 20th century nearly doubled between 1902 and 1907. Immigration reached 1 million per year in 1905, 1906, 1907, 1910, 1913, and 1914. Many Americans worried about the growing influx of immigrants, whose customs seemed unfamiliar and strange to most of the native population. Anti-Catholic sentiments, distrust of political radicalism (usually expressed as anti-socialism), and racist movements gained prevalence and spurred a resurgence of nativism. World War I temporarily slowed the influx of immigrants. Between 1914 and 1915 the number of immigrants dropped by nearly a million, from 1,218,480 to 326,700. By 1918, the final year of the war, only 110,618 immigrants ventured to the United States. However, the heavy flow of immigration started again after the war as people fled the war-ravaged European continent. In 1921, 805,228 immigrants arrived in the United States.

Immigration Act of 1907

The Immigration Act of 1907 barred the immigration of "feeble-minded" people, people with physical or mental defects that might prevent them from earning a living, and people with tuberculosis. Besides increasing the head tax on each arriving immigrant to $5, the 1907 law also officially classified the arriving aliens as either immigrants (people planning to take up residence in the United States) or nonimmigrants (people visiting for a short period to attend school, conduct business, or travel as tourists). All arrivals were required to declare their intentions for permanent or temporary stays in the United States. The law further authorized the president to refuse admission to people he considered harmful to the labor conditions in the nation.

Reflecting national concerns about conflicts between old and new immigrant groups, the Bureau of Immigration and Naturalization proposed in annual reports that the immigrants should be more widely dispersed throughout the rest of the country, instead of being concentrated mostly in northeastern urban areas. Not only would such a distribution of aliens help relieve the nation's urban problems, but also the bureau thought it might promote greater racial and cultural assimilation.

Immigration Act of 1917

The mounting negative feelings toward immigrants resulted in the Immigration Act of 1917, which was passed despite President Woodrow Wilson's (1856–1924) veto. Besides codifying previous immigration legislation, the 1917 act required immigrants over the age of 16 years to pass a literacy test, which proved to be a controversial clause. The new act also cited the following groups to the inadmissible classes of immigrants:

> All idiots, imbeciles, feeble-minded persons, epileptics, insane persons...persons with chronic alcoholism; paupers; professional beggars; vagrants; persons afflicted with tuberculosis in any form or a loathsome or dangerous contagious disease; persons not comprehended within any of the foregoing excluded classes who are found to be and are certified by the examining surgeon as being mentally or physically defective, such physical defect being of a nature which may affect the ability of such alien to earn a living; persons who have been convicted...of a felony or other crime or misdemeanor involving moral turpitude; polygamists, or persons who practice polygamy or believe in and advocate the practice of polygamy; anarchists, or persons who advocate the overthrow by force or violence of the Government of the United States, or of all forms of law...or who advocate the assassination of public

officials, or who advocate and teach the unlawful destruction of property...; prostitutes, or persons coming to the United States for the purpose of prostitution or immoral purposes.

The act also specifically disqualified those coming from the designated Asiatic "barred zone," which encompassed most of Asia and the Pacific Islands. This provision was a continuation of the Chinese Exclusion Act of 1882 and the Gentlemen's Agreement of 1907, in which the Japanese government had agreed to stop the flow of workers to the United States. In 1918 a presidential proclamation announced that passports were required for all entries into the United States.

Denied Entry

Despite increasingly restrictive immigration legislation, only a small percentage of those attempting to immigrate to the United States were turned away. As Table 1.4 shows, 650,252 people were denied entry for a variety of reasons between 1892 and 1990. The largest excluded group consisted of 219,399 people who were considered "likely to become public charge," followed closely by the 204,943 who "attempted entry without inspection or without proper documents" beginning in the 1920s. The 30-year period from 1901 to 1930 was the peak era for exclusion of immigrants deemed likely to become public charges and those considered to be mentally or physically defective or immoral. The 1917 ban on illiterate immigrants excluded 13,679 people over the next 50 years.

First Quota Law

Concern over whether the United States could continue to absorb such huge numbers of immigrants led Congress to introduce a major change in U.S. immigration policy. Other factors influencing Congress included racial fears about the new immigrants and apprehension over some of the immigrants' politically radical ideas.

The Quota Law of 1921 was the first quantitative immigration law. Congress limited the number of aliens of any nationality who could enter the United States to 3% of the number of foreign-born people of that nationality who lived in the United States in 1910 (based on the U.S. census). By 1910, however, many southern and eastern Europeans had already entered the country, a fact legislators had overlooked. Consequently, to restructure the makeup of the immigrant population, Congress approved the National Origins Act of 1924. This act set the first permanent limitation on immigration, called the national origins quota system. The law immediately limited the number of immigrants of each nationality to 2% of the population of that nationality who lived in the United States in 1890.

The 1924 law provided that after July 1, 1927, an overall cap would allow a total of 150,000 immigrants per year. Quotas for each national origin group were to be developed based on the 1920 census. Exempted from the quota limitation were spouses or dependents of U.S. citizens, returning alien residents, or natives of Western Hemisphere countries not subject to quotas (natives of Mexico, Canada, or other independent countries of Central or South America). The 1924 law further required that all arriving nonimmigrants present visas (government authorizations permitting entry into a country for a specific purpose and for a finite amount of time) obtained from a U.S. consulate abroad. U.S. immigration policies adhered to the 1917 and 1924 acts until 1952.

Impact of Quotas

The new laws also barred all Asian immigration, which soon led to a shortage of farm and sugar plantation workers. Filipinos filled the labor gap because the Philippines was a U.S. territory at the time, and they did not come under the immigration quota laws. In addition, large numbers of Caribbean immigrants arrived, peaking during the 1910 to 1919 period, when 120,860 Caribbean immigrants entered the United States. (See Table 1.3.)

Before World War I, Caribbean workers had moved among the islands and to parts of South and Central America. Following the war many went north in search of work. Similarly, after World War II, when agricultural changes in the Caribbean forced many people off farms and into cities, many traveled on to the United States or the United Kingdom.

With the new quota laws, the problem of illegal immigrants arose for the first time. Previously, only a few who had failed the immigration standards tried to sneak in, usually across the U.S.-Mexican or U.S.-Canadian land borders. With the new laws, the number of illegal immigrants began to increase. Subsequently, Congress created the U.S. Border Patrol in 1924 (under the Labor Appropriation Act) to oversee the nation's borders and prevent illegal immigrants from coming into the United States.

IMMIGRATION DURING WORLD WAR II

Immigration dropped well below 100,000 arrivals per year during the Great Depression (1929–1939) because the United States offered no escape from the unemployment that was rampant throughout most of the world. However, in the latter half of the 1930s Nazi persecution caused a new round of immigrants to flee Europe. In 1940 the INS was transferred from the U.S. Department of Labor to the U.S. Department of Justice. This move reflected the growing fear of war, making the surveillance of aliens a question of national security rather than one of how many to admit. The job of the INS shifted from the exclusion of aliens to combating alien criminal and subversive elements. This required closer cooperation with the U.S. attorney general's office and the Federal Bureau of Investigation.

TABLE 1.4

Immigrants denied entry by reason for denial, fiscal years 1892–1990

Year	Total	Subversive or anarchist	Criminal or narcotics violations	Immoral	Mental or physical defect	Likely to become public charge	Stowaway	Attempted entry without inspection or without proper documents	Contract laborer	Unable to read (over 16 years of age)	Other
1892–1990	650,252	1,369	17,465	8,209	82,590	219,399	16,240	204,943	41,941	13,679	44,417
1892–1900	22,515	—	65	89	1,309	15,070	—	—	5,792	—	190
1901–1910	108,211	10	1,681	1,277	24,425	63,311	—	—	12,991	—	4,516
1911–1920	178,109	27	4,353	4,824	42,129	90,045	1,904	—	15,417	5,083	14,327
1921–1930	189,307	9	2,082	1,281	11,044	37,175	8,447	94,084	6,274	8,202	20,709
1931–1940	68,217	5	1,261	253	1,530	12,519	2,126	47,858	1,235	258	1,172
1941–1950	30,263	60	1,134	80	1,021	1,072	3,182	22,441	219	108	946
1951–1960	20,585	1,098	2,017	361	956	149	376	14,657	13	26	932
1961–1970	4,831	128	383	24	145	27	175	3,706	—	2	241
1971–1980	8,455	32	814	20	31	31	30	7,237	—	—	260
1981–1990	19,759	NA	3,675	NA	NA	NA	NA	14,960	—	—	1,124
1981	659	NA	152	NA	NA	NA	NA	486	—	—	21
1982	698	NA	183	NA	NA	NA	NA	478	—	—	37
1983	979	NA	205	NA	NA	NA	NA	728	—	—	46
1984	1,089	NA	160	NA	NA	NA	NA	870	—	—	59
1985	1,747	NA	297	NA	NA	NA	NA	1,351	—	—	99
1986	2,278	NA	270	NA	NA	NA	NA	1,904	—	—	104
1987	1,994	NA	426	NA	NA	NA	NA	1,423	—	—	145
1988	2,693	NA	482	NA	NA	NA	NA	2,043	—	—	168
1989	3,893	NA	712	NA	NA	NA	NA	2,973	—	—	208
1990	3,729	NA	788	NA	NA	NA	NA	2,704	—	—	237

—Represents zero.
NA = Not available.
Note: From 1941–53, statistics represent all exclusions at sea and air ports and exclusions of aliens seeking entry for 30 days or longer at land ports. After 1953, includes aliens excluded after formal hearings.

SOURCE: Adapted from "Table 44. Aliens Excluded by Administrative Reason for Exclusion: Fiscal Years 1892–1990," in *Yearbook of Immigration Statistics: 2004*, U.S. Department of Homeland Security, Office of Policy, Office of Immigration Statistics, January 2006, http://www.dhs.gov/xlibrary/assets/statistics/yearbook/2004/Table44.xls (accessed January 6, 2015)

Alien Registration

World War II began with the German invasion of Poland in September 1939. Growing concern about an increase in refugees that might result from the war in Europe led Congress to pass the Alien Registration Act of 1940 (also known as the Smith Act). Among its provisions, this act required all aliens in the United States to register. Those over 14 years old also had to be fingerprinted. All registration and fingerprinting took place at local post offices between August 27 and December 26, 1940. Each alien was identified by an alien registration number, known as an A-number. For the first time, the government had a means of identifying individual immigrants. The law has been challenged in the courts, but the A-number system was still in use as of 2015. Following registration, each alien received by mail an Alien Registration Receipt Card, which he or she was required to keep as proof of registration. Each alien was also required to report any change of address within five days. Managing such a vast number of registrants and documents in a short time created a monumental challenge for the federal government. The ranks of employees in the Alien Registration Division of the INS increased dramatically in late 1940 and early 1941.

The United States officially entered World War II on December 8, 1941, the day after the Japanese attack on the U.S. naval station in Pearl Harbor, Hawaii. President Roosevelt immediately proclaimed all "nationals and subjects" of nations with which the country was at war to be enemy aliens. According to the INS, on January 14, 1942, the president issued a proclamation requiring further registration of aliens from enemy nations (primarily Germany, Italy, and Japan). All such aliens aged 14 years and older were directed to apply for a Certificate of Identification during the month of February 1942.

Alien registrations were used by a variety of government agencies and private industry to locate possible enemy subversives, such as aliens working for defense contractors, aliens with radio operator licenses, and aliens trained to pilot aircraft. The INS notes that one out of every 23 workers in U.S. industry at that time was a noncitizen.

Japanese Internment

Following the recommendation of military advisers, President Roosevelt issued Executive Order 9066 on February 19, 1942, which authorized the forcible internment of people of Japanese ancestry. Lieutenant General John L. DeWitt (1880–1962) was placed in charge of removal of the Japanese to internment camps, which were located in remote areas in western states, including Arizona, California, Colorado, Idaho, Utah, and Wyoming. Two camps were also established in Arkansas. In *Final Report: Japanese Evacuation from the West Coast 1942*

(1943), DeWitt states that during a period of fewer than 90 days 110,442 people of Japanese ancestry were evacuated from the West Coast. More than two-thirds were U.S. citizens. Relocation began in April 1942. The last camp was vacated in March 1946.

Although the United States was also at war with Germany and Italy, only people of Japanese descent were forced into internment camps. Noncitizens and citizens alike were forced to sell their homes and possessions and to leave their jobs. They lived in tiny, single-room accommodations, sometimes for several years. This treatment, based on fear of Japanese disloyalty, was later widely disparaged as unfair, demeaning, and ineffective as a national-security measure.

Executive Order 9066 was not formally terminated after the war ended. Over the years many Japanese Americans expressed concern that it could be implemented again. In 1976 President Gerald R. Ford (1913–2006) issued a proclamation that officially terminated the provisions of Executive Order 9066 retroactive to December 31, 1946. In 1988 President Ronald Reagan (1911–2004) signed a bill into law that provided $20,000 (about $58,200 in 2015 dollars) in restitution to each of the surviving internees.

POSTWAR IMMIGRATION LAW

A growing fear of communist infiltration, called the Red Scare, arose during the post–World War II period. One result was the passage of the Internal Security Act of 1950, which made membership in communist or totalitarian organizations cause for exclusion (denial of an alien's entry into the United States), deportation, or denial of naturalization. The law also required resident aliens to report their addresses annually and made reading, writing, and speaking English prerequisites for naturalization.

The Immigration and Nationality Act of 1952 added preferences for relatives and skilled aliens, gave immigrants and aliens certain legal protections, made all races eligible for immigration and naturalization, and absorbed most of the Internal Security Act of 1950. The act changed the annual national origin quotas to only one-sixth of 1% of the number of people in the United States in 1920 whose ancestry or national origin was attributable to a specific area of the world. It also allowed aliens to be excluded on ideological grounds, homosexuality, health restrictions, criminal records, narcotics addiction, and involvement in terrorism.

Once again, countries within the Western Hemisphere were not included in the quota system. President Harry S. Truman (1884–1972) vetoed the legislation, but Congress overrode his veto. Although there were major amendments, the Immigration and Nationality Act remained the basic statute governing who could gain entry into the United States until the passage of new laws following the September 11, 2001, terrorist attacks against the United States. These laws reorganized most of the federal government's immigration enforcement and naturalization functions under the umbrella of the newly created Department of Homeland Security, as discussed at greater length in Chapter 2.

During the 1950s a half-dozen special laws allowed the entrance of additional refugees. Many of the laws resulted from World War II, but some stemmed from new developments, including laws that relaxed the quotas for refugees fleeing the failed 1956 Hungarian revolution and those seeking asylum following the 1959 Cuban revolution.

A Two-Hemisphere System

In 1963 President John F. Kennedy (1917–1963) submitted a plan to change the quota system. Two years later Congress passed the Immigration and Nationality Act Amendments of 1965. Since 1924 sources of immigration had changed. During the 1950s immigration from Asia to the United States nearly quadrupled from 34,532 (between 1940 and 1949) to 135,844 (between 1950 and 1959). (See Table 1.3.) During the same period immigrants to the United States from North, Central, and South America increased dramatically.

The 1965 legislation canceled the national origins quota system and made visas available on a first-come, first-served basis. A seven-category preference system was implemented for families of U.S. citizens and permanent resident aliens for the purpose of family reunification. In addition, the law set visa allocations for people with special occupational skills, abilities, or training needed in the United States. It also established an annual ceiling of 170,000 Eastern Hemisphere immigrants with a 20,000 per-country limit, and an annual limit of 120,000 for the Western Hemisphere without a per-country limit or preference system.

The Immigration and Nationality Act Amendments of 1976 extended the 20,000 per-country limit to Western Hemisphere countries. Some legislators were concerned that the 20,000-person limit for Mexico was inadequate, but their objections were overruled. The Immigration and Nationality Act Amendments of 1978 combined the separate ceilings for the Eastern and Western Hemispheres into a single worldwide ceiling of 290,000.

Programs for Refugees

Official U.S. refugee programs began in response to the devastation of World War II, which created millions of refugees and displaced people (DPs). (A displaced person is a person living in a foreign country as a result of having been driven from his or her home country because of war or political unrest.) This was the first time the United States formulated policy to admit people fleeing persecution. The Presidential Directive of December 22, 1945, gave priority in issuing visas to about 40,000 DPs. The directive was followed by the Displaced Persons Act of 1948, which authorized the admission of 202,000 people from Eastern Europe, and the Refugee Relief Act of 1953, which approved entry of another 209,000 defectors from communist countries over a three-year period. The Displaced Persons Act counted the refugees in the existing immigration quotas, whereas the Refugee Relief Act admitted them outside the quota system.

PAROLE AUTHORITY: A TEMPORARY ADMISSION POLICY. In 1956 the U.S. attorney general used the parole authority (temporary admission) under section 212(d) (15) of the Immigration and Nationality Act of 1952 for the first time on a large scale. This section authorized the attorney general to temporarily admit any alien to the United States. Although parole was not admission for permanent residence, it could lead to permanent resident or immigrant status. Aliens already in the United States on a temporary basis could apply for asylum (to stay in the United States) on the grounds they were likely to suffer persecution if returned to their native land. The attorney general was authorized to withhold deportation on the same grounds.

In *Americans at the Gate: The United States and Refugees during the Cold War* (2008), Carl J. Bon Tempo estimates that this parole authority was used to admit approximately 32,000 of the 38,000 Hungarians who fled the failed 1956 Hungarian revolution. The other 6,000 entered under the Refugee Relief Act of 1953 and were automatically admitted as permanent residents. Similarly, in *Defining America through Immigration Policy* (2004), Bill Ong Hing notes that the parole provision was used to accommodate 15,000 refugees leaving China following the communist revolution there in 1949, and was used again in 1962 to admit several thousand Chinese refugees from Hong Kong to the United States.

REFUGEES AS CONDITIONAL ENTRANTS. In 1965, under the Immigration and Nationality Act Amendments, Congress added section 203(a) (7) to the Immigration and Nationality Act of 1952, creating a group of conditional entrant refugees from communist or Middle Eastern countries, with status similar to the refugee parolees. Sections 203(a) (7) and 212(d) (15) were used to admit thousands of refugees, including Czechoslovakians escaping their failed revolution in 1968, Ugandans fleeing a harsh dictatorship during the 1970s, and Lebanese avoiding the civil war in their country during the 1980s.

The United States did not have a general policy governing the admission of refugees until the Refugee Act of 1980. This act eliminated refugees as a category in the preference system and set a worldwide ceiling on immigration of 270,000, not counting refugees. It also removed the requirement that refugees had to originate from a communist or Middle Eastern nation.

Illegal Immigration Becomes a Major Issue

During wartime, the Department of Labor authorized the admission of temporary workers, mainly from Mexico. For example, during World War I nearly 77,000 Mexican workers were admitted to the United States, but only about half of them returned to Mexico. The other half remained in the United States illegally. Then, amid soaring unemployment during the Great Depression, hundreds of thousands of Mexicans were deported or otherwise forced to leave the United States

As the national economy strengthened during World War II, there was a shortage of labor, and President Roosevelt initiated what later came to be known as the Bracero ("manual laborer") Program, which allowed temporary agricultural laborers from Mexico to come to the United States to work. The program expired at the end of the war but was continued via a number of legislative and executive acts before finally being discontinued in 1964. The National Museum of American History indicates in "Opportunity or Exploitation: The Bracero Program" (http://americanhistory.si.edu/onthemove/themes/story_51_5.html) that over 4.5 million Mexicans came to the United States during the 22 years that the Bracero Program was in effect, and the program reinforced existing migration patterns, so that even after it was discontinued, many Mexican workers had come to rely on seasonal agricultural employment in the United States. In the absence of the legal framework for seeking seasonal work in the United States, many Mexicans continued to cross the border illegally. The population of unauthorized immigrants began to grow.

During the 1970s the Vietnam War (1954–1975) divided the nation, oil prices skyrocketed, and gasoline shortages caused long waiting lines at gas stations. Price controls were implemented and removed to control rampant inflation. In this period of political, social, and economic uncertainty, many people saw immigrants as straining the already limited welfare and educational systems. States with growing immigrant populations, such as California, Florida, Illinois, New York, and Texas, pushed Congress for immigration reform.

A surge of refugees from Vietnam and Cambodia as well as Cubans escaping the Fidel Castro (1926–) regime during the mid-1970s added to Americans' concerns. The major source of immigrants had changed from Europe to Latin America and Asia, and some Americans responded unfavorably to the unfamiliar faces and cultures of these new arrivals.

President Ford established the cabinet-level Domestic Council Committee on Illegal Aliens. Its December 1976 report increased border enforcement, recommended sanctions against employers who knowingly hired undocumented workers, and called for legalization for certain unauthorized immigrants who had arrived in the United States before July 1, 1968. In 1979 Congress established the Select Commission on Immigration and Refugee Policy. The commission spent the next two years evaluating the problem. Its 1981 *Final Report* fostered ideas that would become part of major new immigration reform legislation in 1986.

Green Cards

A lawful permanent resident (LPR) card, commonly known as a "green card," gives individuals the right to permanently live in the United States. An LPR carries this document as proof of legal status in the country.

What is known as a green card has come in a variety of different colors at different times in history. The first receipt card, Form AR-3, resulted from the Alien Registration Act of 1940, a national defense measure that was enacted during World War II. The act required all non-U.S. citizens to register at post offices. From there the registration forms were forwarded to the INS. The receipt card was mailed to each alien as proof of his or her compliance with the law. These receipts were printed on white paper.

When the war ended, alien registration became part of the regular immigration procedure. Aliens registered at ports of entry, and the INS issued different types of Alien Registration Receipt Cards based on each alien's admission status. For example, temporary foreign laborers received an I-100a card, visitors received an I-94c card, and permanent residents received an I-151 card. The cards were different colors to make it easy to identify the immigration status of each alien. The permanent resident card, which was necessary to obtain employment, was green.

The Internal Security Act of 1950 made the I-151 card even more valuable. Effective April 17, 1951, any alien holding an AR-3 card (the type that was issued to all aliens during World War II) had to apply to have it replaced with the green I-151 card. Anyone who could not prove his or her legal admission to the United States did not qualify for a green card and could be subject to prosecution for violation of immigration laws.

By 1951 the green card represented security for an immigrant because it indicated the right to permanently live and work in the United States. The Alien Registration Receipt Card, Form I-151, became commonly known to immigrants, immigration attorneys, enforcement officers, and employers by its color. The term *green card* designated not only the document but also the official status so desired by many legal nonimmigrants (students, tourists, and temporary workers) and by unauthorized immigrants.

The green card was so desirable that counterfeiting became a problem. In response to this counterfeiting, the INS issued 19 different designs of the card between 1940 and 1977. The 1964 version was pale blue, and in 1965 the card became dark blue. In January 1977 the INS introduced the machine-readable Alien Registration Receipt Card, Form I-551, which has since been issued in a variety of colors, including pink and a pink and blue combination. Form I-151 and its successor, Form I-551, have such vital meaning to immigrants that despite changes in form number, design, and color, it will probably always be known as a green card.

CHAPTER 2

IMMIGRATION LAWS AND POLICIES SINCE 1980

Before the 1980s U.S. immigration laws changed approximately once in a generation, but the pace of global change quickened at the end of the 20th century and the beginning of the 21st, and the immigrant population of the United States grew steadily, both numerically and as a percentage of total population. As Figure 2.1 shows, the 1970 Census counted 9.6 million foreign-born U.S. residents, who accounted for 4.7% of the total population (the lowest percentage recorded since the U.S. Census Bureau had been counting the foreign-born population). By 2010 the number of foreign-born U.S. residents had more than quadrupled, to 40 million, and as a percentage of total U.S. residents the foreign-born population had more than doubled, to 12.9%. These increases, together with other changes at the national and global political levels, were accompanied by numerous changes to immigration law.

This chapter covers the most significant changes to immigration law and policy made between the 1980s and 2015. Major new immigration legislation was passed in 1986, 1990, and 1996. The September 11, 2001 (9/11), terrorist attacks against the United States led to antiterrorism laws that had considerable impact on immigration policies and procedures, including a reorganization of the federal agencies that oversee most immigration-related affairs. Additionally, since the late 1990s numerous politicians and analysts have routinely called for an overhaul of immigration laws relating to unauthorized immigrants (those in the country without legal authorization, whose numbers have grown rapidly since the 1980s). Throughout the presidential administrations of George W. Bush (1946–) and Barack Obama (1961–), bipartisan proposals to overhaul immigration law were stymied in Congress. Partly in response to the legislative gridlock on the issue, the Obama administration used executive actions to craft significant changes to immigration enforcement policies in 2012 and 2014.

The changes to immigration law discussed in this chapter relate to a number of different federal government agencies. Historically, the Immigration and Naturalization Service (INS) oversaw the major components of immigration policy in the United States. Thus, the INS is frequently referenced below even though the agency was dismantled in the aftermath of 9/11 and replaced by three separate agencies within the newly created Department of Homeland Security (DHS): U.S. Citizenship and Immigration Services (USCIS), Customs and Border Protection (CBP), and Immigration and Customs Enforcement (ICE). The USCIS became the agency responsible for overseeing legal immigration; the CBP was made responsible for preventing the entry of drugs, weapons, terrorists, and others from entering the country illegally; and ICE was charged with enforcing immigration laws when they are violated by people inside the country's borders. In some cases, a particular change in immigration law may be discussed in relation to both the INS (the agency responsible for implementing it at the time of passage) and one or more of the three newly created agencies (which have carried out those implementation functions in the years since the INS was dismantled).

IMMIGRATION REFORM AND CONTROL ACT OF 1986

In November 1986, after a six-year effort to send an acceptable immigration bill through both houses of Congress, President Ronald Reagan (1911–2004) signed the Immigration Reform and Control Act (IRCA) into law. To control illegal immigration, the IRCA adopted three major strategies:

- Legalization of a portion of the undocumented population, thereby reducing the number of immigrants residing illegally in the United States

- Sanctions against employers who knowingly hire illegal immigrants

- Additional border enforcement to impede further unlawful entries

FIGURE 2.1

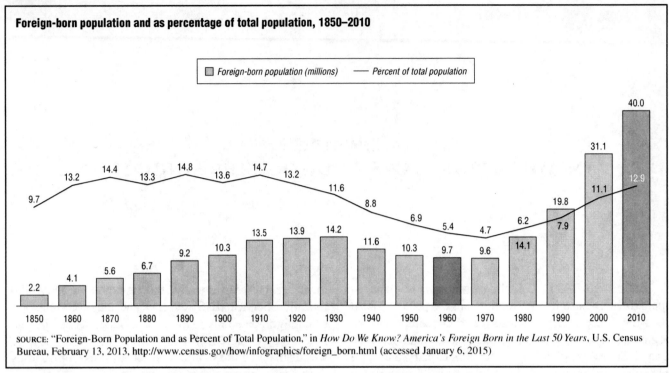

Foreign-born population and as percentage of total population, 1850–2010

SOURCE: "Foreign-Born Population and as Percent of Total Population," in *How Do We Know? America's Foreign Born in the Last 50 Years*, U.S. Census Bureau, February 13, 2013, http://www.census.gov/how/infographics/foreign_born.html (accessed January 6, 2015)

Two groups of immigrants became eligible to apply for legalization under the IRCA. The largest group consisted of immigrants who could prove that they had continuously resided in the United States without authorization since January 1, 1982. This group had entered the United States in one of two ways: they arrived as unauthorized immigrants before January 1, 1982, or they arrived on temporary visas (government authorizations permitting entry into a country) that expired before January 1, 1982.

To adjust to the legal status of permanent resident, immigrants were required to prove eligibility for admission and have at least a minimal understanding and knowledge of the English language, U.S. history, and the U.S. government. They could apply for citizenship five years from the date permanent resident status was granted.

The second group of immigrants that became eligible to apply for legalization under the IRCA were referred to as special agricultural workers (SAWs). This category was created because many fruit and vegetable farmers feared they would lose their workers, many of whom were undocumented, if the IRCA provisions regarding length of continuous residence were applied to seasonal laborers. Most of these workers were migrants who returned home to live in Mexico when there was no work available in the fields. The SAW program permitted unauthorized immigrants who had performed labor in perishable agricultural commodities for a minimum of 90 days between May 1985 and May 1986 to apply for legalization.

How Many Were Legalized?

In *IRCA Legalization Effects: Lawful Permanent Residence and Naturalization through 2001* (October 25, 2002, http://www.dhs.gov/xlibrary/assets/statistics/publications/irca0114int.pdf), Nancy Rytina of the INS estimates that 3 million to 5 million undocumented immigrants were living in the United States in 1986. More than 3 million of these applied for temporary residence status under the IRCA, and nearly 2.7 million (88%) were eventually approved for permanent residence. By 2001 one-third (33%, or 889,033) of these residents had become naturalized citizens. Rytina notes that a majority (75%) of applicants under the IRCA provisions were born in Mexico.

The IRCA barred newly legalized immigrants from receiving most federally funded public assistance for five years. Exceptions included access to emergency care and access to Medicaid for children, pregnant women, the elderly, and the handicapped. The State Legalization Impact Assistance Grant program reimbursed state and local governments the costs for providing public assistance, education, and public health services to the legalized immigrants.

Employer Sanctions

The employer sanctions provision of the IRCA was intended to correct a double standard that prohibited unauthorized immigrants from working in the United States but permitted employers to hire them. The IRCA prohibited employers from hiring, recruiting, or referring for a fee those known to be unauthorized to work in the

United States. Employers who violated the law were subject to a series of civil fines or criminal penalties when a pattern or practice of violations was found.

DOCUMENTING ELIGIBILITY FOR EMPLOYMENT. The burden of proof was on employers to demonstrate that their employees had valid proof of identity and were authorized to work. The IRCA required employers to complete the Employment Eligibility Verification form, known as Form I-9, for each employee hired. In completing the form the employer certified that the employee had presented valid proof of identity and eligibility for employment and that these documents appeared genuine. The IRCA also required employers to retain the completed I-9 forms and produce them in response to an official government request.

Form I-9 was revised a number of times after its 1986 introduction. As of 2015, it consisted of three parts. (See Figure 2.2.) Section 1, to be completed by the employee, required the disclosure of basic personal information and an attestation of legal authorization to work in the United States. Section 2, to be completed by the employer, provided information about the official documents used to establish the employee's legal authorization to work. Section 3 was to be completed by employers who were rehiring an employee within three years of the date the original I-9 form had been completed or when official documents provided on an employee's I-9 form had expired. Form I-9 was available in English and Spanish, but only employers in Puerto Rico could have employees complete the Spanish version for their records. Employers in the 50 states and other U.S. territories were allowed to use the Spanish version as a translation guide for Spanish-speaking employees, but the English version was required for company records. Employees were entitled, however, to use a translator/preparer to assist them in completing the form.

IMMIGRATION MARRIAGE FRAUD AMENDMENTS OF 1986

Before 1986 the INS granted permanent residence fairly quickly to the foreign spouses of U.S. citizens or lawful permanent residents (LPRs). Because marriage represented the quickest method of obtaining LPR status, foreign-born U.S. residents sometimes entered into sham marriages with U.S. citizens or LPRs purely for the sake of gaining permanent residency. Some U.S. citizens or LPRs agreed to marry immigrants for money, and then the marriages were dissolved once the immigrant obtained LPR status. Other cases involved unauthorized immigrants entering into marriages by deceiving citizens or LPRs with declarations of love. According to Vonnell C. Tingle, in "Immigration Marriage Fraud Amendments of 1986: Locking In by Locking Out?" (*Journal of Family Law*, vol. 27, 1988–89), INS statistics showed that between 1978 and 1984 the number of marriage-based

acquisitions of LPR status grew rapidly even though immigration as a whole was declining. The INS believed that a substantial number of those acquiring LPR status were doing so through sham marriages, and the agency broke up multiple criminal organizations that provided marriage-fraud services for immigrants seeking LPR status. These cases resulted in national media attention, and the INS requested that Congress aid it in the attempt to detect sham marriages by passing new legislation.

The Immigration Marriage Fraud Amendments of 1986 specify that individuals basing their immigrant status on a marriage of less than two years are considered conditional immigrants. To remove the conditional immigrant status, the individual must apply for permanent residence within 90 days after the second-year anniversary of receiving conditional status. At that time the conditional immigrant and his or her spouse must show that the marriage remains valid. According to the USCIS, in *Adjudicator's Field Manual—Redacted Public Version* (2015, http://www.uscis.gov/iframe/ilink/docView/AFM/HTML/AFM/0-0-0-1.html), acceptable evidence as of 2015 included documents showing joint ownership of property, leases showing joint tenancy of rental property, documents showing that the spouses' finances are commingled, birth certificates of children born to the two spouses, affidavits submitted by third parties who can testify to the authenticity of the marriage, or other forms of documentation proving that the marriage was not entered into fraudulently. Couples whose marriages are suspected of being fraudulent may be subjected to repeated interviews and lengthy investigations.

The 1986 amendments also provide for cases in which a conditional immigrant may be eligible for permanent residence based on marriage even though a joint petition cannot be filed. Initially, waivers were intended for applicants who would face danger or extreme hardship if forced to return to their home countries, as well as for applicants who could prove that they had entered into a marriage in good faith, but whose marriages had terminated due to death, divorce, or annulment. In 1990 Congress further amended the law to allow conditional immigrant women in abusive relationships to apply for waivers. Spousal abuse is a particular concern given the power imbalance that results when a conditional immigrant must depend on her husband for the continued right to stay in the United States. The U.S. Department of Justice finds cases of alien wives who are virtual prisoners, afraid they will be deported if they defy their husband or report abuse. In addition, some conditional immigrants come from cultures in which divorced women are outcasts with no place in society. Deportation would thus expose them to other forms of abuse. Waiver applications, like joint petitions, require substantial documentation, but they do not have to be filed during the two-year window that applies to the joint petition.

FIGURE 2.2

Form I-9, Employment Eligibility Verification

Employment Eligibility Verification

Department of Homeland Security
U.S. Citizenship and Immigration Services

▶START HERE. Read instructions carefully before completing this form. The instructions must be available during completion of this form.

ANTI-DISCRIMINATION NOTICE: It is illegal to discriminate against work-authorized individuals. Employers **CANNOT** specify which document(s) they will accept from an employee. The refusal to hire an individual because the documentation presented has a future expiration date may also constitute illegal discrimination.

Section 1. Employee Information and Attestation (*Employees must complete and sign Section 1 of Form I-9 no later than the first day of employment, but not before accepting a job offer.*)

Last Name (*Family Name*)	First Name (*Given Name*)	Middle Initial	Other Names Used (*if any*)

Address (*Street Number and Name*)	Apt. Number	City or Town	State ▼	Zip Code

Date of Birth (*mm/dd/yyyy*)	U.S. Social Security Number	E-mail Address	Telephone Number

I am aware that federal law provides for imprisonment and/or fines for false statements or use of false documents in connection with the completion of this form.

I attest, under penalty of perjury, that I am (check one of the following):

☐ A citizen of the United States

☐ A noncitizen national of the United States (*See instructions*)

☐ A lawful permanent resident (Alien Registration Number/USCIS Number): _____

☐ An alien authorized to work until (expiration date, if applicable, mm/dd/yyyy) _____ . Some aliens may write "N/A" in this field.
(*See instructions*)

For aliens authorized to work, provide your Alien Registration Number/USCIS Number **OR** Form I-94 Admission Number:

1. Alien Registration Number/USCIS Number: _____

OR

2. Form I-94 Admission Number: _____

If you obtained your admission number from CBP in connection with your arrival in the United States, include the following:

Foreign Passport Number: _____

Country of Issuance: _____ ▼

Some aliens may write "N/A" on the Foreign Passport Number and Country of Issuance fields. (*See instructions*)

> **3-D Barcode**
> **Do Not Write in This Space**

Signature of Employee:	Date (*mm/dd/yyyy*):

Preparer and/or Translator Certification (*To be completed and signed if Section 1 is prepared by a person other than the employee.*)

I attest, under penalty of perjury, that I have assisted in the completion of this form and that to the best of my knowledge the information is true and correct.

Signature of Preparer or Translator:	Date (*mm/dd/yyyy*):

Last Name (*Family Name*)	First Name (*Given Name*)

Address (*Street Number and Name*)	City or Town	State ▼	Zip Code

STOP *Employer Completes Next Page* STOP

Form I-9 03/08/13 N

Page 7 of 9

FIGURE 2.2

Form I-9, Employment Eligibility Verification [CONTINUED]

Section 2. Employer or Authorized Representative Review and Verification
(Employers or their authorized representative must complete and sign Section 2 within 3 business days of the employee's first day of employment. You must physically examine one document from List A OR examine a combination of one document from List B and one document from List C as listed on the "Lists of Acceptable Documents" on the next page of this form. For each document you review, record the following information: document title, issuing authority, document number, and expiration date, if any.)

Employee Last Name, First Name and Middle Initial from Section 1:

List A	OR	List B	AND	List C
Identity and Employment Authorization		Identity		Employment Authorization

List A	List B	List C
Document Title:	Document Title:	Document Title:
Issuing Authority:	Issuing Authority:	Issuing Authority:
Document Number:	Document Number:	Document Number:
Expiration Date (*if any*) (*mm/dd/yyyy*):	Expiration Date (*if any*) (*mm/dd/yyyy*):	Expiration Date (*if any*) (*mm/dd/yyyy*):
Document Title:		
Issuing Authority:		
Document Number:		
Expiration Date (*if any*) (*mm/dd/yyyy*):		**3-D Barcode** **Do Not Write in This Space**
Document Title:		
Issuing Authority:		
Document Number:		
Expiration Date (*if any*) (*mm/dd/yyyy*):		

Certification

I attest, under penalty of perjury, that (1) I have examined the document(s) presented by the above-named employee, (2) the above-listed document(s) appear to be genuine and to relate to the employee named, and (3) to the best of my knowledge the employee is authorized to work in the United States.

The employee's first day of employment (*mm/dd/yyyy*): _____ (***See instructions for exemptions.***)

Signature of Employer or Authorized Representative	Date (*mm/dd/yyyy*)	Title of Employer or Authorized Representative
Last Name (*Family Name*)	First Name (*Given Name*)	Employer's Business or Organization Name

Employer's Business or Organization Address (*Street Number and Name*)	City or Town	State ▼	Zip Code

Section 3. Reverification and Rehires *(To be completed and signed by employer or authorized representative.)*

A. New Name (*if applicable*) Last Name (*Family Name*) First Name (*Given Name*) Middle Initial	B. Date of Rehire (*if applicable*) (*mm/dd/yyyy*):

C. If employee's previous grant of employment authorization has expired, provide the information for the document from List A or List C the employee presented that establishes current employment authorization in the space provided below.

Document Title:	Document Number:	Expiration Date (*if any*) (*mm/dd/yyyy*):

I attest, under penalty of perjury, that to the best of my knowledge, this employee is authorized to work in the United States, and if the employee presented document(s), the document(s) I have examined appear to be genuine and to relate to the individual.

Signature of Employer or Authorized Representative:	Date (*mm/dd/yyyy*):	Print Name of Employer or Authorized Representative:

Form I-9 03/08/13 N

Page 8 of 9

FIGURE 2.2

Form I-9, Employment Eligibility Verification [CONTINUED]

LISTS OF ACCEPTABLE DOCUMENTS
All documents must be UNEXPIRED

Employees may present one selection from List A or a combination of one selection from List B and one selection from List C.

LIST A		LIST B		LIST C
Documents that Establish Both Identity and Employment Authorization	OR	**Documents that Establish Identity**	AND	**Documents that Establish Employment Authorization**

LIST A	LIST B	LIST C
1. U.S. Passport or U.S. Passport Card	1. Driver's license or ID card issued by a State or outlying possession of the United States provided it contains a photograph or information such as name, date of birth, gender, height, eye color, and address	1. A Social Security Account Number card, unless the card includes one of the following restrictions: (1) NOT VALID FOR EMPLOYMENT (2) VALID FOR WORK ONLY WITH INS AUTHORIZATION (3) VALID FOR WORK ONLY WITH DHS AUTHORIZATION
2. Permanent Resident Card or Alien Registration Receipt Card (Form I-551)		
3. Foreign passport that contains a temporary I-551 stamp or temporary I-551 printed notation on a machine-readable immigrant visa	2. ID card issued by federal, state or local government agencies or entities, provided it contains a photograph or information such as name, date of birth, gender, height, eye color, and address	2. Certification of Birth Abroad issued by the Department of State (Form FS-545)
4. Employment Authorization Document that contains a photograph (Form I-766)	3. School ID card with a photograph	3. Certification of Report of Birth issued by the Department of State (Form DS-1350)
5. For a nonimmigrant alien authorized to work for a specific employer because of his or her status: a. Foreign passport; and b. Form I-94 or Form I-94A that has the following: (1) The same name as the passport; and (2) An endorsement of the alien's nonimmigrant status as long as that period of endorsement has not yet expired and the proposed employment is not in conflict with any restrictions or limitations identified on the form.	4. Voter's registration card	4. Original or certified copy of birth certificate issued by a State, county, municipal authority, or territory of the United States bearing an official seal
	5. U.S. Military card or draft record	
	6. Military dependent's ID card	5. Native American tribal document
	7. U.S. Coast Guard Merchant Mariner Card	6. U.S. Citizen ID Card (Form I-197)
	8. Native American tribal document	7. Identification Card for Use of Resident Citizen in the United States (Form I-179)
	9. Driver's license issued by a Canadian government authority	8. Employment authorization document issued by the Department of Homeland Security
6. Passport from the Federated States of Micronesia (FSM) or the Republic of the Marshall Islands (RMI) with Form I-94 or Form I-94A indicating nonimmigrant admission under the Compact of Free Association Between the United States and the FSM or RMI	**For persons under age 18 who are unable to present a document listed above:**	
	10. School record or report card	
	11. Clinic, doctor, or hospital record	
	12. Day-care or nursery school record	

Illustrations of many of these documents appear in Part 8 of the Handbook for Employers (M-274).

Refer to Section 2 of the instructions, titled "Employer or Authorized Representative Review and Verification," for more information about acceptable receipts.

Form I-9 03/08/13 N

Page 9 of 9

SOURCE: "Form I-9, Employment Eligibility Verification," U.S. Department of Homeland Security, U.S. Citizenship and Immigration Services, March 8, 2013, http://www.uscis.gov/files/form/I-9.pdf (accessed January 6, 2015)

The 1994 Violence against Women Act (VAWA) created additional channels and procedures for abused women and children to petition for LPR status. (The law also applies to abused men, although they are less often the victims of spousal abuse than women.) A VAWA petition allows battered immigrants to apply for status adjustments without the abuser's knowledge. Immigrants who can prove such abuse are typically granted deferred action status (an immigration status indicating that deportation proceedings will not be initiated), and they become eligible for certain public benefits as well as for work authorization. Then they may apply for LPR status based on their eligibility category. When visas are not immediately available, as is often the case with battered immigrants who are the spouses or children of LPRs rather than the spouses or children of citizens, a successful VAWA petition entitles the applicant to work authorization until visas are available.

According to the Office of Immigration Statistics, in *Yearbook of Immigration Statistics: 2013* (October 2014, http://www.dhs.gov/sites/default/files/publications/immigration-statistics/yearbook/2013/LPR/table7d.xls), in fiscal year (FY) 2013, 248,332 people were granted LPR status as a result of their marriage to a U.S. citizen, and 30,582 people were granted LPR status as a result of their marriage to someone with LPR status. The DHS does not keep statistics on immigration marriage fraud, and it is impossible to know how many of these marriages might be fraudulent. Detecting fraudulent marriages requires intensive and time-consuming investigation by immigration officials, so it is likely that a substantial percentage of those who enter into fraudulent marriages are not apprehended or deported. However, most immigration authorities and experts believe that fraudulent marriages account for only a small percentage of marriage-based immigration visas. Devin Dwyer reports in "Immigrant Couples Face Scrutiny in Bid to Root Out Sham Marriages" (ABCNews.com, August 2, 2010), the USCIS denied just over 600 fraudulent marriage-based LPR applications between 2007 and 2009.

IMMIGRATION ACT OF 1990

Shortly after the IRCA was passed, Senators Edward M. Kennedy (1932–2009; D-MA) and Alan K. Simpson (1931–; R-WY) began work to change the Immigration and Nationality Act Amendments of 1965, which provided the framework for legal immigration into the United States. The senators asserted that its family-oriented system allowed one legal immigrant to bring too many relatives into the country. They proposed to cut the number of dependents admitted and replace them with individuals who had the skills or money to immediately benefit the U.S. economy. The result of their efforts was the Immigration Act (IMMACT) of 1990.

Enacted in November 1990, IMMACT represented a major overhaul of immigration law. The focus of the new law was to raise the annual number of immigrants allowed from 500,000 to 700,000 and give greater priority to employment-based immigration. A diversity program encouraged applications from countries with low immigration history by allotting 50,000 visas per year in this category.

Diversity Visa Program

The IMMACT diversity program, which is overseen by the U.S. Department of State, was introduced to encourage immigration from countries that are underrepresented among U.S. immigrants. Diversity visas (DVs), 50,000 of which are distributed by lottery each year, are one of the only available methods of legal immigration for people who do not have close family members or employment agreements in the United States. To be eligible, immigrants must be citizens of countries that have supplied fewer than 50,000 total immigrants over the preceding five years, and no more than 7% of the total

number of DVs can be allocated to the residents of any one country. Applicants must have a high school education or equivalent, or have at least two years of work experience in an occupation that requires a minimum of two years' training or two years' experience within the past five years.

As of 2015, all DV applications had to be submitted electronically, and winners were selected at random by computer. Winners were required to submit further paperwork and undergo interviews, and their spouses and minor children were eligible for derivative DVs. These derivative DVs counted against the yearly limit of 50,000 annual visas under the program. As the State Department notes in "DV 2015—Selected Entrants" (2015, http://travel.state.gov/content/visas/english/immigrate/diversity-visa/dv-2015-selected-entrants.html), those applying for DV admission to the United States during FY 2015 had to apply during the 30-day application period that ran from October 1, 2013, to November 2, 2013. There were 9,388,986 entries (14,397,781 when derivatives are included) for the 50,000 DVs.

Changing Grounds for Exclusion

IMMACT changed the political and ideological grounds for exclusion and deportation. The law repealed the ban against the admission of communists and representatives of other totalitarian regimes that had been in place since 1950. In addition, immigration applicants who had been excluded previously because of associations with communism were provided exceptions if the applicants had been involuntary members of the communist party, had terminated membership, or merely had close relationships with people affiliated with communism.

Temporary Protected Status

IMMACT authorized the U.S. attorney general to grant temporary protected status (TPS) to unauthorized immigrants present in the United States when a natural disaster, ongoing armed conflict, or other extraordinary occurrence in their country posed a danger to their personal safety.

TPS lasts for six to 18 months unless conditions in the immigrant's home country warrant an extension of stay. Thus, the countries whose citizens are eligible for TPS changes constantly, although some war-torn or otherwise troubled countries may stay on the TPS list for many years. TPS does not lead to permanent resident status, although such immigrants can obtain work authorization. Once the TPS designation ends, the foreign nationals resume the same immigrant status they had before TPS (unless that status has expired) or any new status they obtained while in TPS. According to the USCIS, in "Temporary Protected Status" (January 7, 2015, http://www.uscis.gov/humanitarian/temporary-protected-status-deferred-enforced-departure/temporary-protected-status), in early 2015 applicants from the following countries were eligible for TPS: El Salvador, Guinea, Haiti, Honduras, Liberia, Nicaragua, Sierra Leone, Somalia, Sudan, South Sudan, and Syria.

ILLEGAL IMMIGRATION REFORM AND IMMIGRANT RESPONSIBILITY ACT OF 1996

The Illegal Immigration Reform and Immigrant Responsibility Act (IIRIRA) went into effect in September 1996. Among many other provisions, the IIRIRA attempted to combat illegal immigration by making the following changes to immigration law:

- Doubling the number of Border Patrol agents to 5,000 and increasing equipment and technology at points of entry

- Authorizing improvements of southwestern border barriers

- Toughening penalties for immigrant smuggling (up to 10 years in prison, 15 years for third and subsequent offenses) and document fraud (up to 15 years in prison)

- Increasing the number of INS investigators for work-site enforcement, tracking aliens who overstay visas, and investigating alien smuggling

- Instituting a new "expedited removal" proceeding (denial of an alien's entry into the United States without a hearing) to speed deportation of aliens with no documents or with fraudulent documents

- Authorizing three voluntary pilot programs to enable employers to verify the immigrant status of job applicants and to reduce the number and types of documents needed for identification and employment eligibility

- Instituting a bar on admissibility for aliens seeking to reenter the United States after having been unlawfully present in the country (a bar of three years for aliens unlawfully present from six months to a year and a bar of 10 years for those unlawfully present for more than a year)

Verifying Employee Eligibility for Work

To assist employers in complying with the IIRIRA as well as with workplace provisions of the IRCA, the Social Security Administration began in 1997 the Basic Pilot Program, a computerized system that allowed employers to check the validity of Social Security numbers (SSNs) presented by new hires. The system was tested with employers who volunteered in California, Florida, Illinois, and Texas before being expanded in 2004 to employers who volunteered in all states. The program returned a tentative nonconfirmation (known as a TNC) if the name, date of birth, or gender of the new hire did not match Social Security records; if the SSN had never been issued; or if records indicated the person issued that SSN was deceased. The new hire had a set time limit for resolving the problem with the Social Security Administration before the employer could terminate the individual's employment.

The Basic Pilot Program was renamed E-Verify in 2007 and expanded to include a feature that would allow employers to scan a new hire's photo identification to be compared against images stored in DHS immigration databases. Although the program remained voluntary under federal law, 19 states mandated the use of E-Verify in some form as of March 2014, according to *Findings of the E-Verify User Survey* (April 30, 2014, http://www.uscis.gov/sites/default/files/USCIS/Verification/E-Verify/E-Verify_Native_Documents/Everify%20Studies/E-Verify_User_Survey_Report_April2014.pdf), an annual report on the program conducted by the research firm Westat on behalf of the DHS. States requiring all employers (with certain exceptions in some states) to use E-Verify included Alabama, Arizona, Georgia, Mississippi, North Carolina, South Carolina, Tennessee, and Utah. States mandating the use of E-verify for state employees and state contractors but not for other private companies included Colorado, Florida, Idaho, Indiana, Louisiana, Missouri, Nebraska, Oklahoma, Pennsylvania, and Virginia. Minnesota required that the system be used in hiring state contractors only.

According to the USCIS, in FY 2013 E-Verify was used to determine work eligibility in 23.9 million cases nationally. (See Figure 2.3.) Of these employees, 98.8% were found within 24 hours to be authorized to work. Of those not immediately confirmed as authorized, some were confirmed as authorized after an initial mismatch of records, and only 0.98% of the total employees checked were ultimately found to be lacking in work authorization.

PATRIOT ACT OF 2001

Following 9/11 it became apparent that some, if not all, of the perpetrators had entered the United States legally, and many had overstayed their visas with no notice taken by the INS or any other enforcement agency. As a result, several laws were enacted to address immigration concerns related to terrorism. The first such law was the Uniting and Strengthening America by Providing Appropriate Tools Required to Intercept and Obstruct Terrorism Act (known as the Patriot Act), which was signed into law in October 2001. With reference to immigration, the act:

- Mandated that the number of personnel at the northern border be tripled, appropriated funds for technology improvements, and gave the INS access to Federal Bureau of Investigation (FBI) criminal databases. The INS was to begin the task of locating hundreds of

FIGURE 2.3

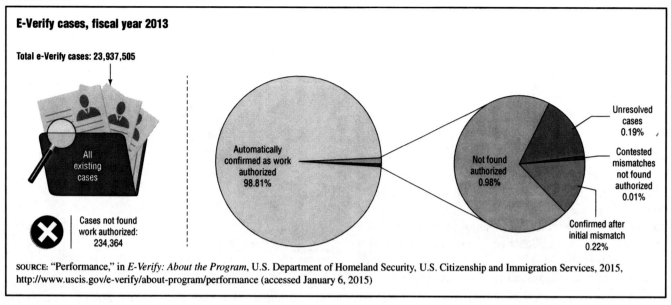

E-Verify cases, fiscal year 2013

Total e-Verify cases: 23,937,505

All existing cases

Cases not found work authorized: 234,364

Automatically confirmed as work authorized 98.81%

Not found authorized 0.98%

Unresolved cases 0.19%

Contested mismatches not found authorized 0.01%

Confirmed after initial mismatch 0.22%

SOURCE: "Performance," in *E-Verify: About the Program*, U.S. Department of Homeland Security, U.S. Citizenship and Immigration Services, 2015, http://www.uscis.gov/e-verify/about-program/performance (accessed January 6, 2015)

thousands of foreigners who had been ordered deported and entering their names into the FBI database.

- Amended the Immigration and Nationality Act of 1952 to clarify that an alien who solicited funds or membership or provided material support to a certified terrorist organization could be detained or removed from the country.

- Directed the U.S. attorney general to implement an entry-exit system, with particular focus on biometric information gathered during the visa application process, and develop tamper-resistant documents. The new system would require certain nonimmigrants to register with the INS and submit fingerprints and photographs on arrival in the United States; report to the INS in person within 30 days of arrival and annually thereafter; and notify an INS agent of their departure. Those who failed to comply could face criminal prosecution.

- Appropriated $36.8 million to implement a foreign-student monitoring system with mandatory participation by all institutions of higher education that enrolled foreign students or exchange visitors. The act expanded the list of participating institutions to include air flight schools, language training schools, and vocational schools.

- Established provisions to ensure that the immigration status of 9/11 victims and their families was not adversely affected as a result of the attacks. The family members of some victims were facing deportation.

The Patriot Act was amended several times over the following decade, and its central features were reauthorized by Congress and President Bush in 2006. In 2011 President Obama signed a bill reauthorizing, through 2015, key provisions that were set to expire.

HOMELAND SECURITY ACT OF 2002

In November 2002 President Bush signed into law the Homeland Security Act, which implemented the largest restructuring of the government in several decades. This act created the cabinet-level U.S. Department of Homeland Security, which consolidated the functions of more than 20 federal agencies into one department that employs over 170,000 people. One of the affected agencies was the INS.

INS Reorganization

Title IV, Section 402 of the Homeland Security Act transferred the responsibilities of the INS from the Justice Department to the DHS. As described earlier, the INS ceased operating under that name. Its functions relating to legal immigration were assumed by the USCIS; the CBP and ICE assumed primary responsibility for the enforcement of immigration law.

Border Security

Section 402 of the Homeland Security Act outlined the responsibilities of the undersecretary for border and transportation security. These included:

- Preventing the entry of terrorists and the instruments of terrorism into the United States

- Securing the borders, territorial waters, ports, terminals, waterways, and air, land, and sea transportation systems of the United States

- Administering the immigration and naturalization laws of the United States, including the establishment of rules governing the granting of visas and other forms of permission to enter the United States to individuals who are not citizens or LPRs

- Administering the customs laws of the United States

- Ensuring the speedy, orderly, and efficient flow of lawful traffic and commerce in carrying out these responsibilities

OTHER POST-9/11 CHANGES

Since 9/11 hundreds of policy changes have been introduced by the Justice Department, the U.S. Department of State, the DHS, and the INS/USCIS. Among the most prominent are changes affecting the issuing of non-immigrant visas to residents of certain countries and to students, as well as changes authorizing local law enforcement agents to participate in the enforcement of immigration law.

In November 2001 the State Department mandated background checks on all male visa applicants between the ages of 16 and 45 from 26 mostly Muslim countries. The Enhanced Border Security and Visa Entry Reform Act of 2002 prohibited issuing nonimmigrant visas to nationals of seven countries (Cuba, Iran, Iraq, Libya, North Korea, Sudan, and Syria) unless it was determined after a thorough background check that the individuals were not security threats. The list of prohibited countries could change as directed by the U.S. attorney general.

After 9/11 the United States also increased visa restrictions for foreign students. The IIRIRA had mandated the creation of a database that stored information about international students, but the system had not yet been launched when the terrorist attacks of 9/11 occurred. In May 2002 the INS launched the Student and Exchange Visitor Information System (SEVIS), an Internet-based system to track foreign nationals who enter the country on student visas. SEVIS, which was overseen by ICE after the creation of the DHS, came online in 2003. A drastic improvement of previous decentralized systems intended to track student visa recipients, SEVIS compiled information across agencies and allowed federal immigration authorities to monitor not only individuals but also the schools and exchange programs that brought students to the United States. According to the Student Exchange Visitor Program (SEVP; the division of ICE that oversees SEVIS), in *Student and Exchange Visitor Information System: General Summary Quarterly Review* (October 2014, http://www .ice.gov/sites/default/files/documents/Document/2014/by-the-numbers.pdf), as of October 2014 the system maintained information on approximately 1.1 million foreign students studying in nearly 9,000 SEVP-certified U.S. schools. The system also tracked 200,782 foreign students who were studying in the United States through a State Department exchange visitor program and

152,704 dependents who were in the country along with visiting students.

Yet another post-9/11 change in immigration policy came when the Justice Department ruled that effective August 2002 local police could detain individuals for immigration violations, a right formerly reserved for federal agents. The measure, like that pertaining to the foreign-student database, was a part of the IIRIRA that had never been finalized. Florida became the test state, initiating a Memorandum of Understanding with the Justice Department, which authorized specially trained local police officers to assist federal agents in locating and detaining wanted aliens.

INTELLIGENCE REFORM AND TERRORISM PREVENTION ACT AND REAL ID ACT

In late 2002 the National Commission on Terrorist Attacks on the United States (also known as the 9/11 Commission) was created by Congress and the president to prepare a complete account of the circumstances surrounding the 9/11 terrorist attacks and the nation's response. The commission was also mandated to provide recommendations that were designed to guard against future attacks. One of the commission's recommendations was to create a national identification program. In December 2004 President Bush signed the Intelligence Reform and Terrorism Prevention Act. This act set national standards for driver's licenses, Social Security cards, and birth certificates.

In May 2005 President Bush signed the REAL ID Act, which mandated federal standards for state-issued driver's licenses. The new act transferred responsibility for driver's license security from the U.S. Department of Transportation to the DHS. The new law required states to develop security upgrades and security clearances for Department of Motor Vehicles personnel; verify all documents with the original issuing agency and verify U.S. citizenship or lawful immigration status before issuing a driver's license or nondriver's ID card; redesign driver's licenses and ID cards so that they contain certain types of security features; and establish new data management, storage, and sharing protocols. States were prohibited from accepting any foreign documents other than an official passport for identity purposes. States were required to be certified by May 11, 2008, in compliance with the DHS and the Transportation Department.

Opposition to the REAL ID Act came from numerous quarters and was initially united across partisan and geographical lines. State governments complained that it would cost them billions of dollars to implement the law. Civil libertarians and privacy experts strongly objected to a national ID system because it would create a massive national database of sensitive personal information without providing sufficient privacy protections. The

American Civil Liberties Union (ACLU) outlines some of the most prominent privacy concerns in its "Real Answers FAQ" (http://www.realnightmare.org/about/2). In creating a single, interlinked database where the most private data of a majority of adults would be stored, the ACLU argued, the system would create a "one-stop shop" for identity thieves. This centralization of data would also enable the federal government to conduct surveillance of ordinary citizens, and the government's invocation of national security as a motivation for such spying would allow the activity to proceed without appropriate judicial oversight. Because REAL ID requirements included a mandate to equip driver's licenses with computerized elements that could be read not only by machines at such locations as airport checkpoints but also by private businesses, there was concern that retailers would be able to scan the machine-readable elements (for example, when requesting identification for a credit card purchase) and use patrons' private data for marketing purposes or sell it to other private businesses without the consent of the individual.

Immigrants, especially those who were not naturalized citizens, were the group the ACLU and other opponents of the REAL ID Act expected to suffer most from its implementation. According to the ACLU, in "Why REAL ID Will Cause New Discrimination against Many US Citizens and Immigrants" (http://www.realnightmare.org/about/5), the law's requirement that department of motor vehicle workers determine a driver's license applicant's citizenship status before issuing REAL ID–compliant identification meant that a form of potentially demeaning immigration law enforcement would occur at the hands of workers with no special expertise in immigration law; in such circumstances, they argued, the likelihood of racial profiling and discrimination was high. Although noncitizens with the legal right to be in the United States had historically been eligible for driver's licenses, many would now be eligible only for a form of license that underlines their immigrant status and publicizes it to retailers, landlords, hotel clerks, building guards, and others, encouraging discrimination. Unlike the 1986 IRCA provisions requiring employers to verify workers' citizenship status, the REAL ID Act contained no antidiscrimination provisions, according to the ACLU.

As a result of these and other objections to the national ID system, many states initially refused to comply with the REAL ID Act. As a result, the DHS repeatedly pushed back its compliance deadlines prior to announcing in December 2013 that it would begin enforcing the new standards in phases beginning in 2014. As reported by the DHS in "REAL ID Enforcement in Brief" (January 30, 2015, http://www.dhs.gov/real-id-enforcement-brief), by mid-2014 the agency was fully enforcing REAL ID Act requirements in restricted areas (areas that are open only to agency

personnel, contractors, and guests) of federal facilities and nuclear power plants. By early 2015 full enforcement was in effect for semirestricted areas (areas that are open to the general public subject to proof of identification) in most federal facilities. The DHS planned to impose REAL ID requirements for boarding aircraft no earlier than 2016.

As of January 2015, according to the DHS, eight states and/or territories (American Samoa, Arizona, Idaho, Louisiana, Maine, Minnesota, New Hampshire, and New York) remained noncompliant with the REAL ID Act. State identification cards from the remaining states/territories were either already in compliance with REAL ID or were acceptable under the terms of a DHS extension granted to those jurisdictions that were moving forward with plans to comply. The DHS estimated that 70% to 80% of U.S. drivers held licenses that met the standards of the act. Those holding licenses from noncompliant states had to submit to alternate access-control protocols when entering the facilities covered by the law, but the use of these licenses for other purposes not covered by the law (such as driving, registering to vote, and applying for federal benefits) was not affected.

In "Real ID Is Slowly Changing State Drivers' Licenses" (USAToday.com, January 22, 2014), Daniel C. Vock notes that state opposition to the law gradually faded as states found that the law's requirements were easier to integrate into their existing systems than initially anticipated. Little had been done to assuage the concerns of civil libertarians and privacy advocates, however, and the burden placed on noncitizen holders of driver's licenses remained. As Vock notes, in the growing number of states where unauthorized immigrants were entitled to obtain driver's licenses, those states planning to comply with REAL ID standards indeed created two tiers of licenses, as the ACLU and others had expected.

DEFERRED ACTION FOR CHILDHOOD ARRIVALS PROGRAM

Although the general trend in post-9/11 immigration legislation had been to restrict the flow of immigrants and/or to enhance border security provisions, there were also frequent calls for legislation that relaxed the legal sanctions imposed on certain unauthorized immigrants. One of the most prominent legislative attempts to provide relief to the unauthorized population was the Development, Relief, and Education for Alien Minors (DREAM) Act, introduced in 2001 by Senators Dick Durbin (1944–; D-IL) and Orrin Hatch (1934–; R-UT). The bill would allow certain young people brought to the United States as children who had graduated from high school and demonstrated good character to remain in the United States for college or to enlist in the military, after which point they would qualify for citizenship. Several versions of the bill appeared in both houses of Congress during the decade that followed, but none mustered sufficient support for passage.

On June 15, 2012, however, Janet Napolitano (1957–), the secretary of homeland security, announced that the United States would cease deporting those young people who met certain criteria outlined in DREAM Act legislation. The Obama administration's new policy was called the Deferred Action for Childhood Arrivals (DACA) program. It went into effect on August 15 of that year. The USCIS explains in "Consideration of Deferred Action for Childhood Arrivals" (January 29, 2014, http://www.uscis.gov/humanitarian/consideration-deferred-action-childhood-arrivals-daca) that the program offered the possibility of relief from deportation to individuals between the ages of 15 and 30 as of June 15, 2012, provided they met the following criteria:

- Was under the age of 16 years at the time of arrival in the United States

- Had continuously resided in the United States for a minimum of five years preceding June 15, 2012, and was physically present in the United States on that date

- Had no lawful immigration status on June 15, 2012

- Was currently a student, a high school graduate, a recipient of a general education development certificate, or an honorably discharged veteran of the military or the U.S. Coast Guard

- Had never been convicted of a felony or of multiple or significant misdemeanors and posed no threat to national security or public safety

Individuals who met these criteria were eligible to apply for deferred action, which consisted of relief from the threat of deportation for two years and eligibility for work authorization. Those granted deferred-action status could apply for renewal at the end of that period. Eligibility to apply for deferred action, however, did not guarantee receipt of that status; applicants were to be judged on a case-by-case basis. The DACA program fell short of DREAM Act proposals in that it did not offer beneficiaries a path to legal permanent residence or citizenship. Additionally, immediate family members and dependents of those granted deferred-action status were ineligible for deferred action. Those who came to the United States after June 15, 2012, were not eligible for deferred action.

Table 2.1 shows statistics for DACA applications processed between August 2012 (the fourth quarter of FY 2012) and September 2014 (the end of FY 2014). A total of 818,050 requests for deferred action were accepted during this time, of which 632,855 had been approved as of October 2014. The total number of requests does not match the total number of immigrants who received relief from deportation, as a substantial portion of 2014 applications were requests to renew an initial application successfully filed at the program's outset. Of the 115,565 requests for renewal that were accepted by the USCIS in 2014, 22,480 had been approved, and 93,080 were still pending as of October 2014. By any accounting, the total number of unauthorized immigrants who received relief from deportation under DACA was significantly lower than the number of those believed to be eligible. As Jens Manuel Krogstad and Jeffrey S. Passel of the Pew Research Center note in "Those from Mexico Will Benefit Most from Obama's Executive Action" (November 20, 2014, http://www.pewresearch.org/fact-tank/2014/11/20/those-from-mexico-will-benefit-most-from-obamas-executive-action), an estimated 1.5 million unauthorized immigrants were eligible for deferred action under the original executive action as of November 2014.

DACA Expansion and Deferred Action for Parents of Americans

On November 20, 2014, President Obama announced a new set of executive actions related to immigration law. Besides measures intended to make it easier for the family members of LPRs to obtain legal status, modernize immigrant and nonimmigrant visa programs, and promote naturalization of LPRs, the executive actions significantly expanded on the DACA program that was already in place, and it added a new program, Deferred Action for Parents of Americans and Lawful Permanent Residents (DAPA).

The USCIS notes in "Executive Actions on Immigration" (January 30, 2015, http://www.uscis.gov/immigrationaction) that the DACA expansion increased the period of relief from the threat of deportation to three years (up from the two years available under the 2012 DACA executive action), and it changed DACA requirements in such a way as to broaden the potential pool of eligible applicants. Under the 2014 proposal, unauthorized immigrants of any age (as opposed to those aged 30 years and under, as the 2012 DACA action stated) could apply for DACA if they came to the United States prior to the age of 16, had lived in the United States continuously since January 1, 2010 (rather than June 15, 2007, as the 2012 DACA action mandated), and met all other DACA guidelines. As with the original DACA program, applicants were subject to approval on a case-by-case basis.

DAPA represented an even larger expansion of the population of unauthorized immigrants eligible for relief from deportation proceedings. In "Executive Actions on Immigration," the USCIS notes that the program was open to any unauthorized immigrants who have lived in the United States continuously since January 1, 2010, had (as of November 20, 2014) a child who was a citizen or LPR, and were not currently in a prioritized category of removal from the United States (priority categorizations primarily consisted of immigrants considered to be

TABLE 2.1

Deferred Action for Childhood Arrivals requests, by intake, biometrics, and case review status, fiscal years 2012–14

	Requests by intake, biometrics and case status								
	Intake[a]				Biometrics[f]	Case review[h]			
Period	Requests accepted[b]	Requests rejected[c]	Total requests received[d]	Average accepted/ day[e]	Biometrics scheduled[g]	Requests under review[i]	Approved[j]	Denied[k]	Pending[l]
Fiscal year—total									
2012	152,423	5,395	157,818	4,763	124,055	29,747	1,686	—	150,737
2013	427,597	16,358	443,955	1,704	445,013	75,122	472,831	11,115	94,388
2014	238,030	24,893	262,923	948	209,670	99,027	158,338	21,285	152,795
2014 initial	122,465	19,135	141,600	488	N/A	N/A	135,858	21,280	59,715
2014 renewal	115,565	5,758	121,323	1,360	N/A	N/A	22,480	D	93,080
Total cumulative	818,050	46,646	864,696	1,532	778,738	99,027	632,855	32,400	152,795
Total cumulative initial	702,485	40,888	743,373	1,316	N/A	N/A	610,375	32,395	59,715
Total cumulative renewal	115,565	5,758	121,323	1,360	N/A	N/A	22,480	D	93,080
Fiscal year 2014 by quarter									
Q1. October–December	31,105	5,646	36,751	502	30,017	56,315	47,628	4,665	73,200
Q2. January–March	31,806	3,384	35,190	521	28,876	49,212	31,473	4,336	69,197
Q3. April–June	42,654	6,343	48,997	666	39,335	53,199	27,724	3,650	80,477
Q3. April–June initial	32,559	5,824	38,383	509	N/A	N/A	27,637	3,649	70,470
Q3. April–June renewal	10,095	519	10,614	481	N/A	N/A	87	D	10,007
Q4. July–September	132,465	9,520	141,985	2,070	111,442	99,027	51,513	8,634	152,795
Q4. July–September initial	26,995	5,824	32,819	422	N/A	N/A	29,120	8,630	59,715
Q4. July–September renewal	105,470	519	105,989	1,648	N/A	N/A	22,393	D	93,080

D = Data withheld to protect requestor's privacy.
—Represents zero.
N/A = not available.
[a]Refers to a request for USCIS to consider deferred removal action for an individual based on Department of Homeland Security guidelines.
[b]The number of new requests accepted at a Lockbox during the reporting period.
[c]The number of requests rejected at a Lockbox during the reporting period.
[d]The number of requests that were received at a Lockbox during the reporting period.
[e]The number of requests accepted per day at a Lockbox as of the end of the reporting period. Also note the average accepted per day for initial plus renewal will not equal the total average.
[f]Refers to capture of requestors' biometrics.
[g]The number of appointments scheduled to capture requestors' biometrics during the reporting period.
[h]Refers to consideration of deferring action on a case-by-case basis during the reporting period.
[i]The number of new requests received and entered into a case-tracking system during the reporting period.
[j]The number of requests approved during the reporting period.
[k]The number of requests that were denied, terminated, or withdrawn during the reporting period.
[l]The number of requests awaiting a decision as of the end of the reporting period.
Notes: Some requests approved or denied may have been received in previous reporting periods. The report reflects the most up-to-date estimate available at the time the report is generated.

SOURCE: "Requests by Intake, Biometrics and Case Status," in *Number of I-821D, Consideration of Deferred Action for Childhood Arrivals by Fiscal Year, Quarter, Intake, Biometrics and Case Status: 2012–2014*, U.S. Department of Homeland Security, U.S. Citizenship and Immigration Services, October 2014, http://www.uscis.gov/sites/default/files/USCIS/Resources/Reports%20and%20Studies/Immigration%20Forms%20Data/All%20Form%20Types/DACA/DACA_fy2014_qtr4.pdf (accessed January 14, 2015)

national security or public safety threats). Again, applicants would not be automatically granted deferred action status but would be evaluated on a case-by-case basis.

Krogstad and Passel of the Pew Research Center estimate that these executive actions would make 3.9 million unauthorized immigrants newly eligible for deferred action. Seven in 10 (2.8 million) of those expected to be newly eligible for deferred action were the parents of children under age 18. Another 700,000 newly eligible immigrants were parents of children over age 18, and 300,000 were individuals who would qualify for DACA under the expanded eligibility guidelines.

The USCIS planned to begin accepting applications for the expanded DACA program in mid-February 2015, and to open the application period for DAPA in mid-2015. However, before implementation had begun, a federal judge in Texas issued an injunction preventing the USCIS from accepting applications. As of April 2015 the judge's ruling was being appealed by the Obama administration, and resolution of the law's status was expected to take several months.

President Obama's 2012 and 2014 executive actions represented a major intervention in immigration law. However, these changes to enforcement protocol were hardly a blanket extension of immigration status to all unauthorized immigrants. As Krogstad and Passel write in "Who Are the Unauthorized Immigrants Ineligible for Obama's Executive Action?" (December 1, 2014, http://www.pewresearch.org/fact-tank/2014/12/01/who-are-the-unauthorized-immigrants-ineligible-for-obamas-executive-action), an estimated 5.8 million unauthorized immigrants would remain at risk of deportation after implementation of the executive actions. Almost all of those (96%) who remained ineligible had no children born in the United States. The ineligible population was heavily male and unmarried, and the ineligible population was slightly more likely (73%) than the eligible population (69%) to be employed.

IMMIGRATION LEGISLATION IN THE STATES

Beginning in the 1990s populist concern about the rising numbers of unauthorized immigrants, especially in border states, led to the proposal of a range of restrictive immigration laws at the state level. Such laws, which sometimes conflict with federal law, were often proposed as remedies to federal inaction on border security and immigration law enforcement, with state governors and legislators typically citing security concerns and/or the necessity of curbing expenditures incurred by law enforcement and other state officials in border states.

The U.S. Supreme Court has consistently upheld the federal government's claims to having exclusive jurisdiction over immigration law, and it has typically overruled state efforts to impose restrictions on immigrants that are inconsistent with federal law. States have no power, for example, to regulate immigration admissions and removals. States and local governments do have some authority to regulate the lives of immigrants who are in the country already, for example by setting policies pertaining to noncitizens' access to education, business licensing, and the provision of health and welfare services. However, there are no clear guidelines establishing the degree of latitude the states have in this area of the law, so the passage of new state immigration legislation is typically accompanied by lawsuits that determine whether or in what form they will proceed to implementation.

Two border states in the Southwest have been at the forefront of efforts to address immigration through state legislation: California and Arizona. During the 1990s California made the highest-profile early attempt to restrict unauthorized immigration, and during the early 21st century Arizona made national headlines by crafting ordinances more restrictive than any in modern U.S. history to that date. Other states followed Arizona's lead in passing increasingly restrictive laws between 2010 and 2012, but adverse rulings at the U.S. Supreme Court (in the case of the Arizona law) and in other federal courts limited the impact of these laws. A backlash to restrictive laws, together with shifting political calculations and the effects of federal policy established by President Obama's executive actions in 2012 and 2014, ushered in a new period of state immigration legislation between 2012 and 2015. Left-leaning states, led by California (in a reversal of its 1990s attempt to restrict immigration), passed an increasing number of immigrant-friendly state laws during this time, many of which were intended to promote the integration of at least some unauthorized immigrants into their communities.

California's Attempt to Restrict Immigrant Rights

Increasing concern about the effects of illegal immigration in California culminated in November 1994, when voters approved Proposition 187. The ballot initiative prohibited unauthorized immigrants and their children from receiving any welfare services, education, or emergency health care. It further required local law enforcement authorities, educators, medical professionals, and social service workers to report suspected unauthorized immigrants to federal and state authorities. It also considered the manufacture, distribution, and sale of fraudulent documents to be a state felony punishable by up to five years in prison.

The day after California voters approved Proposition 187, civil rights groups filed suit in federal district court to block implementation of the ballot initiative. One week later a temporary restraining order was issued. In November 1995 the U.S. district judge Mariana R. Pfaelzer (1926–) ruled unconstitutional Proposition 187's provision that denied elementary and secondary education for undocumented children. Pfaelzer cited the U.S. Supreme Court decision in *Plyler v. Doe* (457 U.S. 202 [1982]), which held that the equal protection clause of the 14th Amendment prohibits states from denying education to illegal immigrant children. Civil rights and education groups had argued that states had no legal rights to regulate immigration, which was a federal responsibility.

In March 1998 Pfaelzer permanently barred Proposition 187's restrictions on benefits for unauthorized immigrants and declared much of the legislation unconstitutional. Pfaelzer did allow, however, the criminal provision to consider as a felony the manufacture, distribution, and use of false documents.

Arizona Succeeds Where California Failed

In November 2004 Arizona voters approved Proposition 200, which required proof of citizenship when registering to vote and applying for public benefits. It also required state, county, and municipal employees to report suspected undocumented immigrants to the authorities. The Mexican American Legal Defense and Educational Fund filed suit to block implementation of Proposition 200. In December 2004 the U.S. district judge David C. Bury (1942–) lifted a temporary order barring implementation of Proposition 200, which allowed it to become law in Arizona.

Proposition 200 proved to be just the beginning of Arizona's restrictive immigration laws. In 2007 Arizona passed one of the toughest immigration laws in the country, the Legal Arizona Workers Act (LAWA), which became effective on January 1, 2008. LAWA provided for the suspension and revocation of the business licenses of Arizona employers who knowingly employ illegal immigrants. It also required employers to verify the work status of newly hired workers through E-Verify.

In 2010 Arizona passed the most restrictive immigration law on record to that date, Arizona Senate Bill 1070 (SB 1070). Signed into law by Governor Jan Brewer (1944–) on April 23, 2010, and subsequently modified, SB 1070 required police officers to determine immigration status during "lawful contact," such as routine traffic stops. The law also required legal immigrants to carry registration documents at all times, making failure to do so a state crime; authorized police to arrest illegal immigrants if they had probable cause to believe that the person had committed an offense that would lead to deportation; and made it illegal for unauthorized workers to solicit or perform work.

SB 1070 faced legal challenges almost immediately. Particular outrage was directed at the so-called "show me your papers" provision, which required law enforcement agencies to ask suspected immigrants for proof of their authorization to be in the United States. Critics argued that the provision legalized racial profiling by essentially requiring police to question the immigration status of anyone who looked Hispanic. Besides a number of other lawsuits attempting to block implementation of the law, the Justice Department filed suit against the state of Arizona in July 2010, asserting that only the federal government had the authority to regulate immigration. Lower courts ruled in favor of the Justice Department, but Arizona appealed and was ultimately granted a hearing before the U.S. Supreme Court. In June 2012 the court issued a 5–3 ruling in *Arizona v. United States* (567 U.S. ___) that struck down much of the law on the grounds that it conflicted with federal law. However, the court upheld the legality of the "show me your papers" provision. The majority opinion, written by Justice Anthony M. Kennedy (1936–), suggested that this provision could later be struck down if a documented pattern of racial profiling resulted from its implementation.

State Immigration Laws Modeled on SB 1070

Arizona's success at passing restrictive immigration laws led other states to follow suit. While SB 1070 was tied up in the courts, the state of Alabama enacted an immigration law that was modeled on the Arizona law but surpassed it in its restrictive character. House Bill 56 (HB 56), signed into law by Alabama Governor Robert Bentley (1943–) in June 2011, contained a "show me your papers" provision similar to Arizona's. It also prohibited unauthorized immigrants from receiving any public services, from attending public colleges and universities, and from applying for jobs. Employers were required to use the E-Verify system to confirm the immigration status of all employees, and the refusal to hire a legal resident while employing an unauthorized immigrant was declared a dis-

criminatory practice. The law prohibited the transportation or harboring of illegal immigrants and the renting of property to illegal immigrants. Meanwhile, primary and secondary public school officials were required to ascertain the immigration status of students and report the number of suspected illegal immigrants to state education officials. Many backers of the law were overt about the intent of HB 56: to make everyday life so difficult for unauthorized immigrants that they would leave the state voluntarily or "self-deport." Josh Lederman reports in "Co-author of Arizona Immigration Law Says 'Self-Deportation' Working" (Hill.com, February 11, 2012) that Kris Kobach (1966–), the secretary of state of Kansas, claimed in February 2012 that HB 56 and SB 1070 had encouraged many illegal immigrants to leave Alabama and Arizona rather than risk arrest and deportation. Kobach helped write both laws.

Much like SB 1070, HB 56 was met with a broad array of legal challenges. A number of HB 56's provisions were temporarily blocked pending the outcome of the court cases, and in August 2012 the U.S. Court of Appeals for the 11th Circuit blocked many of the measures meant to make everyday life difficult for illegal immigrants, including the measures requiring school officials to report students that they suspected of being undocumented. Alabama's appeal of this ruling to the U.S. Supreme Court was denied. As in Arizona, the controversial "show me your papers" provision was upheld. Ongoing lawsuits filed by civil rights and immigrant advocacy groups resulted in a 2013 settlement that ensured the previously invalidated provisions were excised from the law, and the state agreed to pay $350,000 in plaintiffs' attorney fees.

Other states whose governors signed similarly restrictive immigration laws modeled on Arizona's SB 1070 in 2010 and 2011 were Georgia, Indiana, South Carolina, and Utah. Alan Gomez reports in "South Carolina Puts Brakes on Immigration Law" (USAToday.com, March 3, 2014) that by early 2014 only Georgia's law had been implemented in anything resembling its original form, including a provision authorizing the determination of a person's immigration status during any legitimate contact. Most portions of Indiana's law were permanently blocked by a federal judge in 2013, including its version of the "show me your papers" provision (which differed from Arizona's). The "show me your papers" provision of South Carolina's SB 20 was significantly scaled back under the terms of a 2014 settlement between the state and the groups that sued to block implementation of the law. Utah's 2011 HB 497, meanwhile, had initially been heralded as a more humane alternative to Arizona's, since it offered avenues for unauthorized immigrants to apply for work permits provided that they reported themselves and paid a fine. As of 2015 the law had not been enacted, and flagging support for it even among its original supporters made its future uncertain.

A Shift to Immigrant-Friendly State Legislation

As Karthick Ramakrishnan and Pratheepan Gulase-karam of the Center for American Progress, a nonprofit left-leaning advocacy group, report in *Understanding Immigration Federalism in the United States* (March 2014, http://cdn.americanprogress.org/wp-content/uploads/2014/03/StateImmigration-reportv2.pdf), the legal losses suffered by advocates for restrictive state immigration laws were compounded by political losses in the 2012 presidential election. In that election, incumbent Democratic President Barack Obama defeated the Republican candidate, Mitt Romney (1947–), with crucial support from Hispanic and Asian American voters. Obama received an estimated 71% of the Hispanic vote to Romney's 27%, and he received an estimated 73% of the Asian American vote to Romney's 26%. Only eight years earlier, Republican President George W. Bush had won reelection while earning nearly half of both groups' votes.

The precipitous declines in support for Republican candidates by Hispanics and Asian Americans was attributed in part to the party's harsh rhetoric about illegal immigration and its corresponding embrace of policies such as SB 1070 that were perceived as anti-immigrant. The projected increase in the growth of these two populations in the coming decades, resulting from continued immigration as well as births, meant that they would exert a growing amount of power at the ballot box. As a result, Republican politicians and right-leaning pundits began calling for a change in tone on the immigration issue, and many pushed for immigration policy reform at the federal level, in the hopes of appealing to these demographic groups in future elections.

Thus, in the aftermath of the 2012 election, the trend of restrictive state-level immigration ordinances appeared to have peaked. Between 2012 and 2014, in the absence of a broad federal overhaul of immigration legislation, states continued to pass numerous laws relating to their immigrant populations, but these were more likely to be measures intended to promote the integration of immigrants than measures intended to make life harder for them in the hopes of discouraging further unauthorized immigration. No new omnibus immigration legislation (bills attempting to regulate immigration broadly, across numerous sets of issues, such as Arizona's SB 1070 and those modeled after it) appeared during this time. Further, President Obama's announcement of DACA also encouraged this shift in the direction of state immigration laws because it extended rights to certain members of the unauthorized population. DAPA was expected to continue this trend, pending the resolution of legal challenges.

Immigrant-friendly laws had existed before this time. Among the most common measures allowing for the integration of some unauthorized immigrants prior to 2012 were state laws allowing unauthorized students who graduated from public high schools in their state to attend public universities at the in-state tuition rate. Muzaffar Chishti and Faye Hipsman of the nonpartisan Migration Policy Institute note in "As Congress Tackles Immigration Legislation, State Lawmakers Retreat from Strict Measures" (May 23, 2013, http://www.migrationpolicy.org/article/congress-tackles-immigration-legislation-state-lawmakers-retreat-strict-measures) that California and Texas both passed laws to this effect in 2001. Utah and New York enacted similar policies in 2002, and they were followed by Washington and Illinois (2003), Kansas (2004), New Mexico (2005), Nebraska (2006), Wisconsin (2009), and Maryland and Connecticut (2011). Oregon, Colorado, Minnesota, and New Jersey joined this group of states in 2013, and Florida followed suit in 2014. According to the National Conference of State Legislatures, in "Undocumented Student Tuition: Overview" (February 10, 2015, http://www.ncsl.org/research/education/undocumented-student-tuition-overview.aspx), two states, Oklahoma and Rhode Island, allow undocumented students to pay in-state tuition subject to policies set by the Boards of Regents of institutions of higher education; in 2013 the University of Hawaii and the University of Michigan instituted similar policies as a result of decisions by their governing boards, and in 2014 Virginia's attorney general granted the right to in-state tuition to DACA recipients.

Another central issue in states with large populations of unauthorized immigrants was eligibility for driver's licenses. Given the reality that most unauthorized immigrants work and must have a means of transportation to and from their jobs, many law enforcement officials and public-safety experts have long advocated for granting state-issued driver's licenses to at least some portion of the unauthorized population. As noted earlier, the REAL ID Act provided states with options for issuing specially marked driver's licenses to unauthorized immigrants, and states are allowed to impose stricter measures. In the climate of growing restrictionist sentiment that prevailed prior to the Supreme Court ruling on SB 1070 and the 2012 presidential election, seven of 10 states that allowed at least some unauthorized immigrants to obtain driver's licenses (California, Hawaii, Maine, Maryland, Michigan, Oregon, and Tennessee) repealed those policies. Following the 2012 enactment of DACA, which gave legal work authorization to many unauthorized immigrants, the push to extend driving privileges to some or all unauthorized immigrants gained momentum. By 2015, according to the National Immigration Law Center in "State Laws & Policies on Driver's Licenses for Immigrants" (January 2015, http://www.nilc.org/driverlicensemap.html), Nebraska was the only state that continued to deny driver's licenses to DACA recipients. Additionally, in 10 states (California, Colorado, Connecticut, Illinois,

Maryland, Nevada, New Mexico, Utah, Vermont, and Washington) and the District of Columbia, driver's licenses were available to all residents regardless of their immigration status.

Another major element of this new wave of state immigration law focused on the DHS's Secure Communities Program, which had, since 2008, required local law enforcement to cooperate with ICE in detaining unauthorized immigrants who came into contact with police and sheriff's offices. Under this program, for example, immigrants who reported crimes to police or who committed minor traffic violations could be held by law enforcement for 48 hours at ICE's request, and they could be removed from the country as a result of this collaboration between local/state and federal authorities. To combat the growing number of deportations for nonviolent offenses, a number of local police departments and municipal governments stopped cooperating with such requests between 2008 and 2012. In 2013 Connecticut and California became the first to implement noncooperation policies at the state level, in the form of so-called TRUST (Transparency and Responsibility Using State Tools) Acts, which barred state and local law enforcement officers from detaining immigrants at the request of ICE except in cases involving serious crimes.

As San Francisco's CBS TV affiliate reported the following year in "AP Report: California Immigrant Deportations Plummet after Trust Act" (April 6, 2014, http://sanfrancisco.cbslocal.com/2014/04/06/immigration-deportation-trust-act), an Associated Press report found that in the first two months after implementation, 15 of the California sheriff's offices previously responsible for the most deportations in collaboration with ICE, including those in four of the state's five largest counties, saw a 44% drop in deportations in the first two months of 2014. Thus California was squarely in the forefront of states that were relaxing legal requirements and seeking to promote the integration of unauthorized immigrants. This represented a noteworthy turnaround for a state that had two decades earlier led the nation in the attempt to implement restrictive ordinances to combat the surge in illegal immigration.

CHAPTER 3
CURRENT IMMIGRATION STATISTICS

Although the United States has always been a nation of immigrants, the size, characteristics, and geographical distribution of the foreign-born population have changed dramatically with time. The U.S. Census Bureau notes in "How Do We Know? America's Foreign Born in the Last 50 Years" (2013, http://www.census.gov/library/infographics/foreign_born.html) that in 1960 there were an estimated 9.7 million foreign-born residents in the United States. Immigrants at that time represented one out of every 20 U.S. residents, most were from Europe, and they were concentrated in the Northeast and the Midwest. In 2010, by contrast, there were approximately 40 million foreign-born U.S. residents. Immigrants at that time represented one out of every eight U.S. residents, most were from Latin America and Asia, and they were increasingly concentrated in the West and the South.

These changes occurred rapidly and represent a profound shift in the character of the country. However, the relative sizes of the foreign-born and native-born populations in 2010 were not historically unique. Although the percentage of the total population that was foreign born increased steadily between 1970 and 2010, from 4.7% to 12.9%, this last percentage remained below its historic high. (See Figure 2.1 in Chapter 2.) In decennial census counts from 1860 to 1920, the immigrant population was never less than 13.2% of the total U.S. population, and in 1890 the figure stood at an all-time high of 14.8%.

The Census Bureau projects steady growth in the immigrant population in the decades to come, with the foreign-born population eclipsing the record 1890 percentage by the mid-2020s and reaching nearly 19% of the total U.S. population by 2060. (See Table 3.1.) The projected growth in the foreign-born population was expected to be disproportionately driven by the aging of immigrants already in the country. As Table 3.2 shows, between 2015 and 2060 the number of immigrant children was expected to increase from approximately 2.5

million in 2015 to about 3.3 million in 2060 (an increase of 31%, or less than 1% per year), and the population of working-age immigrant adults was expected to increase from 34.4 million to 49.7 million (an increase of 44.5%, or approximately 1% per year). The population of immigrants aged 65 years and older, meanwhile, was projected to grow from 6.4 million in 2015 to 25.3 million in 2060 (an increase of 295%, or about 6.6% per year).

In any event, immigrants will undoubtedly continue to exert a significant influence on the nation's social, cultural, economic, and political life. That influence will, of course, depend not simply on the overall size of the immigrant population but on its specific characteristics. This chapter will focus on statistics relating to the current foreign-born population, including countries of origin, legal status, occupations, and procedures for seeking admission to the country.

COUNTING IMMIGRANTS

In 2013 there were approximately 316.1 million people living in the United States, a large majority of whom were citizens either born in the country (270.2 million), born in a U.S. territory (1.8 million), or born abroad to American parents (2.7 million). (See Table 3.3.) Another 19.3 million U.S. residents were immigrants who had become citizens through the naturalization process, and there were 22.1 million noncitizens. The noncitizen category includes lawful permanent residents (LPRs), people who were in the country legally and temporarily on various types of visas (government permits allowing individuals to enter a country and remain for specific purposes and finite periods), and immigrants without legal authorization to be in the country (some of whom had entered the country illegally, and some of whom had obtained visas to enter the country but remained beyond the time frame specified by the particular visa types).

TABLE 3.1

Population projections, by nativity, 2015–60

[Resident population as of July 1. Numbers in thousands.]

Year	Total			Native born			Foreign born			Percent foreign born
	Population	Numeric change	Percent change	Population	Numeric change	Percent change	Population	Numeric change	Percent change	
2015	321,369	2,621	0.82	278,094	1,696	0.61	43,275	925	2.18	13.47
2016	323,996	2,627	0.82	279,794	1,700	0.61	44,201	927	2.14	13.64
2017	326,626	2,630	0.81	281,498	1,704	0.61	45,128	926	2.10	13.82
2018	329,256	2,631	0.81	283,204	1,706	0.61	46,053	925	2.05	13.99
2019	331,884	2,628	0.80	284,910	1,706	0.60	46,974	922	2.00	14.15
2020	334,503	2,619	0.79	286,611	1,701	0.60	47,892	918	1.95	14.32
2021	337,109	2,606	0.78	288,303	1,692	0.59	48,806	914	1.91	14.48
2022	339,698	2,589	0.77	289,982	1,680	0.58	49,716	910	1.86	14.64
2023	342,267	2,569	0.76	291,645	1,663	0.57	50,622	906	1.82	14.79
2024	344,814	2,547	0.74	293,289	1,643	0.56	51,526	904	1.79	14.94
2025	347,335	2,521	0.73	294,909	1,620	0.55	52,426	901	1.75	15.09
2026	349,826	2,491	0.72	296,503	1,594	0.54	53,323	897	1.71	15.24
2027	352,281	2,456	0.70	298,066	1,564	0.53	54,215	892	1.67	15.39
2028	354,698	2,417	0.69	299,596	1,530	0.51	55,102	887	1.64	15.53
2029	357,073	2,374	0.67	301,090	1,493	0.50	55,983	881	1.60	15.68
2030	359,402	2,329	0.65	302,545	1,455	0.48	56,857	874	1.56	15.82
2031	361,685	2,283	0.64	303,961	1,416	0.47	57,724	867	1.52	15.96
2032	363,920	2,235	0.62	305,337	1,376	0.45	58,583	859	1.49	16.10
2033	366,106	2,187	0.60	306,674	1,337	0.44	59,433	850	1.45	16.23
2034	368,246	2,139	0.58	307,973	1,299	0.42	60,273	840	1.41	16.37
2035	370,338	2,093	0.57	309,235	1,262	0.41	61,103	830	1.38	16.50
2036	372,390	2,052	0.55	310,465	1,230	0.40	61,925	822	1.34	16.63
2037	374,401	2,012	0.54	311,664	1,199	0.39	62,737	813	1.31	16.76
2038	376,375	1,974	0.53	312,835	1,171	0.38	63,541	803	1.28	16.88
2039	378,313	1,938	0.51	313,980	1,145	0.37	64,334	793	1.25	17.01
2040	380,219	1,906	0.50	315,103	1,123	0.36	65,116	782	1.22	17.13
2041	382,096	1,877	0.49	316,209	1,106	0.35	65,888	772	1.19	17.24
2042	383,949	1,852	0.48	317,301	1,092	0.35	66,648	760	1.15	17.36
2043	385,779	1,831	0.48	318,382	1,082	0.34	67,397	749	1.12	17.47
2044	387,593	1,814	0.47	319,459	1,076	0.34	68,134	737	1.09	17.58
2045	389,394	1,801	0.46	320,534	1,076	0.34	68,860	725	1.06	17.68
2046	391,187	1,792	0.46	321,614	1,079	0.34	69,573	713	1.04	17.79
2047	392,973	1,786	0.46	322,699	1,086	0.34	70,273	701	1.01	17.88
2048	394,756	1,783	0.45	323,795	1,095	0.34	70,961	688	0.98	17.98
2049	396,540	1,784	0.45	324,904	1,109	0.34	71,636	675	0.95	18.07
2050	398,328	1,788	0.45	326,030	1,126	0.35	72,299	662	0.92	18.15
2051	400,124	1,795	0.45	327,175	1,146	0.35	72,948	650	0.90	18.23
2052	401,929	1,805	0.45	328,343	1,168	0.36	73,586	637	0.87	18.31
2053	403,744	1,816	0.45	329,535	1,191	0.36	74,210	624	0.85	18.38
2054	405,572	1,828	0.45	330,751	1,216	0.37	74,822	612	0.82	18.45
2055	407,412	1,840	0.45	331,991	1,241	0.38	75,421	599	0.80	18.51
2056	409,265	1,853	0.45	333,258	1,266	0.38	76,007	586	0.78	18.57
2057	411,130	1,865	0.46	334,549	1,291	0.39	76,581	574	0.76	18.63
2058	413,008	1,877	0.46	335,865	1,316	0.39	77,143	562	0.73	18.68
2059	414,896	1,889	0.46	337,204	1,339	0.40	77,693	550	0.71	18.73
2060	416,795	1,898	0.46	338,564	1,361	0.40	78,230	538	0.69	18.77

Note: Data on population change refer to differences in population between July 1 of the preceding year and June 30 of the indicated year. Nativity is determined based on country of birth. Those born in the United States or in U.S. territories are considered native born while those born elsewhere are considered foreign born.

SOURCE: "Table 2. Projections of the Population by Nativity for the United States: 2015 to 2060," in *2014 National Population Projections: Summary Tables*, U.S. Census Bureau, December 2014, http://www.census.gov/population/projections/files/summary/NP2014-T2.xls (accessed January 6, 2015)

In 2013 just over half (21.5 million) of the 41.3 million foreign-born U.S. residents were from Latin America and the Caribbean, and 11.6 million of these immigrants were from Mexico. (See Table 3.4.) Approximately 12.2 million foreign-born residents were from Asia, 4.8 million were from Europe, and 1.8 million were from Africa. Immigrants from Northern America (a Census Bureau classification that includes Canada, Bermuda, Greenland, and the French North Atlantic island territory St. Pierre and Miquelon) made up 846,921 of the foreign-born population, and immigrants from Oceania accounted for 222,390.

The immigrant population is not spread evenly across the United States. As of 2012, the states with the highest concentrations of immigrants were California (where 26.1% of residents were foreign born), New York (22%), and New Jersey (21.5%). (See Figure 3.1.) Another six states (Florida, Hawaii, Maryland, Massachusetts, Nevada, and Texas) and the District of Columbia had immigrant populations ranging from 14.4% to 19.7% of total population, and 10 states (Arizona, Connecticut, Delaware, Georgia, Illinois, New Mexico, Oregon, Rhode Island, Virginia, and Washington) had immigrant populations ranging from 9.6% to 13.8% of total population. In the remaining 31

TABLE 3.2

Projections of the foreign-born population, by sex and selected age groups, 2015–60

[Resident population as of July 1. Numbers in thousands.]

Sex and age	2015	2020	2025	2030	2035	2040	2045	2050	2055	2060
Both sexes	**43,275**	**47,892**	**52,426**	**56,857**	**61,103**	**65,116**	**68,860**	**72,299**	**75,421**	**78,230**
Under 18 years	2,480	2,445	2,622	2,787	2,897	2,996	3,082	3,153	3,211	3,254
Under 5 years	287	308	323	336	348	358	367	374	379	382
5 to 13 years	1,174	1,266	1,388	1,454	1,512	1,563	1,607	1,644	1,673	1,695
14 to 17 years	1,019	871	911	997	1,038	1,075	1,108	1,136	1,159	1,177
18 to 64 years	34,389	37,369	39,651	41,575	43,256	44,651	45,986	47,250	48,485	49,689
18 to 24 years	3,154	3,202	3,057	3,144	3,344	3,471	3,578	3,669	3,744	3,801
25 to 44 years	16,968	17,502	17,996	18,299	18,631	19,146	19,635	20,268	20,891	21,368
45 to 64 years	14,267	16,665	18,598	20,132	21,281	22,035	22,773	23,313	23,850	24,520
65 years and over	6,406	8,079	10,154	12,495	14,950	17,469	19,792	21,895	23,725	25,288
85 years and over	762	890	1,098	1,356	1,791	2,288	2,906	3,581	4,272	4,975
100 years and over	10	11	16	19	23	30	40	59	79	107
16 years and over	41,360	45,934	50,296	54,613	58,770	62,705	66,381	69,764	72,840	75,617
18 years and over	40,795	45,447	49,804	54,070	58,206	62,120	65,778	69,145	72,210	74,977
15 to 44 years	20,929	21,392	21,758	22,221	22,785	23,455	24,078	24,824	25,539	26,087
Male	**21,158**	**23,430**	**25,631**	**27,776**	**29,830**	**31,773**	**33,591**	**35,271**	**36,808**	**38,202**
Under 18 years	1,224	1,218	1,313	1,400	1,456	1,505	1,548	1,584	1,613	1,635
Under 5 years	145	158	166	172	178	184	188	191	194	195
5 to 13 years	574	627	693	727	756	781	803	822	837	848
14 to 17 years	504	433	455	501	522	541	557	571	583	591
18 to 64 years	17,240	18,763	19,935	20,923	21,820	22,576	23,282	23,944	24,547	25,122
18 to 24 years	1,678	1,649	1,571	1,623	1,729	1,795	1,849	1,895	1,932	1,960
25 to 44 years	8,629	9,002	9,273	9,428	9,563	9,785	10,037	10,369	10,686	10,923
45 to 64 years	6,932	8,111	9,091	9,872	10,528	10,996	11,396	11,679	11,930	12,240
65 years and over	2,694	3,449	4,383	5,453	6,554	7,691	8,761	9,743	10,647	11,444
85 years and over	262	307	387	483	656	849	1,090	1,366	1,640	1,930
100 years and over	3	3	4	5	6	8	10	15	21	29
16 years and over	20,219	22,456	24,565	26,650	28,659	30,562	32,347	33,999	35,512	36,890
18 years and over	19,934	22,212	24,319	26,376	28,374	30,267	32,043	33,687	35,194	36,567
15 to 44 years	10,711	10,994	11,196	11,442	11,700	12,003	12,322	12,711	13,073	13,345
Female	**22,117**	**24,463**	**26,795**	**29,081**	**31,273**	**33,343**	**35,269**	**37,028**	**38,613**	**40,029**
Under 18 years	1,256	1,227	1,309	1,387	1,442	1,491	1,533	1,569	1,598	1,619
Under 5 years	142	150	157	164	170	175	179	182	185	187
5 to 13 years	599	639	696	727	756	781	803	822	836	847
14 to 17 years	515	438	456	496	516	535	551	565	576	585
18 to 64 years	17,149	18,606	19,715	20,652	21,436	22,075	22,704	23,307	23,937	24,567
18 to 24 years	1,476	1,553	1,486	1,521	1,615	1,676	1,729	1,774	1,812	1,841
25 to 44 years	8,339	8,499	8,723	8,871	9,068	9,360	9,598	9,899	10,205	10,445
45 to 64 years	7,335	8,554	9,507	10,260	10,753	11,039	11,377	11,634	11,920	12,281
65 years and over	3,712	4,630	5,770	7,042	8,396	9,778	11,031	12,152	13,078	13,843
85 years and over	500	582	711	873	1,135	1,439	1,816	2,215	2,632	3,045
100 years and over	8	8	11	14	17	23	30	43	58	78
16 years and over	21,141	23,479	25,731	27,963	30,111	32,143	34,034	35,765	37,328	38,727
18 years and over	20,861	23,236	25,486	27,694	29,832	31,853	33,735	35,459	37,016	38,410
15 to 44 years	10,217	10,398	10,562	10,779	11,085	11,453	11,756	12,113	12,466	12,742

Note: Nativity is determined based on country of birth. Those born in the United States or in U.S. territories are considered native born while those born elsewhere are considered foreign born.

SOURCE: "Table 5. Projections of the Foreign-Born Population by Sex and Selected Age Groups for the United States: 2015 to 2060," in *2014 National Population Projections: Summary Tables*, U.S. Census Bureau, December 2014, http://www.census.gov/population/projections/files/summary/NP2014-T5.xls (accessed January 6, 2015)

U.S. states, where approximately 40% of the U.S. population lived, immigrants accounted for an average of just 5.2% of residents.

Marriage and Families

In 2012, as in prior years, immigrants were more likely than native-born U.S. residents to be married. (See Table 3.5.) Approximately two-thirds (65.4%) of naturalized citizens aged 15 years and older were married at that time, as were 58.6% of noncitizens, compared with fewer than half (48.7%) of native-born residents. Among the foreign-born population, immigrants from

Asia were the most likely to be married (69.7%), followed by those from Europe (64.1%) and Latin America (57.4%). (See Table 3.6.)

Immigrant women also tend to be more likely than native-born women to have children. Figure 3.2, based on the most recent Census Bureau data available as of 2015, compares the fertility rate (the number of births per 1,000 women) among native-born and foreign-born women aged 15 to 50 years in 2010. In the 12 months preceding the Census Bureau's 2010 survey, 70.3 out of every 1,000 foreign-born women aged 15 to 50 years had given birth

TABLE 3.3

U.S. population by nativity and citizenship status, 2013

	United States Estimate
Total	**316,128,839**
U.S. citizen, born in the United States	270,215,419
U.S. citizen, born in Puerto Rico or U.S. Island Areas	1,815,600
U.S. citizen, born abroad of American parent(s)	2,749,754
U.S. citizen by naturalization	19,294,710
Not a U.S. citizen	22,053,356

Notes: Data are based on a sample and are subject to sampling variability. In data year 2013, there were a series of changes to data collection operations that could have affected some estimates. These changes include the addition of Internet as a mode of data collection, the end of the content portion of Failed Edit Follow-Up interviewing, and the loss of one monthly panel due to the federal government shut down in October 2013. While the 2013 American Community Survey (ACS) data generally reflect the February 2013 Office of Management and Budget (OMB) definitions of metropolitan and micropolitan statistical areas, in certain instances the names, codes, and boundaries of the principal cities shown in ACS tables may differ from the OMB definitions due to differences in the effective dates of the geographic entities. Estimates of urban and rural population, housing units, and characteristics reflect boundaries of urban areas defined based on Census 2010 data. As a result, data for urban and rural areas from the ACS do not necessarily reflect the results of ongoing urbanization.

SOURCE: Adapted from "B05001. Nativity and Citizenship Status in the United States. Universe: Total Population in the United States," in *2013 American Community Survey 1-Year Estimates*, U.S. Census Bureau, 2014, http://factfinder.census.gov/faces/tableservices/jsf/pages/productview.xhtml?pid=ACS_13_1YR_B05001&prodType=table (accessed January 6, 2015)

TABLE 3.4

Foreign-born population, by place of birth, 2013

	United States Estimate
Total	**41,347,945**
Europe	**4,803,059**
Northern Europe	952,872
United Kingdom (inc. Crown Dependencies)	695,489
United Kingdom, excluding England and Scotland	299,942
England	330,357
Scotland	65,190
Ireland	128,350
Denmark	28,521
Norway	28,520
Sweden	44,870
Other Northern Europe	27,122
Western Europe	959,298
Austria	44,688
Belgium	30,726
France	170,394
Germany	584,184
Netherlands	85,085
Switzerland	41,491
Other Western Europe	2,730
Southern Europe	783,755
Greece	137,084
Italy	354,305
Portugal	182,473
Azores Islands	24,803
Spain	102,475
Other Southern Europe	7,418
Eastern Europe	2,096,647
Albania	81,047
Belarus	50,934
Bulgaria	67,941
Croatia	39,026
Czechoslovakia (includes Czech Republic and Slovakia)	64,354
Hungary	74,213
Latvia	24,497
Lithuania	35,514
Macedonia	20,237
Moldova	34,913
Poland	432,601
Romania	157,302
Russia	390,934
Ukraine	345,187
Bosnia and Herzegovina	112,240
Serbia	36,160
Other Eastern Europe	129,547
Europe, n.e.c.	10,487
Asia	**12,176,983**
Eastern Asia	3,803,484
China	2,383,831
China, excluding Hong Kong and Taiwan	1,804,965
Hong Kong	213,034
Taiwan	365,832
Japan	339,970
Korea	1,070,335
Other Eastern Asia	9,348
South Central Asia	3,285,550
Afghanistan	67,169
Bangladesh	203,179
India	2,034,677
Iran	363,972
Kazakhstan	26,334
Nepal	87,456
Pakistan	342,603
Sri Lanka	51,268
Uzbekistan	48,197
Other South Central Asia	60,695

compared with 51.5 per 1,000 native-born women. As with marital status, there were significant variations in the fertility rate among different foreign-born populations. The fertility rate was highest among women from Africa (97.3 per 1,000), Oceania (77.8), and Latin America (75). Women from Mexico had a higher fertility rate (85.2) than the average for women from Latin America. Female immigrants from Asia (62.5 per 1,000), Northern America (57.3), and Europe (55) had lower fertility rates than immigrant women as a whole. These latter three groups were also the least likely of all immigrant groups to have given birth out of wedlock, and immigrant women as a whole were significantly less likely than native-born women to have given birth out of wedlock.

Foreign-born people were more likely than native-born people in 2012 to live in family households (those in which at least one member is related to the person who owns or pays rent for the residence), and immigrant family households were larger, on average, than the family households of the native born. (See Table 3.7.) Whereas 67.3 million of 104 million native-born households (64.7%) were family households, 6.7 million of 8.9 million households headed by a naturalized citizen (75.9%) and 6.5 million of 8.2 million households headed by a noncitizen (78.7%) were family households. Additionally, among families headed by native-born citizens, 46.4% consisted of two people, 22.8% consisted of three people, 18.5% consisted of four people, and 12.3% consisted of five or more people. Among households headed by naturalized citizens, 33.9% consisted of two people, 23.2% consisted of three people, 22.8% consisted of four people, and 20.1% consisted of five or more people.

TABLE 3.4

Foreign-born population, by place of birth, 2013 [CONTINUED]

	United States
	Estimate
South Eastern Asia	4,032,035
Cambodia	164,746
Indonesia	94,600
Laos	196,154
Malaysia	68,956
Burma	116,775
Philippines	1,843,989
Singapore	31,293
Thailand	233,547
Vietnam	1,281,010
Other South Eastern Asia	965
Western Asia	1,010,465
Iraq	200,894
Israel	127,079
Jordan	65,618
Kuwait	22,731
Lebanon	124,256
Saudi Arabia	88,894
Syria	78,934
Yemen	40,548
Turkey	109,667
Armenia	79,122
Other Western Asia	72,722
Asia, n.e.c.	45,449
Africa	**1,825,326**
Eastern Africa	530,019
Eritrea	33,930
Ethiopia	195,805
Kenya	110,678
Other Eastern Africa	189,606
Middle Africa	111,880
Cameroon	46,556
Other Middle Africa	65,324
Northern Africa	321,945
Egypt	176,443
Morocco	63,798
Sudan	41,018
Other Northern Africa	40,686
Southern Africa	98,305
South Africa	95,191
Other Southern Africa	3,114
Western Africa	647,208
Cape Verde	30,744
Ghana	149,377
Liberia	78,909
Nigeria	234,465
Sierra Leone	37,559
Other Western Africa	116,154
Africa, n.e.c.	115,969
Oceania	**222,390**
Australia and New Zealand subregion	107,647
Australia	78,797
Other Australian and New Zealand subregion	28,850
Fiji	38,782
Oceania, n.e.c.	75,961
Americas	**22,320,187**
Latin America	21,473,266
Caribbean	3,953,655
Bahamas	31,403
Barbados	52,499
Cuba	1,144,024
Dominica	31,222
Dominican Republic	991,046
Grenada	32,820
Haiti	593,980
Jamaica	714,743
St. Vincent and the Grenadines	23,868
Trinidad and Tobago	232,026
West Indies	31,055

TABLE 3.4

Foreign-born population, by place of birth, 2013 [CONTINUED]

	United States
	Estimate
Other Caribbean	74,969
Central America	14,751,230
Mexico	11,584,977
Belize	50,296
Costa Rica	78,659
El Salvador	1,252,067
Guatemala	902,293
Honduras	533,598
Nicaragua	240,619
Panama	101,024
Other Central America	7,697
South America	2,768,381
Argentina	170,086
Bolivia	79,924
Brazil	337,040
Chile	97,585
Colombia	677,231
Ecuador	427,906
Guyana	259,815
Peru	440,292
Uruguay	43,541
Venezuela	197,724
Other South America	37,237
Northern America	846,921
Canada	840,192
Other Northern America	6,729

n.e.c. = not elsewhere classified

Notes: This is a modified view of the original table.

Although the American Community Survey (ACS) produces population, demographic and housing unit estimates, it is the Census Bureau's Population Estimates Program that produces and disseminates the official estimates of the population for the nation, states, counties, cities and towns and estimates of housing units for states and counties.

Data are based on a sample and are subject to sampling variability. The degree of uncertainty for an estimate arising from sampling variability is represented through the use of a margin of error. The value shown here is the 90 percent margin of error. The margin of error can be interpreted roughly as providing a 90 percent probability that the interval defined by the estimate minus the margin of error and the estimate plus the margin of error (the lower and upper confidence bounds) contains the true value. In addition to sampling variability, the ACS estimates are subject to nonsampling error. The effect of nonsampling error is not represented in these tables.

In data year 2013, there were a series of changes to data collection operations that could have affected some estimates. These changes include the addition of Internet as a mode of data collection, the end of the content portion of Failed Edit Follow-Up interviewing, and the loss of one monthly panel due to the federal government shut down in October 2013. While the 2013 American Community Survey (ACS) data generally reflect the February 2013 Office of Management and Budget (OMB) definitions of metropolitan and micropolitan statistical areas, in certain instances the names, codes, and boundaries of the principal cities shown in ACS tables may differ from the OMB definitions due to differences in the effective dates of the geographic entities.

Estimates of urban and rural population, housing units, and characteristics reflect boundaries of urban areas defined based on Census 2010 data. As a result, data for urban and rural areas from the ACS do not necessarily reflect the results of ongoing urbanization.

SOURCE: Adapted from "B05006. Place of Birth for the Foreign-Born Population in the United States. Universe: Foreign-Born Population Excluding Population Born at Sea," in *2013 American Community Survey 1-Year Estimates*, U.S. Census Bureau, 2014, http://factfinder.census.gov/faces/tableservices/jsf/pages/productview.xhtml?pid=ACS_13_1YR_B05006&prodType=table (accessed January 6, 2015)

Noncitizens were even more likely to have large families, with two-person families accounting for 21.9% of all family households, three-person families for 22.1%, four-person families for 27.2%, and five-or-more-person families for 28.9%.

The prevalence of family households among all household types varied, as well, when considered by the world region of the householder's birth. (See Table 3.8.)

FIGURE 3.1

Foreign-born population, by state of residence, 1999–2012

State	Foreign born as a percentage of the state population, 2012 (percentage)	Change in the percentage of foreign born in the state population, 1999 to 2012 (percentage points)
Top 3 states, with about one-fifth of U.S. population		
California	26.1	1.7
New York	22.0	2.4
New Jersey	21.5	6.5
All	**24.3**	2.6
Next 7 states, with about one-fifth of U.S. population		
Florida	19.7	2.9
Nevada	18.3	3.1
Texas	16.6	4.3
Hawaii	15.8	−1.5
Maryland	15.6	5.9
District of Columbia	15.3	4.6
Massachusetts	14.4	3.4
All	**17.3**	3.8
Next 10 states, with about one-fifth of U.S. population		
Arizona	13.8	−0.5
Washington	13.7	4.9
Connecticut	13.4	4.8
Illinois	13.3	3.8
Rhode Island	13.1	3.4
Virginia	10.7	4.3
Delaware	10.6	5.2
New Mexico	10.2	4.3
Oregon	9.6	1.2
Georgia	9.6	5.5
All	**12.0**	3.7
Remaining 31 states, with about two-fifths of U.S. population		
All 31 states	5.2	2.0
Total U.S. population		
All states	12.9	2.8

SOURCE: "Exhibit 7. Foreign-Born Population, by State of Residence, 1999 to 2012," in *A Description of the Immigrant Population—2013 Update*, Congressional Budget Office, May 8, 2013, http://www.cbo.gov/sites/default/files/44134_Description_of_Immigrant_Population.pdf (accessed January 14, 2015)

Eight out of 10 households headed by immigrants from Latin America (7 million of 8.7 million, or 80.5%) were family households, compared with 3.8 million of 4.8 million households headed by immigrants from Asia (79.6%) and 1.5 million of 2.3 million households headed by immigrants from Europe (65.4%). The size of family households followed this same pattern. Among Latin American immigrant family households, 21.1% consisted of two people, 22.1% of three people, 25.9% of four people, and 30.9% of five or more people. Relative to Latin American family households, Asian immigrant family households were more likely to consist of two people (29.8%), three people (24.9%), or four people (26.7%), and less likely to consist of five or more people (18.6%). Over half of European immigrant family households (51.5%), meanwhile, consisted of two people, 22.5% of three people, 16.5% of four people, and 9.4% of five or more people.

Employment, Education, Income, and Poverty

In "Foreign-Born Workers: Labor Force Characteristics—2013" (May 22, 2014, http://www.bls.gov/news.release/pdf/forbrn.pdf), the U.S. Bureau of Labor Statistics (BLS) states that in 2013 foreign-born workers made up 16.3% of the U.S. labor force, up slightly from the previous year's figure of 15.8%. (The labor force consists of all people who are either employed or actively seeking work.) Hispanics accounted for nearly half (47.8%) of the foreign-born labor force, and non-Hispanic Asians were the second-largest group in the foreign-born labor force at 24.3%. As Table 3.9 shows, immigrants were more likely than native-born U.S. residents to be part of the labor force, although the participation rates varied by gender. Two out of three (66.4%) foreign-born individuals aged 16 years and older were either working or actively seeking work in 2013, compared with 62.7% of the native-born population. Foreign-born men participated in the labor force at a rate that was well above the rate for native-born men (78.8% versus 68%), but foreign-born women's labor force participation was slightly below that of native-born women (54.6% versus 57.7%). The unemployment rate for foreign-born workers (6.9%) was slightly lower than that for native-born workers (7.5%).

TABLE 3.5

Marital status, by sex, nativity, and citizenship status, 2012

Sex and marital status	Total		Nativity and U.S. citizenship status					
			Native		Naturalized U.S. citizen		Not a U.S. citizen	
	Number	Percent	Number	Percent	Number	Percent	Number	Percent
Both sexes	**247,696**	**100.0**	**209,501**	**100.0**	**17,498**	**100.0**	**20,698**	**100.0**
Married*	125,691	50.7	102,124	48.7	11,436	65.4	12,130	58.6
Spouse present	122,123	49.3	99,975	47.7	11,012	62.9	11,136	53.8
Spouse absent	3,568	1.4	2,150	1.0	424	2.4	995	4.8
Widowed	14,064	5.7	12,282	5.9	1,189	6.8	594	2.9
Divorced	24,923	10.1	22,378	10.7	1,478	8.4	1,066	5.2
Separated	5,671	2.3	4,495	2.1	514	2.9	663	3.2
Never married	77,347	31.2	68,222	32.6	2,881	16.5	6,245	30.2
Male	**119,946**	**100.0**	**101,217**	**100.0**	**8,162**	**100.0**	**10,567**	**100.0**
Married*	62,821	52.4	51,133	50.5	5,706	69.9	5,981	56.6
Spouse present	61,061	50.9	50,191	49.6	5,494	67.3	5,377	50.9
Spouse absent	1,759	1.5	943	0.9	213	2.6	604	5.7
Widowed	2,864	2.4	2,586	2.6	187	2.3	91	0.9
Divorced	10,701	8.9	9,684	9.6	542	6.6	475	4.5
Separated	2,475	2.1	1,990	2.0	213	2.6	272	2.6
Never married	41,085	34.3	35,823	35.4	1,513	18.5	3,748	35.5
Female	**127,751**	**100.0**	**108,284**	**100.0**	**9,336**	**100.0**	**10,131**	**100.0**
Married*	62,870	49.2	50,991	47.1	5,730	61.4	6,149	60.7
Spouse present	61,061	47.8	49,784	46.0	5,519	59.1	5,759	56.8
Spouse absent	1,809	1.4	1,207	1.1	211	2.3	391	3.9
Widowed	11,200	8.8	9,696	9.0	1,001	10.7	503	5.0
Divorced	14,222	11.1	12,694	11.7	937	10.0	591	5.8
Separated	3,196	2.5	2,504	2.3	301	3.2	391	3.9
Never married	36,263	28.4	32,399	29.9	1,367	14.6	2,497	24.6

*Excludes separated.
Note: Numbers in thousands. Universe is the civilian noninstitutionalized population of the United States, plus armed forces members who live in housing units—off post or on post—with at least one other civilian adult.

SOURCE: "Table 1.2. Marital Status of the Population 15 Years and over by Sex, Nativity, and U.S. Citizenship Status: 2012," in *Foreign Born: Current Population Survey—March 2012 Detailed Tables*, U.S. Census Bureau, June 2014, http://www.census.gov/population/foreign/files/cps2012/2012T1.2.xlsx (accessed January 7, 2015)

Compared with native-born workers, in 2013 a greater proportion of foreign-born workers were employed in service occupations; production, transportation, and material moving occupations; and natural resources, construction, and maintenance occupations. For example, 24.8% of foreign-born workers were employed in service occupations (e.g., health care support, building and grounds maintenance, food preparation and serving, and personal care), whereas 16.7% of native-born workers were employed in this field. (See Table 3.10.) Gender was a determinative factor in this occupational category, as well, with 32.9% of foreign-born women working in service professions compared with 19% of foreign-born men, 19.8% of native-born women, and 13.8% of native-born men. Similarly, 15.4% of foreign-born workers were employed in production, transportation, and material moving occupations, compared with 11.1% of native-born workers. In this occupational category, too, there were notable disparities by gender, with 19.4% of foreign-born men working in these professions (which frequently require heavy physical labor), compared with 10% of foreign-born women, 17.1% of native-born men, and 4.6% of native-born women. Meanwhile, native-born workers tended to be more highly concentrated in management, professional, and related occupations (39.5% of native-born workers, compared with 30.3% of foreign-born workers) and sales and office occupations (24.4% of native-born workers, compared with 16.5% of foreign-born workers).

In 2013 the median weekly earnings of immigrants in the work force totaled $643, or 79.9% of the median weekly earnings of native-born workers ($805). (See Table 3.11.) Foreign-born men made less relative to native-born men (74.6%) than foreign-born women made relative to native-born women (84.8%). Foreign-born workers aged 16 to 24 years came the closest to parity with the earnings of their native-born counterparts (90.4%); foreign-born workers in all other age cohorts earned between 75.8% and 81.2% of their native-born counterparts. Comparative median weekly earnings varied significantly by race and ethnicity, with non-Hispanic foreign-born workers of all races earning more than native-born members of those same races. Foreign-born workers of Hispanic or Latino ethnicity earned only 78.2% of their native-born Hispanic or Latino counterparts' median weekly pay.

The disparity in earnings between foreign-born and native-born workers was to a large degree driven by disparities in educational attainment. A much higher

TABLE 3.6

Marital status of the foreign-born population, by sex and world region of birth, 2012

							World region of birth							
							Latin America							
Sex and marital status	Total		Asia		Europe		Total Latin America		Mexico		Other Latin America[a]		Other areas[b]	
	Number	Percent	Number	Percent	Number	Percent	Number	Percent	Number	Percent	Number	Percent	Number	Percent
Both sexes	**38,195**	**100.0**	**10,989**	**100.0**	**4,387**	**100.0**	**20,211**	**100.0**	**11,140**	**100.0**	**9,071**	**100.0**	**2,608**	**100.0**
Married[c]	23,566	61.7	7,663	69.7	2,813	64.1	11,609	57.4	6,869	61.7	4,741	52.3	1,480	56.7
Spouse present	22,148	58.0	7,276	66.2	2,759	62.9	10,744	53.2	6,382	57.3	4,362	48.1	1,369	52.5
Spouse absent	1,418	3.7	387	3.5	55	1.2	866	4.3	487	4.4	379	4.2	111	4.2
Widowed	1,782	4.7	471	4.3	428	9.8	795	3.9	349	3.1	446	4.9	87	3.4
Divorced	2,545	6.7	485	4.4	398	9.1	1,420	7.0	608	5.5	812	9.0	241	9.3
Separated	1,176	3.1	136	1.2	52	1.2	911	4.5	481	4.3	430	4.7	77	3.0
Never married	9,125	23.9	2,234	20.3	695	15.8	5,475	27.1	2,832	25.4	2,642	29.1	722	27.7
Male	**18,729**	**100.0**	**5,069**	**100.0**	**1,980**	**100.0**	**10,326**	**100.0**	**5,952**	**100.0**	**4,375**	**100.0**	**1,353**	**100.0**
Married[c]	11,687	62.4	3,605	71.1	1,319	66.6	6,003	58.1	3,627	60.9	2,376	54.3	760	56.2
Spouse present	10,871	58.0	3,440	67.9	1,302	65.7	5,432	52.6	3,286	55.2	2,147	49.1	696	51.5
Spouse absent	817	4.4	165	3.3	17	0.9	571	5.5	341	5.7	230	5.2	64	4.7
Widowed	279	1.5	45	0.9	70	3.5	150	1.5	74	1.3	76	1.7	14	1.0
Divorced	1,017	5.4	170	3.4	177	8.9	551	5.3	260	4.4	292	6.7	118	8.8
Separated	485	2.6	51	1.0	16	0.8	370	3.6	203	3.4	167	3.8	48	3.6
Never married	5,261	28.1	1,198	23.6	398	20.1	3,252	31.5	1,788	30.0	1,464	33.5	413	30.5
Female	**19,466**	**100.0**	**5,920**	**100.0**	**2,407**	**100.0**	**9,884**	**100.0**	**5,188**	**100.0**	**4,696**	**100.0**	**1,255**	**100.0**
Married[c]	11,879	61.0	4,058	68.5	1,494	62.1	5,606	56.7	3,242	62.5	2,364	50.3	720	57.4
Spouse present	11,277	57.9	3,836	64.8	1,457	60.5	5,312	53.7	3,097	59.7	2,215	47.2	673	53.6
Spouse absent	602	3.1	222	3.8	37	1.6	295	3.0	146	2.8	149	3.2	47	3.8
Widowed	1,504	7.7	426	7.2	358	14.9	645	6.5	275	5.3	370	7.9	74	5.9
Divorced	1,528	7.8	315	5.3	221	9.2	869	8.8	349	6.7	520	11.1	123	9.8
Separated	691	3.6	85	1.4	36	1.5	541	5.5	278	5.4	263	5.6	29	2.3
Never married	3,864	19.9	1,035	17.5	297	12.3	2,223	22.5	1,044	20.1	1,178	25.1	309	24.6

[a]Those born in 'other Latin America' are from all sub-regions of Latin America (Central America, South America, and the Caribbean), excluding Mexico.
[b]Those born in 'other areas' are from Africa, Oceania, Northern America, and born at sea.
[c]Excludes separated.
Note: Numbers in thousands. Universe is the civilian noninstitutionalized population of the United States, plus armed forces members who live in housing units—off post or on post—with at least one other civilian adult.

SOURCE: "Table 3.2. Marital Status of the Foreign-Born Population 15 Years and over by Sex and World Region of Birth: 2012," in *Foreign Born: Current Population Survey—March 2012 Detailed Tables*, U.S. Census Bureau, June 2014, http://www.census.gov/population/foreign/files/cps2012/2012T3.2.xlsx (accessed January 7, 2015)

proportion of foreign-born workers (3.9 million of 16.6 million, or 23.8%) than native-born workers (3 million of 78.5 million, or 3.9%) had less than a high school diploma in 2013. (See Table 3.11.) Smaller disparities were evident in other educational strata. Approximately 4 million foreign-born workers (24.5%) had a high school diploma but no college experience, compared with 21 million native-born workers (26.8%). A substantially smaller proportion of foreign-born workers (2.7 million, or 16.4%) than native-born workers (23.3 million, or 29.7%) had some college or an associate's degree, and a slightly smaller proportion had bachelor's degrees or higher (35.4% to 39.7%). Lower aggregate levels of educational attainment among foreign-born workers could not fully explain the lower overall median weekly earnings for the foreign born, however. With the exception of foreign-born workers with a bachelor's degree or higher, who earned 104% of what their native-born counterparts made, immigrants in every educational cohort earned significantly less than native-born workers in those same cohorts.

The yearly incomes of families headed by immigrants differ substantially by world region of origin. As Table 3.12 shows, 35.3% of Asian immigrant families and 31.9% of European immigrant families reported household incomes of more than $100,000 in 2011. Similar proportions of each group (34.5% and 36.6%, respectively) made less than $50,000 annually and between $50,000 and $99,999 (30.2% and 31.7%, respectively). By contrast, 11.4% of Latin American immigrant families reported incomes of $100,000 or more, and six out of 10 (61.9%) Latin American immigrant families reported incomes of less than $50,000. Unsurprisingly, the household incomes of immigrant families increase the longer those families remain in the United States, at least until the householder reaches an advanced age and earnings fall off. (See Table 3.13.) In 2011, 59.1% of immigrant families whose householder came to the country in the 1970s and 57.1% of those whose householder came to the country in the 1980s made $50,000 or more annually, compared with 43.1% of those whose householder came to the country in 2000 or later.

FIGURE 3.2

Fertility among native and foreign-born women aged 15–50, 2009–10

[Data based on sample]

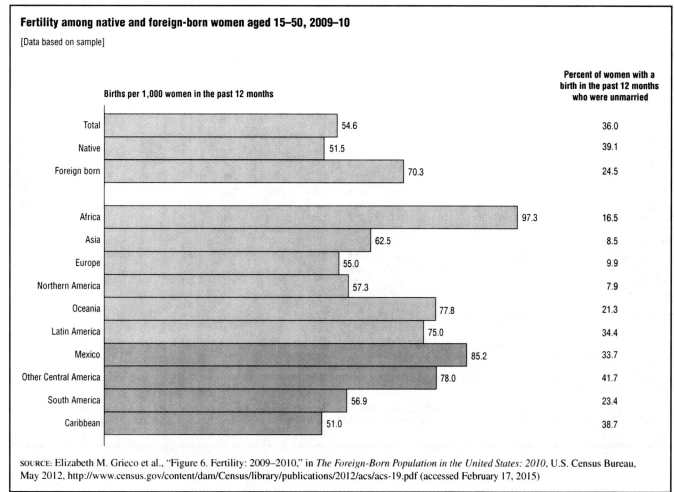

Births per 1,000 women in the past 12 months | Percent of women with a birth in the past 12 months who were unmarried

Category	Births per 1,000 women in the past 12 months	Percent of women with a birth in the past 12 months who were unmarried
Total	54.6	36.0
Native	51.5	39.1
Foreign born	70.3	24.5
Africa	97.3	16.5
Asia	62.5	8.5
Europe	55.0	9.9
Northern America	57.3	7.9
Oceania	77.8	21.3
Latin America	75.0	34.4
Mexico	85.2	33.7
Other Central America	78.0	41.7
South America	56.9	23.4
Caribbean	51.0	38.7

SOURCE: Elizabeth M. Grieco et al., "Figure 6. Fertility: 2009–2010," in *The Foreign-Born Population in the United States: 2010*, U.S. Census Bureau, May 2012, http://www.census.gov/content/dam/Census/library/publications/2012/acs/acs-19.pdf (accessed February 17, 2015)

TABLE 3.7

Household type and size, by nativity and citizenship status of householder, 2012

| Household type and size | Total | | Nativity and U.S. citizenship status | | | | | |
| | | | Native | | Naturalized U.S. citizen | | Not a U.S. citizen | |
	Number	Percent	Number	Percent	Number	Percent	Number	Percent
All households	**121,084**	**100.0**	**103,965**	**100.0**	**8,874**	**100.0**	**8,246**	**100.0**
One person	33,188	27.4	30,090	28.9	1,856	20.9	1,242	15.1
Two people	40,983	33.8	36,687	35.3	2,533	28.5	1,763	21.4
Three people	19,241	15.9	16,118	15.5	1,581	17.8	1,542	18.7
Four people	16,049	13.3	12,696	12.2	1,544	17.4	1,809	21.9
Five or more people	11,622	9.6	8,373	8.1	1,359	15.3	1,890	22.9
Family households*	**80,506**	**100.0**	**67,285**	**100.0**	**6,733**	**100.0**	**6,487**	**100.0**
Two people	34,935	43.4	31,233	46.4	2,284	33.9	1,418	21.9
Three people	18,303	22.7	15,310	22.8	1,563	23.2	1,431	22.1
Four people	15,759	19.6	12,460	18.5	1,533	22.8	1,766	27.2
Five or more people	11,508	14.3	8,282	12.3	1,354	20.1	1,872	28.9
Nonfamily households	**40,578**	**100.0**	**36,679**	**100.0**	**2,141**	**100.0**	**1,758**	**100.0**
One person	33,188	81.8	30,090	82.0	1,856	86.7	1,242	70.6
Two people	6,048	14.9	5,454	14.9	249	11.6	345	19.6
Three people	939	2.3	809	2.2	19	0.9	111	6.3
Four people	289	0.7	235	0.6	11	0.5	43	2.4
Five or more people	114	0.3	91	0.2	5	0.2	18	1.0

*Households in which at least one member is related to the person who owns or rents the occupied housing unit (householder).
Note: Numbers in thousands. Universe is the civilian noninstitutionalized population of the United States, plus armed forces members who live in housing units—off post or on post—with at least one other civilian adult.

SOURCE: "Table 1.4. Household Type by Household Size, Nativity, and U.S. Citizenship Status of the Householder: 2012," in *Foreign Born: Current Population Survey—March 2012 Detailed Tables*, U.S. Census Bureau, June 2014, http://www.census.gov/population/foreign/files/cps2012/2012T1.4.xlsx (accessed January 7, 2015)

TABLE 3.8

Household type and size of foreign-born population, by world region of birth of householder, 2012

Household type and size	Total		Asia		Europe		World region of birth							
							Latin America						Other areas[b]	
							Total Latin America		Mexico		Other Latin America[a]			
	Number	Percent	Number	Percent	Number	Percent	Number	Percent	Number	Percent	Number	Percent	Number	Percent
All households	**17,119**	**100.0**	**4,784**	**100.0**	**2,335**	**100.0**	**8,660**	**100.0**	**4,597**	**100.0**	**4,063**	**100.0**	**1,340**	**100.0**
One person	3,098	18.1	771	16.1	684	29.3	1,296	15.0	484	10.5	812	20.0	347	25.9
Two people	4,296	25.1	1,290	27.0	890	38.1	1,749	20.2	760	16.5	989	24.3	367	27.4
Three people	3,123	18.2	989	20.7	363	15.5	1,603	18.5	758	16.5	845	20.8	169	12.6
Four people	3,353	19.6	1,024	21.4	252	10.8	1,839	21.2	1,048	22.8	792	19.5	238	17.7
Five or more people	3,249	19.0	711	14.9	146	6.3	2,173	25.1	1,548	33.7	626	15.4	219	16.3
Family households[c]	**13,220**	**100.0**	**3,807**	**100.0**	**1,527**	**100.0**	**6,968**	**100.0**	**3,931**	**100.0**	**3,037**	**100.0**	**919**	**100.0**
Two people	3,702	28.0	1,133	29.8	787	51.5	1,473	21.1	642	16.3	831	27.4	309	33.7
Three people	2,993	22.6	949	24.9	344	22.5	1,539	22.1	729	18.5	811	26.7	161	17.5
Four people	3,299	25.0	1,015	26.7	252	16.5	1,802	25.9	1,025	26.1	776	25.6	230	25.0
Five or more people	3,226	24.4	709	18.6	144	9.4	2,154	30.9	1,535	39.1	619	20.4	219	23.8
Nonfamily households	**3,899**	**100.0**	**977**	**100.0**	**809**	**100.0**	**1,692**	**100.0**	**666**	**100.0**	**1,026**	**100.0**	**421**	**100.0**
One person	3,098	79.5	771	78.8	684	84.6	1,296	76.6	484	72.7	812	79.1	347	82.4
Two people	594	15.2	157	16.0	103	12.8	276	16.3	118	17.7	158	15.4	58	13.8
Three people	130	3.3	39	4.0	19	2.3	64	3.8	29	4.4	35	3.4	8	2.0
Four people	54	1.4	9	0.9	—	—	37	2.2	22	3.3	15	1.5	8	1.8
Five or more people	23	0.6	2	0.2	2	0.2	19	1.1	12	1.9	7	0.7	—	—

—Represents zero or rounds to 0.0.

[a]Those born in 'other Latin America' are from all sub-regions of Latin America (Central America, South America, and the Caribbean), excluding Mexico.

[b]Those born in 'other areas' are from Africa, Oceania, Northern America, and born at sea.

[c]Households in which at least one member is related to the person who owns or rents the occupied housing unit (householder).

Note: Numbers in thousands. Universe is the civilian noninstitutionalized population of the United States, plus armed forces members who live in housing units—off post or on post—with at least one other civilian adult.

SOURCE: "Table 3.4. Foreign-Born Households by Household Type, Size, and World Region of Birth of the Householder: 2012," in *Foreign Born: Current Population Survey—March 2012 Detailed Tables*, U.S. Census Bureau, June 2014, http://www.census.gov/population/foreign/files/cps2012/2012T3.4.xlsx (accessed January 7, 2015)

Foreign-born people were more likely than native-born people to be poor in 2011, and poverty status among immigrants varied, like income, according to world region of origin. As Table 3.14 shows, 19% of immigrants lived below the poverty level that year (which was set at $22,350 for a family of four). By comparison, 15.9% of the U.S. population as a whole lived below the poverty line that year. Nearly a quarter (24.1%) of Latin American immigrants lived in poverty, compared with 13.6% of Asian immigrants and 9.7% of European immigrants. (See Table 3.14.) Among Asian and Latin American immigrants (as in the U.S. population at large), children were far more likely than adults to be poor. The poverty rate for Latin American immigrant children was 43.7%, and that of Asian immigrant children was 21.1%. Only 9.4% of European immigrant children lived in poverty. Poverty rates varied among the immigrant population and subpopulations by gender, as well. The poverty rate for all female immigrants was 20.7%, compared with 17.2% for all male immigrants. Female Latin American immigrants experienced poverty at a rate of 27.2% (compared to 21.1% for males), female Asian immigrants at a rate of 13.9% (compared to 13.2% for males), and female European immigrants at a rate of 11.2% (compared to 7.9% for males).

The longer an immigrant had been in the United States as of 2011, the lower the likelihood that he or she lived in poverty. As Table 3.15 shows, the poverty rate was 25.2% for immigrants who had entered the United States in 2000 or later, 18.2% for those who had entered in the 1990s, 14.7% for those who had entered in the 1980s, 12.7% for those who had entered in the 1970s, and 9.7% for those who had entered before 1970. This pattern held for all age groups and both genders, but at all points, children and women were disproportionately likely to live in poverty.

IMMIGRANT STATUS AND ADMISSIONS

Although the term *immigrant* is used commonly to refer to any foreign-born person living in the United States, federal law defines an immigrant as a person who is legally admitted for permanent residence in the United States. Many other foreign-born people live in the United States, some legally under the terms of nonimmigrant temporary visas and some illegally, without government authorization. Among those considered immigrants under the federal definition of the term, some arrive in the country with immigrant visas issued abroad by U.S. Department of State consular offices, and others who are

TABLE 3.9

Employment status of the foreign-born and native-born populations, by selected characteristics, 2012–13

Characteristic	2012						2013					
	Civilian noninstitutional population	Civilian labor force					Civilian noninstitutional population	Civilian labor force				
		Total	Participation rate	Employed	Unemployed			Total	Participation rate	Employed	Unemployed	
					Number	Unemployment rate					Number	Unemployment rate
Total												
Total, 16 years and over	**243,284**	**154,975**	**63.7**	**142,469**	**12,506**	**8.1**	**245,679**	**155,389**	**63.2**	**143,929**	**11,460**	**7.4**
Men	117,343	82,327	70.2	75,555	6,771	8.2	118,555	82,667	69.7	76,353	6,314	7.6
Women	125,941	72,648	57.7	66,914	5,734	7.9	127,124	72,722	57.2	67,577	5,146	7.1
Foreign born												
Total, 16 years and over	**37,727**	**25,026**	**66.3**	**23,006**	**2,021**	**8.1**	**38,162**	**25,328**	**66.4**	**23,582**	**1,746**	**6.9**
Men	18,365	14,424	78.5	13,342	1,082	7.5	18,543	14,615	78.8	13,677	938	6.4
Women	19,362	10,602	54.8	9,663	939	8.9	19,620	10,713	54.6	9,905	809	7.5
Age												
16 to 24 years	3,724	1,905	51.2	1,632	273	14.3	3,719	1,951	52.4	1,702	249	12.7
25 to 34 years	7,674	5,840	76.1	5,373	468	8.0	7,615	5,754	75.6	5,368	386	6.7
35 to 44 years	8,710	6,997	80.3	6,518	479	6.8	8,687	6,937	79.9	6,541	395	5.7
45 to 54 years	7,509	6,071	80.9	5,622	449	7.4	7,691	6,193	80.5	5,789	404	6.5
55 to 64 years	5,021	3,332	66.4	3,051	282	8.5	5,256	3,529	67.2	3,276	254	7.2
65 years and over	5,089	880	17.3	810	70	8.0	5,195	964	18.6	905	59	6.1
Race and Hispanic or Latino ethnicity[a]												
White non-Hispanic or Latino	7,595	4,564	60.1	4,242	322	7.1	7,473	4,485	60.0	4,189	297	6.6
Black non-Hispanic or Latino	3,068	2,166	70.6	1,925	241	11.1	3,175	2,280	71.8	2,041	239	10.5
Asian non-Hispanic or Latino	9,146	5,919	64.7	5,582	337	5.7	9,440	6,143	65.1	5,857	286	4.7
Hispanic or Latino ethnicity	17,507	12,087	69.0	10,988	1,099	9.1	17,658	12,115	68.6	11,210	906	7.5
Educational attainment												
Total, 25 years and over	**34,002**	**23,121**	**68.0**	**21,374**	**1,747**	**7.6**	**34,443**	**23,378**	**67.9**	**21,880**	**1,498**	**6.4**
Less than a high school diploma	9,497	5,688	59.9	5,126	562	9.9	9,520	5,688	59.7	5,229	459	8.1
High school graduates, no college[b]	8,713	5,783	66.4	5,314	469	8.1	8,763	5,786	66.0	5,375	411	7.1
Some college or associate degree	5,670	4,028	71.0	3,713	315	7.8	5,654	4,004	70.8	3,743	262	6.5
Bachelor's degree and higher[c]	10,122	7,621	75.3	7,221	401	5.3	10,507	7,899	75.2	7,533	366	4.6
Native borns												
Total, 16 years and over	**205,558**	**129,948**	**63.2**	**119,464**	**10,485**	**8.1**	**207,517**	**130,061**	**62.7**	**120,348**	**9,713**	**7.5**
Men	98,979	67,903	68.6	62,213	5,690	8.4	100,013	68,052	68.0	62,675	5,376	7.9
Women	106,579	62,046	58.2	57,251	4,795	7.7	107,504	62,009	57.7	57,672	4,337	7.0
Age												
16 to 24 years	35,059	19,379	55.3	16,202	3,177	16.4	35,120	19,430	55.3	16,355	3,075	15.8
25 to 34 years	33,301	27,625	83.0	25,328	2,297	8.3	33,933	27,992	82.5	25,874	2,118	7.6
35 to 44 years	30,932	25,737	83.2	24,058	1,679	6.5	30,926	25,626	82.9	24,109	1,517	5.9
45 to 54 years	36,188	28,983	80.1	27,252	1,731	6.0	35,555	28,274	79.5	26,733	1,541	5.4
55 to 64 years	33,297	21,377	64.2	20,189	1,189	5.6	33,766	21,587	63.9	20,501	1,086	5.0
65 years and over	36,780	6,847	18.6	6,435	412	6.0	38,217	7,152	18.7	6,776	376	5.3
Race and Hispanic or Latino ethnicity[a]												
White non-Hispanic or Latino	152,742	97,328	63.7	90,949	6,379	6.6	153,335	96,826	63.1	91,058	5,768	6.0
Black non-Hispanic or Latino	25,137	15,089	60.0	12,925	2,164	14.3	25,508	15,186	59.5	13,135	2,051	13.5
Asian non-Hispanic or Latino	3,277	2,014	61.5	1,880	134	6.7	3,538	2,207	62.4	2,065	142	6.5
Hispanic or Latino ethnicity	19,252	12,304	63.9	10,890	1,414	11.5	19,860	12,656	63.7	11,305	1,351	10.7

TABLE 3.9

Employment status of the foreign-born and native-born populations, by selected characteristics, 2012–13 [CONTINUED]

	2012						2013					
	Civilian noninstitutional population	Civilian labor force					Civilian noninstitutional population	Civilian labor force				
					Unemployed							Unemployed	
Characteristic		Total	Participation rate	Employed	Number	Unemployment rate		Total	Participation rate	Employed	Number	Unemployment rate
Educational attainment												
Total, 25 years and over	**170,499**	**110,569**	**64.9**	**103,261**	**7,308**	**6.6**	**172,397**	**110,631**	**64.2**	**103,993**	**6,638**	**6.0**
Less than a high school diploma	15,384	5,640	36.7	4,797	843	14.9	14,905	5,317	35.7	4,569	748	14.1
High school graduates, no college[b]	53,099	30,988	58.4	28,404	2,584	8.3	53,186	30,573	57.5	28,244	2,329	7.6
Some college or associate degree	48,624	33,332	68.5	30,992	2,339	7.0	49,384	33,289	67.4	31,182	2,107	6.3
Bachelor's degree and higher[c]	53,392	40,609	76.1	39,067	1,542	3.8	54,923	41,452	75.5	39,998	1,454	3.5

[a]Data for race/ethnicity groups do not sum to totals because data are not presented for all races.
[b]Includes persons with a high school diploma or equivalent.
[c]Includes persons with bachelor's, master's, professional, and doctoral degrees.
Notes: Updated population controls are introduced annually with the release of January data.

SOURCE: "Table 1. Employment Status of the Foreign-Born and Native-Born Populations by Selected Characteristics, 2012–2013 Annual Averages," in *Foreign-Born Workers: Labor Force Characteristics—2013*, U.S. Department of Labor, Bureau of Labor Statistics, May 22, 2014, http://www.bls.gov/news.release/pdf/forbrn.pdf (accessed January 7, 2015)

TABLE 3.10

Employed foreign-born and native-born people, by occupation and sex, 2013

Occupation	Foreign born			Native born		
	Total	Men	Women	Total	Men	Women
Total employed (in thousands)	23,582	13,677	9,905	120,348	62,675	57,672
Occupation as a percent of total employed						
Total employed	100.0	100.0	100.0	100.0	100.0	100.0
Management, professional, and related occupations	30.3	28.2	33.2	39.5	36.3	43.0
Management, business, and financial operations occupations	11.7	11.7	11.7	16.6	18.0	15.1
Management occupations	8.0	8.9	6.8	11.8	13.9	9.5
Business and financial operations occupations	3.7	2.8	4.9	4.9	4.2	5.7
Professional and related occupations	18.6	16.5	21.5	22.9	18.3	27.9
Computer and mathematical occupations	3.9	5.1	2.3	2.5	3.6	1.4
Architecture and engineering occupations	2.2	3.2	0.9	1.9	3.2	0.5
Life, physical, and social science occupations	1.1	1.1	1.1	0.9	0.9	0.9
Community and social service occupations	0.8	0.6	1.1	1.8	1.3	2.3
Legal occupations	0.6	0.4	0.8	1.4	1.3	1.5
Education, training, and library occupations	3.4	2.0	5.4	6.5	3.2	10.1
Arts, design, entertainment, sports, and media occupations	1.3	1.2	1.5	2.1	2.2	2.1
Healthcare practitioner and technical occupations	5.2	2.9	8.5	5.8	2.7	9.1
Service occupations	24.8	19.0	32.9	16.7	13.8	19.8
Healthcare support occupations	2.7	0.7	5.6	2.4	0.5	4.5
Protective service occupations	1.0	1.4	0.5	2.4	3.6	1.1
Food preparation and serving related occupations	7.7	7.5	8.0	5.3	4.3	6.4
Building and grounds cleaning and maintenance occupations	8.6	7.7	9.8	3.0	3.9	2.1
Personal care and service occupations	4.8	1.8	8.9	3.5	1.5	5.7
Sales and office occupations	16.5	12.2	22.4	24.4	17.6	31.8
Sales and related occupations	8.5	7.5	9.9	11.2	11.0	11.3
Office and administrative support occupations	8.0	4.7	12.4	13.2	6.5	20.5
Natural resources, construction, and maintenance occupations	12.9	21.2	1.5	8.3	15.2	0.8
Farming, fishing, and forestry occupations	1.6	2.1	0.9	0.5	0.7	0.2
Construction and extraction occupations	8.3	14.1	0.3	4.3	8.0	0.3
Installation, maintenance, and repair occupations	3.1	5.1	0.3	3.5	6.5	0.3
Production, transportation, and material moving occupations	15.4	19.4	10.0	11.1	17.1	4.6
Production occupations	8.3	9.1	7.4	5.2	7.6	2.7
Transportation and material moving occupations	7.1	10.3	2.7	5.8	9.5	1.9

Note: Updated population controls are introduced annually with the release of January data.

SOURCE: "Table 4. Employed Foreign-Born and Native-Born Persons 16 Years and over by Occupation and Sex, 2013 Annual Averages," in *Foreign-Born Workers: Labor Force Characteristics—2013*, U.S. Department of Labor, Bureau of Labor Statistics, May 22, 2014, http://www.bls.gov/news.release/pdf/forbrn.pdf (accessed January 7, 2015)

already residents in the United States become immigrants when they adjust their status from temporary to permanent residence. The latter category includes individuals who enter the country as foreign students, temporary workers, refugees and asylees (those seeking asylum), and some unauthorized immigrants.

There are various ways to qualify for immigration to the United States and receive a green card (signifying legal status that allows an immigrant to work). However, as the U.S. Citizenship and Immigration Services (USCIS) notes in "Green Card Eligibility" (2015, http://www.uscis.gov/green-card/green-card-processes-and-procedures/green-card-eligibility), immigrant admissions fall into four major categories:

- Family-based
- Employment-based
- Refugee- or asylum-based
- Other ways (a category consisting of specific qualifying groups discussed in this section)

There are different visa limits for the different categories as well as hierarchies of preference within each category. Immediate relatives of U.S. citizens (a category that includes parents, spouses, and unmarried children under the age of 21 years) are granted the highest priority of all classes of immigrants. Visas are always made available for them, and they do not have to wait. Other family members of citizens may apply for family-based visas, but these are subject to availability and the legal priority status of various family relationships. Under the Immigration and Nationality Act (INA) of 1952, a minimum of 226,000 family-based visas are issued each year.

Job- and employment-based immigrants may apply for visas while abroad based on an offer from an employer, but they are subject to preference rankings and must wait accordingly for available visas. There are 140,000 green cards allocated for employment-based immigrants each year, but the number actually issued is larger in some years, as unused family-based visas can be allotted to this category. Workers with "extraordinary abilities, outstanding professors and researchers, and certain multinational

TABLE 3.11

Median weekly earnings of full-time foreign-born and native-born wage and salary workers, by selected characteristics, 2012–13

| | 2012 | | | | | 2013 | | | | |
| | Foreign born | | Native born | | Earnings of foreign born as percent of native born | Foreign born | | Native born | | Earnings of foreign born as percent of native born |
Characteristic	Number	Median weekly earnings	Number	Median weekly earnings		Number	Median weekly earnings	Number	Median weekly earnings	
Total, 16 years and over	**17,089**	**$625**	**85,659**	**$797**	**78.4**	**17,551**	**$643**	**86,712**	**$805**	**79.9**
Men	10,385	665	46,901	898	74.1	10,741	671	47,254	899	74.6
Women	6,704	589	38,758	710	83.0	6,810	610	39,458	719	84.8
Age										
16 to 24 years	994	403	8,036	452	89.2	1,001	415	8,246	459	90.4
25 to 34 years	4,275	591	20,310	729	81.1	4,257	593	20,824	730	81.2
35 to 44 years	4,972	692	19,112	897	77.1	5,065	705	19,238	911	77.4
45 to 54 years	4,267	683	21,079	913	74.8	4,341	699	20,759	916	76.3
55 to 64 years	2,142	667	14,376	929	71.8	2,376	706	14,691	932	75.8
65 years and over	439	628	2,747	778	80.7	510	665	2,954	831	80.0
Race and Hispanic or Latino ethnicity[a]										
White non-Hispanic or Latino	2,906	898	64,284	857	104.8	2,867	952	64,767	864	110.2
Black non-Hispanic or Latino	1,459	640	10,002	623	102.7	1,547	649	10,139	634	102.4
Asian non-Hispanic or Latino	4,213	922	1,385	937	98.4	4,383	951	1,524	936	101.6
Hispanic or Latino ethnicity	8,316	501	7,986	641	78.2	8,529	509	8,330	651	78.2
Educational attainment										
Total, 25 years and over	**16,095**	**652**	**77,623**	**851**	**76.6**	**16,550**	**670**	**78,465**	**860**	**77.9**
Less than a high school diploma	3,879	428	3,131	510	83.9	3,931	428	3,025	511	83.8
High school graduates, no college[b]	3,899	550	21,339	675	81.5	4,047	565	20,997	674	83.8
Some college or associate degree	2,702	673	23,124	758	88.8	2,719	691	23,315	754	91.6
Bachelor's degree and higher[c]	5,615	1,164	30,029	1,165	99.9	5,853	1,235	31,129	1,187	104.0

[a]Data for race/ethnicity groups do not sum to totals because data are not presented for all races.
[b]Includes persons with a high school diploma or equivalent.
[c]Includes persons with bachelor's, master's, professional, and doctoral degrees.
Note: Updated population controls are introduced annually with the release of January data.

SOURCE: "Table 5. Median Usual Weekly Earnings of Full-Time Wage and Salary Workers for the Foreign Born and Native Born by Selected Characteristics, 2012–2013 Annual Averages," in *Foreign-Born Workers: Labor Force Characteristics—2013*, U.S. Department of Labor, Bureau of Labor Statistics, May 22, 2014, http://www.bls.gov/news.release/pdf/forbrn.pdf (accessed January 7, 2015)

executives and managers" are among the individuals who fall into the highest-priority category among job- and employment-based green-card applicants. In descending order of preference, the other employment-based priority categories include workers with advanced degrees, skilled professionals, those affiliated with religious orders, and investors or entrepreneurs.

Foreign-born individuals who are admitted as refugees may apply for green cards one year after entering the United States as a refugee. Likewise, foreign-born residents granted asylum status while already in the United States may apply for a green card one year after being granted asylum status. The spouses and children of refugees and asylees are also eligible for LPR status at the same time. Refugees must apply for a green card at that time to remain within the law. Asylees are not required to apply for a green card within that same time frame, but because changed circumstances in their countries of origin can result in the termination of their asylum status, they are encouraged to do so upon becoming eligible. Refugees and asylees (and their spouses and children) applying for green cards must

have been physically present in the United States for an entire year following their arrival or granting of status, and their refugee or asylum status must still be current. There are no limits on the number of green cards issued in this category.

Although these three categories represent the bulk of the green cards issued in most years, there are also numerous other ways to obtain LPR status. There are 50,000 diversity visas granted annually to applicants from countries with low historic rates of immigration to the United States. Also, a number of small, specific groups of immigrants were eligible for green cards in 2013. The USCIS notes in "Other Ways to Get a Green Card" (2015, http://www.uscis.gov/green-card/other-ways-get-green-card) that these specific groups included children of U.S. citizens born in Korea, Vietnam, Laos, Kampuchea (Cambodia), or Thailand during the years encompassing U.S. military action in Korea and Vietnam; individuals with at least 50% Native American heritage who were born in Canada; individuals who had served as witnesses or informants for U.S. law enforcement agencies; natives of Cuba; Afghan and

TABLE 3.12

Income of foreign-born households, by household type and world region of birth of householder, 2011

Household type and total money income[a]	Total		Asia		Europe		World region of birth — Latin America — Total Latin America		Mexico		Other Latin America[b]		Other areas[c]	
	Number	Percent	Number	Percent	Number	Percent	Number	Percent	Number	Percent	Number	Percent	Number	Percent
Total family households[d]	**13,220**	**100.0**	**3,807**	**100.0**	**1,527**	**100.0**	**6,968**	**100.0**	**3,931**	**100.0**	**3,037**	**100.0**	**919**	**100.0**
$1 to $14,999 or loss	1,355	10.3	268	7.0	88	5.8	897	12.9	572	14.5	325	10.7	102	11.1
$15,000 to $29,999	2,394	18.1	456	12.0	175	11.5	1,627	23.4	1,026	26.1	601	19.8	136	14.8
$30,000 to $39,999	1,511	11.4	317	8.3	150	9.8	965	13.9	601	15.3	364	12.0	79	8.6
$40,000 to $49,999	1,291	9.8	273	7.2	145	9.5	815	11.7	476	12.1	339	11.1	58	6.3
$50,000 to $74,999	2,313	17.5	669	17.6	255	16.7	1,224	17.6	678	17.2	546	18.0	166	18.0
$75,000 to $99,999	1,458	11.0	480	12.6	228	15.0	643	9.2	269	6.8	374	12.3	107	11.7
$100,000 and over	2,898	21.9	1,343	35.3	487	31.9	797	11.4	309	7.9	488	16.1	271	29.5
Median income ($)	50,365	X	71,449	X	69,107	X	39,927	X	35,790	X	46,260	X	61,697	X
Married couple	**9,761**	**100.0**	**3,125**	**100.0**	**1,300**	**100.0**	**4,676**	**100.0**	**2,738**	**100.0**	**1,938**	**100.0**	**661**	**100.0**
$1 to $14,999 or loss	695	7.1	177	5.7	61	4.7	403	8.6	268	9.8	135	7.0	54	8.2
$15,000 to $29,999	1,573	16.1	331	10.6	140	10.8	1,019	21.8	706	25.8	313	16.2	82	12.4
$30,000 to $39,999	1,062	10.9	237	7.6	118	9.1	653	14.0	429	15.7	224	11.5	53	8.1
$40,000 to $49,999	933	9.6	214	6.9	120	9.2	569	12.2	349	12.7	220	11.4	30	4.5
$50,000 to $74,999	1,757	18.0	544	17.4	224	17.2	872	18.7	517	18.9	355	18.3	116	17.6
$75,000 to $99,999	1,193	12.2	411	13.2	195	15.0	510	10.9	221	8.1	289	14.9	77	11.6
$100,000 and over	2,548	26.1	1,209	38.7	441	33.9	650	13.9	248	9.1	401	20.7	248	37.5
Median income ($)	56,572	X	77,634	X	72,109	X	44,078	X	39,046	X	55,060	X	74,377	X
Male family householder, no spouse present	**1,039**	**100.0**	**247**	**100.0**	**62**	**100.0**	**630**	**100.0**	**375**	**100.0**	**255**	**100.0**	**101**	**100.0**
$1 to $14,999 or loss	84	8.1	18	7.2	2	3.4	51	8.1	34	9.1	17	6.5	14	13.6
$15,000 to $29,999	229	22.0	54	22.0	8	13.2	145	23.0	87	23.2	58	22.7	22	21.5
$30,000 to $39,999	141	13.6	23	9.5	11	17.1	100	15.8	64	17.1	36	14.0	8	7.6
$40,000 to $49,999	94	9.0	9	3.5	1	0.9	79	12.6	53	14.0	27	10.5	5	5.0
$50,000 to $74,999	207	20.0	47	19.1	11	18.1	119	19.0	71	18.9	49	19.1	30	29.3
$75,000 to $99,999	121	11.7	28	11.5	13	21.4	64	10.2	29	7.7	36	14.0	15	15.3
$100,000 and over	162	15.6	67	27.2	16	25.8	71	11.3	37	10.0	34	13.2	8	7.7
Median income ($)	46,172	X	60,159	X	70,083	X	41,812	X	40,271	X	46,108	X	50,794	X
Female family householder, no spouse present	**2,420**	**100.0**	**436**	**100.0**	**165**	**100.0**	**1,663**	**100.0**	**818**	**100.0**	**845**	**100.0**	**157**	**100.0**
$1 to $14,999 or loss	576	23.8	73	16.8	25	15.3	443	26.7	270	33.0	173	20.5	34	21.7
$15,000 to $29,999	592	24.5	70	16.1	27	16.1	463	27.9	233	28.5	230	27.3	32	20.4
$30,000 to $39,999	308	12.7	57	13.0	20	12.4	213	12.8	108	13.2	105	12.4	18	11.3
$40,000 to $49,999	264	10.9	50	11.6	24	14.8	167	10.0	75	9.2	92	10.9	23	14.6
$50,000 to $74,999	349	14.4	78	17.8	19	11.6	232	13.9	90	11.0	142	16.8	20	12.6
$75,000 to $99,999	144	5.9	40	9.3	20	12.0	69	4.1	19	2.4	49	5.8	15	9.4
$100,000 and over	188	7.8	67	15.4	29	17.8	76	4.6	23	2.8	53	6.3	16	10.0
Median income ($)	30,986	X	43,609	X	43,505	X	26,894	X	23,362	X	31,443	X	35,703	X
Total nonfamily households[e]	**3,899**	**100.0**	**977**	**100.0**	**809**	**100.0**	**1,692**	**100.0**	**666**	**100.0**	**1,026**	**100.0**	**421**	**100.0**
$1 to $14,999 or loss	1,144	29.3	294	30.1	237	29.3	511	30.2	205	30.7	306	29.9	102	24.3
$15,000 to $29,999	996	25.5	200	20.4	206	25.5	478	28.2	186	27.9	292	28.4	112	26.6
$30,000 to $39,999	393	10.1	98	10.0	83	10.2	176	10.4	68	10.3	108	10.5	36	8.6
$40,000 to $49,999	287	7.4	63	6.5	49	6.1	139	8.2	71	10.7	67	6.6	36	8.6
$50,000 to $74,999	510	13.1	125	12.8	114	14.1	191	11.3	83	12.5	108	10.5	80	18.9
$75,000 to $99,999	274	7.0	101	10.3	39	4.8	115	6.8	34	5.0	81	7.9	20	4.8
$100,000 and over	295	7.6	97	9.9	81	10.0	83	4.9	19	2.9	64	6.2	35	8.2
Median income ($)	26,296	X	29,564	X	26,406	X	24,672	X	23,147	X	25,357	X	28,623	X

TABLE 3.12

Income of foreign-born households, by household type and world region of birth of householder, 2011 [CONTINUED]

Household type and total money income[a]	Total		Asia		Europe		World region of birth — Latin America — Total Latin America		Mexico		Other Latin America[b]		Other areas[c]	
	Number	Percent	Number	Percent	Number	Percent	Number	Percent	Number	Percent	Number	Percent	Number	Percent
Male nonfamily householder	**2,002**	**100.0**	**468**	**100.0**	**338**	**100.0**	**924**	**100.0**	**429**	**100.0**	**495**	**100.0**	**271**	**100.0**
$1 to $14,999 or loss	443	22.1	121	25.8	71	21.1	193	20.9	89	20.9	104	21.0	58	21.3
$15,000 to $29,999	478	23.9	90	19.2	52	15.3	280	30.3	122	28.4	158	31.9	56	20.6
$30,000 to $39,999	217	10.9	45	9.5	43	12.8	99	10.7	44	10.4	54	10.9	31	11.4
$40,000 to $49,999	191	9.5	38	8.1	26	7.6	92	9.9	59	13.7	33	6.7	35	13.0
$50,000 to $74,999	288	14.4	57	12.2	56	16.6	121	13.1	69	16.0	53	10.6	54	19.9
$75,000 to $99,999	168	8.4	58	12.3	26	7.6	75	8.1	27	6.2	48	9.7	10	3.6
$100,000 and over	216	10.8	60	12.9	64	19.0	64	6.9	19	4.4	45	9.1	28	10.2
Median income ($)	31,964	X	34,834	X	42,783	X	29,226	X	30,512	X	28,614	X	35,994	X
Female nonfamily householder	**1,897**	**100.0**	**509**	**100.0**	**470**	**100.0**	**768**	**100.0**	**237**	**100.0**	**531**	**100.0**	**150**	**100.0**
$1 to $14,999 or loss	701	36.9	173	34.0	166	35.3	317	41.3	115	48.6	202	38.1	44	29.6
$15,000 to $29,999	518	27.3	110	21.5	155	32.9	198	25.7	64	26.9	134	25.2	56	37.4
$30,000 to $39,999	175	9.2	53	10.5	39	8.3	78	10.1	24	10.1	54	10.1	5	3.7
$40,000 to $49,999	97	5.1	25	5.0	23	5.0	47	6.1	13	5.4	34	6.4	1	0.6
$50,000 to $74,999	221	11.7	68	13.4	58	12.3	69	9.0	14	6.1	55	10.3	26	17.1
$75,000 to $99,999	106	5.6	43	8.5	13	2.7	40	5.2	7	2.9	33	6.3	11	7.0
$100,000 and over	78	4.1	36	7.1	17	3.5	19	2.5	—		19	3.6	7	4.6
Median income ($)	20,437	X	25,468	X	20,673	X	18,771	X	15,465	X	20,829	X	19,141	X

—Represents zero or rounds to 0.0.

X = Not applicable.

[a]Total money income is the sum of money wages and salaries, net income from self-employment, and income other than earnings.

[b]Those born in 'other Latin America' are from all sub-regions of Latin America (Central America, South America, and the Caribbean), excluding Mexico.

[c]Those born in 'other areas' are from Africa, Oceania, Northern America, and born at sea.

[d]Households in which at least one member is related to the person who owns or rents the occupied housing unit (householder).

[e]Households in which no member is related to the person who owns or rents the occupied housing unit (householder).

Note: Numbers in thousands. Universe is the civilian noninstitutionalized population of the United States, plus armed forces members who live in housing units—off post or on post—with at least one other civilian adult.

SOURCE: Adapted from "Table 3.10. Total Money Income of Foreign-Born Households by Household Type and World Region of Birth of the Householder: 2011," in *Foreign Born: Current Population Survey—March 2012 Detailed Tables*, U.S. Census Bureau, June 2014, http://www.census.gov/population/foreign/files/cps2012/2012T3.10.xlsx (accessed January 7, 2015)

TABLE 3.13

Income of foreign-born households, by household type and year of entry, 2011

Household type and total money income[a]	Total		Year of entry									
			2000 or later[b]		1990–1999		1980–1989		1970–1979		Before 1970	
	Number	Percent	Number	Percent	Number	Percent	Number	Percent	Number	Percent	Number	Percent
Total family households[c]	**13,220**	**100.0**	**3,779**	**100.0**	**3,917**	**100.0**	**2,892**	**100.0**	**1,537**	**100.0**	**1,095**	**100.0**
$1 to $14,999 or loss	1,355	10.3	536	14.2	387	9.9	246	8.5	127	8.3	60	5.4
$15,000 to $29,999	2,394	18.1	798	21.1	754	19.2	434	15.0	202	13.2	205	18.8
$30,000 to $39,999	1,511	11.4	460	12.2	468	12.0	298	10.3	139	9.0	145	13.2
$40,000 to $49,999	1,291	9.8	357	9.4	405	10.3	261	9.0	161	10.5	107	9.8
$50,000 to $74,999	2,313	17.5	578	15.3	643	16.4	579	20.0	314	20.4	199	18.1
$75,000 to $99,999	1,458	11.0	372	9.8	429	10.9	341	11.8	178	11.6	139	12.7
$100,000 and over	2,898	21.9	678	18.0	832	21.2	732	25.3	416	27.1	240	21.9
Median income ($)	50,365	X	42,147	X	48,450	X	57,115	X	58,012	X	52,376	X
Married couple	**9,761**	**100.0**	**2,711**	**100.0**	**2,841**	**100.0**	**2,135**	**100.0**	**1,183**	**100.0**	**891**	**100.0**
$1 to $14,999 or loss	695	7.1	271	10.0	202	7.1	123	5.7	62	5.3	38	4.2
$15,000 to $29,999	1,573	16.1	528	19.5	468	16.5	273	12.8	139	11.7	165	18.5
$30,000 to $39,999	1,062	10.9	308	11.4	326	11.5	203	9.5	102	8.7	123	13.8
$40,000 to $49,999	933	9.6	258	9.5	304	10.7	180	8.4	110	9.3	80	9.0
$50,000 to $74,999	1,757	18.0	452	16.7	464	16.3	431	20.2	247	20.9	163	18.3
$75,000 to $99,999	1,193	12.2	299	11.0	351	12.3	271	12.7	150	12.7	122	13.7
$100,000 and over	2,548	26.1	595	21.9	726	25.6	655	30.7	373	31.5	200	22.5
Median income ($)	56,572	X	49,508	X	54,642	X	65,986	X	66,244	X	53,730	X
Male family householder, no spouse present	**1,039**	**100.0**	**382**	**100.0**	**291**	**100.0**	**211**	**100.0**	**103**	**100.0**	**52**	**100.0**
$1 to $14,999 or loss	84	8.1	41	10.6	17	5.9	6	2.6	21	20.3	—	—
$15,000 to $29,999	229	22.0	95	24.9	62	21.4	45	21.4	14	13.9	12	23.6
$30,000 to $39,999	141	13.6	59	15.4	43	14.7	25	11.9	9	9.1	5	10.1
$40,000 to $49,999	94	9.0	27	7.0	35	12.1	17	8.1	10	9.5	5	9.1
$50,000 to $74,999	207	20.0	69	18.1	61	20.9	51	24.3	20	19.4	6	11.8
$75,000 to $99,999	121	11.7	39	10.1	30	10.3	32	15.0	11	10.7	10	19.4
$100,000 and over	162	15.6	53	13.9	43	14.7	35	16.7	17	17.0	14	26.0
Median income ($)	46,172	X	39,685	X	44,707	X	57,926	X	47,327	X	71,300	X
Female family householder, no spouse present	**2,420**	**100.0**	**686**	**100.0**	**785**	**100.0**	**546**	**100.0**	**251**	**100.0**	**152**	**100.0**
$1 to $14,999 or loss	576	23.8	224	32.7	167	21.3	118	21.7	44	17.5	22	14.3
$15,000 to $29,999	592	24.5	176	25.6	223	28.4	116	21.2	50	19.7	28	18.6
$30,000 to $39,999	308	12.7	93	13.6	100	12.7	70	12.9	27	10.8	17	11.2
$40,000 to $49,999	264	10.9	71	10.4	65	8.3	65	11.8	41	16.4	22	14.5
$50,000 to $74,999	349	14.4	57	8.3	119	15.1	97	17.8	47	18.5	30	19.5
$75,000 to $99,999	144	5.9	34	4.9	48	6.1	38	7.0	17	6.7	7	4.5
$100,000 and over	188	7.8	31	4.5	63	8.0	42	7.7	26	10.3	26	17.4
Median income ($)	30,986	X	23,841	X	30,164	X	34,271	X	40,787	X	44,284	X
Total nonfamily households[d]	**3,899**	**100.0**	**1,139**	**100.0**	**815**	**100.0**	**665**	**100.0**	**487**	**100.0**	**794**	**100.0**
$1 to $14,999 or loss	1,144	29.3	281	24.7	236	29.0	182	27.4	150	30.8	295	37.2
$15,000 to $29,999	996	25.5	280	24.6	184	22.6	153	23.0	109	22.4	269	33.9
$30,000 to $39,999	393	10.1	120	10.5	96	11.8	76	11.4	48	9.8	54	6.8
$40,000 to $49,999	287	7.4	83	7.3	78	9.6	49	7.3	41	8.5	36	4.6
$50,000 to $74,999	510	13.1	198	17.4	78	9.6	91	13.7	69	14.2	73	9.1
$75,000 to $99,999	274	7.0	86	7.5	71	8.8	52	7.8	30	6.2	35	4.4
$100,000 and over	295	7.6	91	8.0	71	8.7	62	9.3	40	8.1	31	3.9
Median income ($)	26,296	X	30,453	X	28,422	X	29,624	X	26,945	X	19,786	X
Male nonfamily householder	**2,002**	**100.0**	**753**	**100.0**	**445**	**100.0**	**387**	**100.0**	**206**	**100.0**	**211**	**100.0**
$1 to $14,999 or loss	443	22.1	161	21.4	85	19.1	94	24.3	53	25.9	49	23.4
$15,000 to $29,999	478	23.9	186	24.7	100	22.5	80	20.6	45	22.0	66	31.4
$30,000 to $39,999	217	10.9	82	10.8	57	12.7	40	10.2	17	8.5	22	10.5
$40,000 to $49,999	191	9.5	66	8.8	50	11.2	36	9.3	23	11.0	16	7.5
$50,000 to $74,999	288	14.4	124	16.4	41	9.1	59	15.3	35	17.0	29	13.9
$75,000 to $99,999	168	8.4	54	7.1	55	12.4	32	8.2	14	6.9	13	6.3
$100,000 and over	216	10.8	80	10.6	57	12.9	47	12.0	18	8.7	15	7.0
Median income ($)	31,964	X	32,136	X	35,187	X	33,574	X	30,654	X	27,178	X

Iraqi translators who had served the U.S. government; battered spouses, children, and parents of citizens or green-card holders; victims of criminal activity and human trafficking; and many others.

The Characteristics of Legal Permanent Residents

According to data released by the U.S. Department of Homeland Security's (DHS) Office of Immigration Statistics (OIS) as part of its *2013 Yearbook of Immigration*

TABLE 3.13

Income of foreign-born households, by household type and year of entry, 2011 [CONTINUED]

Household type and total money income[a]	Total		2000 or later[b]		1990–1999		1980–1989		1970–1979		Before 1970	
	Number	Percent	Number	Percent	Number	Percent	Number	Percent	Number	Percent	Number	Percent
Female nonfamily householder	1,897	100.0	386	100.0	370	100.0	278	100.0	281	100.0	582	100.0
$1 to $14,999 or loss	701	36.9	120	31.0	151	40.8	88	31.7	97	34.3	246	42.2
$15,000 to $29,999	518	27.3	94	24.3	84	22.8	73	26.4	64	22.7	203	34.8
$30,000 to $39,999	175	9.2	38	9.8	39	10.6	36	13.0	30	10.8	32	5.5
$40,000 to $49,999	97	5.1	17	4.4	28	7.5	13	4.5	19	6.6	20	3.5
$50,000 to $74,999	221	11.7	75	19.3	37	10.1	32	11.5	34	12.2	43	7.4
$75,000 to $99,999	106	5.6	32	8.3	16	4.4	21	7.4	16	5.6	22	3.8
$100,000 and over	78	4.1	11	2.9	14	3.7	16	5.6	22	7.7	16	2.8
Median income ($)	20,437	X	25,934	X	19,441	X	22,721	X	22,209	X	17,410	X

X = Not applicable.

[a]Total money income is the sum of money wages and salaries, net income from self-employment, and income other than earnings.

[b]The category '2000 or later' includes 2000–2012.

[c]Households in which at least one member is related to the person who owns or rents the occupied housing unit (householder).

[d]Households in which no member is related to the person who owns or rents the occupied housing unit (householder).

Note: Numbers in thousands. Universe is the civilian noninstitutionalized population of the United States, plus armed forces members who live in housing units—off post or on post—with at least one other civilian adult.

SOURCE: Adapted from "Table 2.10. Total Money Income of Foreign-Born Households by Household Type and Year of Entry: 2011," in *Foreign Born: Current Population Survey—March 2012 Detailed Tables*, U.S. Census Bureau, June 2014, http://www.census.gov/population/foreign/files/cps2012/2012T2.10.xlsx (accessed January 7, 2015)

Statistics (October 2014, http://www.dhs.gov/yearbook-immigration-statistics), 990,553 people obtained LPR status in fiscal year (FY) 2013. (See Table 3.16.) This was the lowest number of LPR visas issued since 2004 and a significant decrease from an LPR peak of 1.3 million in 2006. Figure 3.3 shows the trends in flows of LPRs over the course of the 20th and early 21st centuries. LPR admissions spiked to their all-time highest levels around 1990 as a result of the 2.7 million people admitted under the Immigration Reform and Control Act of 1986.

The United States offers two general methods for foreign-born people to obtain immigrant status. In the first method an alien living abroad can apply for an immigrant visa and then become a legal resident when approved for admission at a U.S. port of entry. The second method of gaining immigrant status is by adjustment of status. This procedure allows certain foreign-born individuals already in the United States to apply for immigrant status, including certain unauthorized residents, temporary workers, foreign students, and refugees. Of the total number of LPR applications granted in 2013, 530,802 (53.6%) were status adjustments and 459,751 were new arrivals. (See Table 3.16.)

As Table 3.16 shows, each year a majority of green cards go to the family members of U.S. citizens and LPRs. Without fail, the largest group annually granted LPR status consists of the immediate family members of U.S. citizens. Of the 990,553 individuals issued green cards in FY 2013, 439,460 (44.4%) were part of this category. An additional 210,303 people (21.2%) were granted LPR status under family-sponsored preferences as members of a citizen's or LPR's extended family.

After these family-based categories, the most commonly issued classes of green cards are employment based: 161,110 applicants were granted LPR status in FY 2013 based on employment. (See Table 3.16.) Of these, 140,009 were status adjustments and 21,101 were new arrivals. Meanwhile, green cards issued to refugees and asylees are all adjustments of status because individuals in this category only become eligible for LPR status after one continuous year of residence in the United States. In FY 2013, 77,395 refugees and 42,235 asylees were granted LPR status. Another 45,618 immigrants were granted diversity visas. Diversity visas overwhelmingly go to new arrivals: the FY 2013 total in this category consisted of 44,113 new arrivals and 1,505 adjustments of status.

As Table 3.17 shows, Asia and North America together supplied more than 70% of LPRs in FYs 2011, 2012, and 2013. In FY 2013, 40.4% of LPRs were Asian, and 31.9% were North American. Another 9.9% of new LPRs came from Africa, 8.7% from Europe, 8.2% from South America, and 0.5% from Oceania. The leading country of origin for new LPR admissions in FY 2013 was Mexico, with 13.6% of the total. Other leading countries of origin among those receiving LPR status were China (the country of origin for 7.2% of new LPRs), India (6.9%), the Philippines (5.5%), and the Dominican Republic (4.2%).

Most of the individuals granted LPR status in FY 2013 resided in high-population states that were already home to large immigrant communities. (See Table 3.18.) Roughly one-fifth (19.4%) of LPRs admitted that year lived in California, 13.5% in New York, 10.4% in Florida, 9.4%

TABLE 3.14

Poverty status of the foreign-born population, by sex, age, and world region of birth, 2011

Sex, age, and poverty status	Total		World region of birth										
			Asia		Europe		Latin America						Other areas[b]	
							Total Latin America		Mexico		Other Latin America[a]			
	Number	Percent	Number	Percent	Number	Percent	Number	Percent	Number	Percent	Number	Percent	Number	Percent
Both sexes	**39,966**	**100.0**	**11,582**	**100.0**	**4,545**	**100.0**	**21,029**	**100.0**	**11,616**	**100.0**	**9,413**	**100.0**	**2,809**	**100.0**
Below poverty level	7,586	19.0	1,575	13.6	441	9.7	5,061	24.1	3,233	27.8	1,828	19.4	509	18.1
At or above poverty level	32,380	81.0	10,007	86.4	4,104	90.3	15,968	75.9	8,383	72.2	7,585	80.6	2,301	81.9
Under 18 years	2,602	100.0	838	100.0	214	100.0	1,273	100.0	736	100.0	537	100.0	277	100.0
Below poverty level	832	32.0	176	21.1	20	9.4	557	43.7	376	51.1	181	33.6	79	28.5
At or above poverty level	1,770	68.0	662	78.9	194	90.6	716	56.3	359	48.9	357	66.4	198	71.5
18 to 64 years	32,399	100.0	9,235	100.0	3,000	100.0	17,880	100.0	10,154	100.0	7,725	100.0	2,284	100.0
Below poverty level	5,962	18.4	1,173	12.7	289	9.6	4,101	22.9	2,670	26.3	1,431	18.5	400	17.5
At or above poverty level	26,436	81.6	8,063	87.3	2,712	90.4	13,779	77.1	7,484	73.7	6,294	81.5	1,883	82.5
65 years and over	4,965	100.0	1,509	100.0	1,331	100.0	1,877	100.0	726	100.0	1,150	100.0	249	100.0
Below poverty level	791	15.9	226	15.0	133	10.0	403	21.5	187	25.7	217	18.8	29	11.8
At or above poverty level	4,174	84.1	1,283	85.0	1,198	90.0	1,473	78.5	539	74.3	934	81.2	220	88.2
Male	**19,616**	**100.0**	**5,350**	**100.0**	**2,049**	**100.0**	**10,775**	**100.0**	**6,223**	**100.0**	**4,551**	**100.0**	**1,442**	**100.0**
Below poverty level	3,370	17.2	707	13.2	161	7.9	2,270	21.1	1,478	23.8	792	17.4	231	16.0
At or above poverty level	16,246	82.8	4,643	86.8	1,888	92.1	8,505	78.9	4,745	76.2	3,759	82.6	1,211	84.0
Under 18 years	1,292	100.0	397	100.0	95	100.0	676	100.0	395	100.0	280	100.0	125	100.0
Below poverty level	399	30.9	70	17.5	9	9.3	288	42.6	199	50.5	88	31.5	33	26.0
At or above poverty level	893	69.1	327	82.5	86	90.7	388	57.4	196	49.5	192	68.5	92	74.0
18 to 64 years	16,252	100.0	4,324	100.0	1,414	100.0	9,298	100.0	5,507	100.0	3,791	100.0	1,216	100.0
Below poverty level	2,686	16.5	554	12.8	106	7.5	1,832	19.7	1,202	21.8	630	16.6	193	15.9
At or above poverty level	13,566	83.5	3,770	87.2	1,308	92.5	7,466	80.3	4,305	78.2	3,161	83.4	1,022	84.1
65 years and over	2,072	100.0	629	100.0	540	100.0	801	100.0	321	100.0	480	100.0	102	100.0
Below poverty level	285	13.8	83	13.2	47	8.6	150	18.7	77	24.0	73	15.2	6	5.6
At or above poverty level	1,787	86.2	546	86.8	494	91.4	651	81.3	244	76.0	407	84.8	96	94.4
Female	**20,350**	**100.0**	**6,232**	**100.0**	**2,497**	**100.0**	**10,254**	**100.0**	**5,393**	**100.0**	**4,862**	**100.0**	**1,367**	**100.0**
Below poverty level	4,216	20.7	868	13.9	280	11.2	2,791	27.2	1,755	32.5	1,036	21.3	277	20.3
At or above poverty level	16,134	79.3	5,364	86.1	2,216	88.8	7,464	72.8	3,638	67.5	3,826	78.7	1,090	79.7
Under 18 years	1,310	100.0	441	100.0	120	100.0	597	100.0	340	100.0	257	100.0	152	100.0
Below poverty level	433	33.1	107	24.2	11	9.4	269	45.0	177	51.9	92	35.9	46	30.6
At or above poverty level	877	66.9	334	75.8	108	90.6	328	55.0	164	48.1	165	64.1	105	69.4
18 to 64 years	16,147	100.0	4,911	100.0	1,587	100.0	8,581	100.0	4,647	100.0	3,934	100.0	1,068	100.0
Below poverty level	3,277	20.3	618	12.6	183	11.5	2,269	26.4	1,468	31.6	800	20.3	207	19.4
At or above poverty level	12,870	79.7	4,293	87.4	1,404	88.5	6,313	73.6	3,179	68.4	3,134	79.7	861	80.6
65 years and over	2,893	100.0	880	100.0	791	100.0	1,076	100.0	405	100.0	671	100.0	147	100.0
Below poverty level	506	17.5	143	16.2	86	10.9	253	23.5	110	27.1	144	21.4	24	16.1
At or above poverty level	2,387	82.5	737	83.8	704	89.1	822	76.5	295	72.9	527	78.6	123	83.9

[a]Those born in 'other Latin America' are from all sub-regions of Latin America (Central America, South America, and the Caribbean), excluding Mexico.
[b]Those born in 'other areas' are from Africa, Oceania, Northern America, and Born at Sea.
Note: Numbers in thousands. Universe is the civilian noninstitutionalized population of the United States, plus armed forces living off post or with their families on post. Poverty status estimates exclude unrelated individuals under 15 years of age.

SOURCE: Adapted from "Table 3.13. Poverty Status of the Foreign-Born Population by Sex, Age, and World Region of Birth: 2011," in *Foreign Born: Current Population Survey—March 2012 Detailed Tables*, U.S. Census Bureau, June 2014, http://www.census.gov/population/foreign/files/cps2012/2012T3.13.xlsx (accessed January 7, 2015)

TABLE 3.15

Poverty status of the foreign-born population, by sex, age, and year of entry, 2011

Sex, age, and poverty status	Total		Year of entry									
			2000 or later[a]		1990–1999		1980–1989		1970–1979		Before 1970	
	Number	Percent	Number	Percent	Number	Percent	Number	Percent	Number	Percent	Number	Percent
Both sexes	**39,966**	**100.0**	**14,950**	**100.0**	**10,946**	**100.0**	**7,090**	**100.0**	**3,867**	**100.0**	**3,112**	**100.0**
Below poverty level	7,586	19.0	3,764	25.2	1,989	18.2	1,040	14.7	491	12.7	301	9.7
At or above poverty level	32,380	81.0	11,186	74.8	8,957	81.8	6,050	85.3	3,375	87.3	2,811	90.3
Under 18 years	2,602	100.0	2,246	100.0	356	100.0	b	b	b	b	b	b
Below poverty level	832	32.0	731	32.6	101	28.4	b	b	b	b	b	b
At or above poverty level	1,770	68.0	1,515	67.4	255	71.6	b	b	b	b	b	b
18 to 64 years	32,399	100.0	12,133	100.0	9,844	100.0	6,367	100.0	2,954	100.0	1,100	100.0
Below poverty level	5,962	18.4	2,895	23.9	1,704	17.3	902	14.2	368	12.4	94	8.6
At or above poverty level	26,436	81.6	9,238	76.1	8,140	82.7	5,465	85.8	2,587	87.6	1,006	91.4
65 years and over	4,965	100.0	571	100.0	746	100.0	723	100.0	913	100.0	2,012	100.0
Below poverty level	791	15.9	139	24.3	184	24.6	138	19.1	124	13.6	207	10.3
At or above poverty level	4,174	84.1	433	75.7	562	75.4	585	80.9	789	86.4	1,805	89.7
Male	**19,616**	**100.0**	**7,512**	**100.0**	**5,290**	**100.0**	**3,597**	**100.0**	**1,898**	**100.0**	**1,319**	**100.0**
Below poverty level	3,370	17.2	1,703	22.7	854	16.2	476	13.2	233	12.3	103	7.8
At or above poverty level	16,246	82.8	5,809	77.3	4,436	83.8	3,121	86.8	1,665	87.7	1,216	92.2
Under 18 years	1,292	100.0	1,122	100.0	169	100.0	b	b	b	b	b	b
Below poverty level	399	30.9	347	30.9	51	30.3	b	b	b	b	b	b
At or above poverty level	893	69.1	775	69.1	118	69.7	b	b	b	b	b	b
18 to 64 years	16,252	100.0	6,165	100.0	4,814	100.0	3,267	100.0	1,469	100.0	537	100.0
Below poverty level	2,686	16.5	1,303	21.1	730	15.2	414	12.7	190	13.0	48	9.0
At or above poverty level	13,566	83.5	4,862	78.9	4,084	84.8	2,854	87.3	1,278	87.0	489	91.0
65 years and over	2,072	100.0	224	100.0	307	100.0	330	100.0	429	100.0	782	100.0
Below poverty level	285	13.8	52	23.4	73	23.9	63	19.0	42	9.9	55	7.0
At or above poverty level	1,787	86.2	172	76.6	234	76.1	267	81.0	387	90.1	727	93.0
Female	**20,350**	**100.0**	**7,438**	**100.0**	**5,655**	**100.0**	**3,493**	**100.0**	**1,969**	**100.0**	**1,794**	**100.0**
Below poverty level	4,216	20.7	2,061	27.7	1,134	20.1	564	16.1	259	13.1	198	11.1
At or above poverty level	16,134	79.3	5,377	72.3	4,521	79.9	2,930	83.9	1,711	86.9	1,595	88.9
Under 18 years	1,310	100.0	1,124	100.0	186	100.0	b	b	b	b	b	b
Below poverty level	433	33.1	384	34.2	50	26.6	b	b	b	b	b	b
At or above poverty level	877	66.9	740	65.8	137	73.4	b	b	b	b	b	b
18 to 64 years	16,147	100.0	5,967	100.0	5,030	100.0	3,100	100.0	1,486	100.0	563	100.0
Below poverty level	3,277	20.3	1,591	26.7	974	19.4	488	15.7	177	11.9	46	8.2
At or above poverty level	12,870	79.7	4,376	73.3	4,056	80.6	2,612	84.3	1,308	88.1	517	91.8
65 years and over	2,893	100.0	347	100.0	439	100.0	393	100.0	483	100.0	1,230	100.0
Below poverty level	506	17.5	86	24.8	110	25.1	76	19.2	81	16.8	152	12.4
At or above poverty level	2,387	82.5	261	75.2	329	74.9	318	80.8	402	83.2	1,078	87.6

[a]The category "2000 or later" includes 2000–2012.
[b]Represents zero or rounds to 0.0.
Note: Numbers in thousands. Universe is the civilian noninstitutionalized population of the United States, plus armed forces members who live in housing units—off post or on post—with at least one other civilian adult. Poverty status estimates exclude unrelated individuals under 15 years of age.

SOURCE: Adapted from "Table 2.13. Poverty Status of the Foreign-Born Population by Sex, Age, and Year of Entry: 2011, in *Foreign Born: Current Population Survey—March 2012 Detailed Tables*, U.S. Census Bureau, June 2014, http://www.census.gov/population/foreign/files/cps2012/2012T2.13.xlsx (accessed January 7, 2015)

in Texas, and 5.4% in New Jersey. The New York City region was the leading metropolitan area of residence for new green-card holders in FY 2013, with 16.9% of new LPRs, followed by the Los Angeles metro area (8.1%), the Miami area (6.7%), the District of Columbia area (4%), and the Chicago area (3.3%). (See Table 3.19.)

New LPRs are typically younger than the native population and are more likely to be female. In FY 2013 the median age of new LPRs was 32 years (see Table 3.20), compared with 35 years for native-born U.S. residents. A majority of LPRs were between the ages of 15 and 44, with smaller numbers of children under five years of age (3.4% of total new LPRs), children aged 5 to 14 years (10.4%), adults aged 45 to 54 years (11.5%), adults aged 55 to 64 years (7.2%), and adults aged 65

years and older (4.9%). Of LPRs admitted in FY 2013, 51.9% were female, and 43.8% were male (the gender of 4.3% of new LPRs was not known). (See Table 3.21.) A majority (58.5%) were married. (See Table 3.22.)

New Arrivals by Adoption

One subgroup of LPRs of particular interest to many observers are children who arrive in the United States via international adoption. These children have received LPR status under the family-based allotment of visas since October 2000, when Congress passed the Child Citizenship Act. This act granted automatic U.S. citizenship to foreign-born biological and adopted children of U.S. citizens, and international adoption became a growing trend in the years that followed.

TABLE 3.16

People obtaining lawful permanent resident status, by type and major class of admission, fiscal years 2004–13

Type and class of admission	2004	2005	2006	2007	2008	2009	2010	2011	2012	2013
Total										
Total	957,883	1,122,257	1,266,129	1,052,415	1,107,126	1,130,818	1,042,625	1,062,040	1,031,631	990,553
Family-sponsored preferences	214,355	212,970	222,229	194,900	227,761	211,859	214,589	234,931	202,019	210,303
First: Unmarried sons/daughters of U.S. citizens and their children	26,380	24,729	25,432	22,858	26,173	23,965	26,998	27,299	20,660	24,358
Second: Spouses, children, and unmarried sons/daughters of alien residents	93,609	100,139	112,051	86,151	103,456	98,567	92,088	108,618	99,709	99,115
Third: Married sons/daughters of U.S. citizens and their spouses and children	28,695	22,953	21,491	20,611	29,273	25,930	32,817	27,704	21,752	21,294
Fourth: Brothers/sisters of U.S. citizens (at least 21 years of age) and their spouses and children	65,671	65,149	63,255	65,280	68,859	63,397	62,686	71,310	59,898	65,536
Immediate relatives of U.S. citizens	417,815	436,115	580,348	494,920	488,483	535,554	476,414	453,158	478,780	439,460
Spouses	252,193	259,144	339,843	274,358	265,671	317,129	271,909	258,320	273,429	248,332
Children*	88,088	94,858	120,064	103,828	101,342	98,270	88,297	80,311	81,121	71,382
Parents	77,534	82,113	120,441	116,734	121,470	120,155	116,208	114,527	124,230	119,746
Employment-based preferences	155,317	246,865	159,075	161,733	164,741	140,903	148,343	139,339	143,998	161,110
First: priority workers	31,291	64,731	36,960	26,697	36,678	40,924	41,055	25,251	39,316	38,978
Second: professionals with advanced degrees or aliens of exceptional ability	32,534	42,597	21,911	44,162	70,046	45,552	53,946	66,831	50,959	63,026
Third: skilled workers, professionals, and unskilled workers	85,969	129,070	89,922	85,030	48,903	40,398	39,762	37,216	39,229	43,632
Fourth: certain special immigrants	5,394	10,121	9,533	5,038	7,754	10,341	11,100	6,701	7,866	6,931
Fifth: employment creation (investors)	129	346	749	806	1,360	3,688	2,480	3,340	6,628	8,543
Diversity	50,084	46,234	44,471	42,127	41,761	47,879	49,763	50,103	40,320	45,618
Refugees	61,013	112,676	99,609	54,942	90,030	118,836	92,741	113,045	105,528	77,395
Asylees	10,217	30,286	116,845	81,183	76,362	58,532	43,550	55,415	45,086	42,235
Parolees	7,121	7,715	4,569	1,999	1,172	2,385	1,592	1,147	758	556
Children born abroad to alien residents	707	571	623	597	637	587	716	633	643	643
Nicaraguan Adjustment and Central American Relief Act (NACARA)	2,292	1,155	661	340	296	296	248	158	183	138
Cancellation of removal	32,702	20,785	29,516	14,927	11,128	8,156	8,180	7,430	6,818	5,763
Haitian Refugee Immigration Fairness Act (HRIFA)	2,451	2,820	3,375	2,448	1,580	552	386	154	93	62
Other	3,809	4,065	4,808	2,299	3,175	5,279	6,103	6,527	7,405	7,270
Adjustments of status										
Total	583,921	738,302	819,248	621,047	640,568	667,776	566,576	580,092	547,559	530,802
Family-sponsored preferences	64,427	70,459	79,709	52,059	56,899	39,787	26,279	28,346	18,560	26,415
First: unmarried sons/daughters of U.S. citizens and their children	7,782	6,389	8,275	7,358	5,650	5,112	3,922	3,343	2,750	2,538
Second: spouses, children, and unmarried sons/daughters of alien residents	45,669	55,362	62,507	37,046	41,881	24,597	11,716	11,985	8,692	6,520
Third: married sons/daughters of U.S. citizens and their spouses and children	4,672	4,164	3,954	3,126	3,811	3,306	4,465	3,085	2,453	1,829
Fourth: brothers/sisters of U.S. citizens (at least 21 years of age) and their spouses and children	6,304	4,544	4,973	4,529	5,557	6,772	6,176	9,933	4,665	15,528
Immediate relatives of U.S. citizens	269,964	266,851	357,127	277,188	251,090	309,073	252,842	243,174	239,986	232,105
Spouses	209,358	208,758	275,676	211,843	191,197	242,123	189,460	178,868	182,276	167,211
Children*	30,706	30,738	43,826	31,351	25,465	28,586	22,750	20,288	18,285	16,519
Parents	29,900	27,355	37,625	33,994	34,428	38,364	40,632	44,018	39,425	48,375
Employment-based preferences	128,232	219,987	121,586	133,082	149,527	127,121	136,010	124,384	126,016	140,009
First: priority workers	27,060	60,240	32,060	23,802	35,082	39,420	39,070	23,605	37,799	37,283
Second: professionals with advanced degrees or aliens of exceptional ability	31,134	41,109	20,939	42,991	68,832	44,336	52,388	65,140	49,414	60,956
Third: skilled workers, professionals, and unskilled workers	65,875	109,713	60,390	62,642	38,981	33,525	34,433	29,757	31,208	34,937
Fourth: certain special immigrants	4,094	8,737	7,917	3,332	6,301	8,855	9,384	5,306	6,644	5,602
Fifth: employment creation (investors)	69	188	280	315	331	985	735	576	951	1,231
Diversity	2,031	1,850	1,853	1,360	1,440	1,277	1,571	1,617	1,356	1,505
Refugees	61,013	112,676	99,609	54,942	90,030	118,836	92,741	113,045	105,528	77,395
Asylees	10,217	30,286	116,845	81,183	76,362	58,532	43,550	55,415	45,086	42,235
Parolees	7,121	7,715	4,569	1,999	1,172	2,385	1,592	1,147	758	556
Children born abroad to alien residents	—	—	—	—	—	—	—	—	—	—
Nicaraguan Adjustment and Central American Relief Act (NACARA)	2,292	1,155	661	340	296	296	248	158	183	138
Cancellation of removal	32,702	20,785	29,516	14,927	11,128	8,156	8,180	7,430	6,818	5,763
Haitian Refugee Immigration Fairness Act (HRIFA)	2,451	2,820	3,375	2,448	1,580	552	386	154	93	62
Other	3,471	3,718	4,398	1,519	1,044	1,761	3,177	5,222	3,175	4,619

The adoption of foreign-born children reached a peak in FY 2004 with a total of 22,991 children admitted as citizens. (See Figure 3.4.) By FY 2013 the number of foreign-born children admitted to the United States through adoption had dropped to 7,092, a decline of 69.2%. This decline was in no small part the result of

TABLE 3.16

People obtaining lawful permanent resident status, by type and major class of admission, fiscal years 2004–13 [CONTINUED]

Type and class of admission	2004	2005	2006	2007	2008	2009	2010	2011	2012	2013
New arrivals										
Total	373,962	383,955	446,881	431,368	466,558	463,042	476,049	481,948	484,072	459,751
Family-sponsored preferences	149,928	142,511	142,520	142,841	170,862	172,072	188,310	206,585	183,459	183,888
First: unmarried sons/daughters of U.S. citizens and their children	18,598	18,340	17,157	15,500	20,523	18,853	23,076	23,956	17,910	21,820
Second: spouses, children, and unmarried sons/daughters of alien residents	47,940	44,777	49,544	49,105	61,575	73,970	80,372	96,633	91,017	92,595
Third: married sons/daughters of U.S. citizens and their spouses and children	24,023	18,789	17,537	17,485	25,462	22,624	28,352	24,619	19,299	19,465
Fourth: brothers/sisters of U.S. citizens (at least 21 years of age) and their spouses and children	59,367	60,605	58,282	60,751	63,302	56,625	56,510	61,377	55,233	50,008
Immediate relatives of U.S. citizens	147,851	169,264	223,221	217,732	237,393	226,481	223,572	209,984	238,794	207,355
Spouses	42,835	50,386	64,167	62,515	74,474	75,006	82,449	79,452	91,153	81,121
Children*	57,382	64,120	76,238	72,477	75,877	69,684	65,547	60,023	62,836	54,863
Parents	47,634	54,758	82,816	82,740	87,042	81,791	75,576	70,509	84,805	71,371
Employment-based preferences	27,085	26,878	37,489	28,651	15,214	13,782	12,333	14,955	17,982	21,101
First: priority workers	4,231	4,491	4,900	2,895	1,596	1,504	1,985	1,646	1,517	1,695
Second: professionals with advanced degrees or aliens of exceptional ability	1,400	1,488	972	1,171	1,214	1,216	1,558	1,691	1,545	2,070
Third: skilled workers, professionals, and unskilled workers	20,094	19,357	29,532	22,388	9,922	6,873	5,329	7,459	8,021	8,695
Fourth: certain special immigrants	1,300	1,384	1,616	1,706	1,453	1,486	1,716	1,395	1,222	1,329
Fifth: employment creation (investors)	60	158	469	491	1,029	2,703	1,745	2,764	5,677	7,312
Diversity	48,053	44,384	42,618	40,767	40,321	46,602	48,192	48,486	38,964	44,113
Refugees	—	—	—	—	—	—	—	—	—	—
Asylees	—	—	—	—	—	—	—	—	—	—
Parolees	—	—	—	—	—	—	—	—	—	—
Children born abroad to alien residents	707	571	623	597	637	587	716	633	643	643
Nicaraguan Adjustment and Central American Relief Act (NACARA)	—	—	—	—	—	—	—	—	—	—
Cancellation of removal	—	—	—	—	—	—	—	—	—	—
Haitian Refugee Immigration Fairness Act (HRIFA)	—	—	—	—	—	—	—	—	—	—
Other	338	347	410	780	2,131	3,518	2,926	1,305	4,230	2,651

—Represents zero.
*Includes orphans.

SOURCE: "Table 6. Persons Obtaining Lawful Permanent Resident Status by Type and Major Class of Admission: Fiscal Years 2004 to 2013," in *Yearbook of Immigration Statistics: 2013*, U.S. Department of Homeland Security, Office of Immigration Statistics, October 2014, http://www.dhs.gov/sites/default/files/publications/immigration-statistics/yearbook/2013/LPR/table6.xls (accessed January 7, 2015)

laws passed in China in 2007 that established tougher criteria for foreigners looking to adopt there. China has long been a leading country of origin for children adopted internationally by U.S. parents, and it remained so in the years that followed, but the number of Chinese-born children adopted by American parents fell dramatically. The State Department indicates in "Statistics" (2015, http://travel.state.gov/content/adoptionsabroad/en/about-us/statistics.html) that adoptions from China fell from 7,903 in FY 2005 to 2,306 in FY 2013. The number of children adopted from other key source countries fell during this time, as well, including Guatemala, the country of origin of 4,726 children adopted into the United States in FY 2007 and only 23 in FY 2013, and South Korea, the country of origin of between 1,600 and 2,000 children adopted into the United States each year between 1999 and 2005, and which was the home country of only 138 in FY 2013.

According to Rachel L. Swarns, in "American Adoptions from Abroad at Their Lowest Level in Years"

(NYTimes.com, January 24, 2013), these declines were attributable to restrictions put in place by source countries themselves, together with the inability of some countries to meet stricter international standards put in place to protect children and prevent human trafficking. Since the peak period of international adoption in the early to middle years of the first decade of the 21st century, China, Russia, and South Korea had each passed policies intended to limit adoptions by U.S. parents and to encourage more adoptions domestically. In late 2012, moreover, the Russian president Vladimir Putin (1952–) signed a ban on all adoptions of Russian children by U.S. parents in retaliation for U.S. attempts to combat alleged human-rights violations in his country. Countries such as Cambodia, Guatemala, and Vietnam, meanwhile, have ceased providing large numbers of adoptive children to countries such as the United States due to allegations of corruption and suggestions that children were taken from their parents under dubious or deceptive circumstances. The State Department thus imposed limits on adoptions from these and other countries. While these limits were

FIGURE 3.3

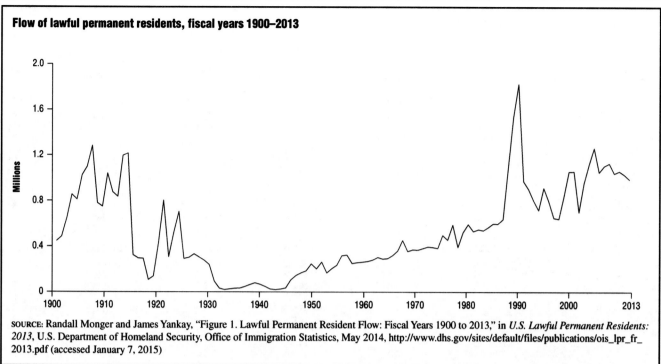

Flow of lawful permanent residents, fiscal years 1900–2013

SOURCE: Randall Monger and James Yankay, "Figure 1. Lawful Permanent Resident Flow: Fiscal Years 1900 to 2013," in *U.S. Lawful Permanent Residents: 2013*, U.S. Department of Homeland Security, Office of Immigration Statistics, May 2014, http://www.dhs.gov/sites/default/files/publications/ois_lpr_fr_2013.pdf (accessed January 7, 2015)

well-meaning, they also left many previously adoptable children stranded in orphanages.

As Table 3.23 shows, China, Ethiopia, Russia, and South Korea were the top source countries for international adoptions from 2009 to 2012. Guatemala supplied the fifth-most adoptees in 2009, before being replaced by Ukraine as the fifth-leading source country in the years that followed. The leading host states for international adoptees varied only slightly during this time, with the largest number of international adoptees finding homes, year after year, in the largest U.S. states of California, Florida, Illinois, New York, and Texas.

NATURALIZATION

Naturalization refers to the conferring of U.S. citizenship on a person after birth. A naturalization court grants citizenship if the naturalization occurs within the United States, whereas a representative of the USCIS confers citizenship when naturalization occurs outside the United States. Beginning in 1992 the Immigration Act (IMMACT) of 1990 also permitted people to naturalize through administrative hearings with the U.S. Immigration and Naturalization Service (now the USCIS). When individuals become U.S. citizens, they pledge allegiance to the United States and renounce allegiance to their former country.

To naturalize, most immigrants must meet certain general requirements. They must be at least 18 years old, have been legally admitted to the United States for permanent residence, and have lived in the country continuously

for at least five years. They must also be able to speak, read, and write English; know how the U.S. government works; have a basic knowledge of U.S. history; and be of good moral character.

The naturalization test covers reading and writing in English as well as basic U.S. history and government. The USCIS provides study materials for both the English test and the civics test at "Study for the Test" (2015, http://www.uscis.gov/citizenship/learners/study-test). Study materials available for the English portion of the test include reading and writing flashcards, the official list of vocabulary words, and self-tests, among other materials. The civics study materials also consist of flash cards and exercises, as well as the official list of 100 questions for the test, and the booklet *Learn about the United States: Quick Civics Lessons for the Naturalization Test* (July 2014, http://www.uscis.gov/sites/default/files/USCIS/Office%20of%20Citizenship/Citizenship%20Resource%20Center%20Site/Publications/PDFs/M-638_red.pdf), which contains short lessons based on each of the 100 questions.

Special Provisions

A small share of people are naturalized under special provisions of the naturalization laws that exempt them from one or more of the general requirements. For example, spouses of U.S. citizens can become naturalized in three years instead of the normal five. Children who immigrated with their parents generally receive their U.S. citizenship through the naturalization of their parents. Aliens with LPR status who served honorably

TABLE 3.17

Lawful permanent resident flow, by region and country of birth, fiscal years 2011–13

Region and country of birth	2013		2012		2011	
	Number	Percent	Number	Percent	Number	Percent
Region						
Total	990,553	100.0	1,031,631	100.0	1,062,040	100.0
Africa	98,304	9.9	107,241	10.4	100,374	9.5
Asia	400,548	40.4	429,599	41.6	451,593	42.5
Europe	86,556	8.7	81,671	7.9	83,850	7.9
North America	315,660	31.9	327,771	31.8	333,902	31.4
Caribbean	122,406	12.4	127,477	12.4	133,680	12.6
Central America	44,724	4.5	40,675	3.9	43,707	4.1
Other North America	148,530	15.0	159,619	15.5	156,515	14.7
Oceania	5,277	0.5	4,742	0.5	4,980	0.5
South America	80,945	8.2	79,401	7.7	86,096	8.1
Unknown	3,263	0.3	1,206	0.1	1,245	0.1
Country						
Total	990,553	100.0	1,031,631	100.0	1,062,040	100.0
Mexico	135,028	13.6	146,406	14.2	143,446	13.5
China, People's Republic	71,798	7.2	81,784	7.9	87,016	8.2
India	68,458	6.9	66,434	6.4	69,013	6.5
Philippines	54,446	5.5	57,327	5.6	57,011	5.4
Dominican Republic	41,311	4.2	41,566	4.0	46,109	4.3
Cuba	32,219	3.3	32,820	3.2	36,452	3.4
Vietnam	27,101	2.7	28,304	2.7	34,157	3.2
Korea, South	23,166	2.3	20,846	2.0	22,824	2.1
Colombia	21,131	2.1	20,931	2.0	22,635	2.1
Haiti	20,351	2.1	22,818	2.2	22,111	2.1
Jamaica	19,400	2.0	20,705	2.0	19,662	1.9
El Salvador	18,260	1.8	16,256	1.6	18,667	1.8
Nigeria	13,840	1.4	13,575	1.3	11,824	1.1
Pakistan	13,251	1.3	14,740	1.4	15,546	1.5
Canada	13,181	1.3	12,932	1.3	12,800	1.2
Ethiopia	13,097	1.3	14,544	1.4	13,793	1.3
Nepal	13,046	1.3	11,312	1.1	10,166	1.0
United Kingdom	12,984	1.3	12,014	1.2	11,572	1.1
Iran	12,863	1.3	12,916	1.3	14,822	1.4
Burma	12,565	1.3	17,383	1.7	16,518	1.6
All other countries	353,057	35.6	366,018	35.5	375,896	35.4

SOURCE: Randall Monger and James Yankay, "Table 3. Lawful Permanent Resident Flow by Region and Country of Birth: Fiscal Years 2011 to 2013," in *U.S. Lawful Permanent Residents: 2013*, U.S. Department of Homeland Security, Office of Immigration Statistics, May 2014, http://www.dhs.gov/sites/default/files/publications/ois_lpr_fr_2013.pdf (accessed January 7, 2015).

in the U.S. military are also entitled to certain exemptions from the naturalization requirements.

Naturalization of Active-Duty Military

Under the terms of the INA, certain foreign-born members and veterans of the U.S. military are eligible for naturalization. The USCIS explains in "Citizenship for Military Members" (2010, http://www.uscis.gov/military/citizenship-military-personnel-family-members/citizenship-military-members) that LPRs who have served honorably in any branch of the armed forces for one year or more and who meet certain basic criteria are often eligible for "peacetime naturalization," and LPRs who have served any length of time (even one day) during hostilities and meet certain basic criteria are eligible for naturalization. The basic criteria for both forms of military naturalization include an ability to read, write, and speak English; knowledge of civics; good moral character; and an attachment to the principles of the U.S. Constitution.

Certain spouses and children of members of the armed forces are also eligible for expedited or overseas naturalization, and certain deceased members of the armed forces are eligible for posthumous naturalization.

Eligible candidates for peacetime naturalization must have been continuously in residence in the United States for five years and physically present for at least 30 months of the five years immediately preceding the date of their application. Naturalization during periods of hostility carries no such residency requirement: applicants who were either admitted as an LPR after entering the military or who were physically present in the United States prior to entering the military are eligible to apply. The periods of hostilities during which military service of any length qualified applicants for naturalization include World War II (1939–1945), the Korean War (1950–1953), the Vietnam War (1954–1975), the Persian Gulf War (1990–1991), and the entire period following September 11, 2001. This last designated period of hostilities

TABLE 3.18

Lawful permanent resident flow, by state of residence, fiscal years 2011–13

State of residence	2013		2012		2011	
	Number	Percent	Number	Percent	Number	Percent
Total	990,553	100.0	1,031,631	100.0	1,062,040	100.0
California	191,806	19.4	196,622	19.1	210,591	19.8
New York	133,601	13.5	149,505	14.5	148,426	14.0
Florida	102,939	10.4	103,047	10.0	109,229	10.3
Texas	92,674	9.4	95,557	9.3	94,481	8.9
New Jersey	53,082	5.4	50,790	4.9	55,547	5.2
Illinois	35,988	3.6	38,373	3.7	38,325	3.6
Massachusetts	29,482	3.0	31,392	3.0	32,236	3.0
Virginia	27,861	2.8	28,227	2.7	27,767	2.6
Maryland	25,361	2.6	24,971	2.4	25,778	2.4
Pennsylvania	24,720	2.5	25,032	2.4	25,397	2.4
Other*	273,039	27.6	288,115	27.9	294,263	27.7

*Includes unknown, U.S. territories and armed forces posts.

SOURCE: Randall Monger and James Yankay, "Table 4. Lawful Permanent Resident Flow by State of Residence: Fiscal Years 2011 to 2013," in *U.S. Lawful Permanent Residents: 2013*, U.S. Department of Homeland Security, Office of Immigration Statistics, May 2014, http://www.dhs.gov/sites/default/files/publications/ois_lpr_fr_2013.pdf (accessed January 7, 2015)

TABLE 3.19

Lawful permanent resident flow, by metropolitan area of residence, fiscal years 2011–13

Metropolitan area of residence	2013		2012		2011	
	Number	Percent	Number	Percent	Number	Percent
Total	990,553	100.0	1,031,631	100.0	1,062,040	100.0
New York-Northern New Jersey-Long Island, NY-NJ-PA	167,393	16.9	179,011	17.4	183,681	17.3
Los Angeles-Long Beach-Santa Ana, CA	79,893	8.1	81,508	7.9	86,161	8.1
Miami-Fort Lauderdale-Pompano Beach, FL	66,636	6.7	66,153	6.4	71,775	6.8
Washington-Arlington-Alexandria, DC-VA-MD-WV	39,170	4.0	38,518	3.7	39,365	3.7
Chicago-Joliet-Naperville, IL-IN-WI	32,819	3.3	34,898	3.4	35,039	3.3
Houston-Sugar Land-Baytown, TX	31,953	3.2	31,738	3.1	31,136	2.9
San Francisco-Oakland-Fremont, CA	30,600	3.1	29,583	2.9	32,433	3.1
Dallas-Fort Worth-Arlington, TX	26,760	2.7	28,010	2.7	28,090	2.6
Boston-Cambridge-Quincy, MA-NH	23,867	2.4	25,042	2.4	25,909	2.4
Atlanta-Sandy Springs-Marietta, GA	20,054	2.0	21,289	2.1	22,035	2.1
Other	471,408	47.6	495,881	48.1	506,416	47.7

Note: Metropolitan areas defined based on Core Based Statistical Areas (CBSAs).

SOURCE: Randall Monger and James Yankay, "Table 5. Lawful Permanent Resident Flow by Metropolitan Area of Residence: Fiscal Years 2011 to 2013," in *U.S. Lawful Permanent Residents: 2013*, U.S. Department of Homeland Security, Office of Immigration Statistics, May 2014, http://www.dhs.gov/sites/default/files/publications/ois_lpr_fr_2013.pdf (accessed January 7, 2015)

had not been terminated as of April 2015; it would end only when the president issued an executive order to that effect.

According to Catherine N. Barry of the Center for American Progress, in "New Americans in Our Nation's Military" (November 8, 2013, https://www.americanprogress.org/issues/immigration/report/2013/11/08/79116/new-americans-in-our-nations-military), as of 2012 there were more than 65,000 immigrants on active duty in the U.S. Armed Forces, and that 24,000 noncitizen immigrants served in the military that year. Each year, approximately 5,000 LPRs enlisted, accounting for 4% of all new recruits.

Naturalization among Different Immigrant Groups

The OIS reports in *2013 Yearbook of Immigration Statistics* that in FY 2013 a total of 779,929 people became naturalized U.S. citizens. Figure 3.5 provides a percentage breakdown of their region of birth. More than one-third (275,700, or 35.4%) of that year's naturalized citizens were from Asia, and nearly as many (271,807, or 34.9%) were from North America. Lower proportions of people naturalized were from Europe (10.3%), Africa (9.2%), South America (9.8%), and Oceania (0.5%). As the *2013 Yearbook of Immigration Statistics* further notes, Mexico was the country of origin for the largest number of naturalized citizens (99,385), followed by

TABLE 3.20

Lawful permanent resident flow, by age, fiscal years 2011–13

Age	2013 Number	2013 Percent	2012 Number	2012 Percent	2011 Number	2011 Percent
Total	990,553	100.0	1,031,631	100.0	1,062,040	100.0
Under 5 years	33,750	3.4	37,495	3.6	38,378	3.6
5 to 14 years	103,191	10.4	115,986	11.2	123,123	11.6
15 to 24 years	165,893	16.7	189,698	18.4	199,114	18.7
25 to 34 years	234,690	23.7	249,111	24.1	252,917	23.8
35 to 44 years	186,102	18.8	187,101	18.1	197,377	18.6
45 to 54 years	113,819	11.5	117,397	11.4	120,797	11.4
55 to 64 years	71,724	7.2	79,206	7.7	77,198	7.3
65 years and over	48,875	4.9	55,628	5.4	53,126	5.0
Unknown age	32,509	3.3	9	—	10	—
Median age (years)	32	X	31	X	31	X

X = Not applicable.
—Figure rounds to 0.0.

SOURCE: Randall Monger and James Yankay, "Table 6. Lawful Permanent Resident Flow by Age: Fiscal Years 2011 to 2013," in *U.S. Lawful Permanent Residents: 2013*, U.S. Department of Homeland Security, Office of Immigration Statistics, May 2014, http://www.dhs.gov/sites/default/files/publications/ois_lpr_fr_2013.pdf (accessed January 7, 2015)

TABLE 3.21

Lawful permanent resident flow, by sex, fiscal years 2011–13

Sex	2013 Number	2013 Percent	2012 Number	2012 Percent	2011 Number	2011 Percent
Total	990,553	100.0	1,031,631	100.0	1,062,040	100.0
Male	434,284	43.8	467,638	43.8	480,679	45.3
Female	513,736	51.9	563,958	54.7	581,351	54.7
Unknown	42,533	4.3	35	—	10	—

—Figure rounds to 0.0.

SOURCE: Randall Monger and James Yankay, "Table 7. Lawful Permanent Resident Flow by Sex: Fiscal Years 2011 to 2013," in *U.S. Lawful Permanent Residents: 2013*, U.S. Department of Homeland Security, Office of Immigration Statistics, May 2014, http://www.dhs.gov/sites/default/files/publications/ois_lpr_fr_2013.pdf (accessed January 7, 2015)

TABLE 3.22

Lawful permanent resident flow, by marital status, fiscal years 2011–13

Marital status	2013 Number	2013 Percent	2012 Number	2012 Percent	2011 Number	2011 Percent
Total	990,553	100.0	1,031,631	100.0	1,062,040	100.0
Single	355,199	35.9	374,559	36.3	405,164	38.1
Married	579,295	58.5	600,961	58.3	599,122	56.4
Other*	51,671	5.2	51,281	5.0	53,017	5.0
Unknown	4,388	0.4	4,830	0.5	4,737	0.4

*Other includes persons who are widowed, divorced, or separated.

SOURCE: Randall Monger and James Yankay, "Table 8. Lawful Permanent Resident Flow by Marital Status: Fiscal Years 2011 to 2013," in *U.S. Lawful Permanent Residents: 2013*, U.S. Department of Homeland Security, Office of Immigration Statistics, May 2014, http://www.dhs.gov/sites/default/files/publications/ois_lpr_fr_2013.pdf (accessed January 7, 2015)

India (49,897), the Philippines (43,489), the Dominican Republic (39,590), China (35,387), Cuba (30,482), Vietnam (24,277), Haiti (23,480), and Colombia (22,196). From FY 2004 to FY 2013, these countries were all among the leading source countries for naturalized citizens, with Mexico consistently leading all nations. El Salvador, Jamaica, and South Korea also posted high totals in one or more of those fiscal years.

FIGURE 3.4

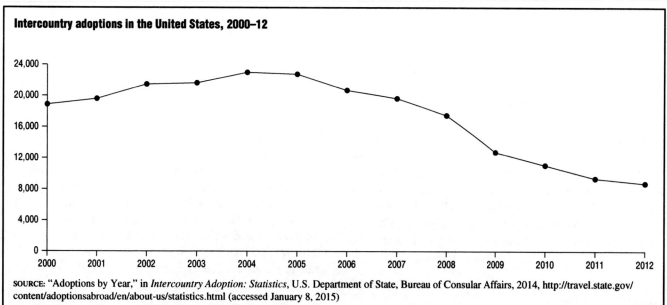

Intercountry adoptions in the United States, 2000–12

SOURCE: "Adoptions by Year," in *Intercountry Adoption: Statistics*, U.S. Department of State, Bureau of Consular Affairs, 2014, http://travel.state.gov/content/adoptionsabroad/en/about-us/statistics.html (accessed January 8, 2015)

TABLE 3.23

Top-5 countries of origin and top-5 destination states for U.S. intercountry adoption, 2009–12

2012

1. China	1. Texas
2. Ethiopia	2. California
3. Russia	3. New York
4. South Korea	4. Florida
5. Ukraine	5. Illinois

2011

1. China	1. California
2. Ethiopia	2. Texas
3. Russia	3. New York
4. South Korea	4. Illinois
5. Ukraine	5. Florida

2010

1. China	1. California
2. Ethiopia	2. New York
3. Russia	3. Texas
4. South Korea	4. Illinois
5. Ukraine	5. Michigan

2009

1. China	1. California
2. Ethiopia	2. New York
3. Russia	3. Texas
4. South Korea	4. Illinois
5. Guatemala	5. Florida

SOURCE: "Top 5 Adopting Countries and States," in "Adoptions by Year," *Intercountry Adoption: Statistics*, U.S. Department of State, Bureau of Consular Affairs, 2014, http://travel.state.gov/content/adoptionsabroad/en/about-us/statistics.html (accessed January 8, 2015)

FIGURE 3.5

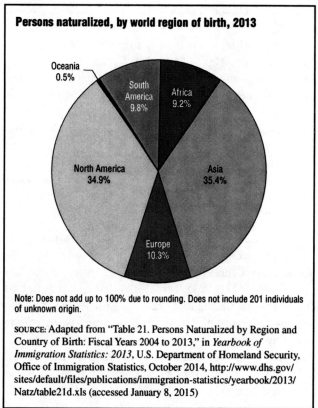

Persons naturalized, by world region of birth, 2013

Note: Does not add up to 100% due to rounding. Does not include 201 individuals of unknown origin.

SOURCE: Adapted from "Table 21. Persons Naturalized by Region and Country of Birth: Fiscal Years 2004 to 2013," in *Yearbook of Immigration Statistics: 2013*, U.S. Department of Homeland Security, Office of Immigration Statistics, October 2014, http://www.dhs.gov/sites/default/files/publications/immigration-statistics/yearbook/2013/Natz/table21d.xls (accessed January 8, 2015)

Naturalization rates vary significantly by country of origin, and the case of Mexican immigrants deserves special attention, given their prevalence among the total immigrant population, the population of LPRs, and the naturalized population. Ana Gonzalez-Barrera et al. of the Pew Hispanic Center report in *The Path Not Taken:*

Two-Thirds of Legal Mexican Immigrants Are Not U.S. Citizens (February 4, 2013, http://www.pewhispanic.org/files/2013/02/Naturalizations_Jan_2013_FINAL.pdf) that Mexican immigrants accounted for 3.9 million of the total 12 million LPRs in 2011, but they became naturalized citizens at much lower rates than other immigrants. Although an increasing percentage of eligible Mexican immigrants chose to become naturalized citizens between 2000 and 2011, only 36% of those eligible in 2011 were naturalized, compared with 68% of the eligible non-Mexican immigrant population.

Gonzalez-Barrera et al. note that the number of Latin American and Caribbean immigrants who were eligible for naturalization but had not applied in 2011 (5.8 million) surpassed the number of immigrants from those regions who had naturalized to that date (5.6 million). It was not a lack of desire that drove the low rates of naturalization among the Hispanic immigrants Pew surveyed: 93% told researchers that they would naturalize if they could. The most commonly cited reasons for not applying for naturalization were personal and administrative barriers, chief among them an insufficient mastery of English and the cost of the application process.

NONIMMIGRANTS

There is no cap on the total number of nonimmigrants allowed to enter the United States, although there are annual limits for some specific types of nonimmigrants. The United States, like most other countries, encourages tourism and tries to attract as many visitors as possible. Although it is easy to get in, strict rules do apply to the conditions of the visit. For example, students can stay only long enough to complete their studies, and businesspeople can stay no longer than six months (although a six-month extension is available). Most nonimmigrants are not allowed to hold jobs while in the United States, but exceptions are made for students and the families of diplomats. An undetermined number of visitors, amounting to many tens of thousands by some estimates, overstay their nonimmigrant visas and continue to live in the United States illegally.

Visas are classified by the type of nonimmigrant visitor. For example, foreign diplomats have A visas, university students have F visas, and many temporary workers have H visas. Table 3.24 lists nonimmigrant admissions, nonimmigrant visa classifications, and the numbers of nonimmigrant visas that were issued by the State Department between FYs 2004 and 2013. In FY 2013 there were 173.1 million nonimmigrant admissions to the country, the highest total since FY 2008, when there were 175.4 million admissions. (Note that the DHS counts admissions rather than individuals, and that the number of admissions does not necessarily provide an accurate estimate of the number of nonimmigrants who enter the United States.) Two groups of visitors account for the bulk of nonimmigrant admissions each year: Canadians who visit the United States for business or pleasure, and Mexicans who have a Nonresident Alien Border Crossing Card (which allows for unlimited travel back and forth between the two countries). These groups are not required to fill out the DHS's I-94 arrival/departure

form, on which nonimmigrants must declare the purpose and length of their visits, their nationality, and other important information. Accordingly, the DHS does not collect detailed data about these visitors.

The remaining 61.1 million nonimmigrant admissions in FY 2013 represented the entries of foreign nationals required to fill out the I-94 form. (See Table 3.24.) These temporary admissions included vacationers (by far the largest group), business visitors, those authorized to work in the United States on a temporary basis, diplomats and their staffs and families, and students, among others. The number of admissions of temporary visitors for pleasure was 48.3 million, up substantially over the preceding years. The number of admissions of temporary visitors for business was 6.3 million, up dramatically from the 4.4 million admissions during the peak of the Great Recession, in FY 2009. There were 3 million admissions for temporary workers and 1.7 million admissions for foreign students in FY 2013.

Temporary Foreign Workers

A temporary worker is a foreign national who comes to the United States to work for a limited period. Most legal temporary workers arrive with H-class visas, which include H-1B/H-1B1 and H-2/H-2A visas. The State Department's Bureau of Consular Affairs notes in *Report of the Visa Office 2013* (2014, http://travel.state.gov/content/visas/english/law-and-policy/statistics/annual-reports/report-of-the-visa-office-2013.html) that over half (55.2%) of individuals admitted to the United States on H-class visas in FY 2013 came from Asia. (See Figure 3.6.) North America (Canada, Mexico, Central America, and the Caribbean) contributed another 34.4% of these workers. Within these regions, certain countries predominated. For example, of the 212,673 Asian workers issued H-class visas that year, 172,284 (81%) came from India. Chinese nationals represented the second-largest group of temporary workers from Asia, at 16,296 (7.7%). Of the 132,390 North American workers issued H-class visas in FY 2013, 118,507 (89.5%) came from Mexico.

H-1 VISA PROGRAM. The H-1 visa program is largely synonymous with the H-1B classification, which allows a temporary worker in a specialty occupation to remain in the United States for an extended period, generally not to exceed six years. There are other H-1 programs (H-1B1, a program specifically for workers from Chile and Singapore, and H-1C, a program for registered nurses), but these constitute a tiny fraction of the overall H-1 program petitions approved yearly by the USCIS.

The USCIS defines the scope of the H-1B program in *Characteristics of H-1B Specialty Occupation Workers: Fiscal Year 2012 Annual Report to Congress, October 1, 2011–September 30, 2012* (June 26, 2013, http://www.uscis.gov/sites/default/files/USCIS/Resources/Reports%20and%20Studies/H-1B/h1b-fy-12-characteristics.pdf):

TABLE 3.24

Nonimmigrant admissions, by class of admission, fiscal years 2004–13

Class of admission	2004	2005	2006	2007	2008	2009	2010	2011	2012	2013
Total all admissions[a]	180,200,000	175,300,000	175,100,000	171,300,000	175,400,000	162,600,000	159,700,000	158,500,000	165,500,000	173,100,000
Total I-94 admissions[b]	30,781,330	32,003,435	33,667,328	37,149,651	39,381,928	36,231,554	46,471,569	53,082,286	53,887,286	61,052,260
Temporary workers and families	1,507,769	1,572,863	1,709,268	1,932,075	1,949,695	1,703,697	2,816,485	3,385,775	3,049,419	2,996,743
Temporary workers and trainees	831,144	882,957	985,456	1,118,138	1,101,938	936,272	1,682,111	2,092,028	1,900,582	1,853,915
CNMI-only transitional workers (CW1)										1,642
Spouses and children of CW1 (CW2)										404
Temporary workers in specialty occupations (H1B)	386,821	407,418	431,853	461,730	409,619	339,243	454,757	494,565	473,015	474,355
Chile and Singapore Free Trade Agreement aliens (H1B1)	4	47	129	170	153	213	163	30	29	8
Registered nurses participating in the Nursing Relief for Disadvantaged Areas (H1C)	70	31	24	49	170	231	295	124		7
Agricultural workers (H2A)[c,d]	22,141		46,432	87,316	173,103	149,763	139,403	188,411	183,860	204,577
Nonagricultural workers (H2B)[c]	86,958		97,279	75,727	104,618	56,381	69,395	79,794	82,906	104,984
Returning H2B workers (H2R)[c,e]			36,792	79,168	5,003	162	104	68	15	9
Trainees (H3)	2,226	2,938	4,134	5,540	6,156	4,168	3,078	3,279	4,081	4,117
Spouses and children of H1, H2, or H3 (H4)	130,847	130,145	133,437	144,136	122,423	105,429	141,571	155,936	156,668	163,786
Workers with extraordinary ability or achievement (O1)	27,127	29,715	31,969	36,184	41,238	45,600	49,995	51,775	53,941	66,604
Workers accompanying and assisting in performance of O1 workers (O2)	6,332	7,635	9,567	10,349	12,497	12,996	13,989	15,949	16,670	20,762
Spouses and children of O1 and O2 (O3)	3,719	4,154	4,674	5,377	6,386	6,533	6,764	6,985	6,853	8,238
Internationally recognized athletes or entertainers (P1)	40,466	43,766	46,205	53,050	57,030	54,432	72,915	84,545	84,209	85,583
Artists or entertainers in reciprocal exchange programs (P2)	3,810	4,423	4,604	4,835	4,358	4,028	11,213	13,359	12,826	12,306
Artists or entertainers in culturally unique programs (P3)	10,038	10,836	12,630	11,900	12,767	11,441	9,669	9,301	9,290	9,512
Spouses and children of P1, P2, or P3 (P4)	1,853	1,938	2,067	2,223	2,229	2,359	2,836	2,944	3,155	3,565
Workers in international cultural exchange programs (Q1)	2,113	2,575	2,423	2,412	3,231	2,555	2,430	2,331	2,494	2,685
Workers in religious occupations (R1)	21,571	22,362	22,706	25,162	25,106	17,362	21,043	19,683	15,906	14,191
Spouses and children of R1 (R2)	6,443	6,712	7,330	6,881	6,421	4,481	7,966	5,682	4,738	4,337
North American Free Trade Agreement (NAFTA) professional workers (TN)	65,970	64,713	73,880	85,142	88,382	99,018	634,116	899,455	733,692	612,535
Spouses and children of TN (TD)	12,635	14,222	17,321	20,787	21,048	19,907	40,409	57,812	56,223	59,708
Intracompany transferees	456,583	455,350	466,009	531,073	558,485	493,992	702,447	788,187	717,893	723,641
Intracompany transferees (L1)	314,484	312,144	320,829	363,536	382,776	333,386	502,723	562,776	498,899	503,206
Spouses and children of L1 (L2)	142,099	143,206	145,180	167,537	175,709	160,606	199,724	225,411	218,994	220,435
Treaty traders and investors	182,934	192,824	216,842	238,936	243,386	229,301	383,694	454,101	386,472	373,360
Treaty traders and their spouses and children (E1)	47,083	49,037	50,230	51,722	50,377	49,111	87,988	110,169	81,337	71,652
Treaty investors and their spouses and children (E2)	135,851	143,786	164,795	177,920	180,270	166,983	281,868	329,230	288,217	279,288
Treaty investors and their spouses and children CNMI only (E2C)										5
Australian Free Trade Agreement principals, spouses and children (E3)			1,817	9,294	12,739	13,207	13,838	14,702	16,916	22,415
Representatives of foreign information media	37,108	41,732	40,961	43,928	45,886	44,132	48,233	51,459	44,472	45,827
Representatives of foreign information media and spouses and children (I1)	37,108	41,732	40,961	43,928	45,886	44,132	48,233	51,459	44,472	45,827
Students	656,373	663,919	740,724	841,673	917,373	951,964	1,595,072	1,788,962	1,653,576	1,669,225
Academic students (F1)	613,221	621,178	693,805	787,756	859,169	895,392	1,514,777	1,702,730	1,566,815	1,577,509
Spouses and children of F1 (F2)	35,771	33,756	35,987	40,178	42,039	40,956	61,036	66,449	67,563	71,167
Vocational students (M1)	6,989	8,378	10,384	13,073	15,496	14,632	17,641	18,824	17,600	19,106
Spouses and children of M1 (M2)	392	607	548	666	669	984	1,618	959	1,598	1,443
Exchange visitors	360,777	382,463	427,067	489,286	506,138	459,408	543,335	526,931	475,232	492,937
Exchange visitors (J1)	321,975	342,742	385,286	443,482	459,126	413,150	484,740	469,993	421,425	433,534
Spouses and children of J1 (J2)	38,802	39,721	41,781	45,804	47,012	46,258	58,595	56,938	53,807	59,403
Diplomats and other representatives	276,817	287,484	292,846	303,290	314,920	323,183	380,241	377,830	365,779	373,330
Ambassadors, public ministers, career diplomatic or consular officers and their families (A1)	28,046	28,488	29,337	30,291	30,882	31,038	38,948	37,692	33,700	34,548
Other foreign government officials or employees and their families (A2)	122,809	126,827	127,296	131,583	136,699	142,315	173,293	175,651	172,096	164,896
Attendants, servants, or personal employees of A1 and A2 and their families (A3)	1,794	1,630	1,496	1,602	1,686	1,766	1,870	1,843	1,553	1,381
Principals of recognized foreign governments (G1)	13,189	13,606	14,523	15,099	15,348	14,876	16,452	15,649	15,669	15,254
Other representatives of recognized foreign governments (G2)	13,685	16,608	15,661	15,160	18,367	17,529	17,711	20,395	17,118	16,011
Representatives of nonrecognized or nonmember foreign governments (G3)	593	740	811	816	844	912	904	967	886	864
International organization officers or employees (G4)	80,515	82,826	85,119	88,374	89,711	92,878	105,040	100,858	100,760	108,478

TABLE 3.24

Nonimmigrant admissions, by class of admission, fiscal years 2004–13 [CONTINUED]

Class of admission	2004	2005	2006	2007	2008	2009	2010	2011	2012	2013
Attendants, servants, or personal employees of representatives (G5)	1,373	1,336	1,411	1,477	1,399	1,389	1,385	1,509	1,190	1,137
North Atlantic Treaty Organization (NATO) officials, spouses, and children (N1 to N7)	14,813	15,423	17,192	18,888	19,984	20,480	24,638	23,266	22,807	30,761
Temporary visitors for pleasure	22,653,699	23,701,858	24,788,438	27,486,177	29,442,168	27,800,027	35,135,270	40,591,607	42,041,426	48,346,018
Temporary visitors for pleasure (B2)	9,185,492	9,758,617	11,269,933	13,087,974	13,371,671	12,680,504	19,144,019	23,806,138	24,476,086	29,915,467
Visa Waiver Program—temporary visitors for pleasure (WT)	13,380,069	13,462,507	12,827,677	13,469,851	15,099,059	14,272,553	14,825,553	15,718,710	16,380,307	17,168,958
Guam Visa Waiver Program—temporary visitors for pleasure to Guam (GT)	88,138	480,734	690,828	928,352	971,438	846,970	120,544	—	—	—
Guam—Commonwealth of Northern Mariana Islands (CNMI) Visa Waiver Program—temporary visitors for pleasure to Guam or Northern Mariana Islands (GMT)	—	—	—	—	—	—	1,045,154	1,066,759	1,185,033	1,261,593
Temporary visitors for business	4,576,783	4,684,164	5,030,779	5,418,884	5,603,668	4,390,888	5,206,234	5,696,503	5,707,218	6,299,533
Temporary visitors for business (B1)	2,352,404	2,432,587	2,673,309	2,928,875	3,052,581	2,408,092	2,944,372	3,055,932	2,972,355	3,498,688
Visa Waiver Program—temporary visitors for business (WB)	2,223,331	2,249,816	2,355,332	2,486,015	2,546,322	1,977,361	2,256,862	2,637,166	2,731,887	2,798,130
Guam Visa Waiver Program—temporary visitors for business to Guam (GB)	1,048	1,761	2,138	3,994	4,765	5,435	904	—	—	—
Guam—Commonwealth of Northern Mariana Islands (CNMI) Visa Waiver Program—temporary visitors for business to Guam or Northern Mariana Islands (GMB)	—	—	—	—	—	—	4,068	3,405	2,976	2,715
Transit aliens	338,170	361,597	378,749	396,383	387,237	346,695	327,572	322,499	313,514	628,711
Aliens in continuous and immediate transit through the United States (C1)	322,187	343,609	357,682	376,451	365,958	326,704	304,012	296,636	289,105	608,396
Aliens in transit to the United Nations (C2)	2,283	2,379	2,854	2,914	2,646	2,613	2,986	4,397	4,158	2,269
Foreign government officials, their spouses, children, and attendants in transit (C3)	13,700	15,609	18,213	17,018	18,633	17,378	20,574	21,466	20,251	18,046
Commuter students	—	33	188	310	1,102	6,488	53,711	108,894	115,561	105,263
Canadian or Mexican national academic commuter students (F3)	—	33	188	307	1,102	6,488	53,711	108,892	115,561	105,263
Canadian or Mexican national vocational commuter students (M3)	—	—	—	3	—	—	—	—	—	—
Alien fiancé(e)s of U.S. citizens and children	33,061	38,027	34,947	38,507	34,863	32,009	34,891	27,700	32,102	29,773
Fiancé(e)s of U.S. citizens (K1)	28,546	32,900	30,021	32,991	29,916	27,754	30,444	24,112	27,977	26,046
Children of K1 (K2)	4,515	5,127	4,926	5,516	4,947	4,255	4,447	3,588	4,125	3,727
Legal Immigration Family Equity (LIFE) Act	70,778	46,727	41,779	37,594	24,172	20,960	38,810	30,099	8,227	3,014
Spouses of U.S. citizens, visa pending (K3)	17,864	16,249	14,739	15,065	12,849	12,937	25,615	17,874	4,534	1,262
Children of U.S. citizens, visa pending (K4)	4,253	4,098	3,692	3,430	2,845	2,578	4,557	3,103	618	417
Spouses of permanent residents, visa pending (V1)	17,866	10,157	9,321	6,960	3,609	2,482	3,620	3,659	1,928	867
Children of permanent residents, visa pending (V2)	15,239	7,159	6,070	5,435	2,270	1,424	2,206	2,546	449	271
Dependents of V1 or V2, visa pending (V3)	15,556	9,064	7,957	6,704	2,599	1,539	2,812	2,917	698	197
Other	433	241	208	100	103	74	92	93	91	87
Unknown	306,670	264,059	222,335	205,372	200,489	196,161	339,856	225,393	125,141	107,626

CNMI = Commonwealth of Northern Mariana Islands.

[a]Estimated admission totals rounded to the nearest hundred thousand. Excludes sea and air crew admissions (D1 and D2 visas).

[b]Beginning in 2010, the number of I-94 admissions greatly exceeds totals reported in previous years due to a more complete count of land admissions.

[c]Data are not available separately for 2005; during 2005 there were 129,327 admissions for H2 classes (H2A, H2B, H2R).

[d]Beginning in 2006, annual increases in H2A admissions may be due to more complete recording of pedestrian admissions along the southwest border.

[e]Issuances of H2R (returning H2B workers not subject to annual numerical limits) ceased at the end of 2007.

[f]Not available.

[g]Not applicable.

[h]Data withheld to limit disclosure.

—Represents zero.

Notes: Admissions represent counts of events, i.e., arrivals, not unique individuals; multiple entries of an individual on the same day are counted as one admission. The majority of short-term admissions from Canada and Mexico are excluded.

SOURCE: Adapted from "Table 25. Nonimmigrant Admissions by Class of Admission: Fiscal Years 2004 to 2013," in Yearbook of Immigration Statistics: 2013, U.S. Department of Homeland Security, Office of Immigration Statistics, October 2014, http://www.dhs.gov/sites/default/files/publications/immigration-statistics/yearbook/2013/NI/table25d.xls (accessed January 8, 2015)

FIGURE 3.6

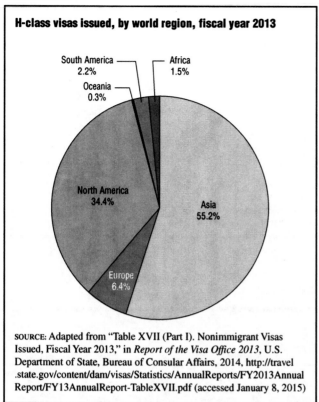

H-class visas issued, by world region, fiscal year 2013

South America 2.2%

Africa 1.5%

Oceania 0.3%

North America 34.4%

Asia 55.2%

Europe 6.4%

SOURCE: Adapted from "Table XVII (Part I). Nonimmigrant Visas Issued, Fiscal Year 2013," in *Report of the Visa Office 2013*, U.S. Department of State, Bureau of Consular Affairs, 2014, http://travel .state.gov/content/dam/visas/Statistics/AnnualReports/FY2013Annual Report/FY13AnnualReport-TableXVII.pdf (accessed January 8, 2015)

The H-1B nonimmigrant classification is a vehicle through which a qualified alien may seek admission to the United States on a temporary basis to work in his or her field of expertise. An H-1B petition can be filed for an alien to perform services in a specialty occupation, services relating to a Department of Defense (DoD) cooperative research and development project or coproduction project, or services of distinguished merit and ability in the field of fashion modeling. Prior to employing an H-1B temporary worker, the U.S. employer must first file a Labor Condition Application with the Department of Labor (DOL) and then file an H-1B petition with the USCIS. The Labor Condition Application specifies the job, salary, length, and geographic location of employment. The employer must agree to pay the alien the greater of the actual or prevailing wage for the position.

The USCIS states that a foreign worker is allowed to remain in H-1 status for up to six continuous years, but each H-1B petition covers a maximum of three years. Employers must file new H-1B petitions to extend the H-1B holder's term of employment to the maximum six years. H-1B petitions may also be filed on behalf of a worker who already has H-1B status with a different employer, and petitions may be filed to revise previous petitions. Therefore, the total number of approved petitions in any given year is likely to exceed the number of foreign individuals who are actually working in the United States under the terms of the program. At the end of the six-year limit for H-1B status, a worker must

either apply for a different immigration status, if eligible, or the individual must leave the United States. Following a year outside of the United States, these workers may be eligible to return to the country under H-1B status for another six-year period.

According to the USCIS, IMMACT set an annual cap on H-1B visas at 65,000 beginning in FY 1992. The USCIS explains, however, that "generally, a petition to extend an H-1B nonimmigrant's period of stay, change the conditions of [his or her] employment, or request new H-1B employment for an H-1B worker already in the United States will not count against the H-1B fiscal year cap." The American Competitiveness and Workforce Improvement Act of 1998 and the American Competitiveness in the Twenty-First Century Act of 2000 introduced important changes to the H-1B program, among them raising the H-1B cap and the introduction of exemptions to the cap. As a result of these initiatives the H-1B cap reached 195,000 in FY 2003, before reverting to the original total of 65,000 in FY 2004. It remained at this level in FY 2012. A number of exemptions remained on the books, however, including an exemption for an annual total of 20,000 foreign nationals who have earned master's or higher degrees in the United States.

As Table 3.25 shows, 262,569 H-1B petitions were approved in FY 2012. These were split almost equally between petitions for initial employment (136,890 petitions, or 52% of the total) and petitions for continuing employment (125,679, or 48%). The initial employment petitions were split nearly equally between workers living outside the United States, and those living inside the United States under the terms of student or other visas. The number of H-1B petitions approved in FY 2012 was in line with the previous year's totals but substantially higher than the numbers for FYs 2009 and 2010, likely due to increased hiring among U.S. businesses as the effects of the Great Recession began to fade.

H-1B petitions were not distributed equally among different nationalities. As Table 3.26 shows, H-1B beneficiaries from India accounted for 168,367 (64.1%) of the total number of approved petitions in FY 2012, and for more than half of both initial and continuing employment petitions that year. Workers from China accounted for the second-highest number of approved H-1B petitions, 19,850, or 7.6% of the total. The concentration of Indian and Chinese workers living in the United States under H-1B status was related to the distribution of jobs that qualified for the program. In FY 2012 over half of all H-1B jobs were in the computer industry. (See Table 3.27.) India's computer industry has grown explosively since the mid-1990s, and the country has developed a renowned infrastructure of educational and training programs that make it a leading international source for technology talent. Likewise, another major source of H-1B petitions, the

TABLE 3.25

H-1B petitions approved, by type, fiscal years 2009–12

Type of petition	Fiscal year 2009	Percent	Fiscal year 2010	Percent	Fiscal year 2011	Percent	Fiscal year 2012	Percent
					Petitions approved			
Total	214,271	100	192,990	100	269,653	100	262,569	100
Initial employment	86,300	40	76,627	40	106,445	39	136,890	52
Aliens outside U.S.	33,283	16	34,848	18	48,665	18	74,997	28
Aliens in U.S.	53,017	25	41,779	22	57,780	21	61,893	24
Continuing employment	127,971	60	116,363	60	163,208	61	125,679	48

Note: Sum of the percent may not add to 100 due to rounding.

SOURCE: "Table 3. H-1B Petitions Approved by Type: FYs 2009 to 2012," in *Characteristics of H1B Specialty Occupation Workers: Fiscal Year 2012 Annual Report to Congress, October 1, 2011–September 30, 2012,* U.S. Department of Homeland Security, U.S. Citizenship and Immigration Services, June 26, 2013, http://www.uscis.gov/sites/default/files/USCIS/Resources/Reports%20and%20Studies/H-1B/h1b-fy-12-characteristics.pdf (accessed January 8, 2015)

TABLE 3.26

H-1B petitions approved by country of birth and type, fiscal years 2011–12

Country of birth	All beneficiaries Fiscal year 2011 Number	Fiscal year 2012 Number	Initial employment Fiscal year 2011 Number	Fiscal year 2012 Number	Continuing employment Fiscal year 2011 Number	Fiscal year 2012 Number
Total	269,653	262,569	106,445	136,890	163,208	125,679
India	156,317	168,367	55,972	86,477	100,345	81,890
China, People's Republic	23,787	19,850	10,165	11,409	13,622	8,441
Canada	9,362	7,999	3,584	3,660	5,778	4,339
Philippines	7,582	5,304	2,020	1,863	5,562	3,441
South Korea	6,689	4,579	3,407	2,662	3,282	1,917
United Kingdom	4,629	3,535	2,573	2,013	2,056	1,522
Mexico	3,473	3,047	1,367	1,528	2,106	1,519
Japan	3,274	2,542	1,276	1,171	1,998	1,371
Taiwan	2,937	2,387	1,455	1,368	1,482	1,019
France	2,653	2,232	1,517	1,377	1,136	855
Pakistan	2,552	1,997	891	851	1,661	1,146
Germany	2,193	1,816	1,210	1,083	983	733
Turkey	2,161	1,774	967	989	1,194	785
Brazil	2,010	1,712	1,105	996	905	716
Nepal	1,566	1,636	719	932	847	704
Venezuela	1,734	1,494	846	807	888	687
Colombia	1,786	1,392	705	623	1,081	769
Italy	1,351	1,332	816	804	535	528
Russia	1,514	1,321	873	829	641	492
Spain	1,198	1,015	684	632	514	383
Other countries	30,885	27,238	14,293	14,816	16,592	12,422

Note: Countries of birth are ranked based on fiscal year 2012 data.

SOURCE: "Table 4A. H-1B Petitions Approved by Country of Birth of Beneficiary and Type of Petition (Number): FYs 2011 and 2012," in *Characteristics of H1B Specialty Occupation Workers: Fiscal Year 2012 Annual Report to Congress, October 11, 2011–September 30, 2012,* U.S. Department of Homeland Security, U.S. Citizenship and Immigration Services, June 26, 2013, http://www.uscis.gov/sites/default/files/USCIS/Resources/Reports%20and%20Studies/H-1B/h1b-fy-12-characteristics.pdf (accessed January 8, 2015)

engineering industry, represents an area in which China's educational system and economy are among the world's strongest.

H-2 VISA PROGRAM. The H-2 Temporary Agricultural Worker Program was authorized by the INA to provide a flexible response to seasonal agricultural labor demands. Since 1964 it has been the only legal program in the United States for temporary foreign agricultural workers. In 1986 the H-2 program was amended to create separate categories of workers: H-2A visas were for temporary workers who performed agricultural services, H-2B visas were for workers who performed other services, and H-2R visas were for former H-2B workers authorized to return to the United States. The H-2R program was discontinued in 2007, but the H-2A and H-2B programs as conceived in 1986 remained in effect in 2015.

Legal and Illegal Immigration

TABLE 3.27

H-1B petitions approved by occupation and type, fiscal years 2011–12

	All beneficiaries		Initial employment		Continuing employment	
	Fiscal year 2011	Fiscal year 2012	Fiscal year 2011	Fiscal year 2012	Fiscal year 2011	Fiscal year 2012
Occupational category	Number	Number	Number	Number	Number	Number
Total	**269,653**	**262,569**	**106,445**	**136,890**	**163,208**	**125,679**
Occupation known	**265,365**	**260,428**	**105,395**	**135,966**	**159,970**	**124,462**
Computer-related occupations	134,873	154,869	51,570	83,444	83,303	71,425
Occupations in architecture, engineering and surveying	29,695	26,329	11,950	13,082	17,745	13,247
Occupations in administrative specializations	21,240	18,204	9,553	9,781	11,687	8,423
Occupations in education	24,321	17,421	9,081	8,492	15,240	8,929
Occupations in medicine and health	18,704	14,083	6,037	5,649	12,667	8,434
Managers and officials N.E.C.*	7,341	6,060	3,187	2,921	4,154	3,139
Occupations in mathematics and physical sciences	5,968	4,969	2,450	2,465	3,518	2,504
Occupations in life sciences	6,375	4,820	2,992	2,505	3,383	2,315
Miscellaneous professional, technical, and managerial	4,944	4,171	2,315	2,266	2,629	1,905
Occupations in social sciences	4,928	3,993	2,346	2,156	2,582	1,837
Occupations in art	3,013	2,619	1,577	1,505	1,436	1,114
Occupations in law and jurisprudence	1,325	1,051	692	580	633	471
Occupations in writing	943	681	486	385	457	296
Miscellaneous	550	463	461	265	89	198
Occupations in entertainment and recreation	556	212	270	119	286	93
Sales promotion occupations	387	165	335	151	52	14
Occupations in museum, library, and archival sciences	202	164	93	107	109	57
Occupation unknown	**4,288**	**2,141**	**1,050**	**924**	**3,238**	**1,217**

*N.E.C. indicates *not elsewhere classified.*
Notes: Occupations ranked based on fiscal year 2012 data.

SOURCE: "Table 8A. H-1B Petitions Approved by Major Occupation Group of Beneficiary and Type of Petition (Number): Fiscal Years 2011 and 2012," in *Characteristics of H1B Specialty Occupation Workers: Fiscal Year 2012 Annual Report to Congress, October 11, 2011–September 30, 2012,* U.S. Department of Homeland Security, U.S. Citizenship and Immigration Services, June 26, 2013, http://www.uscis.gov/sites/default/files/USCIS/Resources/Reports%20and%20Studies/H-1B/h1b-fy-12-characteristics.pdf (accessed January 8, 2015)

The H-2A program is based on employer needs and has no set numerical limits, while the H-2B program is capped at 66,000 new visas per year. The H-2B cap is allocated by half-year, so that 33,000 new visas are issued for the first half of the fiscal year (October 1 to March 31) and 33,000 for the second half of the fiscal year (April 1 to September 30). Unused visas from the first half of the year may be issued for the second half, but unused H-2B visas do not carry over from one fiscal year to the next. H-2B workers who extend their stays in the country while retaining H-2B status are not counted against the yearly limits. According to the DOL's Office of Foreign Labor Certification (OFLC), in *Annual Report, October 1, 2011–September 30, 2012* (July 2013, http://www.foreignlaborcert.doleta.gov/pdf/OFLC-2012_Annual_Report-11-29-2013-Final%20Clean.pdf), in FY 2012, 85,248 workers applying under the H-2A program were certified, and 75,548 workers applying under the H-2B program were certified.

Agricultural employers who anticipate a shortage of domestic workers file an application for H-2A certification with the DOL. These employers must certify that there are not enough U.S. workers able, qualified, and willing to do the work. The employer must also certify that the jobs are not vacant due to a labor dispute. Employers in other industries are eligible to petition for

H-2B workers if their need for labor under the program is considered temporary. An employer's need for employees is considered temporary if it is a one-time occurrence, a seasonal need, a peak-load need (a need related to an anticipated spike in business), or an intermittent need.

Employers utilizing the H-2A and H-2B programs are required to pay wages at a rate that will not adversely affect the prevailing wages for U.S. citizens and permanent residents. These wage floors are typically set as equal to the highest of the following: the average wage paid to local workers in the industry, the federal minimum wage, the state minimum wage, or the local minimum wage. Both programs are also subject to restrictions regarding the countries of origin of participating workers. Each year the DHS publishes a list of countries whose citizens or nationals are authorized to participate in the two programs. As of April 2015, the list included 63 countries. Changes in the list of approved countries does not affect workers currently employed under the program unless they apply for an extension of their visas.

Figure 3.7 shows the top-10 crops worked by H-2A visa holders in FY 2012. Tobacco farmers successfully requested 6,544 H-2A visa recipients, followed by growers of oranges (5,552) and onions (4,055). Plant nurseries and growers of hay, apples, tomatoes, peaches, corn, and sheep all requested more than 2,000 H-2A workers, as well. According to the OFLC, in *Annual Report, October 1, 2011–September 30, 2012*, tobacco growers and their temporary nonimmigrant employees worked mainly in the southern states of Kentucky, North Carolina, Virginia, and Tennessee, as well as in the northeastern state of Connecticut. Orange growers and their workers resided exclusively in Florida. Onion growers and their employees resided in geographically dispersed locations: Georgia, Michigan, Nevada, New York, and Wisconsin.

Figure 3.8 shows the occupations for which H-2B visas were most commonly certified in FY 2012. The OFLC cleared 24,094 individuals to work as laborers and landscapers, by far the most common occupation

FIGURE 3.7

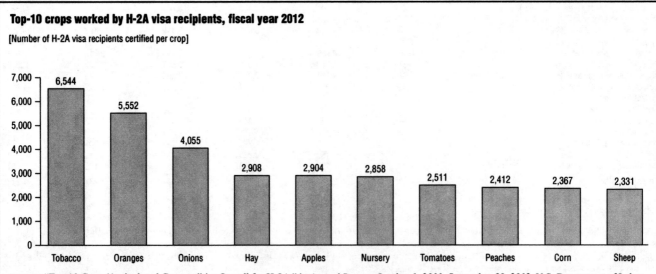

Top-10 crops worked by H-2A visa recipients, fiscal year 2012

[Number of H-2A visa recipients certified per crop]

SOURCE: "Top 10 Crops/Agricultural Commodities Overall for H-2A," in *Annual Report, October 1, 2011–September 30, 2012*, U.S. Department of Labor, Office of Foreign Labor Certification, July 2013, http://www.foreignlaborcert.doleta.gov/pdf/OFLC-2012_Annual_Report-11-29-2013-Final%20Clean.pdf (accessed January 8, 2015)

FIGURE 3.8

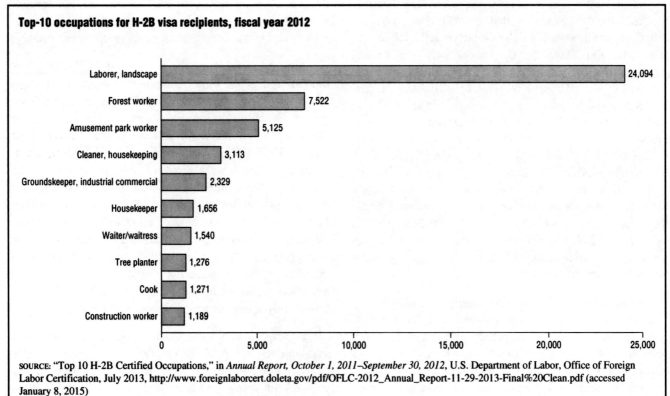

Top-10 occupations for H-2B visa recipients, fiscal year 2012

SOURCE: "Top 10 H-2B Certified Occupations," in *Annual Report, October 1, 2011–September 30, 2012*, U.S. Department of Labor, Office of Foreign Labor Certification, July 2013, http://www.foreignlaborcert.doleta.gov/pdf/OFLC-2012_Annual_Report-11-29-2013-Final%20Clean.pdf (accessed January 8, 2015)

for H-2B visa holders that year. Forest workers (7,522) and amusement park workers (5,125) were the next most-certified types of workers. Smaller numbers of cleaners, groundskeepers, housekeepers, waiters and waitresses, tree planters, cooks, and construction workers were also certified. According to the OFLC, in *Annual Report, October 1, 2011–September 30, 2012*, the average hourly wage for these H-2B positions varied from a low of $7.71 (for amusement park workers) to a high of $11.17 (for tree planters).

Foreign Students at Institutions of Higher Education

According to the Institute of International Education, in *Open Doors Data* (November 2014, http://www .iie.org/research-and-publications/open-doors/data), during the 1948–49 school year there were an estimated 25,464 international students in U.S. colleges and universities, amounting to 1.1% of the total population of 2.4 million higher-education students. (See Table 3.28.) After hovering between 1.3% and 1.6% of the total student population for most of the next three decades, during the late 1970s the foreign-student population surpassed 2% of the total student population. This percentage continued to rise through the early 21st century, flattening temporarily between the 2001–02 school year and the 2006–07 school year, before resuming a dramatic rise. During the 2013–14 academic year there were 886,052 international students receiving education or training in the United States, accounting for 4.2% of all U.S. college and university students.

As Table 3.29 shows, China was by far the leading country of origin for international students during the 2013–14 academic year, accounting for 274,439 (31%) of the total 886,052 international students. Other leading countries of origin included India (102,673 students), South Korea (68,047), Saudi Arabia (53,919), Canada (28,304), Taiwan (21,266), Japan (19,334), Vietnam (16,579), Mexico (14,779), and Brazil (13,286).

The Institute of International Education reports in "International Students: Fields of Study by Place of Origin" (November 2014, http://www.iie.org/en/Research-and-Publications/Open-Doors/Data/International-Students/ Fields-of-Study-Place-of-Origin/2013-14), among most international students, STEM (science, technology, engineering, and math) fields and programs in business and management were by far the most popular in 2013–14. More than 40% of Chinese students were pursuing STEM degrees, and nearly 30% were pursuing business/management degrees. The pursuit of STEM degrees was even more pervasive among Indian students, 78.6% of whom specialized in one or more of these fields.

VISA FEES

In "Fees and Reciprocity Tables" (2015, http://travel .state.gov/content/visas/english/fees/fees-reciprocity-tables .html), the Bureau of Consular Affairs explains that there are two types of fees associated with U.S. visas: service fees and issuance fees. Service fees are charged upon application for a visa or for certain special services. They vary depending on the class of visa and, with a few exceptions, are paid by all applicants. For example, as of April 2015, nonimmigrant visas not requiring petitions (with the exception of E visas) cost $160. Petition-based nonimmigrant visas, including H visas for temporary workers, cost $190. Service fees were higher for those seeking to stay in the United States permanently. Filing an immigrant visa petition for a relative cost $420; a visa for an orphan being adopted internationally cost $720. The processing fee for an employment-based immigrant visa application was $345, and the fee for a diversity visa applicant was $330.

Issuance fees apply only to nonimmigrant visas and are based on reciprocity. Under this concept, the State Department tracks what other countries charge U.S. citizens for various types of visas. For any country where the amount exceeds the U.S. service fee for that type of visa, the United States assesses an issuance fee on visa applicants from that country to make up the cost difference. In other words, issuance fees ensure that any foreigner applying for a nonimmigrant visa to visit the United States pays at least as much for that visa as a U.S. citizen would pay for a visa to visit that foreigner's country of origin. Unlike service fees, issuance fees are only assessed after a visa application has been approved.

FOREIGN NATIONALS NOT ADMITTED TO THE UNITED STATES

State Department officials in foreign countries screen applicants and deny visas for a variety of reasons. An applicant refused a visa can then attempt to "overcome" the issue(s) that caused the denial. In *Report of the Visa Office 2013*, the Bureau of Consular Affairs breaks down the number of foreign nationals refused entry to the United States in FY 2013 according to the reasons for denial. By far the most common reason for denying visas to immigrants was an application's failure to comply with the INA or related regulations. Among the 341,489 total grounds for ineligibility found in the 288,957 immigrant applications that were initially refused in FY 2013, there were 290,369 findings of ineligibility on this basis. (See Table 3.30.) However, 180,022 applicants overcame denials issued for this reason. In all, 194,300 applications for immigrant visas overcame an initial ruling of ineligibility. It should be noted that applications can be denied for more than one reason and that applicants can be denied more than once in a fiscal year, so the total number of denials cataloged in Table 3.30 exceeds the number of individual applicants. Additionally, an applicant can be refused one year and overcome the refusal the following year, so the number of visas refused and the

TABLE 3.28

International student enrollment in colleges and universities, 1948–2014

Year	Enrolled int'l students	Optional Practical Training (OPT)	Total int'l students	Annual % change	Total enrollment	% int'l
1948/49	—	—	25,464	—	2,403,400	1.1
1949/50	—	—	26,433	3.8	2,445,000	1.1
1950/51	—	—	29,813	12.8	2,281,000	1.3
1951/52	—	—	30,462	2.2	2,102,000	1.4
1952/53	—	—	33,675	10.5	2,134,000	1.6
1953/54	—	—	33,833	0.5	2,231,000	1.5
1954/55	—	—	34,232	1.2	2,447,000	1.4
1955/56	—	—	36,494	6.6	2,653,000	1.4
1956/57	—	—	40,666	11.4	2,918,000	1.4
1957/58	—	—	43,391	6.7	3,324,000	1.3
1958/59	—	—	47,245	8.9	no data	—
1959/60	—	—	48,486	2.6	3,640,000	1.3
1960/61	—	—	53,107	9.5	no data	—
1961/62	—	—	58,086	9.4	4,146,000	1.4
1962/63	—	—	64,705	11.4	no data	—
1963/64	—	—	74,814	15.6	4,780,000	1.6
1964/65	—	—	82,045	9.7	5,280,000	1.6
1965/66	—	—	82,709	0.8	5,921,000	1.4
1966/67	—	—	100,262	21.2	6,390,000	1.6
1967/68	—	—	110,315	10.0	6,912,000	1.6
1968/69	—	—	121,362	10.0	7,513,000	1.6
1969/70	—	—	134,959	11.2	8,005,000	1.7
1970/71	—	—	144,708	7.2	8,581,000	1.7
1971/72	—	—	140,126	−3.2	8,949,000	1.6
1972/73	—	—	146,097	4.3	9,215,000	1.6
1973/74	—	—	151,066	3.4	9,602,000	1.6
1974/75*	—	—	154,580	2.3	10,224,000	1.5
1975/76	—	—	179,344	16.0	11,185,000	1.6
1976/77	—	—	203,068	13.2	11,012,000	1.8
1977/78	—	—	235,509	16.0	11,286,000	2.1
1978/79	—	—	263,938	12.1	11,260,000	2.3
1979/80	283,503	2,840	286,343	8.5	11,570,000	2.5
1980/81	308,432	3,450	311,882	8.9	12,097,000	2.6
1981/82	323,419	2,880	326,299	4.6	12,372,000	2.6
1982/83	333,365	3,620	336,985	3.3	12,426,000	2.7
1983/84	335,494	3,400	338,894	0.6	12,465,000	2.7
1984/85	337,803	4,310	342,113	0.9	12,242,000	2.8
1985/86	339,627	4,150	343,777	0.5	12,247,000	2.8
1986/87	344,879	4,730	349,609	1.7	12,504,000	2.8
1987/88	351,387	4,800	356,187	1.9	12,767,000	2.8
1988/89	359,334	7,020	366,354	2.9	13,055,000	2.8
1989/90	379,139	7,712	386,851	5.6	13,539,000	2.9
1990/91	398,759	8,770	407,529	5.3	13,819,000	2.9
1991/92	411,355	8,230	419,585	3.0	14,359,000	2.9
1992/93	427,608	11,010	438,618	4.5	14,487,000	3.0
1993/94	438,319	11,430	449,749	2.5	14,305,000	3.1
1994/95	439,427	13,208	452,635	0.6	14,279,000	3.2
1995/96	438,337	15,450	453,787	0.3	14,262,000	3.2
1996/97	439,859	18,125	457,984	0.9	14,368,000	3.2
1997/98	464,698	16,582	481,280	5.1	14,502,000	3.3
1998/99	474,091	16,842	490,933	2.0	14,507,000	3.4
1999/00	489,866	24,857	514,723	4.8	14,791,000	3.5
2000/01	526,809	21,058	547,867	6.4	15,312,000	3.6
2001/02	560,251	22,745	582,996	6.4	15,928,000	3.7
2002/03	558,530	27,793	586,323	0.6	16,612,000	3.5
2003/04	543,169	29,340	572,509	−2.4	16,911,000	3.4
2004/05	532,040	32,999	565,039	−1.3	17,272,000	3.3
2005/06	526,670	38,096	564,766	−0.05	17,487,000	3.2
2006/07	541,324	41,660	582,984	3.2	17,759,000	3.3
2007/08	567,039	56,766	623,805	7.0	18,248,000	3.4
2008/09	605,015	66,601	671,616	7.7	19,103,000	3.5
2009/10	623,119	67,804	690,923	2.9	20,428,000	3.4
2010/11	647,246	76,031	723,277	4.7	20,550,000	3.5
2011/12	679,338	85,157	764,495	5.7	20,625,000	3.7
2012/13	724,725	94,919	819,644	7.2	21,253,000	3.9
2013/14	780,055	105,997	886,052	8.1	21,216,000	4.2

*The data collection process was changed in 1974/75. Refugees were counted from 1975/76 to 1990/91.

SOURCE: "International Students: Enrollment Trends," in *Open Doors Data*, Institute of International Education, November 2014, http://www.iie.org/Research-and-Publications/Open-Doors/Data/International-Students/Enrollment-Trends/1948-2014 (accessed January 9, 2015)

TABLE 3.29

Top-25 places of origin of international students, 2012–13 and 2013–14

Rank	Place of origin	2012/13	2013/14	2013/14 % of total	Change
	World total	819,644	886,052	100.0	8.1
1	China	235,597	274,439	31.0	16.5
2	India	96,754	102,673	11.6	6.1
3	South Korea	70,627	68,047	7.7	–3.7
4	Saudi Arabia	44,566	53,919	6.1	21.0
5	Canada	27,357	28,304	3.2	3.5
6	Taiwan	21,867	21,266	2.4	–2.7
7	Japan	19,568	19,334	2.2	–1.2
8	Vietnam	16,098	16,579	1.9	3.0
9	Mexico	14,199	14,779	1.7	4.1
10	Brazil	10,868	13,286	1.5	22.2
11	Turkey	11,278	10,821	1.2	–4.1
12	Iran	8,744	10,194	1.2	16.6
13	United Kingdom	9,467	10,191	1.2	7.6
14	Germany	9,819	10,160	1.1	3.5
15	France	8,297	8,302	0.9	0.1
16	Nepal	8,920	8,155	0.9	–8.6
17	Hong Kong	8,026	8,104	0.9	1.0
18	Nigeria	7,316	7,921	0.9	8.3
19	Indonesia	7,670	7,920	0.9	3.3
20	Thailand	7,314	7,341	0.8	0.4
21	Kuwait	5,115	7,288	0.8	42.5
22	Colombia	6,543	7,083	0.8	8.3
23	Venezuela	6,158	7,022	0.8	14.0
24	Malaysia	6,791	6,822	0.8	0.5
25	Spain	5,033	5,350	0.6	6.3

SOURCE: "International Students: Leading Places of Origin," in *Open Doors Data*, Institute of International Education, November 2014, http://www.iie.org/Research-and-Publications/Open-Doors/Data/International-Students/Leading-Places-of-Origin/2012-14 (accessed January 8, 2015)

number of refusals overcome in a given year do not refer to identical pools of individuals.

The second-most-common reason for denying an immigrant application involved an individual's unlawful presence in the United States: 15,964 applications were denied because the applicant had been illegally present for 365 or more days in the preceding 10 years. (See Table 3.30.) Again, many of these denied applicants (15,673) managed to overcome this problem. Other reasons immigrant visas were denied in FY 2013 include lack of required vaccinations, problems with labor certification, prior criminal convictions, smuggling, misrepresentation, and unlawful presence in the United States after previous immigration violations.

The most common reason for initial denial of a nonimmigrant visa in FY 2013 was an application's failure to demonstrate that the individual was entitled to nonimmigrant status. (See Table 3.30.) Over 1.4 million nonimmigrant visas were denied for this reason, and only 17,015 applicants managed to overcome this issue. A large number of nonimmigrant applications (775,201) were denied for failure to comply with the INA or subsequent regulations, but most of the applicants (680,672) managed to overcome this problem. Other reasons that sizable numbers of nonimmigrant applications were denied in FY 2013 include the applicant having been unlawfully present in the United States 365 or more days within the preceding 10 years, misrepresentation, crimes involving moral turpitude,

controlled-substance violations, controlled-substance trafficking, smuggling, the applicant having been unlawfully present in the United States following a prior immigration violation, and falsely claiming citizenship.

Returns and Removals

Having a U.S. visa does not guarantee entry. A visa allows a traveler arriving at a U.S. port of entry to request permission to enter. U.S. Customs and Border Protection inspectors determine the admissibility of aliens who arrive at any of the approximately 300 U.S. ports of entry. Those who arrive without required documents, present improper or fraudulent documents, or are on criminal watch lists are deemed inadmissible. The Illegal Immigration Reform and Immigrant Responsibility Act (IIRIRA) of 1996 provides two options for dealing with the inadmissible individual: removal proceedings and returns (voluntary departure).

Most removal proceedings involve a hearing before an immigration judge, which can result in removal or adjustment to a legal status, such as granting asylum. Removal proceedings can also involve fines or imprisonment. The IIRIRA also empowers immigration officers to order an individual's removal without a hearing or review through a process called expedited removal. This process applies to cases involving fraud, misrepresentation, or the lack of proper documents. Returns are not based on an order of removal; the individual is offered the option to

TABLE 3.30

Immigrant and nonimmigrant visa ineligibilities, by grounds for refusal, fiscal year 2013

[Fiscal year 2013 data is preliminary and subject to change. Any changes would not be statistically significant.]

Grounds for refusal under the Immigration and Nationality Act		Immigrant		Nonimmigrant	
		Ineligibility finding[a]	Ineligibility overcome[b]	Ineligibility finding[a]	Ineligibility overcome[b]
212(a)(1)(A)(i)	Communicable disease	362	377	17	4
212(a)(1)(A)(ii)	Immigrant lacking required vaccinations	3,153	2,566	—	—
212(a)(1)(A)(iii)	Physical or mental disorder	240	84	430	72
212(a)(1)(A)(iv)	Drug abuser or addict	1,052	327	139	29
212(a)(2)(A)(i)(I)	Crime involving moral turpitude	1,263	341	7,043	3,854
212(a)(2)(A)(i)(II)	Controlled substance violators	491	66	4,575	2,536
212(a)(2)(B)	Multiple criminal convictions	101	12	399	119
212(a)(2)(C)(i)	Illicit trafficker in any controlled substance	395	3	3,125	916
212(a)(2)(C)(ii)	Spouse, son, or daughter who benefited from illicit activities of trafficker	12	1	735	53
212(a)(2)(D)(i)	Prostitution (within 10 years)	7	6	46	10
212(a)(2)(D)(ii)	Procuring (within 10 years)	5	1	20	3
212(a)(2)(D)(iii)	Unlawful commercialized vice	2	1	5	2
212(a)(2)(E)	Asserted immunity to avoid prosecution	0	0	1	0
212(a)(2)(G)	Foreign government officials who have engaged in violations of religious freedom	0	0	0	0
212(a)(2)(H)	Significant traffickers in persons	5	0	2	0
212(a)(2)(I)	Money laundering	2	0	15	4
212(a)(3)(A)(i)	Espionage, sabotage, technology transfer, etc.	11	0	209	7
212(a)(3)(A)(ii)	Other unlawful activity	154	0	112	4
212(a)(3)(A)(iii)	Act to overthrow U.S. government	0	0	0	0
212(a)(3)(B)	Terrorist activities	28	0	591	352
212(a)(3)(C)	Foreign policy	0	0	0	0
212(a)(3)(D)	Immigrant membership in totalitarian party	16	5	—	—
212(a)(3)(E)(i)	Participants in Nazi persecutions	0	0	0	0
212(a)(3)(E)(ii)	Participants in genocide	1	0	1	0
212(a)(3)(E)(iii)	Commission of acts of torture or extrajudicial killings	1	0	3	2
212(a)(3)(F)	Association with terrorist organizations	0	0	1	0
212(a)(3)(G)	Recruitment of use of child soldiers	0	0	1	2
212(a)(4)	Public charge	3,544	3,374	349	14
212(a)(5)(A)	Labor certification (immigrants only)	8,523	1,000	—	—
212(a)(5)(B)	Unqualified physician (immigrants only)	2	0	—	—
212(a)(5)(C)	Uncertified foreign health-care workers	0	0	1	0
212(a)(6)(B)	Failure to attend removal proceedings	93	0	10	1
212(a)(6)(C)(i)	Misrepresentation	7,079	2,205	13,911	5,164
212(a)(6)(C)(ii)	Falsely claiming citizenship	466	0	1,883	725
212(a)(6)(E)	Smugglers	2,656	1,236	3,630	1,294
212(a)(6)(F)	Subject of civil penalty (under INA 274C)	0	1	5	1
212(a)(6)(G)	Student visa abusers	0	0	8	1
212(a)(7)(B)	Documentation requirement for nonimmigrants	—	—	89	57
212(a)(8)(A)	Immigrant permanently ineligible for citizenship	0	0	—	—
212(a)(8)(B)	Draft evader	0	0	6	9
212(a)(9)(A)(i)	Ordered removed upon arrival	820	362	1,058	89
212(a)(9)(A)(i)	Ordered removed upon arrival—multiple removals	137	23	72	8
212(a)(9)(A)(i)	Ordered removed upon arrival—convicted aggravated felony	29	2	29	5
212(a)(9)(A)(ii)	Ordered removed or departed while removal order outstanding	1,602	797	855	180
212(a)(9)(A)(ii)	Ordered removed or departed while removal order outstanding—multiple removals	201	46	176	24
212(a)(9)(A)(ii)	Ordered removed or departed while removal order outstanding—convicted aggravated felony	83	8	73	11
212(a)(9)(B)(i)(I)	Unlawfully present 181–364 days (within 3 years)	337	222	772	132
212(a)(9)(B)(i)(II)	Unlawfully present 365 or more days (within 10 years)	15,964	15,673	16,922	1,970
212(a)(9)(C)	Unlawfully present after previous immigration violations	2,235	77	3,985	790
212(a)(10)(A)	Practicing polygamist (immigrants only)	23	2	—	—
212(a)(10)(C)(i)	International child abductor	0	0	5	1
212(a)(10)(C)(ii)	Aliens supporting abductors and relatives of abductors			0	0
212(a)(10)(D)	Unlawful voter	0	0	1	0
212(a)(10)(E)	Former U.S. citizen who renounced citizenship to avoid taxation	0	0	0	0
212(e)	Certain former exchange visitors	22	15	7	6
212(f)	Presidential proclamation	3	0	69	7
214(b)	Failure to establish entitlement to nonimmigrant status	—	—	1,437,959	17,015
221(g)	Application does not comply with provisions of INA or regulations issued pursuant thereto	290,369	180,022	775,201	680,672
222(g)(2)	Alien in illegal status, required to apply for new nonimmigrant visa in country of alien's nationality	—	—	61	7

TABLE 3.30

Immigrant and nonimmigrant visa ineligibilities, by grounds for refusal, fiscal year 2013 [CONTINUED]

[Fiscal year 2013 data is preliminary and subject to change. Any changes would not be statistically significant.]

		Immigrant		Nonimmigrant	
Grounds for refusal under the Immigration and Nationality Act		Ineligibility finding[a]	Ineligibility overcome[b]	Ineligibility finding[a]	Ineligibility overcome[b]
Sec.103 Pub. Law 105–227	Disclosure/trafficking of confidential U.S. business information	0	0	0	0
Sec. 401 Pub. Law 104–114	Helms-Burton refusal	0	0	0	0
Sec. 402 Pub. Law 104–114	Conversion of confiscated U.S. property for gain	0	0	0	0
Sec. 306 Pub. Law 107–173	Inadmissible alien from a country that is a state sponsor of terorrism	0	0	170	4
	Total grounds of ineligibility:	**341,489**	**208,855**	**2,274,777**	**716,156**
	Number of applications:[a]	**288,957**	**194,300**	**2,230,296**	**710,601**

[a]The total grounds of ineligibility may exceed the number of applications refused because one applicant may be found ineligible under more than one section of the Immigration and Nationality Act.
[b]The total of ineligibilities overcome may not necessarily represent the same visa applicants found ineligible and recorded in the total ineligibility findings. A visa may be refused in one fiscal year and the refusal overcome in a subsequent fiscal year. Each action will be separately recorded as part of the appropriate statistical report for the year in which it occurred. A refusal can be overcome by evidence the ineligibility does not apply, by approval of a waiver, or by other relief as provided by law.
Note: The figures at the end of this table show totals of applications refused and refusals overcome. The total of applications refused does not necessarily reflect the number of persons refused during the year. One applicant can apply and be found ineligible more than one time in fiscal year.

SOURCE: "Table XX. Immigrant and Nonimmigrant Visa Ineligibilities (by Grounds for Refusal under the Immigration and Nationality Act), Fiscal Year 2013," in *Report of the Visa Office 2013*, U.S. Department of State, Bureau of Consular Affairs, 2014, http://travel.state.gov/content/dam/visas/Statistics/AnnualReports/FY2013AnnualReport/FY13AnnualReport-TableXX.pdf (accessed January 9, 2015)

FIGURE 3.9

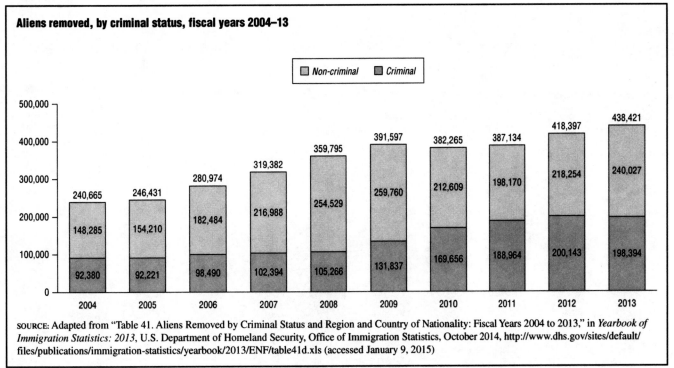

Aliens removed, by criminal status, fiscal years 2004–13

SOURCE: Adapted from "Table 41. Aliens Removed by Criminal Status and Region and Country of Nationality: Fiscal Years 2004 to 2013," in *Yearbook of Immigration Statistics: 2013*, U.S. Department of Homeland Security, Office of Immigration Statistics, October 2014, http://www.dhs.gov/sites/default/files/publications/immigration-statistics/yearbook/2013/ENF/table41d.xls (accessed January 9, 2015)

leave the country. Most such voluntary departures involve unauthorized people who have been apprehended by U.S. Immigration and Customs Enforcement or Customs and Border Protection.

According to the OIS, in *2013 Yearbook of Immigration Statistics*, 438,421 aliens were removed from the United States in FY 2013, 198,394 for criminal reasons and 240,027 for noncriminal reasons. (See Figure 3.9.) Such removals had nearly doubled since 2004, when 240,665 aliens were removed. Of the total number of aliens removed in each fiscal year between 2004 and 2013, the overwhelming majority in each case were from North America. (See Table 3.31.) In FY 2013, removals to other North American countries (chiefly Mexico) accounted for 426,270 (97.2%) of the total 438,421 removals.

TABLE 3.31

Aliens removed, by world region, fiscal years 2004–13

Region	2004	2005	2006	2007	2008	2009	2010	2011	2012	2013
Total	240,665	246,431	280,974	319,382	359,795	391,597	382,265	387,134	418,397	438,421
Africa	2,662	2,372	2,103	2,112	2,064	2,022	1,887	1,663	1,434	1,164
Asia	6,827	6,414	6,366	5,745	5,799	6,240	6,224	5,304	4,331	2,933
Europe	3,574	3,345	3,156	3,164	3,929	4,615	4,007	3,235	2,743	2,009
North America	213,592	219,432	256,952	296,082	335,707	366,261	358,762	367,251	402,022	426,270
Oceania	300	247	219	248	305	317	314	315	256	237
South America	13,618	14,535	12,102	11,988	11,831	12,069	11,012	9,288	7,577	5,775
Unknown	92	86	76	43	160	73	59	78	34	33

Note: Beginning in 2008, excludes criminals removed by Customs and Border Protection (CBP); CBP ENFORCE does not identify if aliens removed were criminals. Refers to persons removed who have a prior criminal conviction.

SOURCE: Adapted from "Table 41. Aliens Removed by Criminal Status and Region and Country of Nationality: Fiscal Years 2004 to 2013," in *Yearbook of Immigration Statistics: 2013*, U.S. Department of Homeland Security, Office of Immigration Statistics, October 2014, http://www.dhs.gov/sites/default/files/publications/immigration-statistics/yearbook/2013/ENF/table41d.xls (accessed January 9, 2015)

CHAPTER 4
THE WORLDWIDE REFUGEE CHALLENGE

WHO IS A REFUGEE?

Every year millions of people around the world are displaced by war, famine, civil unrest, and political turmoil. Others are forced to flee their country to escape the risk of death and torture at the hands of persecutors on account of race, religion, nationality, membership in a particular social group, or political opinion. These refugees, as such persecuted and displaced people are called, are granted special consideration among immigration authorities in the United States and in other countries. Considerable effort is made among those in the international community, led by the Office of the United Nations High Commissioner for Refugees (UNHCR), to respond to refugee crises as they arise.

The United States works with other governmental, international, and private organizations to provide food, health care, and shelter to millions of refugees throughout the world. Resettlement in another country, including the United States, is considered for refugees in urgent need of protection, refugees for whom other long-term solutions are not feasible, and refugees able to join close family members. The United States gives priority to the safe, voluntary return of refugees to their homelands. This policy, recognized in the Refugee Act of 1980, is also the preference of the UNHCR.

LEGALLY ADMITTING REFUGEES

Before World War II (1939–1945) the U.S. government had no arrangements for admitting people seeking refuge. The only way oppressed people were able to enter the United States was through regular immigration procedures.

After World War II refugees were admitted through special legislation that was passed by Congress. The Displaced Persons Act of 1948, which admitted 400,000 East Europeans who had been displaced by the war, was the first U.S. refugee legislation. The Immigration and

Nationality Act of 1952 did not specifically mention refugees, but it did allow the U.S. attorney general parole authority (the authority to grant temporary admission) when dealing with oppressed people. Other legislation (the Refugee Relief Act of 1953, the Fair Share Refugee Act of 1960, and the Indochinese Refugee Act of 1977) responded to particular world events and admitted specific groups.

Refugees were legally recognized for the first time in the Immigration and Nationality Act Amendments of 1965 with a preference category that was reserved for refugees from the Middle East or from countries ruled by a communist government.

Refugee Act of 1980

The Refugee Act of 1980 established a geographically and politically neutral adjudication standard for refugee status. The act redefined the term *refugee* as:

(A) any person who is outside any country of such person's nationality or, in the case of a person having no nationality, is outside any country in which such person last habitually resided, and who is unable or unwilling to return to, and is unable or unwilling to avail himself or herself of the protection of, that country because of persecution or a well-founded fear of persecution on account of race, religion, nationality, membership in a particular social group, or political opinion, or (B) in such circumstances as the President after appropriate consultation ... may specify, any person who is within the country of such person's nationality or, in the case of a person having no nationality, within the country in which such person is habitually residing, and who persecuted or who has a well-founded fear of persecution on account of race, religion, nationality, membership in a particular social group, or political opinion.

The Refugee Act of 1980 required the president, at the beginning of each fiscal year (FY), to determine the number of refugees to be admitted without consideration of any overall immigrant quota. The 1980 law also regulated U.S. asylum policy.

REFUGEES AND ASYLEES. The Refugee Act of 1980 made a distinction between refugees and asylees. A refugee is someone who applies for protection while outside the United States; an asylee is someone who is already in the United States when he or she applies for protection.

The Application Process

The U.S. Refugee Admissions Program (USRAP) is responsible for processing applications to enter the United States as a refugee. In "The United States Refugee Admissions Program (USRAP): Consultation & Worldwide Processing Priorities" (April 8, 2013, http://www.uscis .gov/humanitarian/refugees-asylum/refugees/united-states-refugee-admissions-program-usrap-consultation-worldwide-processing-priorities), the U.S. Citizenship and Immigration Services (USCIS) describes USRAP as "an interagency effort involving a number of governmental and non-governmental partners both overseas and in the United States." The U.S. Department of State's Bureau of Population, Refugees, and Migration (PRM) plays an important role, as does USCIS, other elements of the U.S. Department of Homeland Security (DHS), various nongovernmental organizations, and the UNHCR.

The United States processes applications for refugee and asylum status based on three priority categories. Priority 1 applicants are those individuals and their immediate families who are referred to USRAP by the UNHCR, a U.S. embassy, or a prominent nongovernmental organization. Members of groups of special humanitarian concern are considered Priority 2 applicants, and family members of refugees who have already been admitted to the United States are considered Priority 3 applicants. Due to a difficulty in determining the authenticity of family relationships on Priority 3 applications, which had led to widespread fraud, USRAP suspended the processing of those applications in 2008. As the State Department notes in *Proposed Refugee Admissions for Fiscal Year 2015* (September 18, 2014, http://www.state.gov/j/prm/releases/docsforcongress/231817.htm), processing of Priority 3 applications resumed in late 2012 under stricter guidelines, including DNA verification of parent-child relationships and requirements that applicants register with UNHCR and/or relevant government offices in their countries of origin.

PRM officials conduct prescreening interviews of applicants and assist in the completion of paperwork to be submitted to USCIS. Applicants are then interviewed by USCIS, and if the agency determines that they are eligible for resettlement in the United States, applicants must submit to medical examinations. Those granted refugee status are then provided with assistance in traveling to the United States, obtaining housing and employment, and other services. They may enter and leave the United States thereafter by applying for a refugee travel document, and as discussed in Chapter 3, they may apply for a green card one year from the date of their entry into the United States.

Material Support Denials

Prospective immigrants to the United States can be denied entry to the country if they are found to have provided "material support" to terrorist organizations, which includes such acts as supplying transportation, documents, a safe house, food, monetary contributions, or almost any other form of aid. This reason for denying entry was first codified in the Immigration Act of 1990, but in the wake of the September 11, 2001 (9/11), terrorist attacks, the criteria for determining whether someone could be denied entry for this reason were dramatically broadened. As Bryan Clark and William Holahan write in "Material Support: Immigration and National Security" (*Catholic University Law Review*, vol. 59, no. 4, Summer 2010), the 2001 Patriot Act defined "terrorist organization" much more broadly than previous statutory designations, and the 2005 REAL ID Act further raised the so-called material support bar, or the requirements refugees or asylees must meet to demonstrate that they have no connection to terrorist groups or activities.

As a result, many refugee- and asylum-seekers may have been inappropriately barred from admission to the United States. Clark and Holahan note that those denied admission include victims of terrorism who have aided terrorist organizations under threat of death as well as individuals who have engaged in protests against oppressive governments in their home countries even when those protests were supported by the U.S. government. Refugee admissions decreased dramatically in the wake of these laws' passage, and many legal experts and human rights advocates called for reform of the material support statutes in order to better balance national security with human rights concerns. According to Jordan Fischer, in "The United States and the Material-Support Bar for Refugees: A Tenuous Balance between National Security and Basic Human Rights" (*Drexel Law Review*, vol. 5, no. 1, Fall 2012), "the scales are now tipped too heavily in favor of protecting national security at the cost of denying protection to thousands of meritorious refugees. This imbalance forces refugees to remain in inhumane conditions in violation of their basic human rights."

In response to such concerns, between 2007 and 2014 the DHS and the State Department issued numerous exemptions to the material support bar. There are two categories of exemptions: "Situational Exemptions," which apply to common situations that have prevented legitimate refugees from being admitted to the United States, including those who have been forced to provide support to terrorists; and "Group-Based Exemptions," which apply to specific opposition groups and other organizations that might wrong-fully fall under the definition of terrorist organizations. Individuals qualifying for exemptions under these categories can be admitted as refugees and asylees.

CHARACTERISTICS OF REFUGEES

According to the UNHCR, in *Asylum Trends 2013: Levels and Trends in Industrialized Countries* (March 21, 2014, http://www.unhcr.org/5329b15a9.html), the 44 industrialized countries called on most often to accept refugees fielded an estimated 612,700 asylum applications in 2013. This was the second-highest number of applications in 20 years and the third consecutive yearly increase in the number of applications. Syria was the top source country of asylum seekers, with 56,400 claims, more than double the number registered in 2012 and the highest number in an industrialized country since 1999. The second-leading source country for asylum seekers was Russia (with 39,800 claims), followed by Afghanistan (38,700), Iraq (38,200), and Serbia and Kosovo (34,700). European countries received 484,600 applications for asylum, and 98,700 refugees applied for protection in North America. Smaller numbers of refugees sought asylum in Australia and New Zealand (24,600), Japan (3,300), and South Korea (1,600). Germany received 109,600 asylum applications, more than any other country, followed by the United States (88,400), France (60,100), Sweden (54,300), and Turkey (44,800).

Admissions to the United States

As Figure 4.1 shows, refugee admissions to the United States have declined substantially since the 1990s, peaking at roughly 122,000 refugee arrivals in 1990 before falling to a low of 25,000 in 2002. This decline is largely due to the changes in security procedures and immigration policy following the 9/11 terrorist attacks, and particularly to the material support bar for immigrant admissions. Admissions were on the rise by the end of that decade, however, approaching pre-2001 levels.

Admissions ceilings for refugees are, in keeping with the Refugee Act of 1980, established by the president prior to each fiscal year. The ceiling fell between FY 2011 and FY 2013, from 80,000 to 70,000. (See Table 4.1.) The president also sets ceilings for particular international regions, based on world events. Between FY 2011 and FY 2013 these allocations remained roughly steady, with the most refugee admissions allotted to the Near East/South Asia region, largely to account for refugees from Bhutan, Iran, and Iraq. In FY 2013 the Near East/South Asia region accounted for 46.3% (32,400) of the total refugee ceiling, followed by 16,600 from East Asia (23.7%), 15,950 from Africa (22.8%), 4,400 from Latin America and the Caribbean (6.3%), and 650 from Europe/Central Asia (0.9%). Although the number of refugees admitted each year are limited by these ceilings, the number admitted as refugees does not count against the overall limits on legal immigration.

FIGURE 4.1

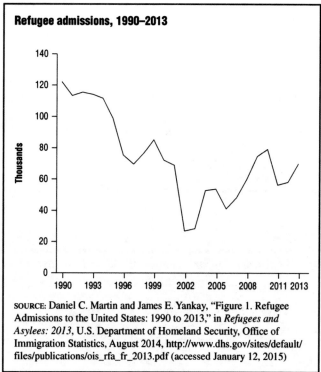
Refugee admissions, 1990–2013

SOURCE: Daniel C. Martin and James E. Yankay, "Figure 1. Refugee Admissions to the United States: 1990 to 2013," in *Refugees and Asylees: 2013*, U.S. Department of Homeland Security, Office of Immigration Statistics, August 2014, http://www.dhs.gov/sites/default/files/publications/ois_rfa_fr_2013.pdf (accessed January 12, 2015)

TABLE 4.1

Refugee admissions ceilings, fiscal years 2011–13

Region	Ceiling		
	2013	2012	2011
Total	**70,000**	**76,000**	**80,000**
Africa	15,950	12,000	15,000
East Asia	16,600	18,000	19,000
Europe/Central Asia	650	2,000	2,000
Latin America/Caribbean	4,400	5,500	5,500
Near East/South Asia	32,400	35,500	35,500
Unallocated reserve	0	3,000	3,000

Note: Ceiling numbers reflect revisions made each fiscal year.

SOURCE: Daniel C. Martin and James E. Yankay, "Table 1. Refugee Admissions Ceilings: 2011 to 2013," in *Refugees and Asylees: 2013*, U.S. Department of Homeland Security, Office of Immigration Statistics, August 2014, http://www.dhs.gov/sites/default/files/publications/ois_rfa_fr_2013.pdf (accessed January 12, 2015)

A total of 69,909 refugees were admitted to the United States during FY 2013. (See Table 4.2.) Of this total, there were 31,698 principal applicants, 11,278 spouses of principal applicants, and 26,933 children of principal applicants. The leading countries of origin for refugees were Iraq, with 19,487 refugee admissions (27.9% of the total); Burma (Myanmar), with 16,299 (23.3%); Bhutan, with 9,134 (13.1%); and Somalia, with 7,608 (10.9%). (See Table 4.3.) Texas accepted 7,466 refugees in FY 2013, 10.7% of the national total and more than any other state. (See Table 4.4.) California was second with 6,379 (9.1%) refugees, followed by

TABLE 4.2

Refugee arrivals, by category of admission, fiscal years 2011–13

Category of admission	2013		2012		2011	
	Number	Percent	Number	Percent	Number	Percent
Total	**69,909**	**100.0**	**58,179**	**100.0**	**56,384**	**100.0**
Principal applicant	31,698	45.3	27,355	47.0	25,075	44.5
Dependents	38,211	54.7	30,824	53.0	31,309	55.5
Spouse	11,278	16.1	9,532	16.4	9,751	17.3
Child	26,933	38.5	21,292	36.6	21,558	38.2

SOURCE: Daniel C. Martin and James E. Yankay, "Table 2. Refugee Arrivals by Category of Admission: Fiscal Years 2011 to 2013," in *Refugees and Asylees: 2013*, U.S. Department of Homeland Security, Office of Immigration Statistics, August 2014, http://www.dhs.gov/sites/default/files/publications/ois_rfa_fr_2013.pdf (accessed January 12, 2015)

TABLE 4.3

Refugee arrivals, by country of nationality, fiscal years 2011–13

[Ranked by 2013 country of nationality]

Country of nationality	2013		2012		2011	
	Number	Percent	Number	Percent	Number	Percent
Total	**69,909**	**100.0**	**58,179**	**100.0**	**56,384**	**100.0**
Iraq	19,487	27.9	12,163	20.9	9,388	16.7
Burma	16,299	23.3	14,160	24.3	16,972	30.1
Bhutan	9,134	13.1	15,070	25.9	14,999	26.6
Somalia	7,608	10.9	4,911	8.4	3,161	5.6
Cuba	4,205	6.0	1,948	3.3	2,920	5.2
Iran	2,579	3.7	1,758	3.0	2,032	3.6
Congo, Democratic Republic	2,563	3.7	1,863	3.2	977	1.7
Sudan	2,160	3.1	1,077	1.9	334	0.6
Eritrea	1,824	2.6	1,346	2.3	2,032	3.6
Ethiopia	765	1.1	620	1.1	560	1.0
All other countries, including unknown	3,285	4.7	3,263	5.6	3,009	5.3

SOURCE: Daniel C. Martin and James E. Yankay, "Table 3. Refugee Arrivals by Country of Nationality: Fiscal Years 2011 to 2013," in *Refugees and Asylees: 2013*, U.S. Department of Homeland Security, Office of Immigration Statistics, August 2014, http://www.dhs.gov/sites/default/files/publications/ois_rfa_fr_2013.pdf (accessed January 12, 2015)

Michigan (4,651, or 6.7%), New York (3,965, or 5.7%), Florida (3,613, or 5.2%), and Arizona (3,052, or 4.4%).

Table 4.5 provides a portrait of the group of refugees admitted to the United States by age, gender, and marital status between FY 2011 and FY 2013. The relative distribution among age groups remained roughly consistent, with children under the age of 18 years accounting for more than one-third of all refugees admitted in each of the three fiscal years. The gender balance and the balance between married and single refugees remained similarly consistent between FYs 2011 and 2013. In FY 2013, 54.1% of admitted refugees were male and 45.9% were female. A majority of refugees (56.3%) were single, whereas 38.3% were married, and 5.3% were either separated, divorced, widowed, or of unknown marital status.

ASYLUM SEEKERS IN THE UNITED STATES

In common usage, refugees are people who are displaced from their home countries due to war, persecution, or other causes discussed in this chapter and who therefore often seek asylum in a country where they will be safe from the threats that forced them to leave. An asylee, then, is simply a refugee who has found asylum. According to U.S. immigration law, however, a refugee is a displaced individual seeking entry to the United States from outside the country, whereas an asylee is a displaced individual who is already in the United States and who is seeking the legal right to remain in the country.

Asylees sometimes enter the United States as tourists and then apply for asylum. Others jump ship in a maritime port of entry. Still others may enter under other nonimmigrant visa status groups, such as foreign students or temporary workers, and then apply to remain on as asylees. Like a refugee applying for entrance into the country, an asylee seeks the protection of the United States because of persecution or a well-founded fear of persecution. Any foreign-born person physically present in the United States or at a port of entry can request asylum. It is irrelevant whether the person is a legal or illegal immigrant. Like refugees, asylum applicants do not count against the worldwide annual U.S. limitation of immigrants.

TABLE 4.4

Refugee arrivals, by state of residence, fiscal years 2011–13

[Ranked by 2013 state of residence]

Country of nationality	2013		2012		2011	
	Number	Percent	Number	Percent	Number	Percent
Total	**69,909**	**100.0**	**58,179**	**100.0**	**56,384**	**100.0**
Texas	7,466	10.7	5,905	10.1	5,627	10.0
California	6,379	9.1	5,167	8.9	4,987	8.8
Michigan	4,651	6.7	3,594	6.2	2,588	4.6
New York	3,965	5.7	3,525	6.1	3,529	6.3
Florida	3,613	5.2	2,244	3.9	2,906	5.2
Arizona	3,052	4.4	2,234	3.8	2,168	3.8
Ohio	2,788	4.0	2,245	3.9	1,691	3.0
Georgia	2,710	3.9	2,516	4.3	2,636	4.7
Pennsylvania	2,507	3.6	2,809	4.8	2,972	5.3
Illinois	2,452	3.5	2,082	3.6	1,937	3.4
Other	30,326	43.4	25,858	44.4	25,343	44.9

SOURCE: Daniel C. Martin and James E. Yankay, "Table 5. Refugee Arrivals by State of Residence: Fiscal Years 2011 to 2013," in *Refugees and Asylees: 2013*, U.S. Department of Homeland Security, Office of Immigration Statistics, August 2014, http://www.dhs.gov/sites/default/files/publications/ois_rfa_fr_2013.pdf (accessed January 12, 2015)

TABLE 4.5

Refugee arrivals, by age, sex, and marital status, fiscal years 2011–13

Characteristic	2013		2012		2011	
	Number	Percent	Number	Percent	Number	Percent
Age						
Total	**69,909**	**100.0**	**58,179**	**100.0**	**56,384**	**100.0**
0 to 17 years	23,647	33.8	18,876	32.4	19,232	34.1
18 to 24 years	10,399	14.9	9,700	16.7	9,588	17.0
25 to 34 years	15,328	21.9	13,491	23.2	11,802	20.9
35 to 44 years	9,543	13.7	7,446	12.8	7,124	12.6
45 to 54 years	5,504	7.9	4,409	7.6	4,230	7.5
55 to 64 years	3,098	4.4	2,441	4.2	2,438	4.3
65 years and over	2,390	3.4	1,816	3.1	1,970	3.5
Sex						
Total	**69,909**	**100.0**	**58,179**	**100.0**	**56,384**	**100.0**
Male	37,792	54.1	31,380	53.9	29,436	52.2
Female	32,117	45.9	26,799	46.1	26,948	47.8
Marital status						
Total	**69,909**	**100.0**	**58,179**	**100.0**	**56,384**	**100.0**
Married	26,789	38.3	22,322	38.4	22,095	39.2
Single	39,392	56.3	32,608	56.0	31,324	55.6
Other`	3,728	5.3	3,249	5.6	2,965	5.3

`Includes persons who were divorced, separated, widowed, or of unknown marital status.

SOURCE: Daniel C. Martin and James E. Yankay, "Table 4. Refugee Arrivals by Age, Sex, and Marital Status: Fiscal Years 2011 to 2013," in *Refugees and Asylees: 2013*, U.S. Department of Homeland Security, Office of Immigration Statistics, August 2014, http://www.dhs.gov/sites/default/files/publications/ois_rfa_fr_2013.pdf (accessed January 12, 2015)

Filing Claims

Asylum seekers must apply for asylum within one year from the date of their last arrival in the United States. If the application is filed past the one-year mark, asylum seekers must show changed circumstances that materially affect their eligibility or extraordinary circumstances that delayed filing. They must also show that they filed within a reasonable amount of time given these circumstances.

An applicant who is ruled ineligible for asylum status and who is not allowed to remain in the United States under another visa status becomes subject to removal proceedings. An applicant who is ruled ineligible for asylum but who is eligible to remain in the United States under another visa status will revert to that prior status for as long as it is valid. Those applicants who are granted asylum status are eligible to work in the United States and to obtain assistance in finding employment. They are also able to participate in social assistance programs and acquire a Social Security card.

The DHS identifies three main types of asylum claims: affirmative, defensive, and follow-to-join. Aliens in the United States can apply for asylum by filing an Application for Asylum (Form I-589) with USCIS. Initiating this process is called an affirmative asylum claim. Aliens who have been placed in removal proceedings and who are in immigration court can request asylum through the Executive Office of Immigration Review. This last-resort effort is called a defensive asylum claim. Follow-to-join asylum status is available to the spouses and children of individuals who have been granted asylum. These derivative asylum applicants do not have to demonstrate that they will be persecuted if not granted asylum because their claims are derived from the application of someone who has already done so. If follow-to-join petitioners are outside the United States at the time that their applications are approved, they are granted asylum status upon entry. If they are inside the United States, they are granted asylum status upon approval of their application.

How Many Are Admitted?

Figure 4.2 shows the trends in affirmative and defensive asylum admissions between 1990 and 2013. The total volume of both types of asylum admissions during the early 1990s was less than 10,000. Defensive asylum admissions increased steadily from less than 3,000 in 1994 to a high of about 14,000 in 2006. Affirmative asylum admissions rose dramatically from about 4,000 in 1991 to a peak of more than 28,000 in 2001, after which date they fell precipitously. Between 2003 and 2010 roughly equal numbers of affirmative and defensive asylees were admitted to the United States annually, and since 2010 more affirmative than defensive asylees have been admitted. (Follow-to-join asylees were not part of DHS statistics until 2011.)

In FY 2013, 15,266 individuals were granted asylum status affirmatively, 9,933 were granted asylum status defensively, and 13,026 were granted follow-to-join asylum status, for a total of 38,225 asylees admitted. (See Table 4.6, Table 4.7, and Table 4.8.) China was by far the leading country of origin for all three types of asylum admissions in FY 2013. That year 4,072 Chinese nationals were granted affirmative asylum, accounting for 26.7% of all successful applicants in that category. The country of origin for the second-highest number of successful affirmative asylum claimants was Egypt, with 3,102 admissions (10.3%). Chinese representation among defensive asylum admissions was even more disproportionate in FY 2013, when 4,532, or 45.6% of all admissions in that category, were of Chinese origin. Ethiopia generated the second-highest number of defensive asylum admissions, with 399 (4%). Similarly, 4,785 Chinese nationals were granted follow-to-join asylee status in FY 2013, representing 36.7% of the total admitted in the category. Haiti accounted for 1,108, or 8.5%, of the total number of follow-to-join asylees.

FIGURE 4.2

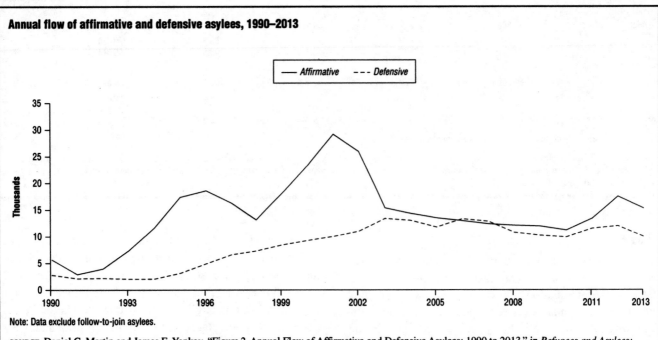

Annual flow of affirmative and defensive asylees, 1990–2013

Note: Data exclude follow-to-join asylees.

SOURCE: Daniel C. Martin and James E. Yankay, "Figure 2. Annual Flow of Affirmative and Defensive Asylees: 1990 to 2013," in *Refugees and Asylees: 2013*, U.S. Department of Homeland Security, Office of Immigration Statistics, August 2014, http://www.dhs.gov/sites/default/ files/publications/ois_rfa_ fr_2013.pdf (accessed January 12, 2015)

TABLE 4.6

Affirmative asylees, by country of nationality, fiscal years 2011–13

[Ranked by 2013 country of nationality]

Country of nationality	2013		2012		2011	
	Number	Percent	Number	Percent	Number	Percent
Total	15,266	100.0	17,389	100.0	13,376	100.0
China, People's Republic	4,072	26.7	4,738	27.2	3,887	29.1
Egypt	3,102	20.3	2,570	14.8	752	5.6
Syria	763	5.0	327	1.9	46	0.3
Iran	612	4.0	607	3.5	366	2.7
Venezuela	608	4.0	960	5.5	898	6.7
Ethiopia	494	3.2	663	3.8	564	4.2
Nepal	473	3.1	572	3.3	417	3.1
Haiti	443	2.9	632	3.6	816	6.1
Iraq	408	2.7	314	1.8	262	2.0
Russia	347	2.3	542	3.1	466	3.5
All other countries, including unknown	3,944	25.8	5,464	31.4	4,902	36.6

Note: Data exclude follow-to-join asylees.

SOURCE: Daniel C. Martin and James E. Yankay, "Table 7. Affirmative Asylees by Country of Nationality: Fiscal Years 2011 to 2013," in *Refugees and Asylees: 2013*, U.S. Department of Homeland Security, Office of Immigration Statistics, August 2014, http://www.dhs.gov/sites/default/files/publications/ois_rfa_fr_2013.pdf (accessed January 12, 2015)

TABLE 4.7

Defensive asylees, by country of nationality, fiscal years 2011–13

[Ranked by 2013 country of nationality]

Country of nationality	2013		2012		2011	
	Number	Percent	Number	Percent	Number	Percent
Total	9,933	100.0	11,978	100.0	11,528	100.0
China, People's Republic	4,532	45.6	5,383	44.9	4,705	40.8
Ethiopia	399	4.0	458	3.8	507	4.4
Nepal	381	3.8	403	3.4	323	2.8
India	322	3.2	282	2.4	262	2.3
Egypt	305	3.1	306	2.6	275	2.4
Soviet Union, former	252	2.5	281	2.3	248	2.2
Eritrea	240	2.4	351	2.9	483	4.2
Russia	187	1.9	176	1.5	195	1.7
El Salvador	181	1.8	191	1.6	164	1.4
Mexico	155	1.6	126	1.1	107	0.9
All other countries, including unknown	2,979	30.0	4,021	33.6	4,259	36.9

Note: Data exclude follow-to-join asylees.

SOURCE: Daniel C. Martin and James E. Yankay, "Table 8. Defensive Asylees by Country of Nationality: Fiscal Years 2011 to 2013," in *Refugees and Asylees: 2013*, U.S. Department of Homeland Security, Office of Immigration Statistics, August 2014, http://www.dhs.gov/sites/default/files/publications/ois_rfa_fr_2013.pdf (accessed January 12, 2015)

Controversy and Uncertainty Surrounding Asylees

Critics charge that many people seek asylum in the United States to avoid dismal economic conditions in their home country rather than for the reasons specified by U.S. law: to escape political or religious persecution or because of a well-founded fear of physical harm or death. Such critics suggest that asylee status is often simply an avenue for unauthorized immigrants to obtain work authorization and access to social services.

Under the Immigration and Nationality Act and subsequent legislation, however, a person can be granted asylum only if he or she establishes a well-founded fear of perse-cution on account of one of five protected grounds: race, religion, nationality, political opinion, or membership in a particular social group. A particular social group has members who share an unchangeable characteristic, such as race, gender, past experience, or kinship ties. Some people argue that the definition for "a particular social group" should be broad and that the intent of the law is to provide a catchall to include all the types of persecution that can occur. Others take a narrow view, seeing the law as a means of identifying and protecting individuals from known forms of harm, not in anticipation of future types of abuse. Amnesty International notes in "Violence against Women Information" (2015, http://www.amnestyusa.org/our-work/

TABLE 4.8

Follow-to-join asylees, by country of nationality, fiscal years 2011–13

Country	2013		2012		2011	
	Number	Percent	Number	Percent	Number	Percent
Total	13,026	100.0	12,145	100.0	11,149	100.0
China, People's Republic	4,785	36.7	4,957	40.8	3,783	33.9
Haiti	1,108	8.5	906	7.5	1,045	9.4
Ethiopia	774	5.9	492	4.1	629	5.6
Nepal	705	5.4	826	6.8	1,082	9.7
India	675	5.2	116	1.0	175	1.6
Unknown	522	4.0	481	4.0	317	2.8
Egypt	501	3.8	322	2.7	175	1.6
Eritrea	485	3.7	228	1.9	221	2.0
Burma	460	3.5	452	3.7	524	4.7
Guatemala	314	2.4	230	1.9	124	1.1
All other countries, including unknown	2,697	20.7	3,135	25.8	3,074	27.6

SOURCE: Daniel C. Martin and James E. Yankay, "Table 9. Follow-to-Join Asylee Travel Documents Issued by Country of Nationality: Fiscal Years 2011 to 2013," in *Refugees and Asylees: 2013*, U.S. Department of Homeland Security, Office of Immigration Statistics, August 2014, http://www.dhs.gov/sites/default/files/publications/ois_rfa_fr_2013.pdf (accessed January 12, 2015)

issues/women-s-rights/violence-against-women/violence-against-women-information) that some asylum adjudicators in the United States do not recognize gender-based violence as a valid claim for asylum protection.

Immigration lawyers and policy experts are unanimous on one aspect of asylum adjudication: the likelihood that asylee applications will be approved depends to a large degree on the individual federal immigration judge who presides over each case. The Transactional Records Access Clearinghouse (TRAC), a data and research organization based at Syracuse University, gathers court data and maintains statistics about the varying rates of asylee application approvals and denials by individual federal judges. In "Judge-by-Judge Asylum Decisions in Immigration Courts, FY 2009–2014" (2014, http://trac.syr.edu/immigration/reports/361/include/denialrates.html), TRAC notes that application approval rates vary broadly across and within jurisdictions. For example, in immigration courts in Atlanta, Georgia, the judge most likely to approve asylee applications between 2009 and 2014 approved 37.6% of all applications, whereas the Atlanta judge least likely to approve applications approved only 6.3% of all applications. Judges in Chicago, Illinois, meanwhile, were more lenient overall, with five judges in that jurisdiction approving more than 50% of applications and one judge approving 82.9%. However, one judge in Chicago was among the nation's least likely to grant asylum status, approving only 4% of applications between 2009 and 2014. Certain border-state immigration courts in Texas and Arizona were exceedingly unlikely to grant asylum status to applicants. Among three immigration judges in El Paso, Texas, one approved only 1% of applications, another approved 4.1%, and a third approved 7.7%. Similarly, the four immigration judges in Eloy, Arizona, approved applications at consistently low rates, ranging from 4% to 5.7%. In Los Angeles, which had 37 immigration judges (more than any other jurisdiction), rates of approval ranged from 5.8% to 76.1%, with an overwhelming majority of judges (25) approving between 25% and 50% of applications.

VICTIMS OF TRAFFICKING AND VIOLENCE

Human trafficking, a term referring to various varieties of modern slavery, is alarmingly widespread in the 21st century. Traffickers often coerce victims into moving far from their homes with promises of good jobs, then force them to work for little or nothing, sometimes as prostitutes, and often under threat of death or extreme brutality. Although the victims of human trafficking frequently work in plain sight in the United States and elsewhere, the conditions allowing traffickers to maintain power over them are hidden. Accurate estimates of the number of victims are accordingly difficult to establish, but the U.S. government devotes substantial resources to combating the problem. As part of this effort, federal immigration law provides for the admission of trafficking victims on the same terms as refugees, and it provides immigration benefits to those who cooperate with investigations into trafficking.

Trafficking victims were made eligible for federal benefits and services through the Trafficking Victims Protection Act (TVPA) of 2000, which also made provisions for the prosecution of traffickers and for prevention efforts in the countries where the crime often originates. The Trafficking Victims Protection Reauthorization Act of 2003 strengthened the law by mandating informational awareness campaigns and creating a new civil action provision that allows victims to sue their traffickers in federal district court. It also required the U.S. attorney general to give an annual report to Congress on the results of U.S. government activities to combat trafficking. Reauthorization bills in 2005, 2008, and 2013 further expanded these laws.

The TVPA designates the U.S. Department of Health and Human Services (HHS) as the agency responsible for helping victims of human trafficking become eligible to receive benefits and services so they may rebuild their lives safely in the United States. Furthermore, the TVPA authorizes certification of adult victims to receive certain federally funded or federally administered benefits and services, such as cash assistance, medical care, food stamps, and housing. Certification obligates victims to cooperate with authorities in the investigation and prosecution of traffickers unless they are unable to do so for reasons relating to physical or psychological trauma. Although not required to be certified by the HHS, minors who are determined to be victims of severe forms of trafficking receive letters of eligibility for the same types of services.

The U.S. attorney general notes in *Attorney General's Annual Report to Congress and Assessment of U.S. Government Activities to Combat Trafficking in Persons, Fiscal Year 2012* (July 2014, http://www.justice.gov/sites/default/files/ag/pages/attachments/2014/10/28/agreporthumantrafficking2012.pdf) that the number of certification letters issued rose consistently in the years after TVPA was enacted. In FY 2001 the HHS issued four eligibility letters to children and 194 certification letters to adults, for a total of 198. (See Table 4.9.) In FY 2005, 34 letters were issued to children and 197 to adults, for a total of 231; and in FY 2011, 101 letters were issued to children and 463 to adults, for a total of 564, the highest annual number since the passage of TVPA. The number of certification letters issued to children rose slightly in FY 2012, to 103, and the number issued to adults declined to 366, for a total of 469. In all, between FY 2001 and FY 2012, 3,650 certification letters were issued.

The number of certification letters is not equivalent to the number of trafficking victims identified as eligible by HHS or other federal agencies. Victims often choose not to come forward for reasons such as language barriers, fears for their safety, and the physical and psychological scars resulting from their traumatic experiences. Some victims also choose to return to their home countries rather than attempt to obtain benefits and residency status in the United States.

The most common country of origin for certified adult victims of trafficking in FY 2012 was Mexico, which accounted for 88 (24% of the total) certification letters. (See Table 4.10.) Other leading countries of origin for trafficking victims were Thailand (61 certifications), the Philippines (46), China (21), India (18), Honduras (15), El Salvador (12), and South Korea (11). In FY 2012, child trafficking victims overwhelmingly came from Central America, with Honduras (33 certifications) and Mexico (29) together accounting for 60% of the total and El Salvador (15) and Guatemala (14) accounting for

TABLE 4.9

Certifications and letters of eligibility issued, fiscal years 2001–12

Fiscal year	Number of eligibility letters to children	Number of certification letters to adults	Total letters issued
2001	4	194	198
2002	18	81	99
2003	6	145	151
2004	16	147	163
2005	34	197	231
2006	20	214	234
2007	33	270	303
2008	31	286	317
2009	50	330	380
2010	92	449	541
2011	101	463	564
2012	103	366	469
Total	**508**	**3,142**	**3,650**

SOURCE: "1. Certifications and Letters of Eligibility," in *Attorney General's Annual Report to Congress and Assessment of U.S. Government Activities to Combat Trafficking in Persons, Fiscal Year 2012*, U.S. Department of Justice, July 2014, http://www.justice.gov/sites/default/files/ag/pages/attachments/2014/10/28/agreporthumantrafficking2012.pdf (accessed January 12, 2015)

TABLE 4.10

Leading countries of origin of adult trafficking victims who received certification letters, fiscal year 2012

Country of origin	Number of adult victims who received certification letters	Percentage of total*
Mexico	88	24
Thailand	61	17
Philippines	46	13
China	21	6
India	18	5
Honduras	15	4
El Salvador	12	3
South Korea	11	3

*Percentages are rounded to the nearest whole number.

SOURCE: "1. Certifications and Letters of Eligibility," in *Attorney General's Annual Report to Congress and Assessment of U.S. Government Activities to Combat Trafficking in Persons, Fiscal Year 2012*, U.S. Department of Justice, July 2014, http://www.justice.gov/sites/default/files/ag/pages/attachments/2014/10/28/agreporthumantrafficking2012.pdf (accessed January 12, 2015)

another 29%. (See Table 4.11.) China was the country of origin for five certified child trafficking victims.

Trafficking victims in the United States are eligible for Continued Presence (CP), T, and U nonimmigrant visas. A CP visa authorizes the victim to remain in the United States for one year as a potential witness in the investigation and prosecution of traffickers, with extensions available as needed for ongoing criminal cases. T and U visa status are also available to certain trafficking victims who are cooperating with investigators or whose removal from the United States would result in extreme hardship. Both T and U nonimmigrant visas are valid for

TABLE 4.11

Leading countries of origin of child trafficking victims who received eligibility letters, fiscal year 2012

Country of origin	Number of child victims who received eligibility letters	Percentage of total*
Honduras	33	32
Mexico	29	28
El Salvador	15	15
Guatemala	14	14
China	5	5

*Percentages are rounded to the nearest whole number.

SOURCE: "1. Certifications and Letters of Eligibility," in *Attorney General's Annual Report to Congress and Assessment of U.S. Government Activities to Combat Trafficking in Persons, Fiscal Year 2012*, U.S. Department of Justice, July 2014, http://www.justice.gov/sites/default/files/ag/pages/attachments/2014/10/28/agreporthumantrafficking2012.pdf (accessed January 12, 2015)

four years. Law enforcement authorities can grant extensions of T and U visas as needed for the investigation and prosecution of crimes. Both T and U visa holders are eligible for green cards, and USCIS is obligated to extend the T and U status during the green-card application process.

The attorney general reports that there were 157 requests for CP visas in FY 2012 and that 199 CP visa requests were approved. (See Table 4.12.) There were fewer applications filed than approvals granted because some of the approvals pertained to applications filed in the preceding fiscal year. Additionally, 220 CP visa extensions were authorized, and 61 CP visa requests were

withdrawn. USCIS approved 1,432 T visas for trafficking victims and their family members in FY 2012, the largest number since the inception of the T visa program. (See Table 4.13.) The number of U visas issued (which are available to victims of crimes other than trafficking) was 17,543 in FY 2012, down slightly from the preceding year. (See Table 4.14.) Although there was a statutory cap of 10,000 on the number of U visas issued to victims and their families, eligible applications above that number were conditionally accepted and placed on a waiting list for the following year's available U visas.

Monitoring Foreign Governments

The TVPA requires the State Department to monitor the efforts of foreign governments to eliminate trafficking. The State Department identifies governments in full compliance with the TVPA (Tier 1); governments not in compliance with minimum standards but that are making progress toward compliance (Tier 2); governments that are not in compliance with the TVPA and have a demonstrated problem with human trafficking, but that are taking action to reduce trafficking (Tier 2 Watch List); and governments that have not taken serious action to stop human trafficking (Tier 3). There were 23 countries listed as Tier 3 in 2014. (See Table 4.15.) Under the TVPA, Tier 3 countries are subject to restrictions on U.S. government assistance (with the exception of humanitarian assistance and trade-related assistance), and they may be deprived of funding for educational and cultural exchange programs. The U.S. also opposes these countries' receiving assistance (again, with the exception of humanitarian and trade-related assistance, as well as some developmental assistance) from interna-

TABLE 4.12

Requests for continued presence visas, fiscal years 2006–12

Fiscal year	2006	2007	2008	2009	2010	2011	2012
Total requests for continued presence	117	125	239	301	198	324	157ª
Number authorized	112	122	225	299	186	283	199
Number withdrawn	5	3	14	2	0	15	61ᵇ
Extensions authorized	20	5	101	148	288	355	220
Countries of origin represented	24	24	31	35	32	41	44
Countries with the highest number of requests	Mexico, El Salvador, and South Korea	Mexico, El Salvador, and China	Mexico, Philippines, and South Korea	Thailand, Philippines, Haiti, and Mexico	Thailand, Mexico, Honduras, and Philippines	Thailand, Philippines, and Mexico	Mexico, Philippines, Thailand, Honduras, and Indonesia
U.S. cities with the highest number of requests	Houston, Newark, and New York	Los Angeles, Newark, Houston, and New York	Miami, Newark, Atlanta, San Francisco, and Los Angeles	Honolulu, Chicago, Miami, and Tampa	Chicago, Honolulu, New York City, and Tampa	Honolulu, Miami, and New Orleans	Honolulu, New Orleans, Chicago, New York, and Atlanta

ªThe primary reason that there are fewer continued presence requests than overall initial continued presence applications authorized is that there were pending cases which had not been adjudicated due to vetting and processing. This resulted in a carryover of cases into the next fiscal year.
ᵇThese cases were withdrawn for various reasons, including victims receiving T or U visas while awaiting continued presence, subjects who departed before adjudication, and the case agent determining that the subject was not a victim.

SOURCE: "Requests for Continued Presence in Fiscal Years 2006–12," in *Attorney General's Annual Report to Congress and Assessment of U.S. Government Activities to Combat Trafficking in Persons, Fiscal Year 2012*, U.S. Department of Justice, July 2014, http://www.justice.gov/sites/default/files/ag/pages/attachments/2014/10/28/agreporthumantrafficking2012.pdf (accessed January 12, 2015)

TABLE 4.13

Applications for T nonimmigrant visas, fiscal years 2002–12

Fiscal year	Victims			Family of victims			Totals		
	Applied	Approved*	Denied*	Applied	Approved*	Denied*	Applied	Approved*	Denied*
2002	163	17	12	234	9	4	397	26	16
2003	750	283	51	274	51	8	1,024	334	59
2004	566	163	344	86	106	11	652	269	355
2005	379	113	321	34	73	21	413	186	342
2006	384	212	127	19	95	45	403	307	172
2007	269	287	106	24	257	64	293	544	170
2008	408	243	78	118	228	40	526	471	118
2009	475	313	77	235	273	54	710	586	131
2010	574	447	138	463	349	105	1,037	796	241
2011	967	557	223	795	722	137	1,762	1,279	360
2012	885	674	194	795	758	117	1,680	1,432	311

*Some approvals and denials are from prior fiscal year filings.

SOURCE: "Applications for T Visas in Fiscal Years 2002–12," in *Attorney General's Annual Report to Congress and Assessment of U.S. Government Activities to Combat Trafficking in Persons, Fiscal Year 2012*, U.S. Department of Justice, July 2014, http://www.justice.gov/sites/default/files/ag/pages/attachments/2014/10/28/agreporthumantrafficking2012.pdf (accessed January 12, 2015)

TABLE 4.14

Applications for U nonimmigrant visas, fiscal years 2009–12

Fiscal year	Victims			Family of victims			Totals		
	Applied	Approved*	Denied*	Applied	Approved*	Denied*	Applied	Approved*	Denied*
2009	6,835	5,825	688	4,102	2,838	158	10,937	8,663	846
2010	10,742	10,073	4,347	6,418	9,315	2,576	17,160	19,388	6,923
2011	16,768	10,088	2,929	10,033	7,602	1,645	26,801	17,690	4,574
2012	24,768	10,122	2,866	15,126	7,421	1,465	39,894	17,543	4,331

*Some approvals and denials are from prior fiscal year filings.

SOURCE: "Applications for U Visas in Fiscal Years 2009–12," in *Attorney General's Annual Report to Congress and Assessment of U.S. Government Activities to Combat Trafficking in Persons, Fiscal Year 2012*, U.S. Department of Justice, July 2014, http://www.justice.gov/sites/default/files/ag/pages/attachments/2014/10/28/agreporthumantrafficking2012.pdf (accessed January 12, 2015)

tional groups such as the World Bank and the International Monetary Fund.

REFUGEE ADJUSTMENT TO LIFE IN THE UNITED STATES

The PRM explains in *FY 2013 Summary of Major Activities* (November 12, 2013, http://www.state.gov/documents/organization/219302.pdf) that in FY 2013 the U.S. government spent just under $2.4 billion in FY 2013 to help process and resettle refugees. The bulk of this budget (83%, or $2 billion) supported overseas assistance, much of it used by the UNHCR and other diplomatic organizations. (See Figure 4.3.) Meanwhile, the costs associated with refugee admissions to the United States totaled $358.9 million (15% of spending), with the remaining funds disbursed for administrative expenses (1%) and humanitarian aid to migrants to Israel (1%).

The State Department makes funds available for the transportation of refugees to resettle in the United States. The cost of transportation is provided to refugees in the form of a loan. Beginning six months after their arrival, refugees become responsible for repaying these loans. Nongovernmental organizations recruit church groups and volunteers from local communities to provide a variety of services and to contribute clothing and household furnishings to meet the needs of arriving refugees. They also become mentors and friends of the refugees by providing orientation to community services, offering supportive services such as tutoring children after school, and teaching families how to shop and handle other essential functions of living in the community.

Mutual assistance associations, many of which have national networks, provide opportunities for refugees to meet their countrymen who are already settled in the United States. These associations also help refugees connect with their ethnic culture through holiday and religious celebrations.

Benefits to Assist Transition

Ongoing benefits for the newly arrived refugees include transitional cash assistance, health benefits, and a wide variety of social services, which are provided

TABLE 4.15

Tier placement of countries, 2014

Tier 1

Armenia	Finland	Luxembourg	Slovenia
Australia	France	Macedonia	Spain
Austria	Germany	Netherlands	Sweden
Belgium	Iceland	New Zealand	Switzerland
Canada	Ireland	Nicaragua	Taiwan
Chile	Israel	Norway	United Kingdom
Czech Republic	Italy	Poland	United States of America
Denmark	Korea, South	Slovak Republic	

Tier 2

Afghanistan	Dominican Republic	Kyrgyz Republic	Portugal
Albania	Ecuador	Latvia	Romania
Argentina	Egypt	Liberia	St. Lucia
Aruba	El Salvador	Lithuania	St. Maarten
Azerbaijan	Estonia	Macau	Senegal
The Bahamas	Ethiopia	Maldives	Serbia
Bangladesh	Fiji	Malawi	Seychelles
Barbados	Gabon	Malta	Sierra Leone
Benin	Georgia	Mauritius	Singapore
Bhutan	Ghana	Mexico	South Africa
Brazil	Greece	Micronesia	Swaziland
Brunei	Guatemala	Moldova	Tajikistan
Bulgaria	Honduras	Mongolia	Trinidad & Tobago
Burkina Faso	Hong Kong	Montenegro	Togo
Cabo Verde	Hungary	Mozambique	Tonga
Cameroon	India	Nepal	Turkey
Chad	Indonesia	Niger	Uganda
Colombia	Iraq	Nigeria	United Arab Emirates
Congo, Republic of	Japan	Oman	Vietnam
Costa Rica	Jordan	Palau	Zambia
Cote D'Ivoire	Kazakhstan	Paraguay	
Croatia	Kiribati	Peru	
Curacao	Kosovo	Philippines	

Tier 2 Watch list

Angola	China (PRC)	Lesotho	Solomon Islands
Antigua & Barbuda	Comoros	Madagascar	South Sudan
Bahrain	Cyprus	Mali	Sri Lanka
Belarus	Djibouti	Marshall Islands	Sudan
Belize	Guinea	Morocco	Suriname
Bolivia	Guyana	Namibia	Tanzania
Bosnia & Herzegovina	Haiti	Pakistan	Timor-Leste
Botswana	Jamaica	Panama	Tunisia
Burma	Kenya	Qatar	Turkmenistan
Burundi	Laos	Rwanda	Ukraine
Cambodia	Lebanon	St. Vincent & the Grenadines	Uruguay

Tier 3

Algeria	Guinea-Bissau	Papua New Guinea	Venezuela*
Central African Republic	Iran	Russia	Zimbabwe
Congo, Democratic Rep. of	Korea, North	Saudi Arabia	
Cuba	Kuwait	Syria	
Equatorial Guinea	Libya	Thailand*	
Eritrea	Malaysia*	Uzbekistan	
The Gambia	Mauritania	Yemen	

Special case

Somalia

*Auto downgrade from Tier 2 watch list.

SOURCE: "Tier Placements," in *Trafficking in Persons Report*, U.S. Department of State, June 2014, http://www.state.gov/documents/organization/226844.pdf (accessed January 12, 2015)

through grants from the HHS's Office of Refugee Resettlement. English-language training is a basic service that is offered to all refugees. The primary focus is preparation for employment through skills training, job development, orientation to the workplace, and job counseling. Early employment leads not only to economic self-sufficiency for the family but also helps establish the family in its new country and community. Special attention is paid to ensure that women have equal access to training and services that lead to job placement. Other services include family strengthening, youth and elderly services, adjustment counseling, and mental health services.

Support for Elderly and Disabled Refugees

Refugees who are elderly or disabled receive benefits from the Social Security Administration, the same as U.S.

FIGURE 4.3

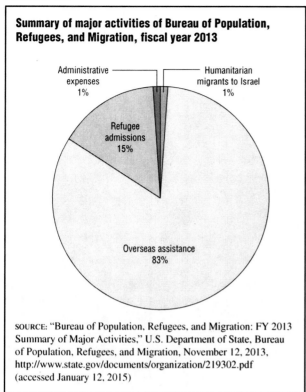

Summary of major activities of Bureau of Population, Refugees, and Migration, fiscal year 2013

Administrative expenses 1%

Humanitarian migrants to Israel 1%

Refugee admissions 15%

Overseas assistance 83%

SOURCE: "Bureau of Population, Refugees, and Migration: FY 2013 Summary of Major Activities," U.S. Department of State, Bureau of Population, Refugees, and Migration, November 12, 2013, http://www.state.gov/documents/organization/219302.pdf (accessed January 12, 2015)

citizens. However, changes by Congress during the late 1990s limit the eligibility of noncitizens to their first seven years in the United States. Time limits for non-citizens do not apply once they become U.S. citizens. The refugee program offers citizenship classes to assist refugees who want to study for the citizenship test.

Unaccompanied Children

As the HHS's Office of Refugee Resettlement (ORR) notes in "Unaccompanied Children Released to Sponsors by State" (2015, http://www.acf.hhs.gov/programs/orr/programs/ucs/state-by-state-uc-placed-sponsors), unac-companied children who are detained by immigration authorities are transferred to the custody of the ORR, which is required by federal law to "feed, shelter, and provide medical care for unaccompanied children until it is able to release them to safe settings and sponsors (usually family members), while they await immigration proceedings." Sponsors undergo background checks to ensure that they are suitable temporary guardians for children. They must ensure that the children appear at immigration hearings to which they are subject and that the children turn themselves over to U.S. Immigration and Customs Enforcement for deportation if and when immigration judges issue removal orders.

The federal government's capacity to carry out this mandate came under extreme pressure in 2013 and 2014, when there was an unprecedented surge in Southwest border crossings by unaccompanied children from Central

America. As Frances Robles reports in "Wave of Minors on Their Own Rush to Cross Southwest Border" (NYTimes.com, June 4, 2014), 47,017 unaccompanied children were apprehended at U.S. border stations in the Southwest between October 2013 and June 2014. (A total of 68,514 children were apprehended at the Southwest border during the fiscal year October 2013 to September 2014, according to the U.S. Customs and Border Patrol. See Chapter 5 for further statistics and information about border apprehensions of unaccompanied children.) Many of these children, as well as a number of mothers appre-hended with small children, appeared to be motivated by a belief that the U.S. government would treat children and mother-child groups more leniently than adult immi-grants who attempted to cross the border illegally.

According to the ORR, in "Unaccompanied Children Released to Sponsors by State," 53,518 unaccompanied children were released to sponsors between October 2013 and September 2014 to await immigration proceedings. Because an unknown number of these children may have been victims of violence, abuse, and/or trafficking, the ORR strictly guards their privacy and does not release specific information about them. Some of these children were likely eligible for asylee status or for visas under TVPA. Those ineligible for such status were subject to deportation proceedings, but laws protecting children from traffickers meant that the deportation process fre-quently moved much more slowly for these children than for adults or families.

Victims of Torture

The International Rehabilitation Council for Torture Victims estimates in "Asylum Seekers, Refugees and Internally Displaced Persons" (2015, http://www.irct .org/our-work/current-focus-areas/asylum-seekers--refugees-and-internally-displace-persons.aspx) that between 4% and 35% of refugees worldwide are likely victims of torture. A nontrivial portion of the overall refugee and asylee population in the United States at any given time, then, is likely to be suffering the aftereffects of torture.

The term *torture*, as defined by U.S. code, refers to acts specifically intended to cause severe physical or mental pain or suffering when these acts are committed by representatives of the law against those in their cus-tody or under their control. The Torture Victims Relief Act (TVRA) of 1998 provides funding to a variety of programs to support refugees, asylees, and asylum seekers who have been victims of torture. As used in the TVRA, the definition of torture explicitly includes the use of rape and other forms of sexual violence. Services available to torture victims under the 1998 law include physical and psychological rehabilitation, social and legal services, research and training for health care providers, and training programs for those who help with the rehabilitation of victims. The ORR notes in "Services for Survivors of Torture Grants" (http://www.acf.hhs.gov/programs/orr/resource/services-for-survivors-of-torture-grants) that between October 2012 and September 2015 there were 31 health care providers, nonprofit programs, or service agencies nationwide who used $10.9 million in TVRA funding to serve torture survivors in the United States.

CHAPTER 5
ILLEGAL IMMIGRATION

BARRIERS TO LEGAL IMMIGRATION

As the preceding chapters make clear, significant constraints regulate the legal immigration process. A foreign national who would like to live in the United States must typically either be a close family member of a U.S. citizen, have a pending contract with an employer who is certified to hire foreign workers, or belong to one of the small groups of people eligible for special visa categories. Even a foreign national who qualifies for immigrant or nonimmigrant visas in one of these ways might have to wait years while pursuing the appropriate documentation to enter the country legally.

Meanwhile, even jobs paying the minimum wage or less in the United States offer incomes significantly larger than jobs in developing countries. Because of their geographic proximity to the United States, people in Mexico and the other countries of Central America are particularly likely to attempt to escape poverty by crossing the U.S. border in the Southwest to find work. They endure significant physical dangers in addition to the legal risks of entering the United States without authorization, and those who manage to find work and remain in the country often send for their families, who take the same risks for the sake of a new life.

Waiting Time for Legal Entry Documents

The annual limit on the number of U.S. employment-based legal admissions is well below the number that is requested by potential immigrants seeking employment. As of January 2015 the employment-based visa applications of priority workers from around the world were being evaluated in a timely manner. (See Table 5.1.) However, those in the second priority group (holders of advanced degrees such as doctorates, as well as highly skilled workers likely to make a positive economic contribution to U.S. companies and the national economy) had been waiting years for a work visa even after securing an employment contract. In January 2015 the State Department was issuing visas to Chinese nationals in the second preference category ("advanced degree holders and persons of exceptional ability") whose applications had been received before February 1, 2010—nearly five years earlier. Workers from India in the same class of applicants had been waiting for nearly 10 years.

The wait for family-based visas could be exceptionally long, as well. The foreign-born spouses and minor children of U.S. citizens, as the highest priority category among all visa applicants, never have to wait for entry into the country. Other family members of citizens are treated very differently under immigration law, however, as are all family members (even spouses and minor children) of green card–holders who are not yet citizens. As of January 2015, for example, if an unmarried adult child of a U.S. citizen was from Mexico, he or she would have been waiting since at least September 15, 1994 (over 20 years), for a family-sponsored visa to be approved. (See Table 5.2.) Likewise, green card–holders who were not citizens could expect to spend years apart from their spouses and children while they worked in the United States. As of January 2015, for applicants from all countries, the State Department was processing visa applications in this category dating from nearly two years prior.

Because of the long waits, many difficult scenarios arise. For example, a parent might learn that a spouse's recent death invalidates immigration applications for their adult children, forcing the children to reapply and wait many additional years. Family members may receive their visas after years in the backlog, only to learn that their children can no longer emigrate with them because they are older than 21 years and must now apply separately as adults or under the lower-priority categories allotted to adult children.

TABLE 5.1

Employment-based visa application backlog, as of January 2015

[In January 2015, the U.S. State Department was issuing employment-based visas for applications received before the dates listed below]

	China	India	Mexico	Philippines	All other countries
1st preference: priority workers	Current applications	Current applications	Current applications	Current applications	Current applications
2nd preference: advanced degree-holders and persons of exceptional ability	February 1, 2010	February 15, 2005	Current applications	Current applications	Current applications
3rd preference: skilled workers and professionals	March 1, 2011	December 15, 2003	June 1, 2013	June 1, 2013	June 1, 2013
3rd preference: other workers	July 22, 2005	December 15, 2003	June 1, 2013	June 1, 2013	June 1, 2013
4th preference: certain special immigrants	Current applications	Current applications	Current applications	Current applications	Current applications
5th preference: investors who create employment	Current applications	Current applications	Current applications	Current applications	Current applications

SOURCE: Adapted from "Employment-Based Preferences," in "Immigrant Numbers for January 2015," *Visa Bulletin*, vol. IX, no. 76, December 9, 2014, http://travel.state.gov/content/dam/visas/Bulletins/visabulletin_January2015.pdf (accessed January 14, 2015)

TABLE 5.2

Family-sponsored visa application backlog, as of January 2015

[In January 2015, the U.S. State Department was issuing employment-based visas for applications received before the dates listed below]

	China	India	Mexico	Philippines	All other countries
1st preference: unmarried adult children of U.S. citizens	July 7, 2008	July 7, 2008	September 15, 1994	December 22, 2004	July 7, 2008
2nd preference A: spouses and minor children of permanent residents	April 15, 2013	April 15, 2013	February 22, 2013	April 15, 2013	April 15, 2013
2nd preference B: unmarried adult children of permanent residents	April 1, 2008	April 1, 2008	November 1, 1994	February 1, 2004	April 1, 2008
3rd preference: married adult children of U.S. citizens	December 22, 2003	December 22, 2003	December 15, 1993	July 8, 1993	December 22, 2003
4th preference: siblings of adult U.S. citizens	March 22, 2002	March 22, 2002	March 22, 1997	July 15, 1991	March 22, 2002

SOURCE: Adapted from "Family-Sponsored Preferences," in "Immigrant Numbers for January 2015," *Visa Bulletin*, vol. IX, no. 76, December 9, 2014, http://travel.state.gov/content/dam/visas/Bulletins/visabulletin_January2015.pdf (accessed January 14, 2015)

ESTIMATES OF THE UNAUTHORIZED IMMIGRANT POPULATION

An unauthorized immigrant is a person who is not a U.S. citizen and who is in the United States in violation of U.S. immigration laws. Other terms commonly used to refer to this population include "undocumented immigrants," "illegal immigrants," and "illegal aliens," although some immigrants and their advocates consider the latter two terms offensive because they equate these individuals' legal violations with their identities.

An unauthorized immigrant can be one of the following:

- A person who enters the United States without a visa, often between land ports of entry

- A person who enters the United States using fraudulent documentation

- A person who enters the United States legally with a temporary visa and then stays beyond the time allowed (an act often called a nonimmigrant overstay or a visa overstay)

- A lawful permanent resident (LPR) who commits a crime after entry, becomes subject to an order of deportation, but fails to depart

Because unauthorized immigrants do not readily identify themselves out of fear of deportation, it is difficult to estimate their numbers accurately. The population further varies between the winter and summer months based on the number of people in agricultural work. However, the Department of Homeland Security's Office of Immigration Statistics (OIS) periodically provides estimates of the size of the unauthorized population as well as a profile of its members. In *Estimates of the Unauthorized Immigrant Population Residing in the United States: January 2012* (March 2013, http://www.dhs.gov/sites/default/files/publications/ois_ill_pe_2012_2.pdf), Bryan Baker and Nancy Rytina of the OIS estimate that as of January 2012 there were approximately 11.4 million unauthorized immigrants living in the United States. (See Figure 5.1.) The Pew Hispanic Center, an affiliate of the widely respected nonprofit fact tank the Pew Research Center, also regularly estimates the unauthorized population. Jeffrey S. Passel and D'Vera Cohn report in *Unauthorized Immigrant Totals Rise in 7 States, Fall in 14* (November 18, 2014, http://www.pewhispanic.org/files/2014/11/2014-11-18_unauthorized-immigration.pdf) that Pew Hispanic's estimate of the unauthorized immigrant population in 2012 was similar to OIS's, at 11.2 million. Passel and Cohn note that unauthorized immigrants accounted for 3.5% of the total U.S. population and 26% of the foreign-born population in 2012.

Both OIS and Pew Hispanic observed a leveling-off of the unauthorized immigrant population beginning in 2009, prior to which the unauthorized population had been growing steadily. The stalled growth in the

FIGURE 5.1

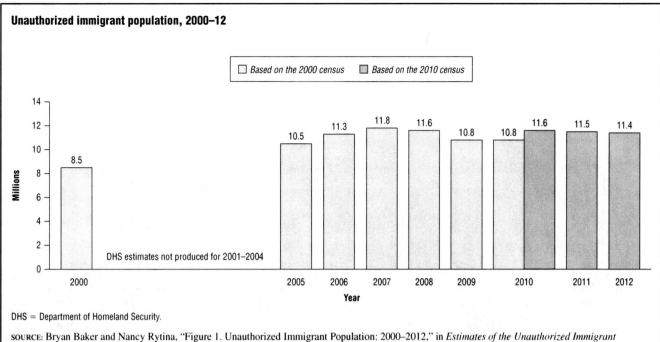

Unauthorized immigrant population, 2000–12

☐ Based on the 2000 census   ▨ Based on the 2010 census

DHS estimates not produced for 2001–2004

Year

DHS = Department of Homeland Security.

SOURCE: Bryan Baker and Nancy Rytina, "Figure 1. Unauthorized Immigrant Population: 2000–2012," in *Estimates of the Unauthorized Immigrant Population Residing in the United States: January 2012*, U.S. Department of Homeland Security, Office of Immigration Statistics, March 2013, http://www.dhs.gov/sites/default/files/publications/ois_ill_pe_2012_2.pdf (accessed January 14, 2015)

unauthorized population was widely attributed to the Great Recession (the most severe economic downturn since the 1930s, which officially lasted from late 2007 through mid-2009 in the United States, but whose effects continued to be felt for years after that time), during which unemployment rates skyrocketed, making it difficult for immigrants to find work. According to the OIS, in *Estimates of the Unauthorized Immigrant Population Residing in the United States*, an estimated 2 million to 4 million unauthorized immigrants were in the United States in 1980. That number increased to an estimated 8.5 million in 2000 and then peaked in 2007 at approximately 11.8 million. (See Figure 5.1.) The period during which the unauthorized population grew most rapidly was 1995 to 2004, when an estimated 6.2 million new unauthorized immigrants, or 54% of those who were present in 2012, entered the country. (See Table 5.3.)

According to OIS estimates, approximately 8.9 million (78%) of the total unauthorized population present in the United States in 2012 were born in North America (Canada, Mexico, the Caribbean, and Central America). (See Figure 5.2.) The next most-common world region of birth for the unauthorized population was Asia, which accounted for 1.3 million of the total, followed by South America (700,000) and Europe (300,000). These numbers were not greatly changed since 2010. In 2012 Mexico remained, as in 2010 and prior years, by far the leading country of birth for members of the unauthorized population, accounting for 6.7 million (59%) of

TABLE 5.3

Period of entry of the unauthorized immigrant population, January 2012

| Period of entry | Estimated population January 2012 | |
	Number	Percent
All years	11,430,000	100
2005–2011	1,540,000	14
2000–2004	3,250,000	28
1995–1999	2,920,000	26
1990–1994	1,720,000	15
1985–1989	1,110,000	10
1980–1984	890,000	8

Note: Detail may not sum to totals because of rounding.

SOURCE: Bryan Baker and Nancy Rytina, "Table 1. Period of Entry of the Unauthorized Immigrant Population: January 2012," in *Estimates of the Unauthorized Immigrant Population Residing in the United States: January 2012*, U.S. Department of Homeland Security, Office of Immigration Statistics, March 2013, http://www.dhs.gov/sites/default/files/publications/ois_ill_pe_2012_2.pdf (accessed January 14, 2015)

the total. (See Table 5.4.) The other leading countries of origin were El Salvador (690,000), Guatemala (560,000), Honduras (360,000), the Philippines (310,000), India (260,000), Korea (230,000), China (210,000), Ecuador (170,000), and Vietnam (160,000).

California had the largest unauthorized population of any state, at 2.8 million or 25%, followed by Texas, at 1.8 million or 16%. (See Table 5.5.) The unauthorized population in California had declined slightly since 2010,

FIGURE 5.2

Unauthorized immigrant population, by world region of birth, January 2012 and January 2010

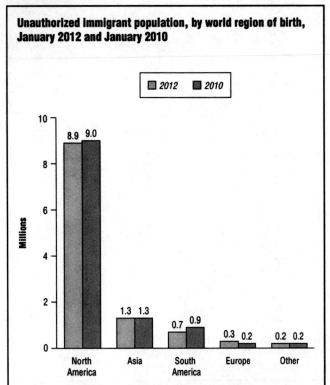

SOURCE: Bryan Baker and Nancy Rytina, "Figure 2. Region of Birth of the Unauthorized Immigrant Population: January 2012 and 2010," in *Estimates of the Unauthorized Immigrant Population Residing in the United States: January 2012*, U.S. Department of Homeland Security, Office of Immigration Statistics, March 2013, http://www.dhs.gov/sites/default/files/publications/ois_ill_pe_2012_2.pdf (accessed January 14, 2015)

TABLE 5.4

Unauthorized immigrant population, by country of birth, January 2012 and January 2010

Country of birth	Estimated population in January		Percent of total	
	2012	2010	2012	2010
All countries	11,430,000	11,590,000	100	100
Mexico	6,720,000	6,830,000	59	59
El Salvador	690,000	670,000	6	6
Guatemala	560,000	520,000	5	4
Honduras	360,000	380,000	3	3
Philippines	310,000	290,000	3	2
India	260,000	270,000	2	2
Korea	230,000	220,000	2	2
China	210,000	300,000	2	3
Ecuador	170,000	210,000	2	2
Vietnam	160,000	190,000	1	2
Other countries	1,760,000	1,720,000	15	15

Note: Detail may not sum to totals because of rounding.

SOURCE: Bryan Baker and Nancy Rytina, "Table 3. Country of Birth of the Unauthorized Immigrant Population: January 2012 and 2010," in *Estimates of the Unauthorized Immigrant Population Residing in the United States: January 2012*, U.S. Department of Homeland Security, Office of Immigration Statistics, March 2013, http://www.dhs.gov/sites/default/files/publications/ois_ill_pe_2012_2.pdf (accessed January 14, 2015)

whereas it had grown slightly in Texas. Other leading states were Florida, with 730,000 unauthorized residents, New York (580,000), Illinois (540,000), New Jersey

TABLE 5.5

Unauthorized immigrant population, by state of residence, January 2012 and January 2010

State of residence	Estimated population in January		Percent of total	
	2012	2010	2012	2010
All states	11,430,000	11,590,000	100	100
California	2,820,000	2,910,000	25	25
Texas	1,830,000	1,780,000	16	15
Florida	730,000	730,000	6	6
New York	580,000	690,000	5	6
Illinois	540,000	550,000	5	5
New Jersey	430,000	440,000	4	4
Georgia	400,000	430,000	3	4
North Carolina	360,000	390,000	3	3
Arizona	350,000	350,000	3	3
Washington	270,000	260,000	2	2
Other states	3,110,000	3,040,000	27	26

Note: Detail may not sum to totals because of rounding.

SOURCE: Bryan Baker and Nancy Rytina, "Table 4. State of Residence of the Unauthorized Immigrant Population: January 2012 and 2010," in *Estimates of the Unauthorized Immigrant Population Residing in the United States: January 2012*, U.S. Department of Homeland Security, Office of Immigration Statistics, March 2013, http://www.dhs.gov/sites/default/files/publications/ois_ill_pe_2012_2.pdf (accessed January 14, 2015)

(430,000), Georgia (400,000), North Carolina (360,000), Arizona (350,000), and Washington (270,000).

Between 2000 and 2012 the increases in the unauthorized population were driven primarily by immigrants from Mexico. (See Table 5.6.) In 2000 there were 4.7 million unauthorized immigrants in Mexico, and in 2012 there were 6.7 million, for an increase of 44%. This increase of 2 million immigrants represented approximately 67% of the total increase of the unauthorized population during this time. Although California was home to the largest population of unauthorized immigrants at all points between 2000 and 2012, most of the population growth occurred in other states. Texas saw the largest increase in number, with the population growing from 1.1 million in 2000 to 1.8 million in 2012, an increase of nearly 68%. Georgia had the largest percentage increase, with an unauthorized population increase of 82%, from 220,000 in 2000 to 400,000 in 2012. Florida's unauthorized population declined over the period, whereas New York's increased modestly, by 40,000. The unauthorized population of New Jersey grew by 80,000, and those of Illinois, North Carolina, and Washington all grew by an estimated 100,000. Arizona's unauthorized population grew rapidly through 2008 and then shrank between 2009 and 2012. Even though part of this decline was likely due to the Great Recession, it was also likely due to restrictive immigration laws passed at the state level, as discussed in Chapter 2. Although these state laws had no authority to increase deportations from the state, they were designed to make conditions difficult for unauthorized immigrants so that they would "self-deport."

TABLE 5.6

Unauthorized immigrant population, by country of birth and state of residence, January 2000 and January 2005–12

Country of birth and state of residence	Estimated population in January									
	2000	2005	2006[a]	2007	2008	2009	2010	2010[b]	2011	2012
Country of birth										
Total	**8,460,000**	**10,490,000**	**11,310,000**	**11,780,000**	**11,600,000**	**10,750,000**	**10,790,000**	**11,590,000**	**11,510,000**	**11,430,000**
Mexico	4,680,000	5,970,000	6,570,000	6,980,000	7,030,000	6,650,000	6,640,000	6,830,000	6,800,000	6,720,000
El Salvador	430,000	470,000	510,000	540,000	570,000	530,000	620,000	670,000	660,000	690,000
Guatemala	290,000	370,000	430,000	500,000	430,000	480,000	520,000	520,000	520,000	560,000
Honduras	160,000	180,000	280,000	280,000	300,000	320,000	330,000	380,000	380,000	360,000
Philippines	200,000	210,000	280,000	290,000	300,000	270,000	280,000	290,000	270,000	310,000
India	120,000	280,000	210,000	220,000	160,000	200,000	200,000	270,000	240,000	260,000
Korea	180,000	210,000	230,000	230,000	240,000	200,000	170,000	220,000	230,000	230,000
China	190,000	230,000	170,000	290,000	220,000	120,000	130,000	300,000	280,000	210,000
Ecuador	110,000	120,000	150,000	160,000	170,000	170,000	180,000	210,000	210,000	170,000
Vietnam	160,000	150,000	150,000	120,000	80,000	110,000	110,000	190,000	170,000	160,000
Other countries	1,940,000	2,300,000	2,340,000	2,170,000	2,100,000	1,700,000	1,610,000	1,830,000	1,670,000	1,760,000
State of residence										
Total	**8,460,000**	**10,490,000**	**11,310,000**	**11,780,000**	**11,600,000**	**10,750,000**	**10,790,000**	**11,590,000**	**11,510,000**	**11,430,000**
California	2,510,000	2,770,000	2,790,000	2,840,000	2,850,000	2,600,000	2,570,000	2,910,000	2,830,000	2,820,000
Texas	1,090,000	1,360,000	1,620,000	1,710,000	1,680,000	1,680,000	1,770,000	1,780,000	1,790,000	1,830,000
Florida	800,000	850,000	960,000	960,000	840,000	720,000	760,000	730,000	740,000	730,000
New York	540,000	560,000	510,000	640,000	640,000	550,000	460,000	690,000	630,000	580,000
Illinois	440,000	520,000	530,000	560,000	550,000	540,000	490,000	550,000	550,000	540,000
New Jersey	350,000	380,000	420,000	470,000	400,000	360,000	370,000	440,000	420,000	430,000
Georgia	220,000	470,000	490,000	490,000	460,000	480,000	460,000	430,000	440,000	400,000
North Carolina	260,000	360,000	360,000	380,000	380,000	370,000	390,000	390,000	400,000	360,000
Arizona	330,000	480,000	490,000	530,000	560,000	460,000	470,000	350,000	360,000	350,000
Washington	170,000	240,000	280,000	260,000	260,000	230,000	200,000	260,000	260,000	270,000
Other states	1,750,000	2,510,000	2,860,000	2,940,000	2,980,000	2,760,000	2,840,000	3,040,000	3,100,000	3,110,000

[a]Revised as noted in the 1/1/2007 unauthorized estimates report published in September 2008.
[b]Revised to be consistent with estimates derived from the 2010 Census.
Note: Detail may not sum to totals because of rounding.

SOURCE: Bryan Baker and Nancy Rytina, "Appendix 2. Country of Birth and State of Residence of the Unauthorized Immigrant Population: January 2000 and 2005–2012," in *Estimates of the Unauthorized Immigrant Population Residing in the United States: January 2012*, U.S. Department of Homeland Security, Office of Immigration Statistics, March 2013, http://www.dhs.gov/sites/default/files/publications/ois_ill_pe_2012_2.pdf (accessed January 14, 2015)

TABLE 5.7

Unauthorized immigrant population, by age and sex, January 2012

Age	Total		Male		Female	
	Number	Percent	Number	Percent	Number	Percent
All ages	**11,430,000**	**100**	**6,100,000**	**100**	**5,330,000**	**100**
Under 18 years	1,120,000	10	580,000	10	530,000	10
18 to 24 years	1,410,000	12	880,000	14	540,000	10
25 to 34 years	3,660,000	32	2,050,000	34	1,600,000	30
35 to 44 years	3,320,000	29	1,750,000	29	1,570,000	29
45 to 54 years	1,400,000	12	650,000	11	750,000	14
55 years and over	520,000	5	190,000	3	330,000	6

Note: Detail may not sum to totals because of rounding.

SOURCE: Bryan Baker and Nancy Rytina, "Table 5. Age by Sex of the Unauthorized Immigrant Population: January 2012," in *Estimates of the Unauthorized Immigrant Population Residing in the United States: January 2012*, U.S. Department of Homeland Security, Office of Immigration Statistics, March 2013, http://www.dhs.gov/sites/default/files/publications/ois_ill_pe_2012_2.pdf (accessed January 14, 2015)

According to OIS estimates, a majority of unauthorized immigrants (7 million, or 61%) were adults between the ages of 25 and 44. (See Table 5.7.) There were more male unauthorized immigrants (6.1 million) than female (5.3 million). The age distribution of the unauthorized population was similar for both sexes, but the male population was slightly younger, with larger percentages of 18-to-34-year-olds, whereas among females there were slightly larger percentages of those aged 45 years and older.

Decline in Immigration from Mexico

According to Passel and Cohn, in *Unauthorized Immigrant Totals Rise in 7 States, Fall in 14*, the unauthorized population as a whole stopped growing between 2009 and 2012 in large part because of a sizable fall-off in immigration from Mexico. Passel and Cohn estimate that the number of unauthorized immigrants from Mexico declined by approximately 500,000 between 2009 and 2012, falling from a peak of 6.4 million to 5.9 million. These numbers differ somewhat from OIS estimates, which suggest that the unauthorized population from Mexico peaked at 7 million in 2008 and fell to 6.7 million by 2012. Although the decline of just over 300,000 is smaller than that estimated by the Pew researchers and the OIS estimate of the Mexican portion of the unauthorized population is larger overall, both sets of researchers agree that the wave of unauthorized immigration from Mexico, which had been growing steadily since the 1990s, had receded as of 2012. Whether this was a temporary phenomenon or a more sustained historical development was unclear as of 2015.

In an earlier Pew Hispanic report, *Net Migration from Mexico Falls to Zero—and Perhaps Less* (April 23, 2012, http://www.pewhispanic.org/2012/04/23/net-migration-from-mexico-falls-to-zero-and-perhaps-less), Passel, Cohn, and Ana Gonzalez-Barrera attribute the decline in unauthorized immigration from Mexico to a convergence of factors. First, there was a decrease in demand for workers during the Great Recession. Additionally, the heightened border security that was initiated after the terrorist attacks in the United States on September 11, 2001 (9/11), had made border crossings far more difficult by the time the recession began. National security concerns and anti-immigrant political pressures had also led to increasing numbers of deportations. The increase in deportations began under the administration of President George W. Bush (1946–) and accelerated under President Barack Obama (1961–). Finally, demographers pointed to the falling birthrate in Mexico, which had begun to relieve some of the pressure that had driven so many in that country to leave home in the preceding decades. In 1960, the Pew authors point out, the average Mexican woman gave birth to 7.3 children. By 2009 the Mexican fertility rate was 2.4 children per woman, only slightly higher than that among U.S. women (2). Together with Mexico's economic growth during that same period, the falling fertility suggested that in the future Mexicans would be better able to find opportunities for personal and professional advancement in their home country.

According to Passel and Cohn, in *Unauthorized Immigrant Totals Rise in 7 States, Fall in 14*, the decline in unauthorized immigration from Mexico between 2009 and 2012 was offset by increases in the unauthorized populations from other parts of the world. The size of unauthorized populations from South America, Europe, and Canada were unchanged during these years, and the populations from Asia, the Caribbean, Central America, and other world regions modestly increased.

Children of Unauthorized Immigrants

From a legal standpoint, there are two distinct populations among the children of unauthorized immigrants: the U.S. born and the foreign born. Those who were born in the United States have what is known as "birthright citizenship," the right to citizenship of anyone born inside the country, even though their parents had no legal right to reside in the country at the time of the birth. Those who were born elsewhere and brought to the United States as children have historically been subject to the same immigration law provisions as all unauthorized immigrants. They have been subject to deportation, ineligible for work authorization and most government benefits, and permanently ineligible for LPR status as well as naturalization.

According to Passel and Cohn, in *Unauthorized Immigrant Totals Rise in 7 States, Fall in 14*, in 2012, 6.9% of all students in grades kindergarten through 12 in the United States had at least one parent who was an unauthorized immigrant. Approximately four times more of these students were U.S. born (5.5% of all U.S. students) than foreign born (1.4%). In 2007, when the unauthorized population was approaching its peak levels, 7.2% of K-12 students had unauthorized parents, with the U.S.-born children of unauthorized immigrants accounting for 4.5% of all students and the foreign-born children of unauthorized immigrants accounting for 2.6% of all students.

This slight decrease in the population of children with unauthorized parents was likely the result of the flattened level of unauthorized immigration overall. Since there were fewer unauthorized immigrants as a percentage of total U.S. population, there were fewer children of unauthorized parents as a percentage of total students, and some children counted in 2007 would have aged beyond secondary school levels by 2012 without being replaced by new arrivals. The shift toward more U.S.-born than foreign-born students in this population was also a result of the slowdown in unauthorized immigration. With fewer new immigrants arriving, the median length of time an unauthorized immigrant had been in the country had increased, and the longer an unauthorized immigrant remains in the United States, the more likely his or her children are to be born in the United States.

As Passel, Cohn, Jens Manuel Krogstad, and Gonzalez-Barrera report in *As Growth Stalls, Unauthorized Immigrant Population Becomes More Settled* (September 3, 2014, http://www.pewhispanic.org/2014/09/03/as-growth-stalls-unauthorized-immigrant-population-becomes-more-settled), in 2000, 2.1 million unauthorized adults (30% of the unauthorized adult population) lived with U.S.-born children who were either minors or adults. By 2012, 4 million unauthorized adults (38%) lived with U.S.-born children. Of the 4 million unauthorized adults who lived with their children, an estimated 3 million (75%) had lived in the United States for a decade or longer, and the median time in the United States for unauthorized parents of U.S.-born children was 15 years.

These two population subsets, U.S.-born and foreign-born children of unauthorized immigrants, became increasingly central to the immigration debate in the first and second decades of the 21st century. As discussed in Chapter 2, the long-running attempt to pass various versions of the Development, Relief, and Education for Alien Minors (DREAM) Act had as one of its central goals the granting of a path to citizenship to many unauthorized immigrants brought to the United States as children. This aspect of the DREAM Act was carried forward in modified form by President Obama's 2012 and 2014 executive actions granting deportation relief to certain unauthorized immigrants. Unauthorized parents of U.S.-born children, meanwhile, were central to the 2014 executive action. The 2012 and 2014 executive actions are discussed at greater length in Chapter 2 as well as later in this chapter.

Unaccompanied Children

As noted in Chapter 4, the period from October 2013 to September 2014 saw an unprecedented surge in southwestern border crossings by unaccompanied children from Central America. According to Frances Robles, in "Wave of Minors on Their Own Rush to Cross Southwest Border" (NYTimes.com, June 4, 2014), large numbers of these children were from the crime-ridden countries of El Salvador, Guatemala, and Honduras, and in many cases they were traveling to the United States on their own after their parents had already made a border crossing as unauthorized immigrants. There was an accompanying, smaller surge in border crossings by mothers with small children (historically an uncommon arrangement among unauthorized immigrants, who have typically crossed the border on their own and sent for their children later). Robles and other observers note that the trend was fueled by widespread rumors that the U.S. government would not deport minors or mother-child groups once they had safely arrived on U.S. soil.

Many right-leaning analysts and politicians blamed the influx of unaccompanied child migrants on President Obama's 2012 Deferred Action for Childhood Arrivals (DACA) program, under which certain unauthorized immigrants brought to the country as children became eligible for relief from deportation. Although the unaccompanied child migrants did not qualify for deportation relief under DACA, critics claimed that DACA sent a message of leniency for would-be border crossers, especially in regard to children. The Obama administration, by contrast, cited rising crime and economic stagnation in Central America as the chief factors driving the surge in border apprehensions.

As Carl Hulse explains in "Immigrant Surge Rooted in Law to Curb Child Trafficking" (NYTimes.com, July 7, 2014), another likely source of the rumors fueling the surge in child migrants was the 2008 reauthorization of the Trafficking Victims Protection Act, which was signed into law by President Bush and implemented during the transition to the Obama administration. Under certain provisions of this legislation, unaccompanied child migrants who were not from Mexico or Canada were subject to increased protections, including a prohibition on quickly deporting them and requirements that they be given legal counsel and a hearing before immigration officials. Although intended to protect traumatized children, to make it possible to reunite them with their families, and to require authorities to deal with them in ways that promote their well-being, the law reportedly made it more difficult to deport unaccompanied children regardless of whether they had experienced or were at risk of trafficking. Robles confirms the influence of the 2008 law on Central Americans' perceptions of U.S. immigration policy. An immigration worker in El Salvador told her that would-be immigrants from her country were keenly aware of a quiet change in U.S. policy. As the United States deported record numbers of unauthorized immigrants to Mexico, few child migrants from El Salvador, Guatemala, or Honduras were seen being returned to their home countries.

As Table 5.8 shows, the surge in unaccompanied children was several years in the making. In fiscal year (FY) 2010, 18,411 children were apprehended along the southwestern border, and in FY 2011, 15,949 children were apprehended. (The fiscal year for the U.S. government runs from October 1 to September 30.) A sharp increase in FY 2012, when 24,481 children were apprehended, was followed by an even sharper increase in FY 2013, when 38,759 children were apprehended. The period from October 2013 to September 2014, however, saw child-migrant numbers rise to what were widely described as crisis levels, with 68,541 children apprehended. In such numbers, unaccompanied children overwhelmed the ability of U.S. Customs and Border Patrol (CBP) to process them, the Office of Refugee Resettlement to care for them (see Chapter 4), and the immigration courts to hear their cases in a timely manner.

As the crisis developed, the Rio Grande Valley, a region encompassing the cities of Brownsville, Harlingen, and McAllen in the extreme southern tip of Texas, was increasingly the most likely border crossing location for unaccompanied children. The CBP officials patrolling

TABLE 5.8

U.S. Border Patrol apprehensions of unaccompanied children aged 0–17, fiscal years 2010–14

Southwest border sector	Fiscal year 2010	Fiscal year 2011	Fiscal year 2012	Fiscal year 2013	Fiscal year 2014
Big Bend	197	189	168	125	256
Del Rio	1,014	1,113	1,618	2,135	3,268
El Centro	448	457	498	434	662
El Paso	1,011	697	659	744	1,029
Laredo	1,570	1,608	2,658	3,795	3,800
Rio Grande Valley	4,977	5,236	10,759	21,553	49,959
San Diego	980	549	524	656	954
Tucson	7,998	5,878	7,239	9,070	8,262
Yuma	216	222	280	247	351
Southwest border total	**18,411**	**15,949**	**24,481**	**38,759**	**68,541**

SOURCE: Adapted from "U.S. Border Patrol Total Monthly UAC Apprehensions by Month, by Sector (FY 2010–FY 2014)," in *Stats and Summaries*, U.S. Department of Homeland Security, U.S. Customs and Border Protection, December 2014, http://www.cbp.gov/sites/default/files/documents/BP%20Total%20Monthly%20UACs%20by%20Sector%2C%20FY10.-FY14.pdf (accessed January 14, 2015)

that border sector apprehended 10,759 of 24,481 (43.9%) total child migrants in FY 2012, 21,553 of 38,759 (55.6%) in FY 2013, and 49,959 of 68,541 (72.9%) in FY 2014. (See Table 5.8.) The area had historically been the primary border-crossing site for unauthorized immigrants from Central America because it is the geographical location closest to their home countries. (See the map of North and Central America, the Bahamas, and the Greater Antilles in Appendix II.) As Daniel Gonzáles reports in "Border Kids: Crossing the River of Hope, Despair" (AZCentral.com, July 14, 2014), children typically traveled to the Rio Grande Valley with the help of smugglers along a well-established network of bus and train lines that followed the eastern coast of Mexico (as well as the route of an oil pipeline) north from El Salvador, Guatemala, and Honduras. Previous waves of adult border crossers from Central America used the Rio Grande's brushy banks to escape notice and were able to further escape detection by blending in with local populations in the U.S. cities close to the border. By contrast, child migrants, as well as children with their mothers, were advised by their smugglers to turn themselves in to the authorities, in keeping with the rumors about immigration officials' likelihood to treat them leniently. "They are surrendering directly to us or the Border Patrol," a local law enforcement officer told Gonzáles. "They actually seek us out."

The CBP notes in "Southwest Border Unaccompanied Alien Children" (2015, http://www.cbp.gov/newsroom/stats/southwest-border-unaccompanied-children) that as of April 2015 the flow of unaccompanied children had slowed considerably since its summer 2014 peak. From October 2014 through March 2015, the CBP apprehended 15,647 unaccompanied children, a 45% decrease from the 28,579 apprehensions for the same period in FY 2014. Whether this decrease represented a reversal of the prior year's surge or a temporary lull remained to be seen.

FEDERAL RESPONSE TO ILLEGAL IMMIGRATION

Law Enforcement and Border Security

As illegal immigration from Mexico and Central America increased through the 1990s and the early years of the following decade, and as comprehensive immigration reform such as the proposals embodied by the DREAM Act foundered in Congress, federal immigration legislation focused intently on the enforcement of laws intended to restrict the flow of unauthorized immigrants. Doris Meissner et al. of the Migration Policy Institute report in *Immigration Enforcement in the United States: The Rise of a Formidable Machinery* (January 2013, http://www.migrationpolicy.org/pubs/enforcementpillars.pdf) that immigration policy in the post-9/11 era has focused on six areas of enforcement: border security, visa controls and the screening of travelers, data-system improvements, workplace enforcement, the pursuit of unauthorized immigrants via the criminal justice system, and the removal of noncitizens.

Resources devoted to securing the U.S. border in the Southwest increased dramatically following the creation of the U.S. Department of Homeland Security (DHS) in 2003. As Meissner et al. note, the number of agents in the U.S. Border Patrol, a part of the CBP, doubled in size between 2005 and 2012, reaching 21,370 as of FY 2012. According to the CBP, in "United States Border Patrol: Sector Profile—Fiscal Year 2014" (http://www.cbp.gov/sites/default/files/documents/USBP%20Stats%20FY2014%20sector%20profile.pdf), the number of Border Patrol agents was 20,863 in FY 2014.

The number of border apprehensions, meanwhile, peaked in 2000, at 1.7 million. By 2005 the number of border apprehensions stood at 1.2 million, and by 2010 at 463,000, the lowest number since the early 1970s. (See Table 5.9.) Since 2010 the number of total apprehensions has fluctuated but remained very low by historic standards, with increased numbers in FY 2013 and FY 2014

TABLE 5.9

U.S. Border Patrol apprehensions, fiscal years 1925–2014

Fiscal year	Apprehensions	Fiscal year	Apprehensions
1925	22,199	1970	231,116
1926	12,735	1971	302,517
1927	16,393	1972	396,495
1928	23,566	1973	498,123
1929	32,711	1974	634,777
1930	20,880	1975	596,796
1931	22,276	1976	696,039
1932	22,735	1977	812,541
1933	20,949	1978	862,837
1934	10,319	1979	888,729
1935	11,016	1980	759,420
1936	11,728	1981	825,290
1937	13,054	1982	819,919
1938	12,851	1983	1,105,670
1939	12,037	1984	1,138,566
1940	10,492	1985	1,262,435
1941	11,294	1986	1,692,544
1942	11,784	1987	1,158,030
1943	11,175	1988	969,214
1944	31,175	1989	891,147
1945	69,164	1990	1,103,353
1946	99,591	1991	1,132,033
1947	193,657	1992	1,199,560
1948	192,779	1993	1,263,490
1949	288,253	1994	1,031,668
1950	468,339	1995	1,324,202
1951	509,040	1996	1,549,876
1952	528,815	1997	1,412,953
1953	835,311	1998	1,555,776
1954	1,028,246	1999	1,579,010
1955	225,186	2000	1,676,438
1956	68,420	2001	1,266,214
1957	46,225	2002	955,310
1958	40,504	2003	931,557
1959	32,996	2004	1,160,395
1960	28,966	2005	1,189,075
1961	29,384	2006	1,089,092
1962	29,897	2007	876,704
1963	38,861	2008	723,825
1964	42,879	2009	556,041
1965	52,422	2010	463,382
1966	79,610	2011	340,252
1967	94,778	2012	364,768
1968	123,519	2013	420,789
1969	172,391	2014	486,651

SOURCE: "U.S. Border Patrol Total Apprehensions FY 1925–FY 2014," in *Stats and Summaries*, U.S. Department of Homeland Security, U.S. Customs and Border Protection, December 2014, http://www.cbp.gov/document/stats/us-border-patrol-total-apprehensions-fy-1925-fy-2014 (accessed January 14, 2015)

likely due to the surge in apprehensions of unaccompanied children discussed earlier. The broad declines in apprehensions since 2000 have been attributed in part to the success of the CBP's deterrence efforts, as well as to the slowing of immigration from Mexico discussed earlier in this chapter.

Demands for increased border security following 9/11 also led to enhancements of the visa screening process that allowed for heightened scrutiny of nonimmigrant visitors and workers. After an initial dramatic drop in nonimmigrant visas, especially those issued to visitors from countries with large populations of Muslims, by 2011 nonimmigrant entries had returned to pre-2001 levels. Additionally, the DHS developed an electronic screening system, U.S. Visitor and Immigrant Status Indicator Technology (US-VISIT), which allows agents to check noncitizens against immigration, criminal, and terrorist databases.

The DHS has also devoted substantial resources to the expansion, upgrading, and interconnection of the information systems used by various executive and law enforcement agencies. The interconnection of databases and computer systems allows for the coordination of antiterrorist, criminal justice, and immigration enforcement efforts at the federal level. Immigration officials are thus armed with much more information than in earlier decades, and they can use this information in making decisions regarding border apprehensions, the issuance of visas, and other activities that affect the movements of unauthorized immigrants.

Although the Immigration Reform and Control Act of 1986 obligated employers to determine the immigration status of employees, enforcement of this part of the act has generally been unsuccessful. One way in which the DHS has sought to remedy this failure is the development of the E-Verify system. As of 2014 the use of E-Verify was voluntary according to federal law, but 19 states mandated the system's use either by all employers, by all state agencies, and/or by all state contractors. As Figure 2.3 in Chapter 2 shows, 23.9 million cases were processed in the E-Verify system in FY 2013, resulting in confirmations that employees were authorized to work in the United States 98.8% of the time.

Between 2006 and 2009, the Bush administration changed the focus on workplace enforcement to target workers rather than employers, undertaking large-scale raids of suspected businesses and arresting scores of unauthorized workers. These raids were extremely unpopular among immigrants regardless of their legal status, and the Obama administration de-emphasized them, returning the focus of workplace enforcement to employer sanctions. Between January 2009 and January 2013, U.S. Immigration and Customs Enforcement (ICE) audited more than 8,000 employers and leveled almost $90 million in fines for workplace violations of immigration law.

Additionally, cooperation has increased between federal, state, and local law enforcement agencies on immigration issues. This trend has been advanced by a number of federal programs aimed at the removal of noncitizens arrested or convicted of criminal offenses. According to Meissner et al., the period between FY 2004 and FY 2011 saw the funding for such programs increase from $23 million to $690 million. One result of this development was that an increasing share of those deported by DHS (half or more in some years) had criminal convictions.

This coordinated approach between the criminal justice and immigration systems is supplemented by an ongoing, broader emphasis on the deportation of unauthorized immigrants and other noncitizens. In FY 2014 ICE partnered with the CBP to remove 213,719 unauthorized immigrants who had recently been apprehended after crossing the border, 91,037 (42.7%) of whom had prior criminal convictions. (See Table 5.10.) That fiscal year ICE removed 102,224 unauthorized immigrants from the interior of the country, 86,923 (85%) of whom had prior criminal convictions. (See Table 5.11.) Mexico was the leading source country for those unauthorized immigrants removed by ICE in FY 2014, accounting for 176,968 removals. (See Table 5.12.) Guatemala (54,423

TABLE 5.10

Noncitizen border removals, by apprehending program and type/priority, fiscal year 2014

Apprehending CBP office	Level/priority	Removals
Office of Border Patrol (OBP)	Convicted criminal	
	Level 1	17,772
	Level 2	19,733
	Level 3	49,948
	Immigration fugitives	1,776
	Repeat immigration violators	54,115
	Other border removals	61,714
	Total OBP	**205,058**
Office of Field Operations (OFO)	Convicted criminal	
	Level 1	1,490
	Level 2	866
	Level 3	1,228
	Immigration fugitives	56
	Repeat immigration violators	995
	Other border removals	4,026
	Total OFO	**8,661**

Note: CBP = U.S. Customs and Border Protection.

SOURCE: "FY 2014 ICE Border Removals by Apprehending Program and Priority," in *ICE Enforcement and Removal Operations Report, Fiscal Year 2014*, U.S. Department of Homeland Security, U.S. Immigration and Customs Enforcement, December 19, 2014, https://www.ice.gov/doclib/about/offices/ero/pdf/2014-ice-immigration-removals.pdf (accessed January 14, 2015)

TABLE 5.11

Noncitizen interior removals, by apprehending program and type/priority, fiscal year 2014

Threat level/priority	Removals
Convicted criminal	
Level 1	43,897
Level 2	22,191
Level 3	20,835
Immigration fugitives	1,629
Repeat immigration violators	7,206
Other removals	6,466
Total	**102,224**

SOURCE: "FY 2014 ICE Interior Removals by Priority," in *ICE Enforcement and Removal Operations Report, Fiscal Year 2014*, U.S. Department of Homeland Security, U.S. Immigration and Customs Enforcement, December 19, 2014, https://www.ice.gov/doclib/about/offices/ero/pdf/2014-ice-immigration-removals.pdf (accessed January 14, 2015)

TABLE 5.12

Top-10 countries of citizenship for those removed by ICE, fiscal year 2014

Citizenship	Total
Mexico	176,968
Guatemala	54,423
Honduras	40,695
El Salvador	27,180
Dominican Republic	2,130
Ecuador	1,565
Nicaragua	1,266
Colombia	1,181
Jamaica	938
Brazil	850
Total	**307,196**

SOURCE: "FY 2014 Top 10 Countries of ICE Removal by Citizenship," in *ICE Enforcement and Removal Operations Report, Fiscal Year 2014*, U.S. Department of Homeland Security, U.S. Immigration and Customs Enforcement, December 19, 2014, https://www.ice.gov/doclib/about/offices/ero/pdf/2014-ice-immigration-removals.pdf (accessed January 14, 2015)

removals), Honduras (40,695), and El Salvador (27,180) were the other leading source countries for those immigrants deported by ICE.

One high-profile attempt to control the flow of unauthorized immigrants across the U.S.-Mexican border involves the building of physical barriers. The first such barrier was a 14-mile (22.5 km) section of fencing built at the westernmost section of the border in San Diego, California. The Secure Fence Act of 2006, signed into law by President Bush, called for the construction of five sections of new fencing covering 850 miles (1,368 km) in locations that were considered most effective at deterring illegal immigration. Congress modified the act in 2007, reducing the required amount of fencing to 700 miles (1,127 km). The most recent data available as of 2015 suggest that approximately 650 to 670 miles (1,046 to 1,078 km) of fencing had been completed at that time. According to John Burnett, in "In South Texas, Few on the Fence over Divisive Border Wall Issue" (NPR.org, August 18, 2014), the construction price for the fencing had reached $2.3 billion, or about $3.5 million per mile, by 2014.

As Burnett notes, many border residents, especially in high-traffic crossing areas such as the Rio Grande Valley, believe that the fencing is ineffective at deterring illegal immigration, as they regularly witness unauthorized immigrants climbing over or moving through gaps in the barriers. CBP officials maintain that the fencing, while not impermeable, is placed strategically in populated areas that are hard to patrol so as to funnel migrants into open countryside where they can be more easily apprehended. "A fence does not seal the border," a Border Patrol agent in the Rio Grande Valley told Burnett. "It helps, but it's not the solution."

Relief from Deportation

Besides border security issues, the large population of unauthorized immigrants in the 21st century posed humanitarian challenges. It was commonly accepted that to some degree the U.S. economy relied on the cheap labor of the millions of unauthorized workers who lived in the country, but federal and state laws subjected these immigrants and their families to a level of instability that many Americans found distasteful. Federal immigration law made no distinction between those unauthorized immigrants who were convicted criminals and those who lived law-abiding, economically productive lives with their families. Thus, for example, a matter as small as a traffic violation could lead to an unauthorized immigrant's deportation, even if he or she had no prior criminal history, had U.S.-born children, and had lived in the country for a decade or more. Likewise, individuals who had been brought to the United States as young children through no fault of their own could find themselves unable to move forward with adult life, as they were not entitled to work authorization and had to guard against the ever-present threat of deportation. In some cases, when they were deported, they were not being sent home to a country they knew but were being sent away from what they considered their home country, the United States.

DEFERRED ACTION FOR CHILDHOOD ARRIVALS. In response to the ongoing failure of Congress to address these and other issues in a comprehensive immigration reform bill, in 2012 the Obama administration took the first of two major unilateral steps to meet the humanitarian dimensions of the illegal immigration problem. As noted in Chapter 2, on June 15, 2012, Janet Napolitano (1957–), the secretary of homeland security, announced the Deferred Action for Childhood Arrivals (DACA) program. Under DACA, unauthorized immigrants who entered the United States as children younger than 16 years old and who were between the ages of 15 and 30 at the time of the announcement would be eligible for relief from deportation for a period of two years, provided that they had continuously resided in the United States since 2007; had no lawful immigration status; were currently enrolled in high school, had a high school diploma or equivalency certificate, or were honorably discharged veterans of the U.S. military; and had never been convicted of significant crimes or posed a threat to public safety. Besides lifting the threat of deportation for two years, DACA recipients were eligible for work authorization and for renewal of their DACA status at the end of the two-year period.

Between August 2012, when the first DACA applications were accepted, and September 2014, 610,375 first-time applicants were granted relief from deportation under the program. (See Table 2.1 in Chapter 2.) The first renewal applications had begun to be processed by Sep-

tember 2014, as well, with 22,480 already approved and another 93,080 pending. Mexico was by far the leading country of origin for DACA recipients, accounting for 488,910 (77.3%) of the 632,855 total approved applications. (See Table 5.13.) El Salvador (22,967 approved applications), Guatemala (15,367), and Honduras (14,884) were the other leading countries of origin among DACA approvals. California was the leading state of residence among successful DACA applicants, accounting for 187,465 (29.6%) of the approved applications. (See Table 5.14.) Texas followed, accounting for 100,271 (15.8%) of the approved applications. Arizona, Florida, Illinois, North Carolina, and New York each accounted for more than 20,000 successful applications.

DACA EXPANSION AND DEFERRED ACTION FOR PARENTS OF AMERICANS. As noted in Chapter 2, in 2014 the Obama administration made another unilateral move toward reforming the immigration enforcement system, and again the move was framed as a remedy to Congressional inaction on the issue. On November 20 of that year, President Obama announced a new set of executive actions intended to extend the scope of DACA and to provide deportation relief for the parents of U.S.-born children and LPRs.

The expansion of the DACA program increased DACA applicants' term of relief from deportation to three years, lifted the age limitation conferring eligibility only on those applicants under age 30, and reset the starting date for the continuous residency requirement to January 1, 2010 (from 2007 under the 2012 executive action). This expansion measure was expected to increase DACA eligibility by approximately 300,000 individuals, according to Krogstad and Passel of the Pew Research Center in "Those from Mexico Will Benefit Most from Obama's Executive Action" (November 20, 2014, http://www.pewresearch.org/fact-tank/2014/11/20/those-from-mexico-will-benefit-most-from-obamas-executive-action).

The Deferred Action for Parents of Americans and Lawful Permanent Residents (DAPA) program, as the second main aspect of President Obama's 2014 immigration-related executive actions was called, represented an extension of deportation relief to another much-discussed group of unauthorized immigrants: the parents of U.S.-born children and of children who were LPRs. DAPA conferred eligibility for relief from deportation on unauthorized immigrants who had lived in the United States continuously since January 1, 2010, had (as of November 20, 2014) a child who was a citizen or LPR, and were not currently in a prioritized category of removal from the country (priority categorizations primarily consisted of immigrants considered to be national security or public safety threats). Krogstad and Passel estimated that 3.5 million parents of children who were in the United States

TABLE 5.13

Deferred Action for Childhood Arrivals requests and approvals, by country of origin, fiscal years 2012–14

Top countries of origin	Accepted to date[a]			Approved to date[b]		
	Initials	Renewals	Total	Initials	Renewals	Total
Mexico	540,575	86,567	627,142	474,138	14,772	488,910
El Salvador	26,417	4,516	30,933	22,069	898	22,967
Guatemala	18,306	2,632	20,938	14,810	557	15,367
Honduras	17,734	2,081	19,815	14,491	393	14,884
South Korea	8,265	3,422	11,687	7,690	1,381	9,071
Peru	8,440	2,121	10,561	7,738	478	8,216
Brazil	7,120	1,367	8,487	6,209	410	6,619
Colombia	6,369	1,350	7,719	5,792	335	6,127
Ecuador	6,333	1,308	7,641	5,519	271	5,790
Philippines	4,311	1,308	5,619	3,895	468	4,363
Argentina	4,126	799	4,925	3,719	196	3,915
India	3,245	983	4,228	2,752	310	3,062
Jamaica	3,625	340	3,965	2,838	79	2,917
Venezuela	2,946	549	3,495	2,607	133	2,740
Dominican Republic	2,926	332	3,258	2,402	75	2,477
Trinidad and Tobago	2,598	326	2,924	2,208	91	2,299
Uruguay	1,962	379	2,341	1,737	86	1,823
Costa Rica	1,961	379	2,340	1,746	86	1,832
Bolivia	1,908	381	2,289	1,747	80	1,827
Poland	1,610	401	2,011	1,431	78	1,509

[a]The number of requests that were accepted to date of the reporting period.
[b]The number of requests that were accepted to date of the reporting period.
Notes: Some requests approved or denied may have been received in previous reporting periods. The report reflects the most up-to-date estimate data available at the time the report is generated.

SOURCE: "Top Countries of Origin," in *Number of I-821D, Consideration of Deferred Action for Childhood Arrivals by Fiscal Year, Quarter, Intake, Biometrics and Case Status: 2012–2014*, U.S. Department of Homeland Security, U.S. Citizenship and Immigration Services, October 2014, http://www.uscis.gov/sites/default/files/USCIS/Resources/Reports%20and%20Studies/Immigration%20Forms%20Data/All%20Form%20Types/DACA/DACA_fy2014_qtr4.pdf (accessed January 14, 2015)

as citizens or LPRs would become newly eligible for deportation relief under the program.

Just before U.S. Citizenship and Immigration Services was set to begin accepting applications for deportation relief under the 2014 executive actions in February 2015, a federal judge in Brownsville, Texas, issued a temporary injunction blocking the law's implementation. As Michael D. Shear and Julia Preston report in "Dealt Setback, Obama Puts Off Immigrant Plan" (NYTimes.com, February 17, 2015), the judge argued that the administration had failed to observe the official procedures for changing federal guidelines. The judge's ruling was hailed by those on the right who had argued since 2012 that President Obama's unilateral decisions to alter immigration policy were unconstitutional in their failure to observe the balance of powers in government. Such critics suggested that the president's changes to enforcement policy represented an attempt to institute laws by executive fiat, rather than through the legislative process. As of April 2015 the administration was appealing the decision, and resolution of the 2014 executive actions' legality was expected to take several months.

STATE RESPONSES TO ILLEGAL IMMIGRATION

In spite of the federal government's deployment of increasing resources to border-security initiatives, and despite its removals of ever-larger numbers of unauthorized

immigrants in the years since 9/11, the perception exists that the federal government is not committed to preventing illegal immigration. Therefore, populist anger over illegal immigration has since the late 1990s been increasingly channeled into state legislative action. Based on the assumption that the states must step in to secure their own borders and protect resources from overuse by unauthorized immigrants, state laws have tested the limits of the federal government's power and remade the terms of the immigration debate.

As discussed in Chapter 2, in the 21st century Arizona has led the way among states seeking to reduce the incoming flow of unauthorized immigrants. Arizona's unprecedentedly restrictive SB 1070, passed in 2010, was the model for similar laws in Alabama, Georgia, Indiana, South Carolina, and Utah. Each of these laws was significantly scaled back by the courts, however. One of the central portions of Arizona's SB 1070, a provision directing law enforcement officials to determine an individual's immigration status during routine traffic stops and interactions, was upheld by a 2012 U.S. Supreme Court ruling, but most of the law's other provisions were invalidated on the grounds that they conflicted with federal law. The other states' immigration laws have met with varying degrees of resistance from federal district courts. As of 2015, none had been implemented in anything like its original form.

TABLE 5.14

Deferred Action for Childhood Arrivals requests and approvals, by state of residence, fiscal years 2012–14

Residence	Accepted to date[a]			Approved to date[b]		
	Initials	Renewals	Total	Initials	Renewals	Total
California	199,781	32,207	231,988	178,717	8,748	187,465
Texas	115,614	21,017	136,631	97,632	2,639	100,271
Illinois	38,369	8,002	46,371	33,081	846	33,927
New York	36,576	4,697	41,273	31,121	1,116	32,237
Florida	29,527	3,938	33,465	24,285	1,029	25,314
Arizona	25,111	5,239	30,350	22,042	1,201	23,243
North Carolina	24,533	2,801	27,334	21,879	495	22,374
Georgia	23,186	3,931	27,117	19,009	973	19,982
New Jersey	19,805	3,864	23,669	16,974	939	17,913
Colorado	15,813	2,385	18,198	13,729	239	13,968
Washington	15,386	2,011	17,397	13,580	216	13,796
Nevada	11,477	1,099	12,576	10,285	202	10,487
Virginia	10,936	1,557	12,493	9,439	329	9,768
Oregon	9,887	1,795	11,682	8,987	187	9,174
Maryland	8,849	1,764	10,613	7,576	332	7,908
Utah	8,729	1,311	10,040	7,739	184	7,923
Indiana	8,749	992	9,741	7,667	142	7,809
Massachusetts	7,107	1,071	8,178	6,002	277	6,279
Tennessee	7,455	711	8,166	6,339	120	6,459
Wisconsin	6,693	1,001	7,694	5,974	106	6,080
Kansas	6,088	1,031	7,119	5,453	131	5,584
Oklahoma	6,112	926	7,038	5,383	197	5,580
South Carolina	5,841	1,188	7,029	5,046	125	5,171
Michigan	5,545	1,033	6,578	4,791	164	4,955
Minnesota	5,560	936	6,496	4,900	119	5,019
New Mexico	5,797	471	6,268	5,052	36	5,088
Pennsylvania	4,999	927	5,926	4,184	175	4,359
Arkansas	4,682	1,047	5,729	4,096	107	4,203
Connecticut	4,285	888	5,173	3,744	155	3,899
Ohio	3,836	793	4,629	3,213	137	3,350
Alabama	3,857	665	4,522	3,281	94	3,375
Missouri	3,072	646	3,718	2,704	177	2,881
Nebraska	3,040	677	3,717	2,639	99	2,738
Kentucky	2,737	449	3,186	2,337	50	2,387
Idaho	2,783	384	3,167	2,516	44	2,560
Iowa	2,458	678	3,136	2,176	122	2,298
Louisiana	1,789	313	2,102	1,477	46	1,523
Mississippi	1,376	267	1,643	1,146	41	1,187
Delaware	1,241	290	1,531	1,105	44	1,149
Rhode Island	1,072	179	1,251	916	29	945
District of Columbia	672	54	726	560	19	579
Wyoming	571	61	632	482	D	486
New Hampshire	317	68	385	269	15	284
Hawaii	326	54	380	252	D	260
South Dakota	209	52	261	171	D	178
Puerto Rico	197	16	213	107	D	107
West Virginia	91	17	108	75	D	78
Alaska	74	15	89	58	D	61
Virgin Islands	84	D	87	40	D	40
North Dakota	63	16	79	45	D	50
Montana	39	D	45	34	D	34
Maine	37	D	44	30	D	32
Not reported[c]	29	D	35	17	D	17
Guam	23	D	32	19	D	21

D = Data withheld to protect requestors' privacy.
[a]The number of requests that were accepted to date of the reporting period.
[b]The number of requests that were accepted to date of the reporting period.
[c]All fields with less than 10 or a blank in the state field are included in the field "not reported."
Notes: Some requests approved or denied may have been received in previous reporting periods. The report reflects the most up-to-date estimate data available at the time the report is generated.

SOURCE: "Residence," in *Number of I-821D, Consideration of Deferred Action for Childhood Arrivals by Fiscal Year, Quarter, Intake, Biometrics and Case Status: 2012–2014*, U.S. Department of Homeland Security, U.S. Citizenship and Immigration Services, October 2014, http://www.uscis.gov/sites/default/files/USCIS/Resources/Reports%20and%20Studies/Immigration%20Forms%20Data/All%20Form%20Types/DACA/DACA_fy2014_qtr4.pdf (accessed January 14, 2015)

The vacuum created by Congressional inaction on the DREAM Act and subsequent legislative proposals has likewise been filled by states and localities interested in integrating their existing immigrants and welcoming new arrivals. A trend toward more immigrant-friendly legislation became noticeable in the wake of the legal setbacks delivered to restrictive state laws, and the trend gained momentum as a result of the 2012 presidential election. The Hispanic vote was crucial to President Obama's reelection, and the Republican Party's embrace of restrictive immigration law was widely regarded as a hindrance to its securing the votes of this population.

Integrative measures existed before this time, as discussed in Chapter 2. Throughout the first decade of the 21st century, numerous states passed laws allowing unauthorized immigrant students to attend public universities at the in-state tuition rate, and others passed laws allowing unauthorized immigrants to obtain driver's licenses. These measures were further legitimized by President Obama's 2012 DACA action. As of 2015 all but one U.S. state (Nebraska) granted driver's licenses to DACA recipients, and 10 states granted driver's licenses to all residents regardless of their immigration status.

In 2013 Connecticut and California intervened in immigration enforcement practices with the passage of similar pieces of legislation known as Transparency and Responsibility Using State Tools (TRUST) Acts. These TRUST Acts were aimed at rolling back a DHS program requiring local law enforcement officers to detain unauthorized immigrants pending ICE investigation even in circumstances when no serious criminal activity was involved. Both TRUST Acts barred law enforcement officers from detaining immigrants at ICE's request unless the detention pertained to the commission of a serious crime.

BORDERS ON THE WATER

The number of unauthorized immigrants attempting to gain entry by boat has fluctuated over time, with Cuban, Dominican, and Haitian nationals typically the most likely to attempt a water crossing and the Gulf of Mexico the primary body of water serving as a route to the United States. The U.S. Coast Guard is responsible for apprehending (or interdicting) unauthorized immigrants at sea, and its interdiction numbers have varied from a low of 171 in FY 1982 to a high of 64,443 in FY 1994. (See Table 5.15.) Interdiction levels have not ranged as widely in the 21st century, varying from a low of 2,088 in FY 2010 to a high of 10,899 in FY 2004. In FY 2014 the Coast Guard interdicted 3,378 unauthorized immigrants, 2,059 of whom were from Cuba, 949 of whom were from Haiti, 293 of whom were from the Dominican Republic, and 48 of whom were from Mexico.

Immigrants from Cuba have enjoyed a special status since 1961, when the country adopted a Communist system of government under Fidel Castro (1926–) and

TABLE 5.15

U.S. Coast Guard migrant interdictions, fiscal years 1982–2014

Fiscal year	Haitian	Dominican	Chinese	Cuban	Mexican	Ecuadorian	Other	Total
2014	949	293	0	2,059	48	0	29	3,378
2013	508	110	5	1,357	31	1	82	2,094
2012	977	456	23	1,275	79	7	138	2,955
2011	1,137	222	11	985	68	1	50	2,474
2010	1,377	140	0	422	61	0	88	2,088
2009	1,782	727	35	799	77	6	41	3,467
2008	1,583	688	1	2,216	47	220	70	4,825
2007	1,610	1,469	73	2,868	26	125	167	6,338
2006	1,198	3,011	31	2,810	52	693	91	7,886
2005	1,850	3,612	32	2,712	55	1,149	45	9,455
2004	3,229	5,014	68	1,225	86	1,189	88	10,899
2003	2,013	1,748	15	1,555	0	703	34	6,068
2002	1,486	177	80	666	32	1,608	55	4,104
2001	1,391	659	53	777	17	1,020	31	3,948
2000	1,113	499	261	1,000	49	1,244	44	4,210
1999	1,039	583	1,092	1,619	171	298	24	4,826
1998	1,369	1,097	212	903	30	0	37	3,648
1997	288	1,200	240	421	0	0	45	2,194
1996	2,295	6,273	61	411	0	2	38	9,080
1995	909	3,388	509	525	0	0	36	5,367
1994	25,302	232	291	38,560	0	0	58	64,443
1993	4,270	873	2,511	2,882	0	0	48	10,584
1992	37,618	588	181	2,066	0	0	174	40,627
1991	2,065	1,007	138	1,722	0	0	58	4,990
1990	871	1,426	0	443	1	0	95	2,836
1989	4,902	664	5	257	30	0	5	5,863
1988	4,262	254	0	60	11	0	13	4,600
1987	2,866	40	0	46	1	0	38	2,991
1986	3,422	189	11	28	1	0	74	3,725
1985	3,721	113	12	51	0	0	177	4,074
1984	1,581	181	0	7	2	0	37	1,808
1983	511	6	0	44	0	0	5	566
1982	171	0	0	0	0	0	0	171

SOURCE: Adapted from "Total Interdictions—Fiscal Year 1982 to Present," in *Alien Migrant Interdiction*, U.S. Coast Guard, October 20, 2014, http://www.uscg.mil/hq/cg5/cg531/amio/FlowStats/FY.asp (accessed January 14, 2015)

became a political enemy of the United States. In the decades that followed, unauthorized immigrants arriving in the United States were treated as refugees, and there were periods of mass migration, including a 1980 event known as the "Mariel boatlift," whereby an estimated 125,000 people left Mariel Harbor in Cuba for asylum in the United States, following Castro's declaration that anyone who wanted to leave the country could do so. Political and economic turmoil in Cuba led to another wave of mass migration to the United States in 1994, and later that year the administration of President Bill Clinton (1946–) enacted a new policy meant to normalize immigration from Cuba. Among the policy's main provisions was what is known as the "wet foot, dry foot" standard for granting asylum status, whereby any refugee who arrived on U.S. soil would be admitted to the country and anyone who was intercepted at sea would be returned to Cuba. This policy has remained in place since that time, even as Castro was succeeded as president by his brother Raúl (1931–) in 2006. In December 2014 the Obama administration moved to normalize diplomatic relations with Cuba, in an effort to end over 50 years of antagonism between the two countries. According to Nick Miroff, in "Fear of Immigration Policy Change Triggers New Wave of Cuban Migrants" (Washington-Post.com, January 27, 2015), fears that normal relations with the United States would change the special immigration status Cubans have long enjoyed led to a surge in immigration from the country following the announcement of the détente.

THE NORTHERN BORDER

The U.S.-Canadian border is the longest nonmilitarized border between two countries in the world. Unlike the U.S.-Mexican border, which has fenced sections and is guarded by nearly 20,000 CBP agents, much of the U.S.-Canadian border is open and seemingly easy to penetrate. It crosses through mountainous terrain, water, and heavily forested areas on its way through 13 U.S. states. Significant portions cross remote prairie farmland through Alaska, the Great Lakes, the St. Lawrence River, and forests and mountains in the American and Canadian Rockies. The border also runs through the middle of the Akwesasne Nation and even divides some communities in Vermont and Quebec.

Although few unauthorized immigrants enter the United States via its northern border, the Canadian border is considered by some to be a greater terrorism risk. As Garrett M. Graff writes in "Fear Canada" (Politico.com, October 16, 2014), entering the country through the southwestern border is impractical for would-be terrorists, since their aims are not compatible with those of the Mexican drug cartels that control the smuggling routes into the United States, and since the demographics of the border region are not conducive to building domestic support networks. By contrast, the relatively lax security on the northern border, together with the existence of terrorist cells on both sides of the border (in the Canadian provinces of Ontario and Quebec as well as in the U.S. states of Michigan and Minnesota), makes the northern border a more logical point of entry. However, as with many issues relating to terrorism, the size of the threat, and therefore the appropriate scale of U.S. response to the threat, was unclear. As Graff notes, "Historically, potential terrorists have done fine arriving in the United States like most other travelers: by purchasing a ticket on a commercial airliner."

The vulnerability of the northern border was quantified in 2010 by the Government Accountability Office (GAO) in "Enhanced DHS Oversight and Assessment of Interagency Coordination Is Needed for the Northern Border" (December 2010, http://www.gao.gov/highlights/d1197 high.pdf). The GAO notes that only 32 miles (51.5 km) of the nearly 4,000-mile (6,400-km) border "had reached an acceptable level of security" in FY 2010. Accordingly, in June 2012 Secretary of Homeland Security Napolitano announced the official U.S. Northern Border Strategy, the primary goals of which are the deterrence and prevention of terrorism and other crimes such as smuggling, trafficking, and illegal immigration; the protection and encouragement of those involved in legal trade, travel, and immigration; and the provision of resources to communities affected by terrorist attacks and other catastrophic events.

The CBP's "United States Border Patrol: Sector Profile—Fiscal Year 2014" indicates that as of September 2014, of the 20,863 total U.S. Border Patrol agents who were active, 2,093 were stationed on the northern border. These agents were responsible for 3,338 apprehensions in FY 2014.

CHAPTER 6
THE COSTS AND BENEFITS OF IMMIGRATION

Although cultural and humanitarian considerations play a major role in the immigration debate, public policy outcomes often hinge on estimates of immigrants' effects on the U.S. economy and on federal and state budgets. Some analysts evaluate the impact of immigration by comparing the economic growth and taxes immigrants provide their local economies against the government services and benefits they might require. Other analysts attempt to estimate the effects of immigration on the U.S. labor market to determine whether immigrants crowd out natives and thus worsen the economic lives of some native-born workers, as is popularly believed. The cost of enforcing existing laws and securing the country's borders is also a key subject of analysis.

IMMIGRANTS AND THE U.S. ECONOMY

In assessing immigrants' impact on the U.S. economy and government budgets, and in particular the impact of large numbers of unauthorized immigrants, a necessary first step is ascertaining the demographic characteristics of noncitizens relative to the characteristics of citizens. Noncitizens include lawful permanent residents (LPRs), residents with temporary visas, and unauthorized immigrants. Citizens can be either U.S.-born or naturalized. Although naturalized citizens typically consider themselves (and are commonly considered) immigrants, in economic terms they closely resemble U.S.-born citizens. Meanwhile, immigrants who have not yet naturalized or who may never naturalize represent the population of most pressing interest to economists and others who study the effects of large-scale immigration. Thus, an overview of the characteristics of noncitizens relative to the characteristics of citizens provides a natural starting point for estimating the costs and benefits of immigration.

According to the Congressional Budget Office (CBO; a nonpartisan government agency that provides economic and budgetary analysis to Congress), in *How Changes in Immigration Policy Might Affect the Federal Budget* (January 2015, https://www.cbo.gov/sites/default/files/cbofiles/attachments/49868-Immigration.pdf), noncitizens and citizens differ significantly by age, marital status, fertility rates, education, labor force status, and income. In 2012 noncitizens were more likely to be between the ages of 25 to 64 years (i.e., of working age), while the citizen population included much larger proportions of people under the age of 25 years and adults over the age of 65 years. (See Table 6.1.) Female noncitizens were significantly more likely to be married or formerly married than female citizens, both at very young ages (15 to 24 years) and at somewhat older ages (25 to 34 years), and their fertility rates significantly exceeded those of female citizens. Male noncitizens were more likely to participate in the labor force (to be employed or looking for a job) than male citizens, whereas female noncitizens were less likely to participate in the labor force than female citizens. Citizens had substantially higher levels of educational attainment: 9% of citizens had less than a high school diploma, compared with 39% of noncitizens. Noncitizens' differences in age and educational attainment, as well as their concentration in lower-paying industries relative to citizens, resulted in earnings disparities between the two groups. Noncitizens' median (the middle value; half were lower and half were higher) earnings ($23,400) were 38% lower than those of citizens ($38,000).

Government Spending and Taxes

Because noncitizens are more likely to live in low-income households than are citizens, the question of whether they receive more in the form of government benefits than they pay in taxes is central to debates about the costs and benefits of immigration. Most noncitizens who work in the United States pay taxes, including income taxes, payroll taxes, sales and excise taxes, and estate and gift taxes. Tax

TABLE 6.1

Demographic characteristics of citizens and noncitizens, 2012

	Percentage of total		Number of people (millions)	
	Citizens	Noncitizens	Citizens	Noncitizens
Age distribution				
Under the age of 25	34	19	101	4
Ages 25 to 64	51	74	150	16
Age 65 or older	15	7	43	1
Total	100	100	294	22
Women currently or formerly married[a]				
Ages 15 to 24	8	17	2	*
Ages 25 to 34	53	66	10	2
Educational attainment, ages 25 to 64				
Less than high school diploma or GED	9	39	13	6
High school diploma or GED	27	23	40	4
Some college or associate's degree	32	15	48	2
Bachelor's degree	21	13	31	2
Master's degree or more	11	10	17	2
Total	101	99	150	16
Labor force participation rate, ages 25 to 64				
Men	82	89	61[b]	7[b]
Women	73	60	56[b]	5[b]
Total	78	75	116[b]	12[b]
Total	93	7	294	22
Memorandum:				
Fertility rates of women, ages 15 to 49[c]	1.8	2.3	n.a.	n.a.
Median earnings in 2010, ages 25 to 64 (dollars)[d]				
Male workers	45,000	26,000	n.a.	n.a.
Female workers	31,700	18,200	n.a.	n.a.
All workers	38,000	23,400	n.a.	n.a.

GED = General Education Development.
*Less than 500,000; n.a. = not applicable.
[a]Consists of all women who are married, divorced, separated, or widowed.
[b]Refers to the number of people participating in the labor force.
[c]The expected number of births experienced by a woman in a particular age range if, at each age within the range, the likelihood that she gave birth was equal to the share of women at the same age who bore a child during the survey year.
[d]Calculated for individuals between the ages of 25 and 64 with positive earnings.
Notes: Demographic information presented here is based on data from the Census Bureau's 2013 American Community Survey as extracted from the Minnesota Population Center's Integrated Public Use Microdata Series. Unemployment information is based on data from outgoing rotation groups of the Census Bureau's monthly Current Population Survey, January 1994 to December 2013.

SOURCE: "Table 2. Demographic Characteristics of Citizens and Noncitizens, 2012," in *How Changes in Immigration Policy Might Affect the Federal Budget*, Congressional Budget Office, January 2015, https://www.cbo.gov/sites/default/files/cbofiles/attachments/49868-Immigration.pdf (accessed January 15, 2015)

liability varies based on the type of visa noncitizens hold and on the length of time they have been in the country. The CBO indicates in *How Changes in Immigration Policy Might Affect the Federal Budget* that half or more of unauthorized residents pay income and payroll taxes. In *Undocumented Immigrants' State and Local Tax Contributions* (July 2013, http://www.itep.org/pdf/undocumentedtaxes.pdf), the Institute on Taxation and Economic Policy finds that in 2010 unauthorized immigrants collectively paid $10.6 billion in state and local taxes, including $1.2 billion in income taxes, $1.2 billion in property taxes, and $8 billion in sales and excise taxes. The effective tax rate (the percentage of total income) of unauthorized immigrants that year was 6.4%, which the institute notes is consistent with the tax rate of low-income natives.

Noncitizens are ineligible for many types of federal benefits under current law. Only LPRs, refugees, and asylees are eligible for most government programs, and some programs mandate a waiting period of five years after an individual has obtained LPR, refugee, or asylee status before he or she becomes eligible. (See Table 6.2.) Unauthorized immigrants are ineligible for almost all government benefits. Those unauthorized immigrants who were granted deferred action under President Barack Obama's (1961–) 2012 Deferred Action for Childhood Arrivals executive action are eligible for Medicare (a federal health insurance program for people aged 65 years and older and people with disabilities) and Social Security and for the earned-income tax credit (a tax refund available to low-income households whose earnings rise above the poverty level). Meanwhile, the U.S.-born children of unauthorized immigrants are eligible for all government programs provided they meet the other applicable income, employment, age, or disability guidelines. According to the CBO, in the short term,

TABLE 6.2

Noncitizens' eligibility for federal programs

	LPRs, refugees, and people granted asylum	Temporary residents	Unauthorized residents[a]
Health care for low-income people			
Medicaid	Only emergency services for the first five years, with some state exceptions for children and pregnant women during those first five years	Emergency services	Emergency services
CHIP	Full coverage for qualified aliens after five years, with some state exceptions for fewer than five years	State option for coverage of prenatal care, labor and delivery, and postpartum care	State option for coverage of prenatal care, labor and delivery, and postpartum care
Premium and cost-sharing assistance[b]	Eligible	Eligible	Not eligible
SNAP	LPRs under the age of 18, refugees, and people granted asylum are immediately eligible; other LPRs must wait five years	Not eligible	Not eligible
Social Security	Eligible	Eligible	Not eligible
SSI	Refugees and people granted asylum are eligible on entrance; LPRs must wait five years and have 40 quarters of work credit	Not eligible	Not eligible
Medicare	Eligible	Eligible	Not eligible
Pell grants and federal student loans	Eligible, no five year-wait	Not eligible	Not eligible
Unemployment insurance	Eligible	Temporary residents with work authorization only	Not eligible
Refundable tax credits	Eligible	Depends on visa, home country, and amount of time in the United States	To receive, a taxpayer must generally file his or her tax return and have either a Social Security number or an ITIN.

LPR = lawful permanent resident; CHIP = Children's Health Insurance Program; SNAP = Supplemental Nutrition Assistance Program; SSI = Supplemental Security Income; ITIN = individual taxpayer identification number.

[a]Formerly unauthorized residents who receive approval for "deferred action"—that is, any removal proceedings initiated against them are delayed for a period of time—are considered lawfully present without legal status. They are eligible to receive Medicare and Social Security benefits, assuming they meet the programs' requirements. In addition, unauthorized residents who are approved for deferred action and receive work authorization have Social Security numbers and therefore can claim the earned income tax credit, if they qualify.
[b]Part of the Affordable Care Act, which comprises the Patient Protection and Affordable Care Act (Public Law 111-148) and the health care provisions of the Health Care and Reconciliation Act of 2010 (P.L. 111-152), as affected by subsequent judicial decisions, statutory changes, and administrative actions.
Notes: In addition to those eligibility requirements stated in the table, people must also meet the usual eligibility requirements for each program.

SOURCE: "Table 1. Noncitizens' Eligibility for Federal Programs," in *How Changes in Immigration Policy Might Affect the Federal Budget*, Congressional Budget Office, January 2015, https://www.cbo.gov/sites/default/files/cbofiles/attachments/49868-Immigration.pdf (accessed January 15, 2015)

increased levels of immigration primarily result in increases in health spending. In the long term, Social Security and Medicare (which are generally available to qualifying individuals aged 65 years and older) represent the chief area of increased costs.

In strict numerical terms, immigrants who have legal authorization to be in the country are theoretically more likely to receive government assistance than are natives, because immigrants have lower median incomes. This is one of the main arguments of those who seek to curtail immigration, especially immigration from low-income countries. For example, Steven A. Camarota of the right-leaning Center for Immigration Studies (CIS) is a leading proponent of this view. In *Immigrants in the United States: A Profile of America's Foreign-Born Population* (August 2012, http://www.cis.org/sites/cis.org/files/articles/2012/immigrants-in-the-united-states-2012.pdf), Camarota maintains that because many immigrants are lacking in education, their financial status lags behind that of the native-born population and exerts a drag on the government. His research suggests that, although immigrants eventually tend to catch up with

their U.S.-born counterparts in financial status, for their first 20 years or more in the United States they are more likely than native-born people to live near or below the poverty line, be among the lowest-earning American workers, and use welfare.

Other analysts maintain that these sorts of comparisons are misleading. According to Marshall Fitz, Philip E. Wolgin, and Patrick Oakford of the left-leaning Center for American Progress, in "Immigrants Are Makers, Not Takers" (February 8, 2013, http://www.americanprogress.org/issues/immigration/news/2013/02/08/52377/immigrants-are-makers-not-takers), comparing any one immigrant household to any one native-born household is equivalent to comparing the socioeconomic status of someone in a developing country to the socioeconomic status of someone in the United States. Immigrants overcome many obstacles on the way to catching up with those who are native born, and the length of time spent adapting to life in the United States is as likely to be a measure of those obstacles as it is to be a measure of immigrants' characteristics. Thus, the researchers maintain that in

FIGURE 6.1

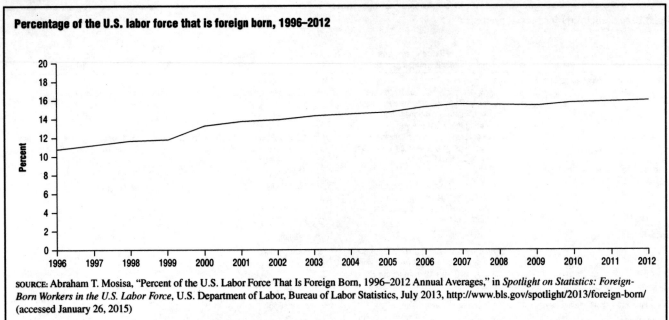

Percentage of the U.S. labor force that is foreign born, 1996–2012

SOURCE: Abraham T. Mosisa, "Percent of the U.S. Labor Force That Is Foreign Born, 1996–2012 Annual Averages," in *Spotlight on Statistics: Foreign-Born Workers in the U.S. Labor Force*, U.S. Department of Labor, Bureau of Labor Statistics, July 2013, http://www.bls.gov/spotlight/2013/foreign-born/ (accessed January 26, 2015)

assessing the economic characteristics of immigrants, the only fair comparison is between immigrants and native-born people at the same level of income. When immigrants and natives of the same income levels are compared, immigrants are not more likely than natives to exert a burden on the government.

The Immigration Policy Center, a nonpartisan research firm that is devoted to fostering fact-based policies on immigration, suggests that a large body of research finds that immigrants contribute more to state and local tax revenues than they receive in the form of services. In "Assessing the Economic Impact of Immigration at the State and Local Level" (April 13, 2010, http://www.immigrationpolicy.org/just-facts/assessing-economic-impact-immigration-state-and-local-level), the Immigration Policy Center provides information about 29 individual studies conducted at the state and local levels during the first decade of the 21st century. All of the cited studies found that immigrants contribute more benefits than costs to state and local governments.

Employment and Wages

Immigrants' impact on the labor force is one of the most contentious subjects in the wider immigration debate. As Figure 2.1 in Chapter 2 shows, the percentage of foreign-born residents within the total U.S. population increased rapidly between 1990 and 2010, from 7.9% to 12.9%. The foreign-born population, which includes both noncitizens and naturalized citizens, has higher labor force participation rates than the U.S.-born population. Thus, immigrants account for an even larger share of the workforce than of the total population, and the number of immigrant workers has steadily grown. In 1996 immigrants represented just under 11% of the U.S. labor force,

and in 2012 immigrants represented approximately 16% of the labor force. (See Figure 6.1.)

Many ordinary citizens and some analysts believe these immigrant gains come at the expense of native-born workers. For example, in "All Employment Growth since 2000 Went to Immigrants" (June 2014, http://cis.org/sites/cis.org/files/camarota-employment_0.pdf), Camarota and Karen Zeigler of the CIS argue that between 2000 and 2014 native-born Americans were responsible for two-thirds of all growth in the working-age population, but that all of the net increase in jobs during this period went to the foreign-born population (including those with and without work authorization). Thus, the total number of employed native-born residents had not increased since 2000 in spite of a significant increase in the number of working-age people from that group, whereas the total number of employed foreign-born residents had risen by 5.7 million. Camarota and Zeigler interpret these facts as evidence that immigrants compete with natives for jobs and that increases in the immigrant population result in job losses for natives.

Economists across the political spectrum typically dismiss such ways of quantifying immigrants' effects on the labor market. For example, Alex Nowrasteh of the right-leaning Cato Institute notes in "Immigration's Real Impact on Wages and Employment" (September 15, 2014, http://www.cato.org/blog/immigrations-real-impact-wages-employment) that statistics such as those presented by the CIS suggest that if those immigrants who currently hold jobs in the United States were not present in the country, more native-born people would be employed. This is a fallacy from the vantage point of economic theory, because it assumes that an economy is equivalent to a "fixed pie" and that there are a limited number of pieces of the pie to be distributed among different groups. In fact, there is no set limit to the number of potential pie pieces in the labor market or any other realm of the economy. Economies are dynamic; when one group finds employment and then its members spend the money they make, the economy as a whole grows. Thus, there are more pieces of the pie than there would be in the absence of immigrant workers. According to Nowrasteh, "A large body of academic economic research has found that immigration has a relatively small effect on U.S-born American wages and their employment prospects....Nowhere will you find a tradeoff where one additional immigrant means that one American loses a job in the economy."

The consensus view among economists that immigrant workers do not exert significant downward pressure on the wages of U.S.-born workers is borne out by the CBO in *The Economic Impact of S.744, the Border Security, Economic Opportunity, and Immigration Modernization Act* (June 2013, https://www.cbo.gov/sites/default/files/44346-Immigration.pdf). The agency notes that most economists approach the issue of immigration's impact on wages by analyzing the degree to which immigrants are able to substitute for U.S.-born workers. If newly arrived immigrants proved to be exact substitutes for U.S.-born workers (in terms of education, job skills, productivity, and other characteristics), then they likely would exert significant downward pressure on wages by increasing the supply of labor. However, immigrants are imperfect substitutes for U.S.-born workers. Most immigrants in the labor force compete either with high-skilled workers or with workers at the lower end of the economic ladder. The CBO's survey of existing research indicates that increases in immigration lower wages very slightly for U.S.-born workers without a high school diploma (by 0.3%) and for workers with a college degree or better (by 0.1%). The wages of U.S.-born high school graduates show no change in response to immigration, and the wages of U.S.-born workers with some college education but without a bachelor's degree increase very slightly (by 0.1%).

Economic Growth

Douglas Holtz-Eakin of the American Action Forum, a right-leaning nonprofit group that focuses on economic growth, makes the economic case for increased immigration in "Immigration Reform, Economic Growth, and the Fiscal Challenge" (April 2013, http://americanactionforum.org/sites/default/files/Immigration%20and%20the%20Economy%20and%20Budget.pdf). He starts by noting the basic premises of his argument: "The building blocks of economic growth are not complex. Total GDP [gross domestic product; the total value of all goods and services produced in the country during a given period] stems from the total number of workers and the average

output per worker, or productivity. The pace of overall population growth will raise the number of workers, and thus raise GDP. In addition, the structure of the population—by age, gender, and education—can influence the fraction of the population at work. Growth in the labor force participation rate can, in turn, raise the rate of GDP above the rate of population growth."

Thus, Holtz-Eakin posits, immigration drives population growth, and population growth drives economic growth. The type of population growth that comes from immigration, he further argues, is of particular importance in the United States, given trends in birth and fertility rates. As Table 6.1 shows, in 2012 the fertility rate for female citizens aged 15 to 49 years was 1.8, or below the "replacement rate" of 2.1 (the number of children that women must have, on average, for the population to remain at its current level). Without some other source of population growth, a nationwide fertility rate of 1.8 will lead to a decline in U.S. population over time. When the population declines, Holtz-Eakin explains, demand for goods and services declines, and the economy shrinks, increasing the ranks of the unemployed. As the number of unemployed increases, the birthrate declines because people are less capable of supporting children.

The structure of U.S. government benefits poses an additional challenge. The programs that benefit the elderly—Social Security and Medicare—are funded through the tax contributions of working-age people. The U.S. population was aging rapidly in the 21st century, as the largest generational cohort in history, the baby boomers (people born between 1946 and 1964), began reaching retirement age amid expectations of ever-increasing life spans. In other words, there was a growing population of elderly people who were likely to live longer after retirement than their predecessors, and there was a shrinking population of younger people to pay for their Social Security and Medicare benefits.

Many experts look to immigrants to meet the country's need for a large enough working-age population to stabilize these federal programs and promote long-term economic growth. Immigrants contribute to the population both through their arrival and through having children once they are in the country. Although the fertility rate for noncitizens has declined over time, in 2012 it remained above the replacement rate, at 2.3. (See Table 6.1.) Gretchen Livingston and D'Vera Cohn of the Pew Research Center note in "U.S. Birth Rate Falls to a Record Low; Decline Is Greatest among Immigrants" (November 29, 2012, http://www.pewsocialtrends.org/2012/11/29/u-s-birth-rate-falls-to-a-record-low-decline-is-greatest-among-immigrants) that foreign-born women account for a disproportionate share of population growth. In 2010 foreign-born women represented 17% of the total population of women aged 15 to 44 years, but they accounted for 23% of all births. Besides having higher fertility rates, noncitizens were more likely than citizens to be of working age. (See Table 6.1.) This is expected to become increasingly important to economic productivity as the U.S.-born population ages and leaves the labor force in increasing numbers.

Immigrants also have a high rate of entrepreneurship. In *The Economic Benefits of Fixing Our Broken Immigration System* (July 2013, http://www.whitehouse.gov/sites/default/files/docs/report.pdf), the White House notes that immigrants' entrepreneurial contributions to the country have been detailed in several independent studies. These include a 2007 report by the Fiscal Policy Institute, which found that small businesses owned by immigrants employed 4.7 million people and had earnings of $776 billion in 2007, as well as a 2012 report by the Partnership for a New American Economy, which found that in 2011 immigrants accounted for 12.9% of the population but started 28% of all new businesses in the country. As the immigrant population has grown, immigrant entrepreneurship has accelerated rapidly. In 1996 immigrants accounted for 13.7% of all U.S. entrepreneurs and the native born for 86.3%; in 2012 immigrants accounted for 27.1% of entrepreneurs and the native born for 72.9%. (See Figure 6.2.)

Immigrant entrepreneurship rates translate into a major force at the level of small businesses. The Fiscal Policy Institute indicates in "Immigrant 'Main Street' Business Owners Playing an Outsized Role" (January 14, 2015, http://fiscalpolicy.org/immigrant-main-street-business-owners-playing-an-outsized-role) that in 2015 immigrants owned 28% of so-called Main Street businesses, a category that encompasses "retail, food services and accommodation, and neighborhood services such as nail salons, beauty shops, and gas stations." Immigrant entrepreneurs were also among U.S. corporate leaders. According to *Forbes*, in "The World's Billionaires" (2015, http://www.forbes.com/billionaires), a substantial number of U.S.-based billionaires came to the country as immigrants, including:

- Russian-born Sergey Brin (1973–) founded Google with partner Larry Page (1973–). They started the company in a garage after dropping out of graduate school in 1998; the company went public in 2004. In 2015 Brin was the world's 20th-richest person, with a fortune of $30.2 billion.

- George Soros (1930–) was born in Hungary and survived the German occupation of Budapest during World War II (1939–1945). He immigrated to the United States in 1945 and founded the Quantum Fund in 1969. In 2015 his personal fortune was worth $24.2 billion.

- Len Blavatnik (1957–) emigrated from Russia in 1978. After earning a master's degree in business administration at Harvard University, he founded the holding company Access Industries in 1986 and was partly responsible for the merger of the Russian oil company TNK-BP. He was worth $20.2 billion in 2015.

- The Australian-born media giant Rupert Murdoch (1931–) renounced his Australian citizenship and became a U.S. citizen in 1985 because of laws that

FIGURE 6.2

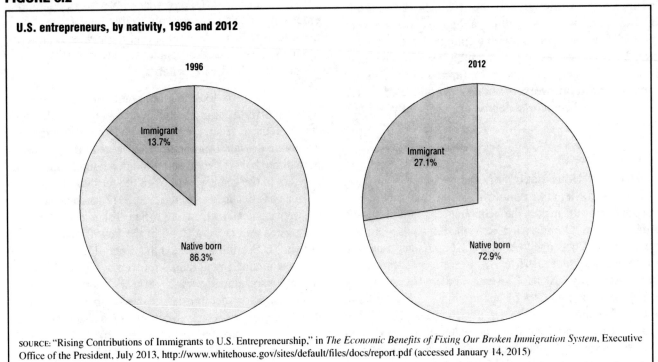

U.S. entrepreneurs, by nativity, 1996 and 2012

SOURCE: "Rising Contributions of Immigrants to U.S. Entrepreneurship," in *The Economic Benefits of Fixing Our Broken Immigration System*, Executive Office of the President, July 2013, http://www.whitehouse.gov/sites/default/files/docs/report.pdf (accessed January 14, 2015) restricted the ownership of U.S. television stations to citizens. In 2015 his personal fortune was $13.9 billion.

- Elon Musk (1971–) was born in South Africa to a Canadian mother and a South African father. He came to the United States in 1995 as a student and became a naturalized citizen in 2002. He founded or cofounded numerous companies, including the payment-processing company PayPal, the private space exploration company SpaceX, and the electric car company Tesla. In 2015 his personal fortune was $12 billion.

- Pierre Omidyar (c. 1967–) was born in France to Iranian immigrant parents. His family immigrated to the United States when he was six years old. He founded an online auction site that in 1997 was renamed eBay, of which he remains chairman. His personal wealth totaled $8 billion in 2015.

Researchers further suggest that the economic benefits of immigration increase in proportion with the extent that immigrants gain legal status and become citizens. In *The Economic Effects of Granting Legal Status and Citizenship to Undocumented Immigrants* (March 2013, http://www.americanprogress.org/wp-content/uploads/2013/03/EconomicEffectsCitizenship-1.pdf), Robert Lynch and Patrick Oakford of the Center for American Progress note that numerous studies show citizens' median incomes are 40% greater (or even higher, depending on the study) than those of noncitizens. (This is consistent with the CBO data presented in Table 6.1.) Immigrants who become naturalized citizens are able to enjoy the same economic and social benefits as the native born, and their earnings rise accordingly. Moreover, immigrants with legal work authorization have been found to make an average hourly wage as much as 28.3% greater than that of unauthorized immigrants. Thus, preventing immigrants from integrating into American life, by denying them work authorization and a pathway to citizenship, all but guarantees that they will remain low-wage workers living on the margins of society. Greater levels of immigrant integration, by contrast, result in greater levels of economic productivity at the individual and the societal level.

ENFORCEMENT COSTS
At the Federal Level

As discussed in Chapter 5, immigration policy at the federal level has focused primarily on enforcement since the last major immigration legislation was passed in 1996. Those federal agencies charged with securing the border and apprehending unauthorized immigrants inside the United States grew dramatically during the 1990s and the following decade, with a particular acceleration of funding levels occurring in the years after the terrorist attacks of September 11, 2001. Enforcement is generally believed to have done comparatively little to slow the numbers of unauthorized immigrants arriving from

Mexico, and indeed, increases in funding corresponded with rapid increases in the population of unauthorized immigrants. Flows of unauthorized immigrants began to slow dramatically as a result of the Great Recession (which lasted from late 2007 to mid-2009), which dimmed employment prospects for both the native born and the foreign born in the years that followed. Although the population of unauthorized immigrants had ceased to grow between 2009 and 2012, funding levels for immigration enforcement continued to increase. These increases were especially noteworthy given the political pressures on most government agencies to cut funding during this period.

As Figure 6.3 shows, a large proportion of the U.S. Department of Homeland Security's (DHS) fiscal year (FY) 2015 budget was devoted specifically to agencies dealing with immigration enforcement. The largest agency

FIGURE 6.3

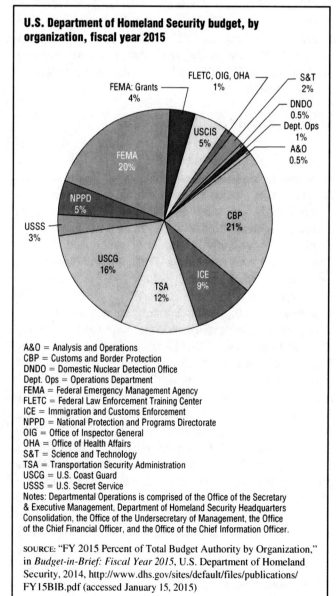

U.S. Department of Homeland Security budget, by organization, fiscal year 2015

A&O = Analysis and Operations
CBP = Customs and Border Protection
DNDO = Domestic Nuclear Detection Office
Dept. Ops = Operations Department
FEMA = Federal Emergency Management Agency
FLETC = Federal Law Enforcement Training Center
ICE = Immigration and Customs Enforcement
NPPD = National Protection and Programs Directorate
OIG = Office of Inspector General
OHA = Office of Health Affairs
S&T = Science and Technology
TSA = Transportation Security Administration
USCG = U.S. Coast Guard
USSS = U.S. Secret Service
Notes: Departmental Operations is comprised of the Office of the Secretary & Executive Management, Department of Homeland Security Headquarters Consolidation, the Office of the Undersecretary of Management, the Office of the Chief Financial Officer, and the Office of the Chief Information Officer.

SOURCE: "FY 2015 Percent of Total Budget Authority by Organization," in *Budget-in-Brief: Fiscal Year 2015*, U.S. Department of Homeland Security, 2014, http://www.dhs.gov/sites/default/files/publications/FY15BIB.pdf (accessed January 15, 2015)

within the DHS by budget allocation was the U.S. Customs and Border Protection (CBP), which received 21% of the total $60.9 billion department budget. The U.S. Immigration and Customs Enforcement (ICE), the other primary federal immigration enforcement agency, was allotted 9% of the total DHS budget. The U.S. Citizenship and Immigration Services, the agency through which all legal immigration occurs, was allotted 5% of the total DHS budget.

Walter A. Ewing of the Immigration Policy Center explains in "The Growth of the U.S. Deportation Machine" (April 9, 2014, http://www.immigrationpolicy.org/just-facts/growth-us-deportation-machine) that CBP's annual budget doubled between FYs 2003 and 2013, growing from $5.9 billion to $11.9 billion, while ICE's annual budget grew 73%, from $3.3 billion to $5.9 billion. Growth in the budget of the U.S. Border Patrol, the unit within the CBP that is responsible for patrolling the border and apprehending unauthorized immigrants who attempt to enter the country, increased by a factor of 10 between FYs 1993 ($363 million) and 2013 ($3.5 billion). According to the DHS, in *Budget-in-Brief: Fiscal Year 2015* (2014, http://www.dhs.gov/sites/default/files/publications/FY15BIB.pdf), the CBP's budget continued to grow in the years that followed, reaching $12.8 billion in FY 2015. ICE's budget declined slightly, to $5.4 billion, in FY 2015.

At the State and Local Levels

States and counties, particularly those on the U.S.-Mexican border, incur substantial costs for law enforcement related to unauthorized immigrants. Under the U.S. Department of Justice's State Criminal Alien Assistance Program (SCAAP), states and counties are partially reimbursed for incarceration expenses related to unauthorized immigrants who commit felonies or two misdemeanors. The program was created in 1995, and funding levels have fluctuated dramatically. In "The State Criminal Alien Assistance Program (SCAAP)" (April 13, 2013, http://www.ncsl.org/research/immigration/state-criminal-alien-assistance-program.aspx), the National Conference of State Legislatures (NCSL) indicates that funding for SCAAP ranged from $130 million in FY 1995 to $565 million in FY 2002, before settling at a level of approximately $400 million between FYs 2006 and 2009. SCAAP funding fell to $330 million in FY 2010, and continued to fall during FYs 2011 through 2013, from $273 million in 2011 to $238 million in 2013. In his annual budgets for FYs 2014 and 2015, President Obama proposed to defund the program entirely. The Department of Justice's Office of Justice Programs notes in *FY 2015 Performance Budget* (March 2014, http://www.justice.gov/sites/default/files/jmd/legacy/2014/02/12/ojp-justification.pdf) that the goals of the program were better served by other federal programs to fund state and county cooperation with ICE, which allowed grantees more flexibility in how they allocated funds. Congress restored funding for the program to $180 million in FY 2014 and to $185 million in FY 2015.

In a February 2015 letter to the majority and minority leaders of the U.S. House of Representatives (http://www.ncsl.org/documents/statefed/House_Immigration_EnforcementLetterSAFE.pdf), the NCSL, the U.S. Conference of Mayors, the National Association of Counties, and the National League of Cities protested against legislation that shifted certain types of immigration law enforcement to states and localities. The leaders of these organizations maintained that under SCAAP states and localities were already being reimbursed for immigration-related expenses at a rate of only 18 cents per dollar. In "Congress Cuts Funds for Jailing Undocumented Criminals" (January 16, 2014, http://www.usatoday.com/story/news/politics/2014/01/16/undocumented-immigrant-incarceration/4536453), Erin Kelly quotes Susan Frederick of the NCSL, who explained the standoff between states/localities and the federal government: "The way [Congress has] rationalized it is by saying they just don't have enough money to go around and that this program is no more or less important than other programs that are being cut. But states are doing everyone a favor by keeping convicted criminals off the streets and keeping our communities safe. They're supposed to get reimbursed for those efforts."

The Projected Costs of More Rigorous Enforcement

In spite of the rapid increases in funding and staffing of the CBP and ICE under both Republican and Democratic presidential administrations, as well as rising levels of deportation, many people concerned with the costs imposed by unauthorized immigrants suggest the federal government should further emphasize apprehension and deportation. They also cite the unfairness of allowing unauthorized immigrants to stay and work in the United States while other foreign nationals wait diligently for visas to enter the country legally. Indeed, by allowing unauthorized immigrants to stay in the country rather than initiating a project of actively locating and deporting everyone who is in the country illegally, the federal government has in effect chosen not to enforce the letter of current immigration law. Some immigration hard-liners, including many members of Congress, insist that the only defensible policy toward unauthorized immigrants is to apprehend and deport them.

Laura Collins and Ben Gitis of the American Action Forum calculate in "The Budgetary and Economic Costs of Addressing Unauthorized Immigration: Alternative Strategies" (March 2015, http://americanactionforum.org/uploads/files/research/The_Budgetary_and_Economic_Costs_of_Addressing_Unauthorized_Immigration.pdf) what it would cost the United States to enforce current immigration law fully and deport the estimated 11.2 million unauthorized immigrants who were in the country as of 2012.

They estimate that announcement of such a policy might prompt up to 20% of the unauthorized population to leave the country on their own and that the DHS would then be responsible for removing approximately 9 million individuals by force. The researchers explain that ICE has the capacity to remove a maximum of 400,000 unauthorized immigrants per year; therefore, the removal of 9 million people would take approximately 20 years. Removal of each individual unauthorized immigrant requires four steps: apprehension, detention, legal processing, and transportation. Based on the current costs to the government of completing this process, Collins and Gitis estimate total costs over 20 years at between $400 billion and $600 billion. Costs would not be limited to the government, however. As noted earlier, unauthorized immigrants are a key part of the U.S. labor force. Removing all unauthorized immigrants would reduce the size of the labor force by just over 11 million people, or 6.4%. This would result in a $1.6 trillion (5.7%) reduction in the GDP.

Collins and Gitis maintain that their estimates should be considered conservative because they do not attempt to calculate the costs of expanding the government's infrastructure, such as the construction costs for building new prisons and court rooms to handle the expanded deportation program. They are also unable to calculate the losses to the labor market that would result from the departure of a substantial number of legal immigrants who have unauthorized family members. Many of these legal immigrants would likely choose to leave the country rather than remain permanently separated from family members, if those family members were certain to be targeted for deportation.

EDUCATION COSTS

In *Plyler v. Doe* (457 U.S. 202 [1982]), the U.S. Supreme Court overturned a Texas law that allowed local school systems to deny public education to children who had entered the country illegally. In its 5–4 ruling, the court maintained that the Texas law violated the 14th Amendment and that public schools have an obligation to educate all children regardless of their immigration status. Because of this, and because extra resources are often necessary to educate children whose first language is not English, educational spending by state and local governments represents by far the largest outlay of funds needed to accommodate the large immigrant population in the United States.

However, no consensus exists as to the price tag for educating the children of immigrants across the United States. The CBO notes in *The Impact of Unauthorized Immigrants on the Budgets of State and Local Governments* (December 2007, http://www.cbo.gov/sites/default/files/12-6-immigration.pdf), the most recent reliable report on this subject as of April 2015, that a number of factors make it difficult to estimate the aggregate level of

state and local spending on immigrants and to compare spending in one state or locality with spending in another. Among these factors are inconsistent data sources across state and local jurisdictions, the wide variance in funding mechanisms and tax collections among different states and municipalities, and the disproportionate concentration of immigrants in certain states and cities, which makes statistical sampling difficult at the national level. Most studies, as the CBO reports, have focused on the effect of unauthorized immigrants and their children on state educational budgets.

Among the state-level data cited by the CBO are studies that focus on education spending in Minnesota and New Mexico during the 2003–04 school year. In that year, state and local governments in Minnesota spent an estimated $79 million to $118 million on education for children who were unauthorized immigrants, as well as approximately $39 million on education for children with birthright citizenship whose parents were unauthorized. The combined amount spent to educate unauthorized immigrants and the children of unauthorized immigrants that year represented less than 3% of the $8 billion in state and local funds spent on public education. Minnesota, however, was experiencing rapid increases in its immigrant population at the time, which can create significant budgetary strain even when the overall spending amount concerned is comparatively small. Between 2000 and 2004 the state's total immigrant student population grew from 9,000 to approximately 16,000. Of the 16,000 immigrant students, between 9,400 and 14,000 were believed to be unauthorized.

The New Mexico study painted a similar portrait of state-level educational spending. In 2003–04 New Mexico had approximately 9,200 unauthorized immigrant students, on whom state and local governments spent an estimated $67 million. This represented approximately 2% of the $3 billion in state and local funds spent on public education.

Besides being required to educate children regardless of their immigration status, state school systems are required to make accommodations for students whose English-language proficiency is limited. As Figure 6.4 shows, the percentage of the foreign-born population that spoke a language other than English at home increased substantially between 1980 and 2010. In 1980, 70.2% of foreign-born U.S. residents over the age of five years spoke a language other than English at home; by 2010, 84.7% spoke a language other than English at home. These percentage increases appeared to have flattened by 2012, when 84.6% of the over-five foreign-born population spoke a language other than English at home. According to Grace Kena et al., in *The Condition of Education 2014* (May 2014, http://nces.ed.gov/pubs2014/2014083.pdf), 9.1% of public school students nationwide were English language

FIGURE 6.4

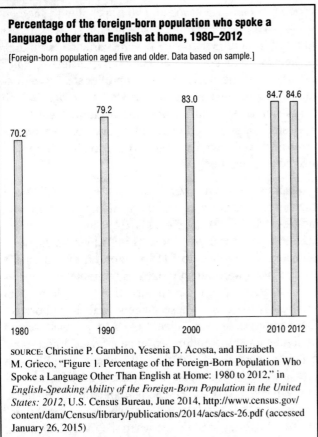

Percentage of the foreign-born population who spoke a language other than English at home, 1980–2012

[Foreign-born population aged five and older. Data based on sample.]

SOURCE: Christine P. Gambino, Yesenia D. Acosta, and Elizabeth M. Grieco, "Figure 1. Percentage of the Foreign-Born Population Who Spoke a Language Other Than English at Home: 1980 to 2012," in *English-Speaking Ability of the Foreign-Born Population in the United States: 2012*, U.S. Census Bureau, June 2014, http://www.census.gov/content/dam/Census/library/publications/2014/acs/acs-26.pdf (accessed January 26, 2015)

FIGURE 6.5

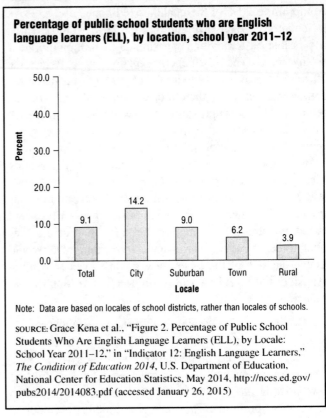

Percentage of public school students who are English language learners (ELL), by location, school year 2011–12

Note: Data are based on locales of school districts, rather than locales of schools.

SOURCE: Grace Kena et al., "Figure 2. Percentage of Public School Students Who Are English Language Learners (ELL), by Locale: School Year 2011–12," in "Indicator 12: English Language Learners," *The Condition of Education 2014*, U.S. Department of Education, National Center for Education Statistics, May 2014, http://nces.ed.gov/pubs2014/2014083.pdf (accessed January 26, 2015)

learners (ELLs) who required special instruction to achieve proficiency in the language. (See Figure 6.5.) The percentage of ELLs was much higher in public schools located in cities (14.2%) than in those located in suburbs (9%), towns (6.2%), or rural areas (3.9%).

Under the terms of the Elementary and Secondary Education Act of 1965, as amended numerous times in subsequent decades, school districts receive federal funds to create and maintain programs to meet the needs of children with limited English proficiency. The U.S. Department of Education (DOE) provides grants to states according to the numbers of English learners in their schools. In "Supporting English Learners" (March 2014, http://www2.ed.gov/about/overview/budget/budget15/crosscuttingissues/englishlearners.pdf), the DOE indicates that it requested $723 million to fund these grants in FY 2015. Other funding for English learners in public schools came from a variety of other DOE programs, including $506 million to the School Improvement Grants Program to aid the country's lowest-performing schools. Approximately 25% of the students in schools receiving these grants were English learners.

THE PROJECTED BENEFITS OF IMMIGRATION REFORM

As noted throughout this book, leaders in both the Democratic and Republican Parties have advocated for comprehensive immigration reform legislation throughout the 21st century. Although many economists have estimated the economic effects of possible reform proposals, costs and benefits depend to a large degree on the specific nature of those proposals. For example, a proposal to expand employment-based visas would generally be expected to increase the size of the labor market and thus to result in GDP gains; however, the size of those gains would be highly dependent on the number of visas made available and the allocation of those visas among different categories of workers.

As of April 2015, the most recent attempt to pass immigration reform legislation was U.S. Senate Bill 744 (S.744), the Border Security, Economic Opportunity, and Immigration Modernization Act of 2013. Cowritten by the so-called Gang of Eight (four Democratic senators and four Republican senators), the bill proposed to:

- Change the family and employment-based visa categories by creating a new class of worker visas that could be expanded based on employer demand

- Overhaul the deportation process so that immigrants would be guaranteed due process protections, the asylum process would be easier to navigate, and judges would have more discretion to make removal decisions on a case-by-case basis

- Create a registry for unauthorized immigrants and allow those registered to apply for legal residency

- Guarantee border security through measures such as the completion of a minimum amount of fencing, a dramatic increase in the number of border patrol agents, and national implementation of the E-Verify system for verifying employees' immigration status

S.744 passed the Senate by a vote of 68–32, but it never reached the floor of the House of Representatives for a vote. Although it was believed that a majority of representatives were prepared to pass the bill (or a similar bill), opposition from the most conservative members of the Republican majority scuttled the effort.

S.744 remains a plausible template for a future immigration reform bill, and numerous economists have analyzed its provisions and projected its impact. The Obama administration, which lobbied unsuccessfully for the bill's passage, makes the case for the bill in *Economic Benefits of Fixing Our Broken Immigration System*, based primarily on the nonpartisan findings of the CBO. In the administration's view, the economic benefits of the bill far outweighed the costs, and passage would bring increases in the GDP, the labor force, productivity, wages, and protections for workers; reduce the federal deficit and the federal debt and make Social Security more solvent; expand entrepreneurship; and support growth in the housing market, the tourism industry, and agriculture. (See Table 6.3.)

In *Economic Impact of S.744, the Border Security, Economic Opportunity, and Immigration Modernization Act*, which analyzed S.744 as it stood prior to passage by the Senate, the CBO concluded that implementation of the bill's provisions would significantly increase the GDP.

TABLE 6.3

Costs of maintaining immigration status quo vs. benefits of comprehensive immigration reform proposed by U.S. Senate Bill S.744

	Costs of maintaining the status quo		Benefits of comprehensive immigration reform
Gross domestic product	U.S. economy does not benefit from higher growth, larger workforce, more innovators, entrepreneurs and capital investment, and increased productivity—and domestic production is lower as a result	+	Economy strengthened as U.S. benefits from a larger labor force, higher productivity, and stronger technology, tourism, hospitality, agriculture, and housing industries. In 2033, US economy is 5.4 percent larger than under status quo
Labor force participation	Labor force participation continues to decline as the baby boom generation retires	+	Higher labor force participation than without immigration reform as new working-age immigrants participate in the labor force at a higher rate
Productivity	U.S. workers and capital do not benefit from productivity gains associated with commonsense immigration reform	+	Productivity of labor and capital increases by 1 percent in 2033
Wages	Because workers do not benefit from productivity gains, average wages are lower: a cost of about $250 annually for the median household by 2033 (in today's dollars)	+	Largely as a result of higher productivity, real wages will rise by 0.5 percent in 2033 relative to current law—the equivalent of about an annual $250 increase today for a median household
Protections for U.S. workers	American workers do not benefit from new protections that help ensure immigrants complement the American workforce	+	Employers must recruit U.S. workers for high-skilled occupations; enhanced portability and wage protections for temporary workers; new safeguards against abuses in recruiting foreign labor
Federal deficits	Federal budget does not benefit from additional taxes paid by new and legalizing immigrants—and deficits are nearly $850 billion higher as a result	+	Over the next twenty years, federal deficits are reduced by nearly $850 billion
Federal debt	By 2023, federal debt as a share of the economy is 3 percentage points higher than it would be under immigration reform	+	U.S. debt falls by 3 percentage points as a share of the economy by 2023, compared to current law
Social Security	Social Security does not benefit from new young and healthier workers balancing out retirement of the Baby Boomer generation	+	Extends the solvency of the Social Security Trust Fund by two years and reduces the 75-year shortfall by nearly half a trillion dollars
Entrepreneurship	Talented entrepreneurs are prevented from starting the next set of Fortune 500 companies in the U.S. and patenting new technologies that fuel innovation and provide Americans with well-paying jobs	+	Entrepreneurial immigrants are eligible for newly created temporary and permanent visas if they demonstrate that they have ideas that attract investment and establish businesses that create jobs
Housing	Housing market does not benefit from higher housing demand, delaying the economic revitalization of communities hit hardest by the recession	+	Housing market recovery is strengthened through stronger demand and higher prices for homes in neighborhoods hardest hit by the recession
Tourism and hospitality	U.S. is unprepared to take advantage of explosive growth in tourism from emerging economies, resulting in fewer tourism and hospitality jobs	+	Provisions in the Senate bill position—including the Visa Waiver Program, new CBP officers, and permanent authorization of the Corporation for Travel Promotion—provide significant boost to these sectors
Agriculture	U.S. agriculture continues to be affected by unpredictable and unstable worker flows, resulting in deportations, employer fines and work stoppages	+	U.S. agricultural output and exports grow over time—supporting a key engine of American economic growth

SOURCE: "Costs of Maintaining the Status Quo, Benefits of Comprehensive Immigration Reform," in *The Economic Benefits of Fixing Our Broken Immigration System*, Executive Office of the President, July 2013, http://www.whitehouse.gov/sites/default/files/docs/report.pdf (accessed January 14, 2015)

Relative to the CBO's GDP projections based on current immigration law, S.744 was expected to increase the GDP 3.3% by 2023 and 5.4% by 2033. (See Figure 6.6.) According to the CBO, the economic gains would be driven by the population boost, which would be one of the law's main immediate results. The agency expected S.744 would add approximately 10 million people to the U.S. population by 2023 and 16 million by 2033. Besides an enlarged population, which results in increased levels of demand for goods and services and thereby drives job creation, passage of the law was expected to increase economic output because of the foreign-born population's higher rate of labor force participation relative to the native born. The CBO did expect an initial rise in the unemployment rate as temporary mismatches between workers' skills and employers' needs were being resolved. Likewise, for about 12 years workers' average wages would fall slightly (by less than 0.5%) relative to wages under current law. By 2025, however, average wages would exceed wages under current law because of increased productivity, and by 2033 average wages would be 0.5% higher than they would be in the absence of the law's implementation. (See Figure 6.7.)

The CBO conducted further analyses of the economic effects of S.744 following its passage in the Senate, during the course of which several changes to the legislation were made. All of the CBO's projections affirmed that passage of S.744 would improve the federal government's fiscal standing. A synthesis of the CBO's projections presented in the White House's *The Economic Benefits of Fixing Our Broken Immigration System* shows that the new tax revenues generated by economic growth and an expanded pool of taxpaying workers was expected to outweigh the costs of implementing the law, reducing federal budget deficits (the difference between

FIGURE 6.6

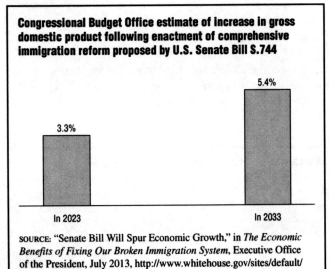

Congressional Budget Office estimate of increase in gross domestic product following enactment of comprehensive immigration reform proposed by U.S. Senate Bill S.744

SOURCE: "Senate Bill Will Spur Economic Growth," in *The Economic Benefits of Fixing Our Broken Immigration System*, Executive Office of the President, July 2013, http://www.whitehouse.gov/sites/default/files/docs/report.pdf (accessed January 14, 2015)

FIGURE 6.7

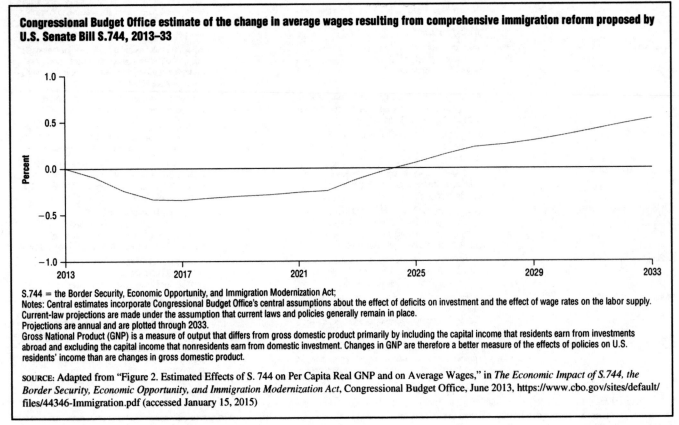

Congressional Budget Office estimate of the change in average wages resulting from comprehensive immigration reform proposed by U.S. Senate Bill S.744, 2013–33

S.744 = the Border Security, Economic Opportunity, and Immigration Modernization Act;
Notes: Central estimates incorporate Congressional Budget Office's central assumptions about the effect of deficits on investment and the effect of wage rates on the labor supply.
Current-law projections are made under the assumption that current laws and policies generally remain in place.
Projections are annual and are plotted through 2033.
Gross National Product (GNP) is a measure of output that differs from gross domestic product primarily by including the capital income that residents earn from investments abroad and excluding the capital income that nonresidents earn from domestic investment. Changes in GNP are therefore a better measure of the effects of policies on U.S. residents' income than are changes in gross domestic product.

SOURCE: Adapted from "Figure 2. Estimated Effects of S. 744 on Per Capita Real GNP and on Average Wages," in *The Economic Impact of S.744, the Border Security, Economic Opportunity, and Immigration Modernization Act*, Congressional Budget Office, June 2013, https://www.cbo.gov/sites/default/files/44346-Immigration.pdf (accessed January 15, 2015)

FIGURE 6.8

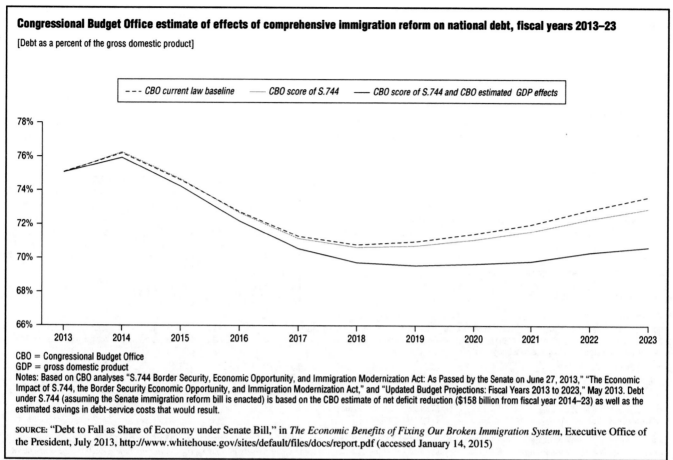

Congressional Budget Office estimate of effects of comprehensive immigration reform on national debt, fiscal years 2013–23

[Debt as a percent of the gross domestic product]

CBO = Congressional Budget Office

GDP = gross domestic product

Notes: Based on CBO analyses "S.744 Border Security, Economic Opportunity, and Immigration Modernization Act: As Passed by the Senate on June 27, 2013," "The Economic Impact of S.744, the Border Security Economic Opportunity, and Immigration Modernization Act," and "Updated Budget Projections: Fiscal Years 2013 to 2023," May 2013. Debt under S.744 (assuming the Senate immigration reform bill is enacted) is based on the CBO estimate of net deficit reduction ($158 billion from fiscal year 2014–23) as well as the estimated savings in debt-service costs that would result.

SOURCE: "Debt to Fall as Share of Economy under Senate Bill," in *The Economic Benefits of Fixing Our Broken Immigration System*, Executive Office of the President, July 2013, http://www.whitehouse.gov/sites/default/files/docs/report.pdf (accessed January 14, 2015)

the amount of money the government spends versus the amount it receives in a given year) $158 billion by 2023 and $700 billion by 2033. These lower deficits would in turn reduce the U.S. government's debt (the cumulative value of all prior budget deficits over the country's history) as a share of GDP by around four percentage points. (See Figure 6.8.)

In a letter to Senator Patrick Leahy (1940–; D-VT; July 3, 2013, https://www.cbo.gov/sites/default/files/s744aspassed.pdf) following the bill's Senate passage, the CBO provides details about the bill's impact on "off-budget" revenue increases and deficits. In federal budgetary parlance, off-budget refers to those government expenses that are not subject to the yearly budgeting process, during which spending on individual programs is often modified as the president and Congress come to an agreement on the coming year's fiscal priorities. Over time, fewer and fewer government expenses have remained off-budget. The only major program that remained off-budget in the 21st century was Social Security, whose trust fund was deemed too important to be subject to the yearly demands of the budgeting process.

Thus, in Table 6.4 and Table 6.5, the rows providing data for off-budget revenues and deficits refer to Social

Security revenues (receipts derived from workers' tax payments) and deficits (the difference between yearly revenues and the amount paid out in benefits). Although both on-budget and Social Security revenues were expected to increase markedly as a result of the law's provisions during the first 10 years, the Social Security deficit was expected to fall dramatically (by $209.8 billion) as a result of the law. (See Table 6.4.) This decrease in the Social Security deficit was expected to accelerate in the second decade after the law's passage. Between 2024 and 2033 S.744 was expected to generate $575 billion in savings for the program. (See Table 6.5.)

Groups such as the CIS and the Federation for American Immigration Reform, both of which oppose any increase in immigration or any path to legal status for the unauthorized population, objected to the CBO's scoring of S.744, believing the agency's projections of economic and budgetary benefits were based on mistaken assumptions. However, neither organization produced a competing set of economic projections, and their criticisms did not measurably affect expert opinions on the issue. Meanwhile, the CBO projections confirmed many earlier economic studies, including Holtz-Eakin's "Immigration Reform, Economic Growth, and the Fiscal Challenge" and Raúl Hinojosa-Ojeda's

TABLE 6.4

Congressional Budget Office estimate of budgetary effects of comprehensive immigration reform proposed by U.S. Senate Bill S.744, 2014–23

	By fiscal year, in billions of dollars											
	2014	**2015**	**2016**	**2017**	**2018**	**2019**	**2020**	**2021**	**2022**	**2023**	**2014–2018**	**2014–2023**
Changes in direct spending												
Estimated outlays	7.6	11.2	18.1	23.9	28.2	29.1	35.2	40.8	48.3	55.7	89.0	298.1
On-budget	7.6	11.2	18.1	23.8	28.2	28.9	35.0	40.4	47.8	55.0	88.9	296.0
Off-budget	0	*	*	*	0.1	0.1	0.2	0.3	0.5	0.7	0.1	2.1
Changes in revenues												
Estimated revenues	2.1	11.5	27.9	39.0	44.8	47.4	54.8	64.4	77.0	86.8	125.3	455.8
On-budget	1.6	6.5	13.5	19.3	22.7	23.6	28.9	35.4	43.0	49.4	63.7	244.0
Off-budget	0.5	5.0	14.4	19.7	22.2	23.8	25.9	29.0	34.0	37.4	61.7	211.9
Net increase or decrease (−) in the deficit from changes in direct spending and revenues												
Estimated impact on deficit	5.5	−0.3	−9.8	−15.1	−16.6	−18.4	−19.7	−23.7	−28.7	−31.1	−36.3	−157.7
On-budget	6.0	4.7	4.6	4.5	5.5	5.4	6.0	5.0	4.8	5.6	25.2	52.1
Off-budget	−0.5	−5.0	−14.4	−19.6	−22.1	−23.7	−25.7	−28.7	−33.5	−36.7	−61.5	−209.8
Changes in spending subject to appropriation												
Estimated authorization level	7.5	1.6	1.3	1.6	1.9	1.6	1.7	1.9	2.0	2.2	13.9	23.4
Estimated outlays	2.6	2.5	2.5	2.2	2.2	2.0	2.0	2.1	2.2	2.4	12.0	22.7

Memorandum:

Estimated deficit impact from changes in direct spending and revenues for S.744 as reported by the judiciary committee. (The memorandum shows the Congressional Budget Office's and Joint Committee of Taxation's estimate of the net increase or decrease (−) in the deficit from changes in direct spending and revenues for the committee-approved version of S.744, as previously reported by the Congressional Budget Office on June 18, 2013.)

	2014	**2015**	**2016**	**2017**	**2018**	**2019**	**2020**	**2021**	**2022**	**2023**	**2014–2018**	**2014–2023**
Estimated impact on the deficit	2.5	−4.7	−14.0	−19.3	−20.5	−21.1	−23.1	−27.6	−33.2	−36.2	−55.9	−197.1
On-budget	3.0	0.3	0.4	0.3	1.7	2.8	2.9	1.4	0.6	0.9	5.7	14.2
Off-budget	−0.5	−5.0	−14.4	−19.7	−22.2	−23.9	−25.9	−29.0	−33.8	−37.1	−61.7	−211.4

*An increase of less than $50 million; components may not sum to totals because of rounding.
Note: The changes in direct spending would affect budget authority by similar amounts.

SOURCE: "Table 1. Summary of Estimated Budgetary Effects of S.744, as Passed by the Senate," in *Letter to the Honorable Patrick J. Leahy Providing an Estimate for S.744, the Border Security, Economic Opportunity, and Immigration Modernization Act, as Passed by the Senate on June 27, 2013*, Congressional Budget Office, July 3, 2013, http://www.cbo.gov/publication/44397 (accessed January 15, 2015)

"The Economic Benefits of Comprehensive Immigration Reform" (*Cato Journal*, vol. 32, no. 1, Winter 2012). As of April 2015, no competing economic interpretation of any mainstream proposal for immigration reform had achieved the same level of expert consensus as the CBO studies of S.744.

TABLE 6.5

Congressional Budget Office estimate of budgetary effects of comprehensive immigration reform proposed by U.S. Senate Bill S.744, 2024–33

	Billions of dollars
	2024–2033
Changes in direct spending	
Low-income health programs	400
Social Security and Medicare	65
Refundable tax credits	265
Supplemental Nutrition Assistance Program	40
Other direct spending	30
Subtotal, direct spending	**800**
On-budget	755
Off-budget	45
Changes in revenues	
Estimated revenues	1,485
On-budget	865
Off-budget	620
Net increase or decrease (−) in the defecit from changes in direct spending and receipts*	
Estimated impact on deficit	−685
On-budget	−110
Off-budget	−575
Memorandum:	
Gross domestic product (billions of dollars)	330,000
Impact on deficit as a percentage of GDP	−0.2

*In addition, CBO estimates that implementing S.744 would have significant effects on discretionary spending. CBO estimates those costs would total $23 billion over the 2014–2023 period and between $75 billion and $80 billion over the 2024–2033 period, including the costs for the additional border patrol agents that were paid for with a direct appropriation during the 2014–2023 period.
CBO = Congressional Budget Office.
GNP = gross national product.
Note: Components may not sum to totals because of rounding.

SOURCE: "Table 2. Estimated Budgetary Impact of S.744, as Passed by the Senate, over the 2024–2033 Period," in *Letter to the Honorable Patrick J. Leahy Providing an Estimate for S.744, the Border Security Economic Opportunity, and Immigration Modernization Act, as Passed by the Senate on June 27, 2013*, Congressional Budget Office, July 3, 2013, http://www.cbo.gov/publication/44397 (accessed January 15, 2015)

CHAPTER 7

IMMIGRATION'S ROLE IN RESHAPING THE UNITED STATES

The large-scale economic effects of immigration discussed in Chapter 6 represent only one facet of immigrants' impact on life in the United States. Indeed, in spite of the economic consensus on the benefits of immigration, the topic remains politically controversial because of other, more visible changes in communities, in the populations of individual states, and in the nation's character. Regardless of whether the immigration system is reformed, immigrants, their children, and their grandchildren are projected to exert an increasing influence on the United States in the decades ahead.

WHAT WILL THE UNITED STATES LOOK LIKE IN 2060?

In December 2014 the U.S. Census Bureau released its annual series of population projections for the coming decades. The 2014 projections maintain that in the period from 2015 to 2060, the U.S. population will become older and more diverse. Although net migration into the United States is expected to slow during this period, the effects of the preceding decades' immigration boom have already laid the groundwork for enormous demographic change. Continuing immigration and the flourishing of second- and third-generation immigrants (people born in the United States but who in many cases still strongly identify with their culture of origin) are expected to transform the United States from a majority-white nation into a nation where no ethnic or racial group constitutes a majority of the population.

Table 7.1 shows the predicted numerical changes in population, the rate of change, and the components of the changes between 2015 and 2060. Falling birthrates, together with medical and technological advances that have extended the average life span considerably, translate into a population that is heavily weighted toward older residents. The Census Bureau predicts that the rate of population loss due to deaths will increasingly approach the rate of population gain due to births, resulting in increasingly smaller annual "natural increases" in the population (the difference between the number of births and the number of deaths). The annual natural increase is expected to fall from 1.4 million in 2015 to a low of 314,000 in 2049, before rising slowly during the 2050s. The increase in net international migration (the difference in the number of immigrants that arrive in the United States and the number of U.S. citizens that migrate to other countries) is projected to be modest over the course of these decades. Accordingly, the growth of the total U.S. population is expected to decelerate, falling steadily from an annual rate of 0.82% in 2015 to a low of 0.45% between 2048 and 2056.

Despite a slowdown in the total U.S. population growth between 2015 and 2060, population growth projections among different ethnic and racial groups will likely vary. (See Table 7.2.) Growth of the non-Hispanic portion of the U.S. population is expected to decline steadily through 2050, from an increase of 6.3 million between 2015 and 2020 to an increase of only 2 million between 2045 and 2050, before growth recovers slightly between 2050 and 2060. Among all subgroups of the non-Hispanic population, growth rates are also expected to vary. The non-Hispanic white population's growth is expected to fall precipitously, from 1 million between 2015 and 2020 to 467,000 between 2020 and 2025, after which declines in the non-Hispanic white population become the norm and grow increasingly large through 2050. By contrast, the non-Hispanic African American population is expected to trend only slightly downward, growing by 1.8 million between 2015 and 2020 and by 1.4 million between 2040 and 2045. The non-Hispanic Asian American population is also expected to grow at a stable rate, ranging from a high of 2.4 million between 2025 and 2030 to a low of 2.2 million in 2055 and 2060.

TABLE 7.1

Population projections and components of population change, 2015–60

[Resident population as of July 1. Numbers in thousands.]

| Year | Population | Numeric change | Percent change | Natural increase | Vital events | | Net international migration* |
					Births	Deaths	
2015	321,369	2,621	0.82	1,380	3,999	2,619	1,241
2016	323,996	2,627	0.82	1,377	4,027	2,650	1,250
2017	326,626	2,630	0.81	1,374	4,055	2,681	1,256
2018	329,256	2,631	0.81	1,369	4,080	2,712	1,262
2019	331,884	2,628	0.80	1,361	4,104	2,743	1,267
2020	334,503	2,619	0.79	1,349	4,125	2,777	1,271
2021	337,109	2,606	0.78	1,331	4,142	2,811	1,275
2022	339,698	2,589	0.77	1,307	4,155	2,848	1,282
2023	342,267	2,569	0.76	1,279	4,165	2,887	1,291
2024	344,814	2,547	0.74	1,246	4,174	2,927	1,301
2025	347,335	2,521	0.73	1,210	4,181	2,971	1,310
2026	349,826	2,491	0.72	1,171	4,187	3,016	1,320
2027	352,281	2,456	0.70	1,127	4,191	3,064	1,329
2028	354,698	2,417	0.69	1,079	4,194	3,115	1,338
2029	357,073	2,374	0.67	1,028	4,196	3,168	1,347
2030	359,402	2,329	0.65	974	4,198	3,224	1,355
2031	361,685	2,283	0.64	919	4,200	3,281	1,363
2032	363,920	2,235	0.62	864	4,203	3,339	1,371
2033	366,106	2,187	0.60	808	4,207	3,399	1,379
2034	368,246	2,139	0.58	753	4,212	3,459	1,386
2035	370,338	2,093	0.57	699	4,219	3,520	1,394
2036	372,390	2,052	0.55	651	4,227	3,576	1,401
2037	374,401	2,012	0.54	604	4,235	3,631	1,407
2038	376,375	1,974	0.53	560	4,245	3,685	1,414
2039	378,313	1,938	0.51	518	4,255	3,737	1,420
2040	380,219	1,906	0.50	479	4,266	3,787	1,426
2041	382,096	1,877	0.49	445	4,278	3,833	1,432
2042	383,949	1,852	0.48	414	4,290	3,876	1,438
2043	385,779	1,831	0.48	388	4,303	3,916	1,443
2044	387,593	1,814	0.47	365	4,317	3,952	1,448
2045	389,394	1,801	0.46	348	4,332	3,984	1,453
2046	391,187	1,792	0.46	335	4,347	4,012	1,458
2047	392,973	1,786	0.46	324	4,362	4,038	1,462
2048	394,756	1,783	0.45	317	4,377	4,060	1,466
2049	396,540	1,784	0.45	314	4,391	4,077	1,470
2050	398,328	1,788	0.45	315	4,406	4,091	1,473
2051	400,124	1,795	0.45	319	4,420	4,101	1,477
2052	401,929	1,805	0.45	325	4,433	4,108	1,480
2053	403,744	1,816	0.45	333	4,446	4,113	1,483
2054	405,572	1,828	0.45	342	4,458	4,116	1,485
2055	407,412	1,840	0.45	352	4,470	4,117	1,488
2056	409,265	1,853	0.45	363	4,480	4,117	1,490
2057	411,130	1,865	0.46	374	4,491	4,117	1,491
2058	413,008	1,877	0.46	384	4,500	4,116	1,493
2059	414,896	1,889	0.46	395	4,510	4,115	1,494
2060	416,795	1,898	0.46	403	4,519	4,116	1,495

*Net international migration includes the international migration of both native and foreign-born populations. Specifically, it includes: (a) the net international migration of the foreign born, (b) the net international migration of the native born, and (c) the net migration between the United States and Puerto Rico.
Note: Data on population change and components of change refer to events occurring between July 1 of the preceding year and June 30 of the indicated year.

SOURCE: "Table 1. Projections of the Population and Components of Change for the United States: 2015 to 2060," in *2014 National Population Projections: Summary Tables*, U.S. Census Bureau, December 2014, http://www.census.gov/population/projections/files/summary/NP2014-T1.xls (accessed January 26, 2015)

Meanwhile, the Hispanic population is expected to grow by much larger numerical amounts each half-decade, ranging from a high of 7.1 million between 2030 and 2035 to a low of 6.7 million between 2055 and 2060. (See Table 7.2.) The other group whose growth is expected to be especially noteworthy is the mixed-race population. The population of those identifying as a mix of two or more races (independent of Hispanic origin) is projected to grow at steadily accelerating rates throughout the 45 years of the Census Bureau's projections, increasing from a growth rate of 1.4 million between 2015 and 2020 to a growth rate of 2.6 million between 2055 and 2060.

As Table 7.3 shows, rapid declines in the non-Hispanic white population relative to other racial and ethnic populations are expected in the 45 years covered by the Census Bureau's projections. Overall, the non-Hispanic population is projected to decline steadily, from 82.3% of total population in 2015 to 71.4% in 2060, whereas the Hispanic population is projected to increase steadily, from 17.7% in 2015 to 28.6% in 2060.

TABLE 7.2

Population projections, by race and Hispanic origin, 2015–60

[Numbers in thousands]

Hispanic origin and race	2015–2020	2020–2025	2025–2030	2030–2035	2035–2040	2040–2045	2045–2050	2050–2055	2055–2060
	Numeric change in resident population as of July 1.								
Total population	**13,135**	**12,831**	**12,067**	**10,936**	**9,881**	**9,175**	**8,934**	**9,084**	**9,382**
One race	11,751	11,305	10,401	9,135	7,931	7,064	6,656	6,640	6,775
White	6,988	6,468	5,634	4,522	3,465	2,706	2,350	2,340	2,471
Black	2,134	2,135	2,043	1,910	1,808	1,759	1,763	1,810	1,876
AIAN	238	232	220	201	179	158	138	124	113
Asian	2,331	2,409	2,448	2,449	2,428	2,394	2,361	2,327	2,279
NHPI	60	60	57	54	51	47	43	39	36
Two or more races	1,384	1,526	1,666	1,801	1,950	2,111	2,278	2,444	2,607
Race alone or in combination[a]									
White	8,287	7,905	7,207	6,231	5,324	4,725	4,536	4,689	4,982
Black	2,926	3,029	3,041	3,011	3,025	3,103	3,239	3,417	3,614
AIAN	454	454	442	418	392	369	351	340	332
Asian	2,846	2,978	3,069	3,123	3,159	3,183	3,208	3,232	3,243
NHPI	145	153	156	157	160	163	166	169	174
Not Hispanic	**6,338**	**5,943**	**5,044**	**3,856**	**2,798**	**2,157**	**2,028**	**2,285**	**2,687**
One race	5,253	4,745	3,742	2,456	1,287	523	266	397	684
White	1,045	467	−463	−1,593	−2,613	−3,278	−3,500	−3,380	−3,110
Black	1,812	1,811	1,714	1,575	1,468	1,418	1,426	1,477	1,546
AIAN	73	67	56	41	26	14	5	b	−4
Asian	2,277	2,354	2,390	2,390	2,367	2,333	2,301	2,268	2,220
NHPI	46	46	44	41	39	37	34	33	31
Two or more races	1,085	1,198	1,302	1,400	1,511	1,633	1,763	1,887	2,004
Race alone or in combination[a]									
White	2,067	1,599	772	−258	−1,167	−1,708	−1,802	−1,557	−1,171
Black	2,443	2,525	2,509	2,449	2,431	2,479	2,590	2,742	2,908
AIAN	192	188	173	150	128	112	104	102	101
Asian	2,710	2,830	2,906	2,946	2,966	2,975	2,988	2,998	2,990
NHPI	108	113	114	113	113	114	115	117	118
Hispanic	**6,797**	**6,889**	**7,023**	**7,080**	**7,083**	**7,018**	**6,906**	**6,799**	**6,695**
One race	6,498	6,561	6,660	6,679	6,643	6,541	6,391	6,242	6,092
White	5,943	6,002	6,097	6,115	6,079	5,984	5,851	5,719	5,581
Black	322	324	329	334	339	341	337	333	330
AIAN	165	165	164	159	153	144	134	124	116
Asian	54	56	57	59	61	61	60	59	60
NHPI	14	14	13	12	12	11	9	7	5
Two or more races	299	328	363	401	439	478	515	557	603
Race alone or in combination[a]									
White	6,219	6,306	6,435	6,489	6,491	6,433	6,337	6,246	6,154
Black	483	504	531	562	594	624	648	675	706
AIAN	262	266	269	268	264	257	247	238	230
Asian	136	148	162	177	193	207	220	235	254
NHPI	37	40	42	45	47	49	51	52	55
	Percent change in resident population as of July 1.								
Total population	**4.09**	**3.84**	**3.47**	**3.04**	**2.67**	**2.41**	**2.29**	**2.28**	**2.30**
One race	3.75	3.48	3.09	2.64	2.23	1.94	1.80	1.76	1.76
White	2.81	2.53	2.15	1.69	1.27	0.98	0.85	0.83	0.87
Black	5.03	4.79	4.37	3.92	3.57	3.35	3.25	3.23	3.24
AIAN	5.93	5.48	4.91	4.28	3.66	3.11	2.64	2.31	2.05
Asian	13.29	12.13	10.99	9.91	8.93	8.09	7.38	6.77	6.21
NHPI	8.07	7.47	6.63	5.81	5.17	4.59	4.01	3.52	3.13
Two or more races	16.76	15.83	14.92	14.04	13.33	12.73	12.19	11.65	11.13
Race alone or in combination[a]									
White	3.24	2.99	2.65	2.23	1.87	1.63	1.54	1.56	1.64
Black	6.34	6.17	5.84	5.46	5.20	5.07	5.04	5.06	5.10
AIAN	6.86	6.43	5.87	5.24	4.67	4.20	3.84	3.58	3.37
Asian	13.86	12.74	11.64	10.61	9.70	8.91	8.25	7.68	7.15
NHPI	9.77	9.37	8.75	8.12	7.62	7.22	6.85	6.54	6.30
Not Hispanic	**2.40**	**2.19**	**1.82**	**1.37**	**0.98**	**0.75**	**0.70**	**0.78**	**0.91**
One race	2.04	1.80	1.40	0.90	0.47	0.19	0.10	0.14	0.25
White	0.53	0.23	−0.23	−0.80	−1.32	−1.68	−1.82	−1.79	−1.68
Black	4.55	4.35	3.95	3.49	3.14	2.94	2.88	2.90	2.95
AIAN	3.09	2.77	2.25	1.62	1.01	0.51	0.17	−0.02	−0.13
Asian	13.41	12.22	11.06	9.96	8.97	8.11	7.40	6.79	6.23
NHPI	8.34	7.76	6.91	6.04	5.35	4.78	4.29	3.91	3.59
Two or more races	16.46	15.60	14.67	13.76	13.05	12.48	11.97	11.45	10.91

TABLE 7.2

Population projections, by race and Hispanic origin, 2015–60 [CONTINUED]

[Numbers in thousands]

Hispanic origin and race	2015–2020	2020–2025	2025–2030	2030–2035	2035–2040	2040–2045	2045–2050	2050–2055	2055–2060
					Percent change in resident population as of July 1.				
Race alone or in combination[a]									
White	1.01	0.78	0.37	−0.12	−0.56	−0.82	−0.88	−0.76	−0.58
Black	5.72	5.59	5.26	4.88	4.62	4.50	4.50	4.56	4.63
AIAN	4.51	4.23	3.73	3.11	2.57	2.20	2.00	1.93	1.87
Asian	13.89	12.73	11.60	10.54	9.60	8.78	8.11	7.53	6.98
NHPI	9.52	9.08	8.40	7.69	7.14	6.72	6.38	6.09	5.82
Hispanic	11.98	10.84	9.97	9.14	8.38	7.66	7.00	6.44	5.96
One race	11.80	10.65	9.77	8.93	8.15	7.42	6.75	6.18	5.68
White	11.88	10.73	9.84	8.98	8.20	7.46	6.78	6.21	5.71
Black	12.04	10.82	9.90	9.15	8.52	7.88	7.23	6.66	6.19
AIAN	10.02	9.12	8.28	7.45	6.65	5.88	5.15	4.56	4.08
Asian	9.72	9.09	8.54	8.08	7.70	7.23	6.61	6.09	5.80
NHPI	7.32	6.66	5.84	5.18	4.66	4.04	3.17	2.35	1.75
Two or more races	17.96	16.72	15.87	15.10	14.39	13.67	12.98	12.41	11.96
Race alone or in combination[a]									
White	12.08	10.93	10.05	9.21	8.44	7.71	7.05	6.49	6.01
Black	14.10	12.87	12.03	11.36	10.79	10.22	9.64	9.15	8.77
AIAN	11.09	10.15	9.32	8.50	7.71	6.95	6.25	5.68	5.20
Asian	13.27	12.80	12.42	12.08	11.74	11.29	10.77	10.37	10.15
NHPI	10.56	10.27	9.83	9.44	9.09	8.70	8.22	7.84	7.68

Black = black or African American. AIAN = American Indian and Alaska Native. NHPI = Native Hawaiian and other Pacific Islander.
[a]"In combination" means in combination with one or more other races. The sum of the five race groups adds to more than the total change because individuals may report more than one race.
[b]Rounds to zero.
Note: Hispanic origin is considered an ethnicity, not a race. Hispanics may be of any race. Responses of "some other race" from the 2010 Census are modified.

SOURCE: "Table 12. Projected Change in Population Size by Hispanic Origin and Race for the United States: 2015 to 2060," in *2014 National Population Projections: Summary Tables*, U.S. Census Bureau, December 2014, http://www.census.gov/population/projections/files/summary/NP2014-T12.xls (accessed January 26, 2015)

Within the non-Hispanic population, non-Hispanic whites are expected to decline significantly as a share of total population. In 2015 non-Hispanic whites accounted for 61.7% of the total population. By 2045 this group will fall below 50% of the U.S. population and continue to decline, to 43.7% in 2060. The non-Hispanic African American population is expected to grow slightly in relation to other groups, from 12.4% of total population in 2015 to 13% in 2060, and the non-Hispanic Asian American population is expected to grow rapidly, from 5.3% of the population in 2015 to 9.1% in 2060.

As Table 7.4 demonstrates, this sweeping change, whereby Hispanics are expected to account for a rapidly increasing share of the total U.S. population, Asians for a measurably larger share than they previously constituted, and non-Hispanic whites for a rapidly diminishing share of total population, is an effect of both immigration and the natural rate of increase among different demographic groups. The annual number of non-Hispanic white births is projected to decline, from 2 million in 2015 to 1.5 million in 2060, whereas the annual number of deaths for this group is projected to increase from 2 million in 2015 to a peak of approximately 2.6 million in 2040 and 2050, before declining slightly to 2.4 million in 2060. Meanwhile, although Hispanic death rates are projected to rise in approximate proportion to non-Hispanic death rates,

annual births among Hispanics are expected to increase substantially, from 995,000 in 2015 to 1.6 million in 2060. Thus, the Hispanic birthrate is expected to remain well above the replacement level (see Chapter 6), resulting in a steady natural increase over time, whereas the non-Hispanic white population's birthrate is expected to fall below replacement level after 2020, with deaths increasingly outpacing births through 2060. Births among the Asian population are expected to grow enough to maintain net natural increases.

Besides maintaining net natural increases in population, Hispanics are expected to continue to account for a large share of net international immigrants, as are Asians and non-Hispanic whites. (See Table 7.4.) However, Hispanic immigrants are expected to arrive in approximately twice the numbers of non-Hispanic white immigrants. Asian net immigration numbers are expected to rise slightly more rapidly than those of Hispanics, but at their projected peak of 406,000 in 2050 they will equal only 72% of Hispanic net immigration.

As these population projections indicate, the radical reshaping of the United States' racial and ethnic makeup that is expected between 2015 and 2060 is predicated on three basic factors: the low birthrates of non-Hispanic whites relative to the size of the non-Hispanic white

TABLE 7.3

Percentage distribution of projected population, by race and Hispanic origin, 2015–60

[Percent of total resident population as of July 1.]

Hispanic origin and race	2015	2020	2025	2030	2035	2040	2045	2050	2055	2060
Total population	**100.00**	**100.00**	**100.00**	**100.00**	**100.00**	**100.00**	**100.00**	**100.00**	**100.00**	**100.00**
One race	97.43	97.12	96.79	96.43	96.05	95.64	95.20	94.74	94.25	93.76
White	77.28	76.34	75.38	74.42	73.44	72.44	71.43	70.42	69.42	68.45
Black	13.21	13.33	13.45	13.57	13.68	13.80	13.93	14.06	14.19	14.32
AIAN	1.25	1.27	1.29	1.31	1.32	1.33	1.34	1.35	1.35	1.35
Asian	5.46	5.94	6.41	6.88	7.34	7.79	8.22	8.63	9.00	9.35
NHPI	0.23	0.24	0.25	0.26	0.26	0.27	0.28	0.28	0.28	0.29
Two or more races	2.57	2.88	3.21	3.57	3.95	4.36	4.80	5.26	5.75	6.24
Race alone or in combination:*										
White	79.56	78.91	78.27	77.65	77.04	76.44	75.85	75.29	74.76	74.27
Black	14.35	14.66	14.99	15.34	15.70	16.08	16.50	16.95	17.41	17.88
AIAN	2.06	2.11	2.17	2.22	2.26	2.31	2.35	2.38	2.41	2.44
Asian	6.39	6.99	7.59	8.19	8.79	9.39	9.99	10.57	11.13	11.65
NHPI	0.46	0.49	0.51	0.54	0.57	0.59	0.62	0.65	0.68	0.70
Not Hispanic	**82.34**	**81.00**	**79.72**	**78.45**	**77.17**	**75.90**	**74.67**	**73.50**	**72.42**	**71.44**
One race	80.29	78.71	77.16	75.61	74.04	72.46	70.89	69.36	67.91	66.55
White	61.72	59.61	57.54	55.48	53.41	51.34	49.29	47.30	45.42	43.65
Black	12.38	12.43	12.50	12.55	12.61	12.67	12.73	12.80	12.88	12.96
AIAN	0.73	0.73	0.72	0.71	0.70	0.69	0.68	0.66	0.65	0.63
Asian	5.28	5.76	6.22	6.68	7.13	7.56	7.98	8.38	8.75	9.09
NHPI	0.17	0.18	0.18	0.19	0.20	0.20	0.21	0.21	0.21	0.22
Two or more races	2.05	2.30	2.56	2.83	3.13	3.44	3.78	4.14	4.51	4.89
Race alone or in combination:*										
White	63.54	61.66	59.84	58.05	56.26	54.50	52.77	51.14	49.61	48.22
Black	13.29	13.49	13.72	13.96	14.21	14.48	14.78	15.09	15.43	15.78
AIAN	1.32	1.33	1.34	1.34	1.34	1.34	1.34	1.33	1.33	1.32
Asian	6.07	6.64	7.21	7.78	8.35	8.91	9.46	10.00	10.51	10.99
NHPI	0.35	0.37	0.39	0.41	0.43	0.44	0.46	0.48	0.50	0.52
Hispanic	**17.66**	**19.00**	**20.28**	**21.55**	**22.83**	**24.10**	**25.33**	**26.50**	**27.58**	**28.56**
One race	17.14	18.41	19.62	20.82	22.00	23.18	24.31	25.37	26.34	27.21
White	15.56	16.73	17.84	18.94	20.03	21.11	22.15	23.12	24.01	24.80
Black	0.83	0.90	0.96	1.02	1.08	1.14	1.20	1.26	1.31	1.36
AIAN	0.51	0.54	0.57	0.60	0.62	0.64	0.67	0.69	0.70	0.71
Asian	0.17	0.18	0.19	0.20	0.21	0.22	0.23	0.24	0.25	0.26
NHPI	0.06	0.06	0.06	0.07	0.07	0.07	0.07	0.07	0.07	0.07
Two or more races	0.52	0.59	0.66	0.74	0.82	0.92	1.02	1.13	1.24	1.35
Race alone or in combination:*										
White	16.02	17.25	18.43	19.60	20.78	21.94	23.08	24.15	25.15	26.06
Black	1.07	1.17	1.27	1.38	1.49	1.61	1.73	1.85	1.98	2.10
AIAN	0.73	0.78	0.83	0.88	0.93	0.97	1.01	1.05	1.09	1.12
Asian	0.32	0.35	0.38	0.41	0.44	0.48	0.52	0.57	0.61	0.66
NHPI	0.11	0.12	0.12	0.13	0.14	0.15	0.16	0.17	0.18	0.19

Black = black or African American; AIAN = American Indian and Alaska Native; NHPI = Native Hawaiian and other Pacific Islander.
*"In combination" means in combination with one or more other races. The sum of the five race groups adds to more than the total within each grouping because individuals may report more than one race.
Note: Hispanic origin is considered an ethnicity, not a race. Hispanics may be of any race. Responses of "some other race" from the 2010 Census are modified.

SOURCE: "Table 11. Percent Distribution of the Projected Population by Hispanic Origin and Race for the United States: 2015 to 2060," in *2014 National Population Projections: Summary Tables*, U.S. Census Bureau, December 2014, http://www.census.gov/population/projections/files/summary/NP2014-T11.xls (accessed January 26, 2015)

elderly population, the comparatively higher birthrates of Hispanic and Asian immigrants and their descendants, and the continued high levels of Hispanic and Asian immigration. Thus, the two factors driving projected population increases in the United States are directly related to immigration.

THE CHANGING GEOGRAPHY OF IMMIGRATION

The changes brought about by immigration have historically been concentrated in large-population states with major metropolitan centers, such as California, Florida, Illinois, New Jersey, New York, and Texas. These states remain home to the largest immigrant populations in the United States, but since the 1990s rapid growth of the immigrant population in other states has changed the nature of the public discussion of immigration. As Figure 3.1 in Chapter 3 shows, between 1999 and 2012 a number of states not known for their ethnic and cultural diversity, such as Connecticut, Delaware, Georgia, Virginia, and Washington, have seen their immigrant populations grow rapidly. Even in the smallest states in the country by population, increased immigrant populations became noticeable. In the 31 most sparsely populated states, immigrants accounted for 5.2% of the population on average.

TABLE 7.4

Projected components of population change, by race and Hispanic origin, 2015–60

[Numbers in thousands]

Component, race, and Hispanic origin	2015	2020	2030	2040	2050	2060
Total population change	**2,621**	**2,619**	**2,329**	**1,906**	**1,788**	**1,898**
One race	2,361	2,331	1,986	1,503	1,319	1,364
White	1,429	1,368	1,043	620	460	504
Black	418	431	398	356	355	380
AIAN	47	47	43	34	26	22
Asian	455	473	491	483	470	451
NHPI	12	12	11	10	8	7
Two or more races	260	288	344	403	469	534
Non-Hispanic white alone	251	175	−181	−590	−699	−600
Hispanic	1,345	1,366	1,413	1,414	1,372	1,330
Natural increase	**1,380**	**1,349**	**974**	**479**	**315**	**403**
One race	1,141	1,082	654	101	−129	−106
White	706	640	283	−168	−337	−283
Black	289	290	230	158	125	118
AIAN	38	38	33	24	16	11
Asian	100	106	102	83	64	47
NHPI	7	8	6	5	3	2
Two or more races	239	266	320	378	444	509
Non-Hispanic white alone	26	−58	−432	−855	−973	−877
Hispanic	809	834	864	851	808	780
Births	**3,999**	**4,125**	**4,198**	**4,266**	**4,406**	**4,519**
One race	3,735	3,831	3,839	3,836	3,895	3,926
White	2,867	2,909	2,874	2,833	2,831	2,803
Black	596	624	628	633	660	684
AIAN	59	62	63	63	62	62
Asian	203	225	262	296	331	365
NHPI	10	11	11	12	12	12
Two or more races	263	294	359	430	511	593
Non-Hispanic white alone	2,017	2,000	1,846	1,711	1,628	1,510
Hispanic	995	1,066	1,210	1,334	1,441	1,563
Deaths	**2,619**	**2,777**	**3,224**	**3,787**	**4,091**	**4,116**
One race	2,595	2,749	3,185	3,735	4,024	4,032
White	2,161	2,269	2,592	3,001	3,168	3,086
Black	306	334	398	475	535	567
AIAN	21	24	31	39	46	50
Asian	104	119	160	213	267	318
NHPI	3	3	5	7	9	11
Two or more races	24	28	38	52	67	84
Non-Hispanic white alone	1,991	2,058	2,278	2,565	2,601	2,387
Hispanic	186	233	346	484	632	783
Net international migration	**1,241**	**1,271**	**1,355**	**1,426**	**1,473**	**1,495**
One race	1,220	1,249	1,332	1,402	1,448	1,470
White	723	728	760	788	797	787
Black	129	141	168	198	230	263
AIAN	9	9	10	10	10	10
Asian	355	367	388	400	406	404
NHPI	4	5	5	5	5	5
Two or more races	21	22	23	25	25	25
Non-Hispanic white alone	226	233	251	264	273	277
Hispanic	535	533	549	564	564	550

Black = black or African American. AIAN = American Indian and Alaska Native. NHPI = Native Hawaiian and other Pacific Islander.

Note: Data on population change and components of change refer to events occurring between July 1 of the preceding year and June 30 of the indicated year. Hispanic origin is considered an ethnicity, not a race. Hispanics may be of any race. Responses of "some other race" from the 2010 Census are modified.

SOURCE: "Table 15. Projected Components of Change by Race and Hispanic Origin for the United States: 2015 to 2060," in *2014 National Population Projections: Summary Tables*, U.S. Census Bureau, December 2014, http://www.census.gov/population/projections/files/summary/NP2014-T15.xls (accessed January 26, 2015)

Although this percentage of immigrants was low compared with larger states, the figure had increased by two percentage points since 1999—a near doubling of the immigrant population as a share of total population in these states.

Moreover, outside of established immigrant destinations such as California, Florida, New Jersey, New York, and Texas, growth in the immigrant population was likely more noticeable to residents who were unaccustomed to integrating newcomers of diverse cultural backgrounds. Some new immigrant destinations were towns that had not witnessed the arrival of new immigrants since the early 20th century. Common fears regarding economic competition, crime, the rise of foreign-language speaking and instruction, and rising demand for social services led in some cases to the proposal of restrictive legislation at the local and state levels, as discussed in Chapters 2 and 5.

Miriam Jordan reports in "Heartland Draws Hispanics to Help Revive Small Towns" (WSJ.com, November 8, 2012) on the growing numbers of Hispanic immigrants who have left immigrant-rich parts of the western United States for the more sparsely populated midwestern and southern states. These immigrants settled in out-of-the-way small towns, Jordan relates, because of the combination of good jobs, lower housing costs, and safe neighborhoods. According to Jordan, the 2010 census found that the Hispanic population in the Midwest grew by 49% between 2000 and 2010, contributing much to the overall population growth in the region (which was only 4%). The states of Indiana (82%), Iowa (82%), Nebraska (77%), and Minnesota (74.5%) saw particularly high growth in their Hispanic populations between 2000 and 2010.

Some of the localities subject to rapid influxes of Hispanic residents responded by passing ordinances meant to deter unauthorized immigrants from settling, and cultural and economic anxieties were common. Additionally, the rapid growth of Hispanic populations, which tend to vote heavily Democratic in state and national elections, threatened to upset the balance of political power in the small towns of the Midwest and the Southeast, many of which were Republican strongholds.

In "Can Immigration Save Small-Town America? Hispanic Boomtowns and the Uneasy Path to Renewal" (*Annals of the American Academy of Political and Social Science*, vol. 641, no. 1, May 2012), Patrick J. Carr, Daniel T. Lichter, and Maria J. Kefalas tell a similar story, while further assessing the significance of the wave of Hispanic migration to small towns. The researchers note that the overwhelming movement of the U.S. population to metropolitan areas during the late 20th and early 21st centuries had left many small towns in the Midwest on the brink of collapse: "Any demographic and economic effects have been exacerbated by who is leaving, namely, young adults of reproductive age and the most educated and talented.... While young people have always left small towns, the exodus comes at a time when opportunities for those who stay have been severely reduced by consolidation in agriculture and the globalization of manufacturing.... The net result is that the jobs remaining in nonmetro America are fewer and often pay less than they did even a decade ago."

A primary driver of the growth in the Hispanic population in these areas is the very consolidation of the agribusiness industry that played a role in undermining the career opportunities of many of the native-born residents of the Midwest. Many Hispanic immigrants have been drawn to these midwestern towns by the relocation of food-processing facilities away from cities. These slaughterhouses and meatpacking plants have relocated to rural areas to be closer to raw materials (beef, chicken, and pork) and because of lower labor costs, a result of lower costs of living and a lack of unions. These jobs pay less and are more dangerous than many of the manufacturing or agricultural jobs native-born residents in the Midwest had enjoyed in previous decades. Food-processing companies have actively courted Hispanic immigrants to work in their plants, and immigrants have arrived in large numbers.

Carr, Lichter, and Kefalas analyze the responses of two small middle America towns, Hazleton, Pennsylvania, and St. James, Minnesota, to the growth of their Hispanic populations. Prior to 2000 Hazleton, a town of around 25,000, had been losing population for seven decades because of deindustrialization. Over the course of the next decade, the town's Hispanic population grew rapidly, from 4.9% of the total population to 37.3%, and the town as a whole grew by approximately 2,000 residents, even though the death rate of its native-born population outpaced its birthrate. Anti-immigration activists such as the national television personality Lou Dobbs (1945–) pointed to Hazleton as symptomatic of the larger threat that immigration posed to the American way of life, and several local politicians made anti-immigrant rhetoric the cornerstone of their agendas, claiming that many of the new residents were unauthorized immigrants and that their arrival had driven crime rates higher. In fact, as Carr, Lichter, and Kefalas point out, although there were isolated instances of high-profile crimes allegedly committed by unauthorized immigrants, Hazleton's violent crime rate declined during the period of rapid Hispanic population growth. Nevertheless, Hazleton became a test case for restrictive immigration law, passing a local measure that became a model for other municipalities. Although the law caused widespread tension and attracted national media scrutiny, its effect on the growth of the Hispanic population was inconclusive at best. Meanwhile, Carr, Lichter, and Kefalas note, even those politicians who back the restrictive law acknowledge that Hispanic in-migration has revitalized the town economically and greatly improved the fiscal health of local government.

Although many observers point to Hazleton as emblematic of the complex response to immigration in the 21st century, Carr, Lichter, and Kefalas offer an alternative view of how immigration plays out in their analysis of the experience of St. James. Smaller than Hazleton, St. James, a town with 4,600 residents, saw more gradual growth in its immigrant population. Hispanics began coming to the area during the 1970s and 1980s, when they were recruited from south Texas by a local food-processing plant. Like Hazleton, St. James saw its fortunes become increasingly dependent on its immigrant population. During the mid-1990s a strategic planning group assembled by local leaders and composed entirely of white natives discovered, as part of their information-gathering process, that new arrivals to the town frequently felt excluded and uncomfortable. In response to this information, St. James began focusing on integrating its immigrant community through the newly formed Family Services Collaborative, which mediated the concerns of immigrants, school systems, and social services providers and generated numerous spin-off initiatives. However, tensions remained between the new arrivals and the natives.

THE SITUATION IN MAJOR CITIES

Large U.S. metropolitan areas experience their own complex challenges as a result of immigration, but these challenges take very different forms from those in small towns, given the vast differences in scale and diversity of both the immigrant and native-born populations. Among U.S. metropolitan areas, New York City, Los Angeles County, and Miami-Dade County have long been on the front lines of immigration-related change. The foreign born constitute over one-third of the population of all three metro areas, and a large proportion of residents in each area are second-generation immigrants. Andy Kiersz notes in "Here Are the Most Popular Destinations for Immigrants Coming to America" (BusinessInsider .com, March 27, 2014) that between July 2012 and July 2013 the New York metro area saw net immigration of 128,042 people. This was more than double the level of net immigration to Miami (52,706 people), the second-leading immigrant destination during this period, followed closely by Los Angeles (49,798 people).

Non-Hispanic whites are a minority in these metro areas, and all three have long histories as entry points for immigrants to the United States. Accordingly, the challenges brought by immigration relate more to the changing nature of the immigrant populations and the scale of the challenges than to straightforward resistance to or anxiety about immigration. Although all three metro areas are rich in immigrant culture and history, their immigrant populations are distinct from one another. New York is the most diverse of the three metro areas, with large numbers of immigrants from dozens of countries, whereas the immigrant population in Los Angeles is dominated by immigrants from Mexico and a handful of Asian countries. Miami, long the country's top destination for Cuban immigrants, has in the 21st century also become a top destination for South Americans.

New York City

Throughout its history New York City has been defined by a large and ever-changing immigrant population, and the city continues to attract large numbers of immigrants in the 21st century. According to the Census Bureau (2014, http://factfinder.census.gov), in 2013 the city was home to approximately 8.4 million people, of whom 3.1 million (37%) were foreign born. These numbers make New York one of the most diverse cities in the world. It should also be noted that these numbers do not account for the sprawling complex of cities and suburbs that make up the New York metro area, which encompasses parts of New Jersey and Pennsylvania and had a total population of 19.9 million in 2013, according to the Census Bureau (2014, http://www.census.gov/newsroom/releases/pdf/CB14-51_countymetropopest2013tables.pdf).

Although New York, like many other areas of the country, saw rapid increases in the size of its immigrant population in the latter decades of the 20th century and the beginning of the 21st, the composition of the city's immigrant population differed substantially from that of the country at large. Latin America was the leading region of origin among New York immigrants, as in the country at large, but only 182,266 (5.9%) of New York's 3.1 million foreign-born residents had been born in Mexico, whereas 28% (11.6 million of 41.3 million) of the total U.S. foreign born came from Mexico. (See Table 7.5 and Table 3.4 in Chapter 3.) Instead, over half of New York's 1.6 million Latin American immigrants came from the Caribbean, including 415,902 people from the Dominican Republic (13.4% of the total foreign-born population), the largest group of immigrants by country of birth. Chinese immigrants (including immigrants from Hong Kong and Taiwan) accounted for 377,768 (12.2% of the total). Other leading countries of origin among the city's immigrant population were also located in the Caribbean, including Jamaica (172,476), Haiti (86,855), and Trinidad and Tobago (80,316). South America was also a leading region of birth for the city's immigrants, with especially large numbers coming from Guyana (136,604), Ecuador (128,706), and Colombia (64,591). South Central Asian immigrants from Bangladesh (76,323), India (70,737), and Pakistan (42,109); East Asian immigrants from South Korea (64,965); and Southeast Asian immigrants from the Philippines (50,573) were all present in numbers exceeding the size of many small cities. The same was true of immigrants from Russia (68,266), Ukraine (60,663), Italy (50,246), and Poland (50,241).

Nearly half (49%) of all New Yorkers over the age of five years spoke a language other than English at home, and 23.2% of New Yorkers over the age of five years spoke English less than "very well." (See Table 7.6.) Nearly one-third (31.4%) of natives spoke languages other than English at home, which is a measure of the large number of second-generation immigrants in the city. Meanwhile, over three-quarters (76.3%) of foreign-born residents spoke another language at home, and

TABLE 7.5

Immigrant population of New York City, by place of birth, 2013

	New York City, New York
	Estimate
Total	**3,106,661**
Europe	**473,940**
Northern Europe	50,755
United Kingdom (inc. Crown Dependencies)	29,787
United Kingdom, excluding England and Scotland	14,415
England	14,297
Scotland	1,075
Ireland	14,819
Denmark	1,400
Norway	923
Sweden	2,984
Other Northern Europe	842
Western Europe	46,899
Austria	3,541
Belgium	2,810
France	16,561
Germany	17,999
Netherlands	2,736
Switzerland	3,203
Other Western Europe	49
Southern Europe	87,510
Greece	23,491
Italy	50,246
Portugal	2,079
Azores Islands	0
Spain	9,621
Other Southern Europe	2,073
Eastern Europe	288,016
Albania	18,819
Belarus	12,909
Bulgaria	5,984
Croatia	4,008
Czechoslovakia (includes Czech Republic and Slovakia)	4,201
Hungary	8,493
Latvia	1,995
Lithuania	1,416
Macedonia	4,346
Moldova	4,769
Poland	50,241
Romania	13,817
Russia	68,266
Ukraine	60,663
Bosnia and Herzegovina	959
Serbia	2,989
Other Eastern Europe	24,141
Europe, n.e.c.	760
Asia	**863,700**
Eastern Asia	462,266
China	377,768
China, excluding Hong Kong and Taiwan	318,496
Hong Kong	34,279
Taiwan	24,993
Japan	19,498
Korea	64,965
Other Eastern Asia	35
South Central Asia	237,687
Afghanistan	3,224
Bangladesh	76,323
India	70,737
Iran	6,029
Kazakhstan	3,772
Nepal	4,661
Pakistan	42,109
Sri Lanka	3,577
Uzbekistan	22,579

TABLE 7.5

Immigrant population of New York City, by place of birth, 2013 [CONTINUED]

	New York City, New York
	Estimate
Other South Central Asia	4,676
South Eastern Asia	93,460
Cambodia	2,250
Indonesia	4,403
Laos	171
Malaysia	9,443
Burma	4,692
Philippines	50,573
Singapore	2,109
Thailand	6,982
Vietnam	12,837
Other South Eastern Asia	0
Western Asia	68,381
Iraq	1,471
Israel	19,649
Jordan	2,275
Kuwait	468
Lebanon	4,463
Saudi Arabia	1,291
Syria	4,182
Yemen	8,838
Turkey	9,320
Armenia	1,869
Other Western Asia	14,555
Asia, n.e.c.	1,906
Africa	**138,998**
Eastern Africa	7,141
Eritrea	1,472
Ethiopia	2,417
Kenya	1,475
Other Eastern Africa	1,777
Middle Africa	4,036
Cameroon	580
Other Middle Africa	3,456
Northern Africa	26,792
Egypt	16,355
Morocco	5,599
Sudan	2,561
Other Northern Africa	2,277
Southern Africa	2,996
South Africa	2,917
Other Southern Africa	79
Western Africa	83,283
Cape Verde	436
Ghana	26,622
Liberia	3,567
Nigeria	19,583
Sierra Leone	3,994
Other Western Africa	29,081
Africa, n.e.c.	14,750
Oceania	**9,034**
Australia and New Zealand subregion	8,216
Australia	6,690
Other Australian and New Zealand subregion	1,526
Fiji	0
Oceania, n.e.c.	818
Americas	**1,620,989**
Latin America	1,597,321
Caribbean	874,981
Bahamas	1,891
Barbados	21,272
Cuba	15,305
Dominica	10,469
Dominican Republic	415,902
Grenada	19,203
Haiti	86,855
Jamaica	172,476

TABLE 7.5

Immigrant population of New York City, by place of birth, 2013 [CONTINUED]

	New York City, New York
	Estimate
St. Vincent and the Grenadines	13,158
Trinidad and Tobago	80,316
West Indies	11,995
Other Caribbean	26,139
Central America	300,860
Mexico	182,266
Belize	7,903
Costa Rica	5,302
El Salvador	32,449
Guatemala	26,852
Honduras	24,998
Nicaragua	3,679
Panama	16,536
Other Central America	875
South America	421,480
Argentina	13,121
Bolivia	4,666
Brazil	17,486
Chile	5,540
Colombia	64,591
Ecuador	128,706
Guyana	136,604
Peru	31,265
Uruguay	2,929
Venezuela	10,681
Other South America	5,891
Northern America	23,668
Canada	22,962
Other Northern America	706

n.e.c. = not elsewhere classified.

Notes: Data are based on a sample and are subject to sampling variability. The degree of uncertainty for an estimate arising from sampling variability is represented through the use of a margin of error. The value shown here is the 90 percent margin of error. The margin of error can be interpreted roughly as providing a 90 percent probability that the interval defined by the estimate minus the margin of error and the estimate plus the margin of error (the lower and upper confidence bounds) contains the true value. In addition to sampling variability, the American Community Survey (ACS) estimates are subject tononsampling error. The effect of nonsampling error is not represented in these tables.

In data year 2013, there were a series of changes to data collection operations that could have affected some estimates. These changes include the addition of Internet as a mode of data collection, the end of the content portion of Failed Edit Follow-Up interviewing, and the loss of one monthly panel due to the federal government shut down in October 2013. While the 2013 ACS data generally reflect the February 2013 Office of Management and Budget (OMB) definitions of metropolitan and micropolitan statistical areas, in certain instances the names, codes, and boundaries of the principal cities shown in ACS tables may differ from the OMB definitions due to differences in the effective dates of the geographic entities.

Estimates of urban and rural population, housing units, and characteristics reflect boundaries of urban areas defined based on Census 2010 data. As a result, data for urban and rural areas from the ACS do not necessarily reflect the results of ongoing urbanization.

SOURCE: Adapted from "B05006. Place of Birth for the Foreign-Born Population in the United States: New York City, New York," in *2013 American Community Survey 1-Year Estimates*, U.S. Census Bureau, 2014, http://factfinder.census.gov/faces/tableservices/jsf/pages/productview.xhtml?pid=ACS_13_1YR_B05006&prodType=table (accessed January 26, 2015)

49.3% of the over age-five immigrant population spoke English less than "very well." A large percentage of households in the city (14.8%) included no one over the age of 14 years who spoke English "very well."

The diversity of languages spoken by the city's immigrants presents municipal officials with a range of challenges regarding the delivery of services and the enforcement of human rights and fair business and labor practices. As Table 7.6 indicates, 358,877 of the city's 2.1 million students were foreign born, and many second-generation immigrants also required language accommodation in the schools. Hospitals are required by state law to provide translation services to those who request them, but the task is greatly complicated by more than 100 languages spoken by the city's residents. To address language barriers, the city's Commission on Human Rights prints educational literature about human rights laws and discrimination in Arabic, Chinese, Creole, French, Korean, Polish, Russian, Spanish, and Urdu. In July 2008 Mayor Michael Bloomberg (1942–) issued Executive Order 120 (http://www.nyc.gov/html/imm/html/eoll/eo120.shtml), which, to ensure equal access to public services, directed all city agencies to provide language services to all New Yorkers for whom English was not their primary language.

Immigrants face challenges beyond language barriers in adjusting to the culture of their new country. They can become victims of discrimination and exploitation because they do not understand U.S. laws and standards. Immigrants often do not seek help because they feel unwelcome outside their own community or, based on experiences in their homeland, do not trust government officials. New York City attempts to address these problems through a variety of channels, including agencies such as the Mayor's Office of Immigrant Affairs (2015, http://www.nyc.gov/html/imm/html/about/about.shtml), which "promotes the well-being of immigrant communities by recommending policies and programs that facilitate successful integration of immigrant New Yorkers into the civic, economic, and cultural life of the City." Additionally, the Commission on Human Rights offers extensive education programs for immigrants regarding fair housing—the right of people to housing opportunity without regard to their age, familial status, religion, or sex (according to federal law) or to their citizenship status, lawful occupation, marital status, or sexual orientation (according to the New York City Human Rights Law). The Neighborhood Human Rights Program works to foster positive relations among residents of diverse racial, ethnic, and religious backgrounds. It offers mediation and conflict resolution services through community service centers.

Los Angeles County

The Census Bureau (2014, http://factfinder.census.gov) indicates that Los Angeles County, whose total population was 10 million in 2013, was home to an immigrant population of approximately 3.5 million. As with New York City, these numbers do not account for the entirety of greater Los Angeles, a metro area whose population was 13.1 million in 2013, according to the Census Bureau (2014, http://www.census.gov/newsroom/

TABLE 7.6

Native and immigrant populations of New York City, by school enrollment and language characteristics, 2013

Subject	Total Estimate	Native Estimate	Foreign born Estimate	Foreign born; naturalized citizen Estimate	Foreign born; not a U.S. citizen Estimate
New York City, New York					
Total population	**8,405,837**	**5,299,176**	**3,106,661**	**1,672,546**	**1,434,115**
School enrollment					
Population 3 years and over enrolled in school	2,081,141	1,722,264	358,877	145,499	213,378
Nursery school, preschool	6.5%	7.7%	1.1%	0.6%	1.4%
Elementary school (grades K–8)	41.7%	46.1%	20.5%	13.0%	25.6%
High school (grades 9–12)	19.2%	19.2%	18.9%	15.1%	21.4%
College or graduate school	32.6%	27.0%	59.6%	71.3%	51.6%
Language spoken at home and ability to speak English					
Population 5 years and over	7,850,081	4,760,466	3,089,615	1,669,245	1,420,370
English only	51.0%	68.6%	23.7%	27.8%	18.9%
Language other than English	49.0%	31.4%	76.3%	72.2%	81.1%
Speak English less than "very well"	23.2%	6.3%	49.3%	41.6%	58.3%
Selected characteristics					
Households with no one age 14 and over who speaks English only or speaks English "very well"	14.8%	3.6%	29.2%	25.7%	35.4%

Notes: This is a modified view of the original table.

Although the American Community Survey (ACS) produces population, demographic and housing unit estimates, it is the Census Bureau's Population Estimates Program that produces and disseminates the official estimates of the population for the nation, states, counties, cities and towns and estimates of housing units for states and counties.

Data are based on a sample and are subject to sampling variability. The degree of uncertainty for an estimate arising from sampling variability is represented through the use of a margin of error. The value shown here is the 90 percent margin of error. The margin of error can be interpreted roughly as providing a 90 percent probability that the interval defined by the estimate minus the margin of error and the estimate plus the margin of error (the lower and upper confidence bounds) contains the true value. In addition to sampling variability, the ACS estimates are subject to nonsampling error. The effect of nonsampling error is not represented in these tables.

In data year 2013, there were a series of changes to data collection operations that could have affected some estimates. These changes include the addition of Internet as a mode of data collection, the end of the content portion of Failed Edit Follow-Up interviewing, and the loss of one monthly panel due to the federal government shut down in October 2013.

These data for the occupied housing units lines refer to the native or foreign-born status of the householder.

Due to methodological changes to data collection for data year 2013, comparisons of current-year language estimates to past years' language estimates should be made with caution.

Industry codes are 4-digit codes and are based on the North American Industry Classification System 2012.

Occupation codes are 4-digit codes and are based on Standard Occupational Classification 2010.

Telephone service data are not available for certain geographic areas due to problems with data collection.

While the 2013 ACS data generally reflect the February 2013 Office of Management and Budget (OMB) definitions of metropolitan and micropolitan statistical areas, in certain instances the names, codes, and boundaries of the principal cities shown in ACS tables may differ from the OMB definitions due to differences in the effective dates of the geographic entities. Estimates of urban and rural population, housing units, and characteristics reflect boundaries of urban areas defined based on Census 2010 data. As a result, data for urban and rural areas from the ACS do not necessarily reflect the results of ongoing urbanization.

SOURCE: Adapted from "S0501. Selected Characteristics of the Native and Foreign-Born Populations: New York City, New York," in *2013 American Community Survey 1-Year Estimates*, U.S. Census Bureau, 2014, http://factfinder.census.gov/faces/tableservices/jsf/pages/productview.xhtml?pid=ACS_13_1YR_S0501&prodType=table (accessed January 26, 2015)

releases/pdf/CB14-51_countymetropopest2013tables.pdf). Over nine out of 10 Los Angeles County immigrants were arrivals from Latin America (2 million, or 58.1%) and Asia (1.2 million, or 34.3%). (See Table 7.7.) As with the country at large, a majority of these Latin American immigrants were from Mexico. Mexican immigrants accounted for almost 39% of the county's foreign-born population. In fact, were Los Angeles County's Mexican-born population a city, it would have been among the 10 largest cities in the United States in 2013, with 1.4 million people (slightly more than the population of Dallas, Texas). The primary countries of origin for Los Angeles County's 1.2 million Asian immigrants were China (263,168, including those from Hong Kong and Taiwan), the Philippines (228,959), South Korea (158,354), Iran (106,890), Vietnam (99,912), Armenia (55,685), and India (51,519).

As with New York City, language barriers play a major role in the dispensation of municipal services in Los Angeles County. Over half (56.7%) of the 9.4 million Los Angeles County residents over the age of five years spoke a language other than English at home, and 25.5% spoke English less than "very well." (See Table 7.8.) Among the 5.9 million natives over the age of five years, 36% spoke a language other than English at home, again likely pointing to a large second-generation immigrant population. Nearly all (92.1%) of the 3.5 million immigrants over the age of five years spoke a language other than English at home, and 61.3% of immigrants over the age of five years spoke English less than "very well." An estimated 30.6% of immigrant households and 14% of all county households had no member over the age of 14 years who spoke English "very well."

According to the California Immigrant Policy Center, in "Looking Forward: Los Angeles" (2014, http://www.scribd.com/doc/238495903/Looking-Forward-Los-Angeles), immigrants represented 43% of the labor force in greater Los Angeles and a majority of the labor force in industries such as grounds cleaning and maintenance (76%); farming, fishing, and forestry (73%); production

TABLE 7.7

Immigrant population of Los Angeles County, by place of birth, 2013

	Los Angeles County, California
	Estimate
Total	**3,467,880**
Europe	**170,545**
Northern Europe	40,629
United Kingdom (inc. crown dependencies):	31,068
United Kingdom, excluding England and Scotland	13,084
England	15,032
Scotland	2,952
Ireland	3,285
Denmark	1,296
Norway	736
Sweden	3,066
Other Northern Europe	1,178
Western Europe	34,883
Austria	2,066
Belgium	950
France	10,394
Germany	14,584
Netherlands	4,902
Switzerland	1,702
Other Western Europe	285
Southern Europe	18,346
Greece	4,267
Italy	8,229
Portugal	1,520
Azores Islands	122
Spain	4,208
Other Southern Europe	122
Eastern Europe	75,761
Albania	480
Belarus	1,946
Bulgaria	2,032
Croatia	1,801
Czechoslovakia (includes Czech Republic and Slovakia)	2,513
Hungary	5,612
Latvia	1,024
Lithuania	1,647
Macedonia	90
Moldova	924
Poland	7,503
Romania	6,740
Russia	20,821
Ukraine	15,857
Bosnia and Herzegovina	970
Serbia	821
Other Eastern Europe	4,980
Europe, n.e.c.	926
Asia	**1,188,386**
Eastern Asia	458,156
China	263,168
China, excluding Hong Kong and Taiwan	166,972
Hong Kong	26,504
Taiwan	69,692
Japan	35,466
Korea	158,354
Other Eastern Asia	1,168
South Central Asia	186,137
Afghanistan	3,260
Bangladesh	6,115
India	51,519
Iran	106,890
Kazakhstan	1,685
Nepal	2,875
Pakistan	8,041
Sri Lanka	3,827
Uzbekistan	1,594

	Los Angeles County, California
	Estimate
Other South Central Asia	331
South Eastern Asia	408,269
Cambodia	28,064
Indonesia	12,731
Laos	2,356
Malaysia	4,609
Burma	9,104
Philippines	228,959
Singapore	1,949
Thailand	20,531
Vietnam	99,912
Other South Eastern Asia	54
Western Asia	133,920
Iraq	8,299
Israel	14,482
Jordan	3,667
Kuwait	1,286
Lebanon	20,866
Saudi Arabia	3,217
Syria	13,027
Yemen	96
Turkey	6,202
Armenia	55,685
Other Western Asia	7,093
Asia, n.e.c.	1,904
Africa	**52,244**
Eastern Africa	12,469
Eritrea	938
Ethiopia	7,315
Kenya	1,467
Other Eastern Africa	2,749
Middle Africa	1,462
Cameroon	994
Other Middle Africa	468
Northern Africa	18,266
Egypt	14,444
Morocco	2,303
Sudan	52
Other Northern Africa	1,467
Southern Africa	5,638
South Africa	5,638
Other Southern Africa	0
Western Africa	11,893
Cape Verde	0
Ghana	856
Liberia	519
Nigeria	9,269
Sierra Leone	447
Other Western Africa	802
Africa, n.e.c.	2,516
Oceania	**13,336**
Australia and New Zealand subregion	6,129
Australia	5,099
Other Australian and New Zealand subregion	1,030
Fiji	3,316
Oceania, n.e.c.	3,891
Americas	**2,043,369**
Latin America	2,013,508
Caribbean	31,838
Bahamas	156
Barbados	455
Cuba	17,166
Dominica	0
Dominican Republic	2,849
Grenada	188
Haiti	938
Jamaica	5,310

TABLE 7.7

Immigrant population of Los Angeles County, by place of birth, 2013 [CONTINUED]

	Los Angeles County, California
	Estimate
St. Vincent and the Grenadines	477
Trinidad and Tobago	3,498
West Indies	80
Other Caribbean	721
Central America	1,881,802
Mexico	1,350,253
Belize	16,202
Costa Rica	4,197
El Salvador	264,620
Guatemala	178,934
Honduras	37,704
Nicaragua	26,724
Panama	2,677
Other Central America	491
South America	99,868
Argentina	14,490
Bolivia	2,933
Brazil	9,686
Chile	7,733
Colombia	16,728
Ecuador	12,871
Guyana	586
Peru	28,416
Uruguay	718
Venezuela	3,792
Other South America	1,915
Northern America	29,861
Canada	29,669
Other Northern America	192

n.e.c. = not elsewhere classified

Notes: Data are based on a sample and are subject to sampling variability.
In data year 2013, there were a series of changes to data collection operations that could have affected some estimates. These changes include the addition of Internet as a mode of data collection, the end of the content portion of Failed Edit Follow-Up interviewing, and the loss of one monthly panel due to the federal government shut down in October 2013. While the 2013 American Community Survey (ACS) data generally reflect the February 2013 Office of Management and Budget (OMB) definitions of metropolitan and micropolitan statistical areas, in certain instances the names, codes, and boundaries of the principal cities shown in ACS tables may differ from the OMB definitions due to differences in the effective dates of the geographic entities.
Estimates of urban and rural population, housing units, and characteristics reflect boundaries of urban areas defined based on Census 2010 data. As a result, data for urban and rural areas from the ACS do not necessarily reflect the results of ongoing urbanization.

SOURCE: Adapted from "B05006. Place of Birth for the Foreign-Born Population in the United States: Los Angeles County, California," in *2013 American Community Survey 1-Year Estimates*, U.S. Census Bureau, 2014, http://factfinder.census.gov/faces/tableservices/jsf/pages/productview.xhtml?pid=ACS_13_1YR_B05006&prodType=table (accessed January 26, 2015)

(70%); and construction (58%). The area's immigrants were upwardly mobile, with a majority (65%) of those who arrived prior to 1980 having become homeowners as of 2010–12, compared with 34% of those who arrived after 1990. This disparity suggests that it typically takes immigrants in the region an extended period to achieve prosperity and that their progress toward the American dream of homeownership and economic security accelerates markedly during their second decade of life in the country.

Miami-Dade County

The Census Bureau (2014, http://factfinder.census.gov) notes that Miami-Dade County had a total population

of 2.6 million in 2013. Its total metro area population, however, was much larger, at 5.8 million, according to the Census Bureau (2014, http://www.census.gov/newsroom/releases/pdf/CB14-51_countymetropopest2013tables.pdf). Both Miami's metro area and urban core populations were substantially smaller than the comparable municipal units in the New York and Los Angeles areas, but of the three localities, it had the highest proportion of immigrants among its total population. According to Census Bureau figures for Miami-Dade County, the area's total 2013 population was 2.6 million, 1.4 million (51.8%) of whom were foreign born. Miami's immigrant population was neither as diverse as New York's nor as nationally representative as Los Angeles County's. The primary factors shaping immigration in Miami have historically been the city's proximity to Cuba and the federal government's liberal immigration policy for Cubans who came to the United States to escape the Fidel Castro (1926–) regime. Of the 1.4 million immigrants in the Miami area, 654,118 (48.2%) were from Cuba. (See Table 7.9.) This was a larger Cuban population than in all Cuban cities excluding the country's capital of Havana, and yet it does not fully account for Miami's Cuban population, which is also rich in second- and third-generation immigrants.

Although arrivals from Cuba remained the dominant group in Miami's immigrant population from the second half of the 20th century through 2013, South American arrivals have begun to noticeably reshape the cultural fabric of the area. Lizette Alvarez states in "Influx of South Americans Drives Miami's Reinvention" (NYTimes.com, July 20, 2014) that "well-educated, well-off South Americans," both immigrants and visitors, "have transformed Miami's once recession-dampened downtown, enriched its culture and magnified its allure for businesses around the world as a crossroads of the Spanish-speaking world." As Table 7.9 shows, Colombians (90,029), Venezuelans (45,348), Peruvians (37,385), Argentines (22,545), Ecuadorians (15,213), and Brazilians (13,172) were all present in large numbers in Miami-Dade County in 2013. Central Americans were also a major presence, especially those from Nicaragua (78,655), Honduras (41,226), Mexico (24,096), Guatemala (21,041), and El Salvador (15,093); as were Caribbean immigrants from Haiti (80,010), the Dominican Republic (38,961), and Jamaica (28,358).

Nearly three-quarters (71.6%) of the 2.5 million Miami-Dade County residents over the age of five years spoke a language other than English at home, and 34.6% spoke English less than "very well." (See Table 7.10.) Among the 1.1 million natives over the age of five years, 48% spoke a language other than English at home, again a measure of the size of the second-generation immigrant population. As in Los Angeles, nearly all (91%) of the county's 1.4 million immigrants over the age of five years spoke a language other than English at home, and

TABLE 7.8

Native and immigrant populations of Los Angeles County, by school enrollment and language characteristics, 2013

Subject	Los Angeles County, California				
	Total	Native	Foreign born	Foreign born; naturalized citizen	Foreign born; not a U.S. citizen
	Estimate	Estimate	Estimate	Estimate	Estimate
Total population	**10,017,068**	**6,549,147**	**3,467,921**	**1,683,732**	**1,784,189**
School enrollment					
Population 3 years and over enrolled in school	2,748,844	2,413,874	334,970	108,021	226,949
Nursery school, preschool	5.7%	6.4%	1.2%	0.9%	1.4%
Elementary school (grades K–8)	41.5%	44.7%	18.3%	8.9%	22.8%
High school (grades 9–12)	21.3%	21.2%	21.7%	13.4%	25.7%
College or graduate school	31.4%	27.7%	58.7%	76.8%	50.1%
Language spoken at home and ability to speak English					
Population 5 years and over	9,376,923	5,920,745	3,456,178	1,681,252	1,774,926
English only	43.3%	64.0%	7.9%	10.3%	5.6%
Language other than English	56.7%	36.0%	92.1%	89.7%	94.4%
Speak English less than "very well"	25.5%	4.7%	61.3%	51.5%	70.7%
Selected characteristics					
Households with no one age 14 and over who speaks English only or speaks English "very well"	14.0%	1.3%	30.6%	25.1%	37.9%

Notes: Data are based on a sample and are subject to sampling variability. In data year 2013, there were a series of changes to data collection operations that could have affected some estimates. These changes include the addition of Internet as a mode of data collection, the end of the content portion of Failed Edit Follow-Up interviewing, and the loss of one monthly panel due to the federal government shut down in October 2013. These data for the occupied housing units lines refer to the native or foreign-born status of the householder. Due to methodological changes to data collection for data year 2013, comparisons of current-year language estimates to past years' language estimates should be made with caution. Industry codes are 4-digit codes and are based on the North American Industry Classification System 2012. The industry categories adhere to the guidelines issued in Clarification Memorandum No. 2, "NAICS Alternate Aggregation Structure for Use By U.S. Statistical Agencies," issued by the Office of Management and Budget. Occupation codes are 4-digit codes and are based on Standard Occupational Classification 2010. Telephone service data are not available for certain geographic areas due to problems with data collection. While the 2013 American Community Survey (ACS) data generally reflect the February 2013 Office of Management and Budget (OMB) definitions of metropolitan and micropolitan statistical areas, in certain instances the names, codes, and boundaries of the principal cities shown in ACS tables may differ from the OMB definitions due to differences in the effective dates of the geographic entities. Estimates of urban and rural population, housing units, and characteristics reflect boundaries of urban areas defined based on Census 2010 data. As a result, data for urban and rural areas from the ACS do not necessarily reflect the results of ongoing urbanization.

SOURCE: Adapted from "S0501. Selected Characteristics of the Native and Foreign-Born Populations: Los Angeles County, California," in *2013 American Community Survey 1-Year Estimates*, U.S. Census Bureau, 2014, http://factfinder.census.gov/faces/tableservices/jsf/pages/productview.xhtml?pid=ACS_13_1YR_S0501&prodType=table (accessed January 26, 2015)

58.1% of immigrants over the age of five years spoke English less than "very well." An estimated 38.3% of immigrant households and 25.8% of all county households had no member over the age of 14 years who spoke English "very well."

AMERICAN VIEWS ON IMMIGRATION

Concerns about immigration's effect on the United States were hardly uniform in the 21st century. Although Republican voters and politicians tended to support more restrictive immigration policies than Democratic voters and politicians, and although Democrats were more likely to support pathways to work authorization and citizenship for the unauthorized population than Republicans, the immigration issue did not divide people along partisan lines with the precision of other domestic issues. Indeed, immigration reform that includes integration of unauthorized residents and a relaxation of employer-based visas enjoyed strong support among centrist and fiscal-oriented Republicans during Barack Obama's (1961–) second term in office, a time when few Republicans and Democrats agreed on any substantive political issues. Thus, the political divide on immigration was largely a divide within the Republican Party, with passage of future legislation dependent on whether the party's centrists or its more extreme members exercised the most influence over the intraparty debate. The party's most conservative members, including many politicians from border states and the South, largely advocated for an enforcement-only approach to immigration policy, whereas others in the party were more inclined to consider a combination of enforcement and integration, in keeping with mainstream Democratic views of the issue.

In "The Real GOP Split on Immigration" (Politico.com, January 14, 2015), Daniel J. McGraw argues that there was also a geographic split on the issue within the Republican Party. According to McGraw, party leaders in the Midwest were much more likely to favor policies integrating immigrants, including the unauthorized population. This was largely a function of the economic distress the region had been experiencing for decades. In a political context defined by population declines in major cities such as Detroit, Michigan, and Cleveland, Ohio, and by economic stagnation at the regional level, the economic argument for immigration was especially influential. McGraw explains, "The main thrust of the Midwestern pro-immigration argument is based on two points: first, that immigrants tend

TABLE 7.9

Immigrant population of Miami-Dade County, by place of birth, 2013

	Miami-Dade County, Florida
	Estimate
Total	1,356,053
Europe	44,592
Northern Europe	6,059
United Kingdom (inc. crown dependencies)	4,343
United Kingdom, excluding England and Scotland	2,211
England	2,092
Scotland	40
Ireland	439
Denmark	374
Norway	25
Sweden	741
Other Northern Europe	137
Western Europe	9,824
Austria	378
Belgium	684
France	3,956
Germany	3,380
Netherlands	910
Switzerland	516
Other Western Europe	0
Southern Europe	15,850
Greece	485
Italy	3,791
Portugal	886
Azores Islands	0
Spain	10,645
Other Southern Europe	43
Eastern Europe	12,814
Albania	176
Belarus	87
Bulgaria	464
Croatia	142
Czechoslovakia (includes Czech Republic and Slovakia)	969
Hungary	1,149
Latvia	365
Lithuania	72
Macedonia	0
Moldova	269
Poland	1,570
Romania	757
Russia	3,533
Ukraine	2,321
Bosnia and Herzegovina	46
Serbia	157
Other Eastern Europe	737
Europe, n.e.c.	45
Asia	40,098
Eastern Asia	9,468
China	8,234
China, excluding Hong Kong and Taiwan	6,461
Hong Kong	459
Taiwan	1,314
Japan	700
Korea	361
Other Eastern Asia	173
South Central Asia	12,314
Afghanistan	0
Bangladesh	1,161
India	6,113
Iran	2,400
Kazakhstan	187
Nepal	0
Pakistan	1,998
Sri Lanka	346
Uzbekistan	109

TABLE 7.9

Immigrant population of Miami-Dade County, by place of birth, 2013 [CONTINUED]

	Miami-Dade County, Florida
	Estimate
Other South Central Asia	0
South Eastern Asia	9,940
Cambodia	119
Indonesia	146
Laos	0
Malaysia	57
Burma	0
Philippines	5,722
Singapore	52
Thailand	953
Vietnam	2,891
Other South Eastern Asia	0
Western Asia	8,025
Iraq	51
Israel	4,158
Jordan	81
Kuwait	99
Lebanon	1,434
Saudi Arabia	614
Syria	144
Yemen	0
Turkey	1,204
Armenia	59
Other Western Asia	181
Asia, n.e.c.	351
Africa	5,169
Eastern Africa	1,068
Eritrea	182
Ethiopia	440
Kenya	121
Other Eastern Africa	325
Middle Africa	179
Cameroon	44
Other Middle Africa	135
Northern Africa	2,115
Egypt	600
Morocco	892
Sudan	0
Other Northern Africa	623
Southern Africa	435
South Africa	435
Other Southern Africa	0
Western Africa	1,372
Cape Verde	0
Ghana	98
Liberia	5
Nigeria	1,084
Sierra Leone	0
Other Western Africa	185
Africa, n.e.c.	0
Oceania	715
Australia and New Zealand subregion	715
Australia	245
Other Australian and New Zealand subregion	470
Fiji	0
Oceania, n.e.c.	0
Americas	1,265,479
Latin America	1,259,853
Caribbean	817,224
Bahamas	5,717
Barbados	1,076
Cuba	654,118
Dominica	632
Dominican Republic	38,961
Grenada	955
Haiti	80,010
Jamaica	28,358

TABLE 7.9

Immigrant population of Miami-Dade County, by place of birth, 2013 [CONTINUED]

	Miami-Dade County, Florida
	Estimate
St. Vincent and the Grenadines	375
Trinidad and Tobago	4,347
West Indies	390
Other Caribbean	2,285
Central America	194,790
Mexico	24,096
Belize	1,726
Costa Rica	6,722
El Salvador	15,093
Guatemala	21,041
Honduras	41,226
Nicaragua	78,655
Panama	6,159
Other Central America	72
South America	247,839
Argentina	22,545
Bolivia	3,465
Brazil	13,172
Chile	9,186
Colombia	90,029
Ecuador	15,213
Guyana	2,661
Peru	37,385
Uruguay	7,772
Venezuela	45,348
Other South America	1,063
Northern America	5,626
Canada	5,507
Other Northern America	119

n.e.c. = not elsewhere classified

Notes: Data are based on a sample and are subject to sampling variability. In data year 2013, there were a series of changes to data collection operations that could have affected some estimates. These changes include the addition of Internet as a mode of data collection, the end of the content portion of Failed Edit Follow-Up interviewing, and the loss of one monthly panel due to the federal government shut down in October 2013. While the 2013 American Community Survey (ACS) data generally reflect the February 2013 Office of Management and Budget (OMB) definitions of metropolitan and micropolitan statistical areas, in certain instances the names, codes, and boundaries of the principal cities shown in ACS tables may differ from the OMB definitions due to differences in the effective dates of the geographic entities. Estimates of urban and rural population, housing units, and characteristics reflect boundaries of urban areas defined based on Census 2010 data. As a result, data for urban and rural areas from the ACS do not necessarily reflect the results of ongoing urbanization.

SOURCE: Adapted from "B05006. Place of Birth for the Foreign-Born Population in the United States: Miami-Dade County, Florida," in *2013 American Community Survey 1-Year Estimates*, U.S. Census Bureau, 2014, http://factfinder.census.gov/faces/tableservices/jsf/pages/productview.xhtml?pid=ACS_13_1YR_B05006&prodType=table (accessed January 26, 2015)

to be more entrepreneurial than native-borns and therefore are job creators; and second, Midwestern colleges and universities have large numbers of foreign students, and the region wants to keep them after they graduate by opening up the number of visas available."

Public polling tends to show a country whose views on immigration are much closer to Democrats' and centrist Republicans' than to conservative Republicans'. The Gallup Organization asks questions annually in an attempt to track views on immigration over time. According to Gallup, in *Immigration* (2015, http://www.gallup.com/poll/1660/immigration.aspx), the poll results indicate

that public opinion supporting a reduction in immigrant flows peaked at 65% during the mid-1990s, and that as of 2014, 41% of respondents believed immigration should be decreased, compared with 33% who believed immigration should be kept at present levels and 22% who believed it should be increased. These percentages did not vary substantially among non-Hispanic whites, non-Hispanic African Americans, and Hispanics. When asked, "On the whole, do you think immigration is a good thing or a bad thing for this country today?" 63% of respondents in 2014 chose "a good thing," 33% chose "a bad thing," 3% expressed mixed feelings, and 1% had no opinion. These percentages had fluctuated only minimally since 2001. When questioning respondents about specific legislative priorities for dealing with illegal immigration, Gallup found an overwhelming consensus in favor of the main elements of S.744, the immigration reform bill passed by the U.S. Senate in 2013 but scuttled by conservative opposition in the U.S. House of Representatives. At the time the bill was under discussion in the Senate, Gallup found that 83% of Americans favored tightening security at U.S. borders, 84% favored requiring business owners to check the immigration status of employees, 76% favored expanding the number of work visas for in-demand workers, and 88% favored allowing unauthorized immigrants already in the country to become citizens provided that they meet certain requirements such as paying tax penalties, passing a criminal background check, and learning English.

In "Like Bush, Many Republicans Are Moderate on Immigration" (FiveThirtyEight.com, April 12, 2014), an analysis of 2014 polling data on a number of political questions, Nate Silver finds that the partisan divide on immigration is highly sensitive to the presentation of questions. He notes that when pollsters ask whether individuals support a pathway to citizenship for unauthorized immigrants without any conditions, Republicans and Democrats are separated by 32 percentage points, with only 37% of Republicans expressing support, compared with 69% of Democrats. Nevertheless, when pollsters ask whether individuals support a pathway to citizenship provided that unauthorized immigrants first satisfy certain conditions such as paying back taxes and passing criminal background checks, 72% of Republicans and 83% of Democrats expressed support. Thus, the partisan gap on this particular aspect of the immigration question was only 11 percentage points, one of the smallest gaps among all political issues.

In late 2014, just before Obama's announcement of his second set of executive actions on immigration, the Pew Research Center conducted a survey asking a representative group of Americans about their immigration

TABLE 7.10

Native and immigrant populations of Miami-Dade County, by school enrollment and language characteristics, 2013

Subject	Total Estimate	Native Estimate	Foreign born Estimate	Foreign born; naturalized citizen Estimate	Foreign born; not a U.S. citizen Estimate
			Miami-Dade County, Florida		
Total population	**2,617,176**	**1,261,123**	**1,356,053**	**741,564**	**614,489**
School enrollment					
Population 3 years and over enrolled in school	647,903	494,509	153,394	60,493	92,901
Nursery school, preschool	6.6%	8.3%	1.1%	0.1%	1.7%
Elementary school (grades K–8)	41.4%	47.5%	21.9%	11.9%	28.4%
High school (grades 9–12)	19.9%	19.7%	20.9%	15.7%	24.3%
College or graduate school	32.0%	24.5%	56.1%	72.3%	45.6%
Language spoken at home and ability to speak English					
Population 5 years and over	2,462,579	1,111,758	1,350,821	740,957	609,864
English only	28.4%	52.0%	9.0%	9.9%	7.9%
Language other than English	71.6%	48.0%	91.0%	90.1%	92.1%
Speak English less than "very well"	34.6%	6.1%	58.1%	50.0%	68.0%
Selected characteristics					
Households with no one age 14 and over who speaks English only or speaks English "very well"	25.8%	3.2%	38.3%	33.6%	46.7%

Notes: Data are based on a sample and are subject to sampling variability. In data year 2013, there were a series of changes to data collection operations that could have affected some estimates. These changes include the addition of Internet as a mode of data collection, the end of the content portion of Failed Edit Follow-Up interviewing, and the loss of one monthly panel due to the federal government shut down in October 2013. These data for the occupied housing units lines refer to the native or foreign-born status of the householder. Due to methodological changes to data collection for data year 2013, comparisons of current-year language estimates to past years' language estimates should be made with caution. Industry codes are 4-digit codes and are based on the North American Industry Classification System 2012. The industry categories adhere to the guidelines issued in Clarification Memorandum No. 2, "NAICS Alternate Aggregation Structure for Use By U.S. Statistical Agencies," issued by the Office of Management and Budget. Occupation codes are 4-digit codes and are based on Standard Occupational Classification 2010. Telephone service data are not available for certain geographic areas due to problems with data collection. While the 2013 American Community Survey (ACS) data generally reflect the February 2013 Office of Management and Budget (OMB) definitions of metropolitan and micropolitan statistical areas, in certain instances the names, codes, and boundaries of the principal cities shown in ACS tables may differ from the OMB definitions due to differences in the effective dates of the geographic entities. Estimates of urban and rural population, housing units, and characteristics reflect boundaries of urban areas defined based on Census 2010 data. As a result, data for urban and rural areas from the ACS do not necessarily reflect the results of ongoing urbanization.

SOURCE: Adapted from "S0501. Selected Characteristics of the Native and Foreign-Born Populations: Miami-Dade County, Florida," in *2013 American Community Survey 1-Year Estimates*, U.S. Census Bureau, 2014, http://factfinder.census.gov/faces/tableservices/jsf/pages/productview.xhtml?pid=ACS_13_1YR_S0501&prodType=table (accessed January 26, 2015)

policy priorities. Pew notes in "More Prioritize Border Security in Immigration Debate" (September 3, 2014, http://www.people-press.org/2014/09/03/more-prioritize-border-security-in-immigration-debate) that 33% of respondents said better border security and tougher enforcement of immigration laws should be prioritized, 23% said creating a way for unauthorized immigrants to become citizens if they meet certain conditions should be the top priority, and 41% said both should be given equal priority.

CHAPTER 8
THE UNITED STATES NEEDS MORE TOLERANT IMMIGRATION LAWS

REMARKS BY PRESIDENT BARACK OBAMA IN ADDRESS TO THE NATION ON IMMIGRATION, NOVEMBER 20, 2014

My fellow Americans, tonight, I'd like to talk with you about immigration.

For more than 200 years, our tradition of welcoming immigrants from around the world has given us a tremendous advantage over other nations. It's kept us youthful, dynamic, and entrepreneurial. It has shaped our character as a people with limitless possibilities—people not trapped by our past, but able to remake ourselves as we choose.

But today, our immigration system is broken—and everybody knows it.

Families who enter our country the right way and play by the rules watch others flout the rules. Business owners who offer their workers good wages and benefits see the competition exploit undocumented immigrants by paying them far less. All of us take offense to anyone who reaps the rewards of living in America without taking on the responsibilities of living in America. And undocumented immigrants who desperately want to embrace those responsibilities see little option but to remain in the shadows, or risk their families being torn apart.

It's been this way for decades. And for decades, we haven't done much about it.

When I took office, I committed to fixing this broken immigration system. And I began by doing what I could to secure our borders. Today, we have more agents and technology deployed to secure our southern border than at any time in our history. And over the past six years, illegal border crossings have been cut by more than half. Although this summer, there was a brief spike in unaccompanied children being apprehended at our border, the number of such children is now actually lower than it's been in nearly two years. Overall, the number of people trying to cross our border illegally is at its lowest level since the 1970s. Those are the facts.

Meanwhile, I worked with Congress on a comprehensive fix, and last year, 68 Democrats, Republicans, and independents came together to pass a bipartisan bill in the Senate. It wasn't perfect. It was a compromise. But it reflected common sense. It would have doubled the number of border patrol agents while giving undocumented immigrants a pathway to citizenship if they paid a fine, started paying their taxes, and went to the back of the line. And independent experts said that it would help grow our economy and shrink our deficits.

Had the House of Representatives allowed that kind of bill a simple yes-or-no vote, it would have passed with support from both parties, and today it would be the law. But for a year and a half now, Republican leaders in the House have refused to allow that simple vote.

Now, I continue to believe that the best way to solve this problem is by working together to pass that kind of common sense law. But until that happens, there are actions I have the legal authority to take as President—the same kinds of actions taken by Democratic and Republican presidents before me—that will help make our immigration system more fair and more just.

Tonight, I am announcing those actions.

First, we'll build on our progress at the border with additional resources for our law enforcement personnel so that they can stem the flow of illegal crossings, and speed the return of those who do cross over.

Second, I'll make it easier and faster for high-skilled immigrants, graduates, and entrepreneurs to stay and contribute to our economy, as so many business leaders have proposed.

Third, we'll take steps to deal responsibly with the millions of undocumented immigrants who already live in our country.

I want to say more about this third issue, because it generates the most passion and controversy. Even as we are a nation of immigrants, we're also a nation of laws. Undocumented workers broke our immigration laws, and I believe that they must be held accountable—especially those who may be dangerous. That's why, over the past six years, deportations of criminals are up 80 percent. And that's why we're going to keep focusing enforcement resources on actual threats to our security. Felons, not families. Criminals, not children. Gang members, not a mom who's working hard to provide for her kids. We'll prioritize, just like law enforcement does every day.

But even as we focus on deporting criminals, the fact is, millions of immigrants in every state, of every race and nationality still live here illegally. And let's be honest—tracking down, rounding up, and deporting millions of people isn't realistic. Anyone who suggests otherwise isn't being straight with you. It's also not who we are as Americans. After all, most of these immigrants have been here a long time. They work hard, often in tough, low-paying jobs. They support their families. They worship at our churches. Many of their kids are American-born or spent most of their lives here, and their hopes, dreams, and patriotism are just like ours. As my predecessor, President Bush, once put it: "They are a part of American life."

Now here's the thing: We expect people who live in this country to play by the rules. We expect that those who cut the line will not be unfairly rewarded. So we're going to offer the following deal: If you've been in America for more than five years; if you have children who are American citizens or legal residents; if you register, pass a criminal background check, and you're willing to pay your fair share of taxes—you'll be able to apply to stay in this country temporarily without fear of deportation. You can come out of the shadows and get right with the law. That's what this deal is.

Now, let's be clear about what it isn't. This deal does not apply to anyone who has come to this country recently. It does not apply to anyone who might come to America illegally in the future. It does not grant citizenship, or the right to stay here permanently, or offer the same benefits that citizens receive—only Congress can do that. All we're saying is we're not going to deport you.

I know some of the critics of this action call it amnesty. Well, it's not. Amnesty is the immigration system we have today—millions of people who live here without paying their taxes or playing by the rules while politicians use the issue to scare people and whip up votes at election time.

That's the real amnesty—leaving this broken system the way it is. Mass amnesty would be unfair. Mass deportation would be both impossible and contrary to our character. What I'm describing is accountability—a common-sense, middle-ground approach: If you meet the criteria, you can come out of the shadows and get right with the law. If you're a criminal, you'll be deported. If you plan to enter the U.S. illegally, your chances of getting caught and sent back just went up.

The actions I'm taking are not only lawful, they're the kinds of actions taken by every single Republican President and every single Democratic President for the past half century. And to those members of Congress who question my authority to make our immigration system work better, or question the wisdom of me acting where Congress has failed, I have one answer: Pass a bill....

Most Americans support the types of reforms I've talked about tonight. But I understand the disagreements held by many of you at home. Millions of us, myself included, go back generations in this country, with ancestors who put in the painstaking work to become citizens. So we don't like the notion that anyone might get a free pass to American citizenship.

I know some worry immigration will change the very fabric of who we are, or take our jobs, or stick it to middle-class families at a time when they already feel like they've gotten the raw deal for over a decade. I hear these concerns. But that's not what these steps would do. Our history and the facts show that immigrants are a net plus for our economy and our society. And I believe it's important that all of us have this debate without impugning each other's character.

Because for all the back and forth of Washington, we have to remember that this debate is about something bigger. It's about who we are as a country, and who we want to be for future generations.

Are we a nation that tolerates the hypocrisy of a system where workers who pick our fruit and make our beds never have a chance to get right with the law? Or are we a nation that gives them a chance to make amends, take responsibility, and give their kids a better future?

Are we a nation that accepts the cruelty of ripping children from their parents' arms? Or are we a nation that values families, and works together to keep them together?

Are we a nation that educates the world's best and brightest in our universities, only to send them home to create businesses in countries that compete against us? Or are we a nation that encourages them to stay and create jobs here, create businesses here, create industries right here in America?

That's what this debate is all about. We need more than politics as usual when it comes to immigration. We need reasoned, thoughtful, compassionate debate that focuses on our hopes, not our fears. I know the politics of this issue are tough. But let me tell you why I have come to feel so strongly about it.

Over the past few years, I have seen the determination of immigrant fathers who worked two or three jobs without taking a dime from the government, and at risk any moment of losing it all, just to build a better life for their kids. I've seen the heartbreak and anxiety of children whose mothers might be taken away from them just because they didn't have the right papers. I've seen the courage of students who, except for the circumstances of their birth, are as American as Malia or Sasha; students who bravely come out as undocumented in hopes they could make a difference in the country they love.

These people—our neighbors, our classmates, our friends—they did not come here in search of a free ride or an easy life. They came to work, and study, and serve in our military, and above all, contribute to America's success.

Tomorrow, I'll travel to Las Vegas and meet with some of these students, including a young woman named Astrid Silva. Astrid was brought to America when she was four years old. Her only possessions were a cross, her doll, and the frilly dress she had on. When she started school, she didn't speak any English. She caught up to other kids by reading newspapers and watching PBS, and she became a good student. Her father worked in landscaping. Her mom cleaned other people's homes. They wouldn't let Astrid apply to a technology magnet school, not because they didn't love her, but because they were afraid the paperwork would out her as an undocumented immigrant—so she applied behind their back and got in. Still, she mostly lived in the shadows—until her grandmother, who visited every year from Mexico, passed away, and she couldn't travel to the funeral without risk of being found out and deported. It was around that time she decided to begin advocating for herself and others like her, and today, Astrid Silva is a college student working on her third degree.

Are we a nation that kicks out a striving, hopeful immigrant like Astrid, or are we a nation that finds a way to welcome her in? Scripture tells us that we shall not oppress a stranger, for we know the heart of a stranger—we were strangers once, too.

My fellow Americans, we are and always will be a nation of immigrants. We were strangers once, too. And whether our forebears were strangers who crossed the Atlantic, or the Pacific, or the Rio Grande, we are here only because this country welcomed them in, and taught them that to be an American is about something more than what we look like, or what our last names are, or how we worship. What makes us Americans is our shared commitment to an ideal—that all of us are created equal, and all of us have the chance to make of our lives what we will.

That's the country our parents and grandparents and generations before them built for us. That's the tradition we must uphold. That's the legacy we must leave for those who are yet to come.

Thank you. God bless you. And God bless this country we love. (https://www.whitehouse.gov/the-press-office/2014/11/20/remarks-president-address-nation-immigration)

STATEMENT OF JANET MURGUÍA, PRESIDENT AND CHIEF EXECUTIVE OFFICER OF THE NATIONAL COUNCIL OF LA RAZA, BEFORE THE U.S. SENATE, COMMITTEE ON THE JUDICIARY, HEARING ON "THE BORDER SECURITY, ECONOMIC OPPORTUNITY, AND IMMIGRATION MODERNIZATION ACT, S.744," APRIL 22, 2013

I am the President and CEO of the National Council of La Raza (NCLR), the largest national Hispanic civil rights and advocacy organization in the United States, an American institution recognized in the book *Forces for Good* as one of the highest impact nonprofits in the nation. We represent some 300 Affiliates—local, community-based organizations in 41 states, the District of Columbia, and Puerto Rico—that provide education, health, housing, workforce development, and other services to millions of Americans and immigrants annually.

NCLR has a long legacy of engaging in immigration, evidenced through our work in the Hispanic community and in Washington, DC. We helped shape the Immigration Reform and Control Act of 1986, the Immigration Act of 1990 to preserve family-based immigration, and the Nicaraguan Adjustment and Central American Relief Act....We also led four successful efforts to restore safety net systems that promote immigrant integration. We have worked with Presidents Ronald Reagan, George H. W. Bush, Bill Clinton, and George W. Bush to achieve the best results possible for our community and for the country. We know that working with both parties is the only way to get things done.

Fixing our broken immigration system is in the best interest of our country. That is why it is so important to acknowledge the work of the bipartisan group of senators who last week reached a critically important breakthrough in the push for immigration reform with the introduction of S.744, the "Border Security, Economic Opportunity, and Immigration Modernization Act of 2013." ...

As I noted in my previous testimony, NCLR's principles for immigration reform are very clear that reform should (1) restore the rule of law by creating a roadmap to legalization and citizenship for the 11 million aspiring Americans, and include smart enforcement that improves safety, supports legal immigration channels, and prevents discrimination; (2) preserve the rule of law by creating workable legal immigration channels that reunite families, strengthen our economy, and protect workers' rights;

and (3) strengthen the fabric of our society by adopting proactive measures that advance the successful integration of new immigrants....

The Time Is Now

There are three potent threads aligning that make this moment different and the opportunity for reform stronger: the moral, economic, and political imperatives for immigration reform.

- The moral imperative for reform has been made clear for years, with a wide ranging set of organizations raising awareness about the untold damage our broken immigration system has had on immigrants and families, a plight that found its most potent symbol recently in the courageous activism of DREAMers. And the magnitude of that devastation is much larger, as the lives and fate of immigrants are fundamentally interwoven with those of citizens and impacts how those who are deemed to be immigrants are treated.

- The economic imperative for reform has been gaining strength particularly in the last couple of years, with the consequences of deportation policies, state anti-immigrant laws, and an outdated legal immigration system, affecting more industries. Simultaneously, more and more studies show the economic benefit to our country of implementing legalization, promoting citizenship, and bringing in the best and brightest talent from around the globe.

- Election Day made the political imperative crystal clear. Adding to the strong participation by African American voters, according to the exit polls, Asian American and Pacific Islander voters were 3% of the electorate and Latinos were 10%. Latinos were decisive in Nevada, Colorado, and Florida, and an essential part of the winning coalition in places like Pennsylvania and Wisconsin, as were Asian American voters in Minnesota and Virginia.

These three imperatives, and the conditions that created them, have brought together the multi-sector voices and constituencies on the left and right of the debate necessary to help immigration reform become a reality. We understand that failure to achieve reform will mean a continued erosion of the family unit, working rights, community wellbeing, and civil rights protections that start with the vulnerable undocumented community and reverberate well beyond....

A Roadmap to Citizenship

Our country places a high regard on the successful integration of immigrants into the socio-economic fabric of the nation. And we must remember that the American public puts a special premium on citizenship, because citizenship signifies fully embracing our country and accepting the contract that all of our ancestors at some

point made: to be fully American. The American people want to see immigrants all in—not partially in, not in a special status, but in the same boat as everyone else.

We believe Senate bill 744 recognizes the importance of that process of integration, and seeks to strike a balance that can reflect our national principles and priorities. And it also recognizes the fact that, if we are serious about restoring the rule of law, it is essential that we acknowledge that no healthy society can tolerate the existence of a subclass of people outside the scope and protection of the law. Those living in the shadows are easily exploited by employers, thus lowering the wages and labor standards for all workers and undercutting businesses that play by the rules. They are afraid to report crimes that they may experience or witness, undermining public safety.

In addition, the lives of undocumented immigrants are inextricably linked with ours. Most of them are long-term U.S. residents; they work hard, pay taxes, and otherwise abide by our laws. They provide for U.S. citizen spouses and children; they are our fellow churchgoers and children's playmates. Some of them came to this country as children, and this is the only country they know and consider home. Many have contributed to the revitalization of the cities where they live, and are providing the services the aging Baby Boom generation requires.

The notion that we are going to hunt down and deport 11 million people is a fantasy, and one the American public neither buys nor supports. So the question then is, what do we do? The majority of Americans support an earned legalization with a roadmap to citizenship as an essential component of immigration reform—and Senate bill 744 offers that possibility....

The benefits to our country of allowing these immigrants to earn legalization are significant, both economically and socially. No longer could unscrupulous employers pit undocumented workers against other workers. Legalization is also the only way to reduce the ability of unscrupulous employers from exploiting them or threatening to deport them for reporting labor law violations, thereby endangering wages and working conditions for all workers.

And bringing stability through earned legality to this population would mean opportunity for deepening roots, as well as higher earnings and therefore higher tax revenue—which studies have estimated would add billions of dollars just in the next 10 years alone. Legalized immigrants would be able to invest and spend more as they would be able to work towards their dreams—starting a business, buying a home for their families, helping their children succeed....

Family Unity

Keeping families together and strong is a core principle and a fundamental value of American life. In every religion, in every culture, in every wave of immigrants that have come to this country, the family unit has been critical both to the survival of immigrants in a strange land, and to their success in adapting and contributing to their newly adopted nation. It also promotes the economic stability of immigrants and their integration into our country, and we must continue our historic commitment to this idea.

We are glad that the bipartisan legislation seeks to address the unnecessary separation of families who are kept apart by extraordinarily long wait times for certain family visas. Millions of close family members of U.S. citizens and permanent residents are stuck waiting outside the U.S. for visas to become available; many wait for more than two decades. It is also important to remember that the family is not only a social unit, but a powerful economic engine. Close relatives are able to make vital contributions to the U.S. economy as productive workers and entrepreneurs. By clearing out the backlogs in the family and employment based categories and removing the limitation on the number of visas that are requested by legal permanent residents who apply for their spouses and minor children, the legislation would help promote the economic stability of immigrant families and their integration into our country....

Future Flow of Workers

Unlike previous immigration reforms, which have tightened enforcement but failed to establish effective legal avenues that respond to the needs of our economy and protect the American workforce, this bill has a series of provisions offering the opportunity for future workers to eventually pursue legal permanent residency and then citizenship. This is the best way to prevent the nation from having another debate in the future about legalizing yet another group of workers who live and work unlawfully in the U.S. It is imperative that our legal immigration system keep pace with our economy and our changing society.

As such, the sponsors of the bipartisan senate bill took into account the needs of both our country and its workers, from the fields all the way to Silicon Valley, by providing multiple ways for immigrant workers to enter the U.S. through safe and legal channels to meet legitimate workforce needs across sectors of our economy. The proposed legislation includes provisions that are complex and need further analysis. However, it appears it would create a 21st century process intended to be responsive to U.S. labor needs in a regulated, orderly fashion—while breaking precedent by providing labor rights and protections. We strongly believe that immigrant workers should have the same rights and responsibilities as other U.S. workers, including whistleblower protections and back-pay owed to them for their labor.

Immigrant Integration

Americans hold immigrant integration in high regard and want to see immigrants pledge allegiance to our country. So we are very pleased to see that the bipartisan legislation also includes many measures designed to achieve the successful integration of immigrants into American society. Its provisions would help enhance social cohesion among neighbors and coworkers in communities across the United States. The legislation would prohibit the use of race and ethnicity in federal law enforcement activities and requires data collection and new regulations to ensure a prohibition of racial profiling is implemented effectively. It also establishes an Office of New Americans, a New Americans taskforce and includes additional initiatives to help immigrants learn English, American civics and integrate into local communities. From financial counseling to English and civics courses, there is a dramatic need for increased resources and collaboration across government agencies to achieve the full integration of immigrants. And immigrants want to learn English and make greater contributions to the nation—I know it, because my organization and our hundreds of Affiliates help immigrants on this journey every day of the week....

Conclusion

...We acknowledge that compromises will have to be made by all parties. Significant concessions have already been made in this legislation, many that cut deeply into the interests of the Hispanic community. If each of us was looking at only individual pieces of this bill from our own parochial perspective, there is much we would be forced to oppose. But just as we are asking others to set aside some of their preferences to advance our nation's interests, we recognize that all of us have to accept some compromises to advance our common goal of producing a bill that reflects a strong, effective, and sustainable immigration policy for the 21st Century.

A bright line will soon emerge between those who seek to preserve a status quo, which serves no one except those who profit from a broken system, and those who are working in good faith to reach compromise and deliver a solution the country desperately needs. Put in stark terms, those who oppose progress are not just advocates for doing nothing, in essence, they are advocating for worse than nothing. Opponents of progress are supporting the continued existence of a subclass of 11 million people living outside the scope and protection of the law and an enforcement regime that separates families, turns a blind eye to racial profiling and the detention and even deportation of U.S. citizens and lawful residents. They would do nothing to address the growing gap between on the one hand, the family values of a 21st century society and the economic needs of a 21st Century economy and on the other, a legal immigration system that has remained unchanged for nearly three decades. They are opposing improved labor law enforcement, leveling the field for American workers, and laying the foundation for the accelerated integration of today's immigrants and those yet to arrive. In short, they offer the same feeble failed policies that may advance their political interests but don't produce real results, or they hold out for dystopian ends that cannot be achieved.

This bright line will be burnt indelibly in the minds of Latino voters. Those who created the game-changing moment for this debate in November, and the additional 14.4 million U.S. born and raised prospective Hispanic voters that will join the electorate between now and 2028. Our community will be engaged and watching closely to ensure that the legalization process is real, enforcement is accountable, and families and workers are protected. (http://www.nclr.org/images/uploads/publications/nclrtestimony_sjc_42213_1.pdf)

TESTIMONY OF GROVER NORQUIST, PRESIDENT OF AMERICANS FOR TAX REFORM, BEFORE THE U.S. SENATE, COMMITTEE ON THE JUDICIARY, HEARING ON "THE BORDER SECURITY, ECONOMIC OPPORTUNITY, AND IMMIGRATION MODERNIZATION ACT, S.744," APRIL 22, 2013

Chairman Leahy, Ranking Member Grassley, and Members of the Committee, my name is Grover Norquist, and I am President of Americans for Tax Reform (ATR). ATR is a nonprofit advocacy organization that promotes free market principles and a fiscally conservative approach to public policymaking.

Mr. Chairman, people are an asset, not a liability. America is the most immigrant-friendly country in the world, and we are the richest country in the world. This is not a coincidence. Those who would make us less immigrant-friendly would make us less successful, less prosperous, and less American.

Now, how do we evaluate the specific legislation before the Senate? The Border Security, Economic Opportunity, and Immigration Modernization Act of 2013's stated aim is to uphold America's tradition of strengthening its economy by maintaining its openness to immigrants.

Dynamic Analysis: A Conservative Consensus

The consensus conservative, free market approach to evaluating any public policy change is to do so dynamically. Dynamic scoring takes into account both the costs and benefits of any policy change. Specific to immigration, providing a tough but fair pathway to legal status for America's undocumented population while facilitating an adequate future flow of legal immigrants will increase the size and productivity of our workforce and thus lead to accelerated economic growth for all Americans.

Wall Street Journal editorial board member Jason Riley made the case for dynamic scoring in his 2008 book:

> Supply siders have for decades been critical of the way federal agencies like the Congressional Budget Office and the Joint Committee on Taxation estimated, or "scored," the effects of tax cuts on revenue without figuring in their effects on the overall economy. And rightly so. Under static modeling, for instance, if a state doubles its cigarette tax, it will double its revenue from that tax. But that doesn't take into account, as a dynamic model would, the fact that the tax increase will affect behavior. Smokers, for example, may quit or smoke less. The tobacco taxes they previously paid would be lost to the state, offsetting some of the additional revenue anticipated by increasing the tax rate. Similarly, a tax cut might not result in a revenue reduction if it stimulates more economic activity.

Riley also provides a history of conservative policy organizations driving the center-right consensus on dynamic scoring:

> Along with other conservative outfits like the National Center for Policy Analysis and the Institute for Policy Innovation, [the Heritage Foundation] helped pioneer the use of dynamic analysis. Whether the issue was trade liberalization or tax policy, free-market conservatives regularly mocked economic studies that took into account only static impacts. "[No] matter how many times a 'static' analysis is disproved," Heritage Foundation president Ed Feulner once wrote, "Congress keeps doing business in the same wrongheaded way." When President Bush's 2007 budget proposal included a plan to create a Dynamic Analysis division inside the Treasury Department to assess how tax laws affect economic activity, William Beach, Heritage's top numbers cruncher, praised the move. "Inside the Beltway, this type of work is called 'dynamic analysis,'" Beach wrote in *BusinessWeek*. "Outside the Beltway, this is called 'economics.'"

Indeed, any sound conservative evaluation of public policy changes must include an accounting of the legislation's costs and benefits....

Dynamic Scoring Specific to the Immigration Debate

To score legislation dynamically we need to understand its impact on the economy first. The broad issue of dynamic scoring applies specifically to immigration reform because immigrants increase both the supply and demand sides of the economy. On the supply side, immigrants work and thereby increase economic production and the productivity of Americans. Because immigrants have different skills, they are complements rather than competitors to the vast majority of Americans. On the demand side, immigrants purchase and rent goods, services, and real estate produced by other Americans, thus incentivizing production.

Immigrants and Americans, in the face of such changes, do not respond statically. Both groups change their behavior in response to incentives, and it is incumbent upon us to measure the economic effects of these behavioral changes dynamically. For instance, immigrant incomes increase over time just as incomes increase during the working life of Americans. After the legalization of immigrants during the Reagan amnesty, their incomes rose by an average 15 percent just by gaining legal status. Those immigrants today are making much more than they did then and, as a result, paying more in taxes. In response to immigration, Americans also increase their investments in machines and capital to invest in a faster growing and productive workforce. Those are just two changes but they illustrate the magnitude of dynamic changes to the economy. Since both the supply and demand sides change in relation to each other, we have to use a dynamic scoring process to accurately estimate the broad effects.

The broader economic impacts are gigantic. A 2009 study prepared for the Cato Institute by economists Peter Dixon and Maureen Rimmer employed a dynamic economic model called USAGE to estimate the effects of changes in the U.S. economy due to an immigration policy change very similar to today's Senate legislation. It found that the incomes of U.S. households would increase by $180 billion a year. Increased legal immigration will add millions of consumers, workers, renters, and others who will make our economy larger by working with Americans to produce more of the goods and services we demand.

Another similar study commissioned by Cato and written by Professor Raul Hinojosa-Ojeda of UCLA employed a similar analysis using a dynamic model called the GMig2. The study found that an additional $1.5 trillion in GDP growth would occur ten years after immigration reform similar to the Senate's plan.

As a comparison, Professor Hinojosa-Ojeda ran a simulation on the GMig2 model whereby immigration reform was instead replaced by an effective enforcement-only policy that produced the mass removal of all illegal immigrants—a policy desired by immigration restrictionists. The result of that simulation was a $2.6 trillion decrease in estimated GDP growth over the same decade.

Most recently, American Action Forum President Douglas Holtz-Eakin, former Director of the Congressional Budget Office, authored a dynamic study on the economic impact of immigration reform. While not specifically related to the legislation before us today, Holtz-Eakin's study measures the costs and benefits of a "benchmark immigration reform," concluding that significantly increasing legal immigration would boost GDP growth by 0.9 points annually....

Additionally, Holtz-Eakin cites the entrepreneurial vigor associated with immigrants as further evidence that more immigration will lead to higher rates of economic growth. This assertion is supplemented by the Kauffman Foundation, which found that immigrants in 2011 were twice as likely as native-born Americans to start a new business.

Immigrants and Productivity Gains

To get a sense of how the productivity of today's undocumented workers might increase once they have earned legal status, imagine the converse. If your siblings or your children were denied the ability to have a driver's license and therefore fly on airplanes or drive themselves to and from work, how productive would they be? How would their income suffer? How many career opportunities would they be denied?

Allowing undocumented workers to move from job to job, travel easily and safely, search out and interview for different jobs in different sectors and locations would greatly increase their productivity, and they would become greater contributors to their own well-being and the wealth of our nation.

The majority of those undocumented immigrants currently here are low-skilled. Some argue that we should not be importing or legalizing this type of talent. But in reality, the U.S. economy demands an enormous number of low-skilled workers. They work in construction, retail, hospitality, food preparation, agriculture, manufacturing, and other industries. But the domestic labor supply is inadequate for these types of jobs. We need immigrant labor to fill demand for low-skill jobs....

Increasing the supply of low-skilled immigrants doesn't only ensure that more vacant jobs are filled. It increases the overall productivity of the American economy by injecting talent that is complementary to the existing domestic labor supply. Immigrants are generally either lower-skilled or higher-skilled than most native-born workers. That means they aren't competing with Americans for the type of jobs they are qualified to do. Instead, they fill jobs that complement the existing American labor supply, raising productivity and wages across the board.

Think about this in the context of a restaurant. Immigrants, because of their low skills and lesser English speaking proficiency, work in non-communications jobs like dishwashing, cooking, bussing tables, and janitorial work. The Americans who filled these jobs in previous generations are now performing higher-paid jobs like waiting tables, hosting, and managing the restaurant. The availability of lower-skilled labor allows native-born Americans to work better jobs and earn more money.

By the same account, high-skilled immigrants are vital to America's dynamic economy. Similar to low-skilled immigrants, they rarely directly compete with native-born workers, but for different reasons. High-skilled labor is extremely entrepreneurial. They grow the economic pie by innovating and building new businesses. They directly create opportunity for Americans.

Immigrants or their children founded more than 40 percent of Fortune 500 companies. Those immigrant-founded Fortune 500s employ more than 10 million people worldwide, and have combined global revenues of $4.2 trillion.

Baseless Criticism

Some people who choose to play politics with this issue have ignored dynamic analysis and instead considered only the inflated costs of reform. Errors found in pseudo-analysis by anti-immigration groups include:

- Exaggerating public benefit costs by citing household costs, rather than individual immigrant costs. By counting welfare costs on a household basis, critics [are] including millions of native-born American spouses and children into their estimation. This is a misleading trick that inflates the true cost of public benefits for immigrants, and assumes native-born Americans are only public charges because of their association with their immigrant spouses or parents.

- Portraying impossible levels of welfare use. Putting aside the evidence that immigrants come to America to pursue economic opportunity, it is important to point out that leading criticisms of increased immigration predict levels of welfare use that are impossible under this bill. Most undocumented immigrants are barred from accepting public benefits, including Obamacare, for 13 years at the earliest. Those on a quicker path—agricultural workers and DREAMers—still must wait eight years. Yet prominent criticisms of the bill assume immediate adoption welfare benefits by those legalized.

- Assuming immigrant wages will remain stagnant throughout their lives. With legalization comes labor market flexibility and productivity gains, resulting in higher wages. After the 1986 Reagan amnesty, immigrant wages increased immediately after they became legal, sometimes by as much as 15 to 25 percent.

- Ignoring the costs of an enforcement-only approach. Professor Raul Hinojosa-Ojeda of UCLA using the GMig2, a dynamic bilateral labor flows model, to estimate the economic effects of a successful enforcement-only policy that mass removed of all illegal immigrants—a policy desired by immigration restrictionists. The result of that simulation was a $2.6 trillion decrease in estimated GDP growth over the same decade, decreasing tax revenues. Direct government costs of such a program are also enormous. Economist Rajeev Goyle estimated that deporting 11 million people would cost the government $206 billion over a five year period. More conservatively, Immigration and Customs Enforcement (ICE) assumed that the marginal immigrant costs $12,500 to deport which, assuming no increase in marginal costs, would cost the government approximately $140 billion to deport 11 million unauthorized immigrants.

- Conceding the size of the current welfare state, rather than working to reform it. Building a wall around the welfare state is a far more effective and economically beneficial policy than building a wall around the country. It is also politically possible.

There are groups that oppose growing the American economy via more immigration because of their extreme environmental and population control views, because they have a flawed Malthusian view of the economy, and because they don't understand free markets. Their failed arguments against immigration are also arguments against having children. These groups view people not as assets, but as liabilities. This is a fatally flawed argument, and completely inconsistent with conservative principles.

Some argue that the fiscal burden of America's entitlement programs make more immigration cost prohibitive. That is a false choice. That our entitlement systems are broken is not an argument for less immigration; it is an argument to fix our entitlement systems.

The legislation before us today puts at least 13 years between legal status and access to public benefits for most undocumented immigrants, mitigating the negative fiscal impacts of our bloated entitlement programs. Those who insist or imagine that this bill would impose trillions of dollars in new entitlement costs have not read the legislation, nor do they understand the current eligibility requirements.

Furthermore, immigrants come at the beginning of their working lives, which means they will have years to pay taxes and contribute to the economy before being eligible for entitlements. The American Community Survey estimates that the average age of immigrants who have come since the year 2000 is 31 while the average native-born American is 36 years old. Immigrants typically arrive in their mid-20s after their home countries pay for their education so they can begin to work and pay taxes in the U.S. immediately. By coming at such a young working age the government does not have to pay for their education but they could work around 40 years before being eligible for entitlements if they decide to stay.

Also, many low-skilled immigrants work for years in the U.S. before returning home with their savings as part of a phenomenon called circular migration. Forcing them to work in the illegal market means they will stay here longer than they otherwise would because if they did leave the U.S., there would be no guarantee they could come back later to make money if they had to. Allowing them to come legally or to legalize the ones here would reignite circular migration, allowing immigrants to plan on coming here for a few years to work and pay taxes and then returning home with their savings. Princeton Sociologist Doug Massey has observed that 20 percent to 30 percent of Mexican immigrants from 1965 to 1986 followed that pattern.

For almost all means-tested federal welfare programs, immigrants are substantially restricted access until they have had a green card for at least five years. Programs they are restricted from include: Medicaid, Supplemental Nutrition Assistance Program, Temporary Assistance for Needy Families, and Supplemental Security Income. The current legislation would construct even larger barriers to welfare, with a 10-year waiting period for most newly legalized immigrants to receive a green card, and then another 3 years until access to means-tested public benefits. That is a high wall around the welfare state....

Mr. Chairman, it is my belief that a position in favor of more legal immigration and a fair and humane path to citizenship for those undocumented immigrants already here is wholly consistent with the ideals of the center-right movement I have worked my entire life to help build. I believe that free markets lead to economic growth and prosperity for all. This includes free and flexible labor markets, which will benefit not only those who wish to come here to pursue the American Dream, but also those of us blessed enough to have been born in the United States of America.

CHAPTER 9
THE UNITED STATES NEEDS TOUGHER IMMIGRATION LAWS

TESTIMONY OF SHAWN MORAN, VICE PRESIDENT OF THE NATIONAL BORDER PATROL COUNCIL, BEFORE THE U.S. SENATE, COMMITTEE ON HOMELAND SECURITY AND GOVERNMENTAL AFFAIRS, HEARING ON "DEFERRED ACTION ON IMMIGRATION: IMPLICATIONS AND UNANSWERED QUESTIONS," FEBRUARY 4, 2015

Chairman Johnson, Ranking Member Carper, members of the Committee, on behalf of the 16,500 Border Patrol Agents whom I represent, I would like to thank you for having this hearing.

My name is Shawn Moran and I am the Vice President and national spokesperson of the National Border Patrol Council. I am a 17 year veteran of the Border Patrol and have spent the majority of my career in the Imperial Beach and El Cajon Border Patrol Stations in California. I have also been temporarily assigned to several sectors and stations along the southwest border during that time.

Before I discuss how I believe the President's decision will impact border security, I want to be clear that I am not a lawyer. I am not here to comment on the legality of the President's actions. I am here as a federal law enforcement agent to discuss how the amnesty provided in November will impact border security. Unfortunately, I do not believe the border security implications were fully considered prior to the issuance of the executive order and that concrete actions need to be taken by Congress and the Administration this year to bolster border security.

Albert Einstein's definition of insanity is doing the same thing over and over again and expecting a different result. If you look at the history of our response to illegal immigration we certainly meet that definition. In 1986 Congress passed and President Reagan signed the Immigration Reform and Control Act (IRCA). This legislation was supposed to "solve" the illegal immigration problem

in this country and in the process legalized illegal aliens who had been in the country prior to 1982.

What was the result? Illegal immigration exploded. The Pew Research Center estimates that the population of illegal aliens in this country in 1990, immediately following the passage of IRCA, was 3.5 million. By 2007 that population had swelled to 12.2 million. Cities like San Diego, where I am stationed, and El Paso were nearly overrun.

In my career, I have arrested and interviewed thousands of illegal aliens. In deciding whether or not to attempt to enter this country illegally, these individuals weigh the risks and potential rewards. These individuals are risking not only a lifetime of savings to pay the smugglers but literally their own lives in the process. They know the border is a dangerous place. They know that they are opening themselves up to predation from smugglers in addition to the physical hazards of crossing the Rio Grande River, the Arizona desert, or even the Montana wilderness.

Unfortunately since the passage of IRCA there is a perception among illegal aliens that if you can get over the border and can hide in the shadows long enough, eventually there will be a pathway to legal status. This pathway may be by virtue of the duration you have been here or through your children. We need only look to the debacle last summer with unaccompanied minors to see how prevalent this perception is among potential illegal aliens.

Last year the Administration took great pains to point out that their most recent expansion of Deferred Action for Childhood Arrivals (DACA) was a continuation of deferred actions that had been taken by previous Administrations. We were all told that there was precedent for their actions. The Administration was completely correct. There were ample amounts of precedent and therein lies the problem. We will never be able to stop illegal immigration until potential illegal aliens believe that it is a losing proposition. They need to know that they will be found and that hiding in the shadows will do them no good. Employers need to know that if they hire illegal aliens, there will be credible sanctions.

The question then becomes what steps this Committee, within your jurisdiction, can take to strengthen border security before the next wave of illegal immigration comes. Several suggestions that I have include:

- Increased manpower—Currently there are 21,370 Border Patrol Agents in this country. Under sequestration we effectively lost 1,500 full time equivalents (FTEs) that have thankfully been restored under the Border Patrol Pay Reform Act introduced by Senators [Jon] Tester and [John] McCain. We do not have to double the size of the Border Patrol to gain operational control of the border. But we are, in my opinion, approximately 5,000 Agents short of where we should be. NBPC [National Border Patrol Council] would advocate that of this number, 1,500 be sent to the northern border which is woefully understaffed and the remaining 3,500 positions allocated to interior enforcement.

- Supervising staffing levels—The Border Patrol is an extremely top heavy organization with far too many layers of management and a convoluted chain of command. Although Congress has provided the funding to double the size of the Border Patrol we have not doubled the number of Agents at the border. Let me explain, the average large police department has one supervisor for every 10 officers. The Border Patrol has one supervisor for every 4 Agents. The Committee should mandate a 10:1 ratio and achieve it through attrition in the supervisory ranks. The second problem is that we have Agents doing duties like processing and transportation that could be handled more cost effectively by non-law enforcement personnel.

- Interior enforcement—Every night we effectively play goal line defense because all of our resources and assets are concentrated right at the border instead of having a defense in depth. Let me give you an example, we have 7,000 Agents in Arizona and do you know how many Agents we have assigned to Phoenix, which is an important transit point for traffickers? The answer is zero. The Border Patrol's northernmost station in Arizona is Casa Grande, which is 50 miles south of Phoenix.

- Better training—During the buildup of the Border Patrol during the Bush Administration the Academy's duration was reduced from approximately 20 weeks to as little as 54 days if you spoke Spanish. This is simply not enough time to properly train an Agent and weed out those who are not up to the challenge. The Committee should require that the Academy revert back to 20 weeks.

Again, I want to thank the Committee for the opportunity to testify. If you have any questions I would be happy to answer them to the best of my ability. (http://www.hsgac.senate.gov/download/?id=0292d3f5-e39d-45b6-8027-e961a693b61a)

TESTIMONY OF MICHAEL W. CUTLER, SENIOR SPECIAL AGENT, U.S. IMMIGRATION AND NATURALIZATION SERVICE (RETIRED), BEFORE THE U.S. SENATE, COMMITTEE ON THE JUDICIARY, HEARING ON "BUILDING AN IMMIGRATION SYSTEM WORTHY OF AMERICAN VALUES," MARCH 20, 2013

Good afternoon Chairman Leahy, Senator Coons, Ranking Member Grassley, other members of the Judiciary Committee, fellow witnesses, ladies and gentlemen.

I greatly appreciate the opportunity to provide my perspectives at this important hearing concerning how America's immigration system be made reflective and worthy of American values. For me personally, immigration is the story of my own family and it has virtually been my life's work. As you may know, I was sworn in as an Immigration Inspector in October 1971 at the New York District Office of the former Immigration and Naturalization Service [INS]. Thus began my career with the INS that would span some 30 years. At the end of my career with the INS I was a Senior Special Agent assigned to the Organized Crime, Drug Enforcement Task Force.

My career provided me with a unique front row seat to the true importance of America's immigration laws to nearly every challenge and threat confronting America and Americans.

Rather than simply being a single issue, immigration is a *singular* issue that impacts everything from national security, criminal justice and community safety to the economy, unemployment, healthcare and public health, education and the environment to name the most prominent.

America's immigration laws were enacted to achieve two critical goals—protect innocent lives and protect the jobs of American workers.

A review of Title 8, United States Code, Section 1182 will make the purpose and intentions of our immigration laws clear. This section of the Immigration and Nationality Act enumerates the categories of aliens who are ineligible to enter the United States. Among these categories are aliens who have dangerous communicable diseases, suffer extreme mental illness and are prone to violence or are sex offenders. Criminals who have committed serious crimes are also excludible as are spies, terrorists, human rights violators and war criminals. Finally, aliens who would work in violation of law or become public charges are also deemed excludible.

It is vital to note that there is nothing in our immigration laws that would exclude aliens because of race, religion or ethnicity.

Our valiant members of the armed forces are charged with keeping our enemies as far from our borders as possible while the DHS [U.S. Department of Homeland Security] is charged with securing our borders from within. While mentioning our borders it is vital to understand that any state that has an international airport or has access to a seaport is as much a border state as are those states that are found along America's northern and southern borders.

We are constantly told that the immigration system is broken. What is never discussed is the fact that for decades the federal government has failed to effectively secure America's borders and enforce and administer the immigration laws. These failures convinced desperate people from around the world that the United States is not serious about its borders or its laws. This impression was further exacerbated by the Amnesty created by IRCA in 1986 which enabled more than 3.5 million illegal aliens to acquire lawful status and a pathway to United States citizenship.

This supposed one-time program that was to finally restore integrity to the immigration system was an abysmal failure. It could be argued that the failures to effectively enforce the immigration laws especially where the employer sanctions provisions of IRCA was concerned, to balance the amnesty provisions, provided a huge incentive for aliens to enter the United States in violation of America's borders and laws and consequently, the United States witnessed the largest influx of illegal aliens in history.

Respect for America's immigration laws have been further eroded by other factors such as the advocacy by the administration, and some Congressional leaders, for the creation of a program under the aegis of "Comprehensive Immigration Reform" that, if enacted, would provide unknown millions of illegal aliens, whose true identities and entry data are unverifiable, with pathways to citizenship. There are many reasons that programs such as these are problematic, but first and foremost is the undeniable fact that there is no way to determine the true identities of these aliens nor any way to verify how or when they entered the United States. This lack of integrity also plagues the program known as DACA (Deferred Action for Childhood Arrivals) that the administration created under the guise of "prosecutorial discretion" to provide illegal aliens who claim to have entered the United States as teenagers with temporary lawful status and employment authorization. It has been estimated that this program may ultimately provide between one million and two million such illegal aliens with official identity documents and employment authorization. The identity documents enable those to whom these documents are issued to obtain Social Security cards, driver's licenses and other such official identity documents even though it is virtually impossible to be certain of the true identities of the aliens to whom these documents are issued.

These are essentially the same aliens who would have been eligible for lawful status under the failed legislation known as the DREAM Act. As a former INS special agent I can tell you that there is no magical way to verify the information contained in the applications for participation in Comprehensive Immigration Reform or DACA is accurate or honest. The best chance to do this would be to conduct full field investigations—investigations that ICE [U.S. Immigration and Customs Enforcement] and USCIS [U.S. Citizenship and Immigration Services] do not have the resources to conduct. Time and again the GAO [U.S. Government Accountability Office] and OIG [Office of Inspector General] have pointed to a lack of integrity to the immigration benefits program. Fraud undermines the immigration system and national security as well.

Here are two important excerpts from the 9/11 Commission Staff Report on Terrorist Travel.

First of all, here is the first paragraph from the preface of that report:

"It is perhaps obvious to state that terrorists cannot plan and carry out attacks in the United States if they are unable to enter the country. Yet prior to September 11, while there were efforts to enhance border security, no agency of the U.S. government thought of border security as a tool in the counterterrorism arsenal. Indeed, even after 19 hijackers demonstrated the relative ease of obtaining a U.S. visa and gaining admission into the United States, border security still is not considered a cornerstone of national security policy. We believe, for reasons we discuss in the following pages, that it must be made one."

Here is a paragraph under the title "Immigration Benefits" found on page 98:

"Terrorists in the 1990s, as well as the September 11 hijackers, needed to find a way to stay in or embed themselves in the United States if their operational plans were to come to fruition. As already discussed, this could be accomplished legally by marrying an American citizen, achieving temporary worker status, or applying for asylum after entering. In many cases, the act of filing for an immigration benefit sufficed to permit the alien to remain in the country until the petition was adjudicated. Terrorists were free to conduct surveillance, coordinate operations, obtain and receive funding, go to school and learn English, make contacts in the United States, acquire necessary materials, and execute an attack."

On December 7, 2012, the DHS OIG issued a report that was entitled:

"Improvements Needed for SAVE to Accurately Determine Immigration Status of Individuals Ordered Deported"

In conducting its investigation and preparing the report, the OIG examined the SAVE (Systematic Alien Verification for Entitlements) program. The results of the review were disconcerting, to say the least. The report noted that failures to update the data in the system could potentially affect the more than 800,000 individuals who have been ordered deported, removed, and excluded but who are still in the United States. That report went on to note that a random statistical sample test of individuals who had been ordered deported but still remained in the United States identified a 12 percent error rate in immigration status verification. In other words, these individuals had no status, but were erroneously identified as having lawful immigration status.

Adding this to the clearly stated policies of the administration which invoked "Prosecutorial Discretion" to not arrest or seek the removal of illegal aliens unless the aliens in question have been convicted of committing serious crimes.

Most recently the administration has engaged in a program to release thousands of illegal aliens from custody who have criminal histories. This program undermines any vestiges of integrity that the immigration law enforcement program might have had. I cannot imagine how a clearer message could be sent to people around the world that our nation is not only willing to ignore violations of law but reward violations of laws that were enacted to protect innocent lives and the jobs of American workers.

Meanwhile leaders of some cities and states openly demonstrate their disdain and contempt for our immigration laws by declaring that they have created "sanctuaries" for illegal aliens; yet the federal government refuses to take action against them.

Each of these actions, or lack of action, has served to encourage, induce, aid or abet aliens to violate our immigration laws. Sanctuary cities and states also serve to shield illegal aliens from detection by the federal government. It is important to note that this all represents violations of Title 8, United States Code, Section 1324 that addresses alien smuggling, harboring, inducing and, in general facilitating the entry of illegal aliens into the United States.

This would be wrong at any time but my concern is that today our nation is threatened by international terrorist organizations and transnational criminals from the four corners of our planet, and the pernicious gangs and criminal organizations that they often belong to.

Notwithstanding these threats and the fact that the American economy is hobbled by extraordinarily high unemployment and underemployment rates, the immigration component of these challenges has been ignored. Each month the United States lawfully admits tens of thousands of foreign workers who are authorized to work in the United States, while failures to effectively secure our borders and enforce the immigration laws from within the interior of the United States provides unfair competition for American workers desperate to find decent jobs. By not routinely enforcing the immigration laws and by its latest decision to release thousands of criminal aliens, the entire immigration system has come to lack integrity and fails to provide the deterrence against foreign nationals who would enter the United States intent on working illegally or, perhaps, with far more nefarious goals in mind.

Law enforcement is at its best when it creates a climate of deterrence to convince those who might be contemplating violating the law that such an effort is likely to be discovered and that if discovered, adverse consequences will result for the law violators. Current policies and statements by the administration, in my view, encourage aspiring illegal aliens around the world to head for the United States. In effect the starter's pistol has been fired and for these folks, the finish line to this race is the border of the United States.

Back when I was an INS special agent I recall that Doris Meissner who was, at the time, the commissioner of the INS, said that the agency needed to be "customer oriented." Unfortunately, while I agree about the need to be customer oriented what Ms. Meissner and too many politicians today seem to have forgotten is that the "customers" of the INS and of our government in general, are the citizens of the United States of America.

I look forward to your questions. (http://www.judiciary.senate.gov/imo/media/doc/3-20-13CutlerTestimony.pdf)

TESTIMONY OF RUSSELL PEARCE, PRESIDENT OF BANAMNESTYNOW.COM, BEFORE THE U.S. SENATE, COMMITTEE ON THE JUDICIARY, SUBCOMMITTEE ON IMMIGRATION, REFUGEES, AND BORDER SECURITY, HEARING ON "EXAMINING THE CONSTITUTIONALITY AND PRUDENCE OF STATE AND LOCAL GOVERNMENTS ENFORCING IMMIGRATION LAW," APRIL 24, 2012

Good Morning. I'm Russell Pearce, the author of, and driving force behind [the controversial 2010 Arizona immigration law] Support Our Law Enforcement and Safe Neighborhoods Act, known as "SB 1070," which is overwhelmingly supported by citizens across the nation.

Thank you, Chairman Schumer, for inviting me here today. It is an honor for me to appear before this Committee. As you well know, the illegal alien problem is a critical issue, not only in Arizona, but across the country.

The adverse effects of illegal immigration ripple throughout our society.

In addressing this problem, we must begin by remembering that we are a nation of laws. We must have the courage—the fortitude—to enforce, with compassion but without apology, those laws that protect the integrity of our borders and the rights of our citizens from those who break our laws.

SB1070, in full accordance with federal law, removes the political handcuffs from state and local law enforcement. All law enforcement agencies have the legal authority, and a moral obligation, to uphold our laws, such as Sheriff Joe Arpaio, who is keeping his Oath and doing the job he was hired to do. His deputies were trained by ICE on how they want federal law enforced. And yet the Obama Justice Department continues to attack and threaten him.

The invasion of illegal aliens we face today—convicted felons, drug cartels, gang members, human traffickers and even terrorists—pose one of the greatest threats to our nation in terms of political, economic and national security. During the debate of SB1070, a rancher friend of mine, Rob Krentz, was murdered on the border by an illegal alien. I have attended funerals of many citizens and law enforcement officers murdered by illegal aliens. My own son, a Deputy Sheriff, was critically wounded in a gun battle with an illegal alien while serving a warrant. I have been in public service most of my life and I have seen the real costs and damage caused by the presence of illegal aliens in our country.

In Arizona alone, the annual cost of illegal immigration is approximately $2.6 billion and that is just to educate, medicate and incarcerate illegal aliens in Arizona. Nationally, the cost is in the tens of billions of dollars and the taxpayers foot the bill. And those numbers do not reflect the costs of crimes committed by those here illegally, or the jobs lost by legal residents. Government's failure to enforce our laws and secure our border is unforgivable and the total cost is staggering.

Had law enforcement enforced our immigration laws we would have averted 9/11. The terrorist attacks of September 11, 2001, underscored for all Americans the link between immigration law enforcement and terrorism. Four of the five leaders of the 9/11 attack were in violation of our immigration laws and had contact with law enforcement but were not arrested. Nineteen alien terrorists had been able to violate our immigration laws, overstay their visas or violate their Immigration statuses with impunity, and move freely within the Country without significant interference from federal or local law enforcement. The abuse of U.S. Immigration laws was instrumental in the deaths of nearly 3,000 people on that tragic day in America.

Yet, instead of addressing enforcing the law, the Obama administration does the opposite, by encouraging further law breaking. Under federal law, "Sanctuary Policies" plainly are illegal. But the Obama administration does not sue those cities that are openly in violation of federal law for having these illegal sanctuary policies. Instead, it chooses to sue Arizona for *enforcing* the law, *protecting* our citizens, *protecting* jobs for lawful residents, and *protecting* the taxpayers and the citizens of this Republic in attempting to secure our borders.

Contrary to the view of the Obama Justice Department, not every state action related to illegal aliens is preempted by federal law. America has a system of dual sovereignty. Only state laws that regulate immigration are preempted by federal law.

Almost 40 years ago, the Supreme Court made it clear that the mere fact aliens are the subject of a state statute does not render it a regulation of immigration. Only the determination of who should or should not be admitted into the country, and the conditions under which that person may remain, is the *regulation* of immigration.

During my eleven years in the Arizona State Legislature, I authored numerous legislative initiatives designed to protect the State of Arizona from the adverse effects of illegal immigration and most importantly, to uphold the rule of law. They include:

- Proposition 200 in 2004, which requires individuals to show identification at the polls prior to voting (passed by 57% of the voters);

- Proposition 100 in 2006, a State constitutional amendment to deny bond to any person unlawfully present in the United States who commits a serious crime in Arizona (passed by 78% of the voters, including 60% of Hispanics);

- Proposition 102, 2006, which states that a person unlawfully present in the United States who sues an American citizen cannot receive punitive damages (passed by 75% of the voters);

- In 2007, The "Legal Arizona Workers Act," prohibiting employers from hiring unauthorized workers and requiring use of federal E-Verify system to confirm employee eligibility (upheld by the Supreme Court in 2011 by a 5 to 3 vote).

I am also proud to say that each of these initiatives has become law and survived various legal challenges. In fact, the last time that I was in Washington, the Supreme Court upheld the Legal Arizona Workers Act against what I consider an unpatriotic challenge by the Chamber of Commerce and anti-rule of law challenge/attack by the Obama administration.

Because of these accomplishments, the citizens of Arizona are safer. According to the Phoenix Law Enforcement

Association, the organization that represents the rank-and-file police officers in Phoenix:

> Since SB1070, Phoenix has experienced a 30-year low crime rate. 600 police vacancies, budget cuts, and old policing strategies didn't bring about these falling crime rates. SB1070 did. When hard-working rank-and-file Phoenix Police Officers were given access to the tool of SB1070, the deterrence factor this legislation brought about was clearly instrumental in our unprecedented drop in crime. And all of this without a single civil rights, racial profiling, or biased policing complaint. To ignore the positive impact of SB1070 in the City of Phoenix is to ignore the huge elephant in the middle of the room.

In other words, although city hall will not acknowledge the effect of my legislative initiatives on crime rates, the Phoenix Law Enforcement Association has no doubts: the various law enforcement provisions enacted by the Arizona State Legislature have worked.

Therefore, I am pleased to be here today to highlight for this Committee the importance of SB 1070 in combating rampant illegal immigration and upholding the rule of law.

Let me take a moment to reiterate why we are here today. We are here because the federal government has decided not to enforce the law. When I was at the Supreme Court in December 2010 listening to the oral arguments in the legal challenge to my E-Verify law, Justice [Antonin] Scalia commented that "nobody would [have thought] that ... the Federal Government would not enforce [immigration laws]. Of course, no one would have expected that." States, such as Arizona, have no choice but to take action to address the adverse effects of the federal government's failure to enforce the law.

Everyone knows that proactive state laws work. It is clear in Arizona. Neither the federal government nor the interest groups challenging the various laws around the country claim that these laws do not protect the public from additional lawlessness. Yet, they have taken unprecedented steps to prevent enforcement of state laws. Therefore, the only issue is whether a specific state law is "preempted" by some federal law.

And, importantly, as the Supreme Court has held, only the determination of who should or should not be admitted into the country, and the conditions under which that person may remain, is the regulation of immigration. Therefore, as long as states do not interfere with the federal government's enforcement activity, states indisputably have the authority to legislate in areas touching on immigration.

Again, let me be clear, SB 1070 does not regulate immigration. Instead, it utilizes Arizona's inherent "police powers" and regulates unlawfully present aliens consistent with the objectives of federal law. SB 1070 specifically authorizes and directs Arizona law enforcement officers to cooperate and communicate with federal officials regarding the enforcement of federal immigration law and imposes penalties under Arizona law for non-compliance with federal law. In other words, SB 1070 mirrors federal objectives while furthering entirely legitimate state goals.

A brief review of the actual provisions of SB 1070 at issue before the Supreme Court tomorrow demonstrates this point:

Section 2 of the law simply provides Arizona police officers with additional guidance as to how to interact with individuals who may not be lawfully present. It does nothing more than define a police officer's available discretion consistent with existing federal law to inquire about a person's immigration status. In addition, for Section 2 to even apply there must be a lawful stop, detention, or arrest and there must be reasonable suspicion that a person is an alien and is not lawfully present in the United States.

Section 3 simply reinforces federal law as it essentially makes it a state crime for unlawfully present aliens in Arizona to violate federal registration laws. Under federal law, every alien who has been issued a registration document is required to carry that document on his or her person at all times. Therefore, Section 3 only creates state law penalties for failing to comply with federal law. Such a practice is common in other areas that the federal government regulates. In other words, an unlawfully present alien only violates Section 3 if he violates federal law.

Section 5 also reinforces federal law. Under federal law, it is unlawful to knowingly hire an illegal alien for employment. To assist employers in complying with this federal law, Section 5 was carefully crafted to ensure that only those who may lawfully work would apply for jobs. In other words, this provision does no more than protect the jobs of those who may lawfully work from those who are not eligible to work under federal law. And, with unemployment still at record levels, it is a critical function of state governments to protect available jobs for all legal workers.

And finally, Section 6 defines the existing warrantless arrest authority of Arizona law enforcement officers and is not preempted. It is undisputed under that law that state and local law enforcement officers have authority to enforce criminal provisions of federal immigration laws. Therefore, Section 6 simply makes clear that Arizona law enforcement officers have authority to arrest without a warrant individuals who have willfully failed or refused to depart after having been ordered to be removed by a federal immigration judge.

Contrary to what is reported in the press, it is only these simple and clear law enforcement measures that are before the Supreme Court tomorrow. This common sense law is fully within the authority of Arizona—and any other state—as it protects Arizona citizens from the effects of illegal immigration and upholds the rule of law. And protecting our citizens, I believe, is the highest duty of any public official.

Thank you and God bless you and may God continue to bless this Republic. (http://www.judiciary.senate.gov/imo/media/doc/12-4-24PearceTestimony.pdf)

TESTIMONY OF MARK KRIKORIAN, EXECUTIVE DIRECTOR, CENTER FOR IMMIGRATION STUDIES, BEFORE THE U.S. SENATE, COMMITTEE ON THE JUDICIARY, HEARING ON "THE BORDER SECURITY, ECONOMIC OPPORTUNITY, AND IMMIGRATION MODERNIZATION ACT, S.744," APRIL 22, 2013

There may be circumstances under which an amnesty for certain illegal aliens would make sense. Given the pervasive and deliberate non-enforcement of the immigration laws for so many years, and the resulting large population of illegal aliens, one could make a case for clearing the decks, as it were, and making a fresh start. This would be a distasteful proposition, to be sure, given that virtually all illegal aliens are guilty of multiple felonies, among them identity theft, document fraud, tax evasion, and perjury. Nonetheless, for practical reasons conferring legal status on established, non-violent illegal aliens may well, at some point, be a policy option worth discussing.

But only *after* the problem that allowed the mass settlement of illegal aliens has been addressed.

S 744 takes the opposite approach. It legalizes the illegal population *before* the necessary tools are in place to avoid the development of yet another large illegal population. As such, it paves the way for yet more demands for amnesty a decade or so in the future, as those who entered in, say 2015, are so well-established by 2023 that we will be told that we have to permit them to stay as well.

What's more, the legalization provisions of the bill make widespread fraud very likely.

Much has been made of the so-called triggers in Sec. 3 that would permit the Registered Provisional Immigrants (RPI) to receive permanent residence. Tying the green card to achievement of these benchmarks—which include an employment authorization system for all employers, biographical exit tracking at airports and seaports, and substantial completion of two border strategies—is presented as a guarantee that this scenario of serial amnesties would not happen. Unfortunately, those triggers are, in a very real sense, beside the point.

The other triggers mentioned in Sec. 3—those allowing the granting of the initial RPI status—are the submission by the Department of Homeland Security of two plans: A "Comprehensive Southern Border Security Strategy" and a "Southern Border Fencing Strategy."

Since similar plans have been frequently offered over the years, this isn't much of a hurdle.

And yet it's the only hurdle that matters because receipt of Registered Provisional Immigrant status *is* the amnesty—that is to say, it represents the transformation of the illegal alien into a person who is lawfully admitted to the United States.

RPI status brings with it work authorization, a legitimate Social Security account, driver's license, travel documents—in effect, Green Card Lite. It is only the upgrade of this status to that of lawful permanent resident—Green Card Premium, if you will—that is on hold until the enforcement benchmarks are satisfied. But the political and bureaucratic incentives to press for the achievement of those enforcement benchmarks are blunted by the fact that the amnesty has already happened. With people "out of the shadows" and no longer "undocumented," the urgency to meet enforcement deadlines would evaporate, especially in the face of determined opposition to enforcement by business and civil liberties groups.

To use an analogy, if you're flying to the West Coast, it doesn't ultimately matter whether you're in coach or first class—your destination is the same. By the same token, whether or not the beneficiary of the RPI amnesty is upgraded to a green card, the destination is the same—the ability to live and work in the United States. An upgrade from coach to first class may actually be more consequential than the upgrade from RPI to permanent residence; while the former results in wider seats and free drinks, all a green card offers that RPI status does not is the right to apply for citizenship, something most recipients of green cards from the IRCA amnesty had not done a quarter century after the enactment of the law.

And many of those who receive the RPI amnesty are likely to do so fraudulently. Reading Sec. 2101 harkens back to the 1986 Immigration Reform and Control Act's Special Agricultural Worker program, which the *New York Times* called "one of the most extensive immigration frauds ever perpetrated against the United States Government." The Justice Department's Office of Inspector General described it this way:

> To be eligible for adjustment of status under the SAW provisions, the applicant had to prove with documentation that he or she had worked in an agricultural enterprise in the United States for 90 days in each calendar year from 1984 through 1986, or for 90 days between May 1985 and May 1986. The evidence of having engaged in such work, INS employees believed, was often forged and sold to undocumented individuals seeking U.S. residency. *Given the crush of applications under the program and the relative fewer investigative resources, INS approved applications absent explicit proof that they were in fact fraudulent.*

("An Investigation of the Immigration and Naturalization Service's Citizenship USA Initiative," USDoJ [U.S. Department of Justice] OIG, July 2000, http://www.justice.gov/oig/special/0007/listpdf.htm, p. 72; emphasis added)

When Sec. 2101 of S 744 is considered in this light, the sources of fraud become apparent:

• If IRCA created a "crush" of applications when only three million people applied, what should we call the workload that DHS will face when triple the number of people—at least—apply for the RPI amnesty? The administrative capacity does not exist to handle this properly, which all but guarantees that most applications will be rubber-stamped by overwhelmed DHS staff.

• The bill says DHS "may interview," not "shall interview," applicants for the RPI amnesty. Given the aforementioned crush, it is unlikely many will be interviewed. In fact, the current DACA amnesty … is a good model for how the administration would manage S 744's amnesty provisions. DACA processing is almost entirely paper-based, with few interviews, resulting in the approval of 99.5 percent of applications. And yet the number of cases so far decided amounts to perhaps one-fiftieth the number likely to apply for the RPI amnesty.

• S 744 allows affidavits by non-relatives regarding the work or education history of RPI amnesty applicants. Fraudulent affidavits were common among IRCA applicants, with some small farmers claiming to have employed hundreds of illegal-alien farmworkers. The temptation to fraud will be great in any program giving away something as valuable as the RPI amnesty, but the ability to investigate fraudulent affidavits will be extremely limited given the millions of applicants. And there is no realistic level of fees or penalties that could raise enough money to hire enough staff to follow up on questionable affidavits. They will be approved, as in the 1980s, absent specific proof that they're fraudulent.

• The current bill also contains a confidentiality clause, prohibiting the use of any information provided by illegal alien applicants for other purposes. This means illegal aliens with little likelihood of approval are free to apply and try their luck, knowing that there's no downside, and a significant upside.

• As a corollary to this, there is no requirement that rejected applicants be immediately taken into custody and deported. In fact, the bill specifically says that failure to qualify does not require DHS to commence removal proceedings. Again, unqualified applicants would have nothing to lose in applying, in the hope that they could fall through the cracks and get approved, something certain to happen to a significant number of people.

• As an additional incentive to fraudulent applicants, S 744 provides de facto work authorization to those merely *applying* for the RPI amnesty, pending the adjudication of the application. Application alone also forestalls removal, making a frivolous application an attractive option for illegal aliens with no chance at amnesty.

We don't have to speculate about the consequences of such widespread fraud. Mahmoud "The Red" Abouhalima was an Egyptian illegal alien driving a cab in New York when he fraudulently—and successfully—applied for amnesty as a farmworker. This legal status allowed him to travel to Afghanistan for terrorist training, which he put to use in the first World Trade Center attack in 1993.

A co-conspirator, Mohammed Salameh, also applied for the 1986 amnesty but was, remarkably, turned down. But since that amnesty, like the one in S 744, did not mandate the removal of failed applicants, Salameh was able to remain and assist in the 1993 bombing.

S 744 thus places amnesty before enforcement, and ensures an amnesty process that would reward fraud. A better approach would be to make the *initial* legalization dependent on the bill's enforcement provisions, rather than a future upgrade in status. The enforcement provisions themselves would have to be strengthened by requiring, for instance, biometric exit-tracking at all ports of entry, not just airports and seaports—as it already required in current law and as was recommended by the 9/11 Commission. Another trigger for initial legalization would have to be an explicit statement by Congress that states and localities are not preempted from enforcing civil immigration law.

And any future amnesty would need to be constructed differently. Not only should all lies, however small, be punished with criminal prosecution, but the amnesty might best be conducted piecemeal, rather than addressing millions of people effectively all at once. That is to say, candidates might be considered as they are apprehended for traffic stops or factory raids or what have you, with those who fail to qualify be removed.

Thank you for the opportunity to speak on this important matter and I look forward to any questions you might have. (http://www.cis.org/Testimony/Krikorian-Senate-Bill-744)

APPENDIX I: FEDERAL PROTECTIONS AGAINST NATIONAL ORIGIN DISCRIMINATION—U.S. DEPARTMENT OF JUSTICE
POTENTIAL DISCRIMINATION AGAINST IMMIGRANTS BASED ON NATIONAL ORIGIN

This brochure, which was issued in October 2008 and is reprinted virtually in its entirety here, is available on the U.S. Department of Justice website (http://www.justice.gov/crt/legalinfo/nordwg_brochure.php). The brochure is also published in Arabic, Cambodian, Chinese, Farsi, French, Haitian Creole, Hindi, Hmong, Korean, Laotian, Punjabi, Russian, Spanish, Tagalog, Urdu, and Vietnamese.

INTRODUCTION

Federal laws prohibit discrimination based on a person's national origin, race, color, religion, disability, sex, and familial status. Laws prohibiting national origin discrimination make it illegal to discriminate because of a person's birthplace, ancestry, culture or language. This means people cannot be denied equal opportunity because they or their family are from another country, because they have a name or accent associated with a national origin group, because they participate in certain customs associated with a national origin group, or because they are married to or associate with people of a certain national origin.

The Department of Justice's Civil Rights Division is concerned that national origin discrimination may go unreported in the United States because victims of discrimination do not know their legal rights, or may be afraid to complain to the government. To address this problem, the Civil Rights Division has established a National Origin Working Group to help citizens and immigrants better understand and exercise their legal rights....

CRIMINAL VIOLATIONS OF CIVIL RIGHTS

- A young man of South Asian descent is assaulted as he leaves a concert at a nightclub. The assailant, a member of a skinhead group, yells racial epithets as he beats the victim unconscious in the club's parking lot with fists and a pipe.

- At Ku Klux Klan meetings, a Klansman tells other members that Mexicans and Puerto Ricans should go "back where they came from." They burn a cross in the front yard of a young Hispanic couple in order to frighten them and force them to leave the neighborhood. Before burning the cross, the defendant displays a gun and gives one of his friends another gun in case the victims try to stop them.

- An American company recruits workers in a small Mexican town, promising them good work at high pay. The company smuggles the Mexicans to the United States in an empty tanker truck. When they finally arrive in the U.S., the workers are threatened, told that if they attempt to leave their factory they will be killed.

The Criminal Section of the Civil Rights Division prosecutes people who are accused of using force or violence to interfere with a person's federally protected rights because of that person's national origin. These rights include areas such as housing, employment, education, or use of public facilities. You can reach the Criminal Section at (202) 514-3204....

DISABILITY RIGHTS

- An HMO that enrolls Medicaid patients tells a Mexican American woman with cerebral palsy to come back another day for an appointment while it provides immediate assistance to others.

This example may be a violation of federal laws that prohibit discrimination because of disability as well as laws that prohibit discrimination because of national origin. If you believe you have been discriminated against because you have a disability you may contact the Disability Rights Section at (800) 514-0301 (voice) or 800-514-0383 (TTY)....

EDUCATION

- A child has difficulty speaking English, but her school does not provide her with the necessary assistance to help her learn English and other subjects.

- A majority Haitian school does not offer honors classes. Other schools in the district that do not have many Haitian students offer both honors and advanced placement courses.

These examples may be violations of federal law, which prohibits discrimination in education because of a person's national origin. The Division's Educational Opportunities Section enforces these laws in elementary and secondary schools as well as public colleges and universities. The Education Section's work addresses discrimination in all aspects of education, including assignment of students to schools and classes, transportation of students, hiring and placement of faculty and administrators, distribution of school resources, and provision of educational programs that assist limited English speaking students in learning English.

To file a complaint or for more information, contact the Education Section at (202) 514-4092....

EMPLOYMENT

- A transit worker's supervisor makes frequent racial epithets against the worker because his family is from Iran. Last week, the boss put up a fake sign on the bulletin board telling everyone not to trust the worker because he is a terrorist.

- A woman who immigrated from Russia applies for a job as an accountant. The employer turns her down because she speaks with an accent even though she is able to perform the job requirements.

- A food processing company requires applicants who appear or sound foreign to show work authorization documents before allowing them to complete an employment application while native born Caucasian applicants are not required to show any documents before completing employment applications. Moreover, the documents of the ethnic employees are more closely scrutinized and more often rejected than the same types of documents shown by native born Caucasian employees.

These examples may be violations of the law that prohibits discrimination against an employee or job applicant because of his or her national origin. This means an employer cannot discipline, harass, fire, refuse to hire or promote a person because of his or her national origin. If you believe an employer, labor organization or employment agency has discriminated against you because of your national origin, contact:

Equal Employment Opportunity Commission

(800) 669-4000

(Employers with 15 or more employees)

Office of Special Counsel

(800) 255-7688

(Employers with 4 to 14 employees)

Employment Litigation Section

(202) 514-3831

(State or local government employer with a pattern or practice of illegal discrimination)

In addition, an employer may violate federal law by requiring specific work authorization documents, such as a green card, or rejecting such documents only from applicants of certain national origins. For more information or to file a charge, contact the Division's Office of Special Counsel at the above... toll-free number.

HOUSING

- A Native Hawaiian family is looking for an apartment. They are told by the rental agent that no apartments are available, even though apartments are available and are shown to white applicants.

- A realtor shows a Latino family houses only in Latino neighborhoods and refuses to show the family houses in white neighborhoods.

These examples may be violations of the federal Fair Housing Act. That law prohibits discrimination because of national origin, race, color, sex, religion, disability, or familial status (presence of children under 18) in housing. Individual complaints of discrimination may be reported to the Department of Housing and Urban Development (HUD) at (800) 669-9777. If you believe there is a pattern or practice of discrimination, contact the Division's Housing and Civil Enforcement Section at (202) 514-4713.

LENDING

- A Latina woman is charged a higher interest rate and fees than white male customers who have similar financial histories and apply for the same type of loan.

This example may be a violation of federal laws that prohibit discrimination in lending because of national origin, race, color, sex, religion, disability and marital status or because any of a person's income comes from public assistance. If you believe you have been denied a loan because of your national origin or other protected reason, you may ask the lender for an explanation in writing of why your application was denied.

If the loan is for a home mortgage, home improvement, or other housing-related reasons, you may file a complaint with the Department of Housing and Urban Development at (800) 669-9777. If the loan is for purposes other than housing (such as a car loan), you may file a complaint either with the Division's Housing and Civil Enforcement Section or with the lender's regulatory agency. If your experience was part of a pattern or practice of discrimination you may also call the Housing and Civil Enforcement Section at (202) 514-4713, to obtain more information about your rights or to file a complaint.

PUBLIC ACCOMMODATIONS

- In a restaurant, a group of Asian Americans waits for over an hour to be served, while white and Latino customers receive prompt service.

- Haitian American visitors to a hotel are told they must pay in cash rather than by credit card, are charged higher rates than other customers, and are not provided with the same amenities, such as towels and soap.

These examples may be violations of federal laws that prohibit discrimination because of national origin, race, color, or religion in places of public accommodation. Public accommodations include hotels, restaurants, and places of entertainment. If you believe you have been denied access to or equal enjoyment of a public accommodation where there is a pattern or practice of discrimination, contact the Housing and Civil Enforcement Section at (202) 514-4713....

POLICE MISCONDUCT

- Police officers constantly pull over cars driven by Latinos, for certain traffic violations, but rarely pull over white drivers for the same violations.

- A police officer questioning a man of Vietnamese origin on the street gets angry when the man is unable to answer his questions because he does not speak English. The Officer arrests the man for disorderly conduct.

These examples may be violations of the Equal Protection Clause of the United States Constitution. They may also be violations of the Omnibus Crime Control and Safe Streets Act of 1968. That law prohibits discrimination because of national origin, race, color, religion, or sex by a police department that gets federal funds through the U.S. Department of Justice. They may also violate Title VI of the Civil Rights Act of 1964, which prohibits discrimination by law enforcement agencies that receive any federal financial assistance, including asset forfeiture property.

Complaints of individual discrimination can be filed with the Coordination and Review Section ... at 1-888-848-5306.

Complaints of individual discrimination may also be filed with the Office of Justice Programs...at (202) 307-0690.

The Special Litigation Section investigates and litigates complaints that a police department has a pattern or practice of discriminating on the basis of national origin. To file a complaint, contact the Special Litigation Section at (202) 514-6255....

CIVIL RIGHTS OF INSTITUTIONALIZED PERSONS

- A jail will not translate disciplinary hearings for detainees who do not speak English.

- A state's psychiatric hospital has no means of providing treatment for people who do not speak English.

These examples may be violations of the Equal Protection Clause of the United States Constitution. The Special Litigation Section enforces the constitutional rights of people held in state or local government institutions, such as prisons, jails, juvenile correctional facilities, mental health facilities, developmental disability or mental retardation facilities, and nursing homes. If you are a resident of any such facility and you believe there is a pattern or practice of discrimination based on your national origin, contact the Special Litigation Section at (202) 514-6255....

FEDERALLY ASSISTED PROGRAMS

- A local social services agency does not provide information or job training in Korean even though one quarter of local residents speak only Korean.

- A hospital near the Texas/Mexico border dresses its security officers in clothes that look like INS uniforms to scare Latinos away from the emergency room. Latino patients are told to bring their own translators before they can see a doctor.

These examples may be violations of federal laws that prohibit discrimination because of national origin, race or color by recipients of federal funds. If you believe you have been discriminated against by a state or local government agency or an organization that receives funds from the federal government, you may file a complaint with the Division's Coordination and Review Section at (888) 848-5306.... The Coordination and Review Section will refer the complaint to the federal funding agency that is primarily responsible for enforcing non-discrimination prohibitions applicable to its recipients.

VOTING

- Despite requests from voters in a large Spanish-speaking community, election officials refuse to provide election materials, including registration forms and sample ballots, in Spanish or to allow Spanish speakers to bring translators into the voting booth.

- A polling official requires a dark-skinned voter, who speaks with a foreign accent and has an unfamiliar last name, to provide proof of American citizenship, but does not require proof of citizenship from white voters.

The election officials' conduct may violate the federal laws prohibiting voting discrimination. The Voting Rights Acts do not specifically prohibit national origin discrimination. However, provisions of the Acts make it illegal to limit or deny the right to vote of any citizen not only because of race or color, but also because of membership in a language minority group. In addition, the Acts also require in certain jurisdictions that election materials and assistance be provided in languages other than English.

Additionally, Section 208 of the Voting Rights Act allows voters, who need help because of blindness, disability or because they cannot read or write, to bring someone (other than an employer or union representative) to help. This means that a voter who needs help reading the ballot in English can bring a friend or family member to translate. In some places, election officials must provide information, such as voter registration and the ballot, in certain language(s) other than English. This can include interpreters to help voters vote.

If you believe that you have been discriminated against in voting or denied assistance in casting your ballot, you may contact the Division's Voting Section at (800) 253-3931....

When you call any of the offices listed in this brochure, the phone will be answered in English. If you need an interpreter, tell the operator what language you speak. The operator will put you on hold while an interpreter is found. Please do not hang up. Through a language interpreter service, we are equipped to assist callers in all languages.

Note: For persons with disabilities, this document will be available in large print, audio tape, computer disc, and Braille.

APPENDIX II
MAPS OF THE WORLD

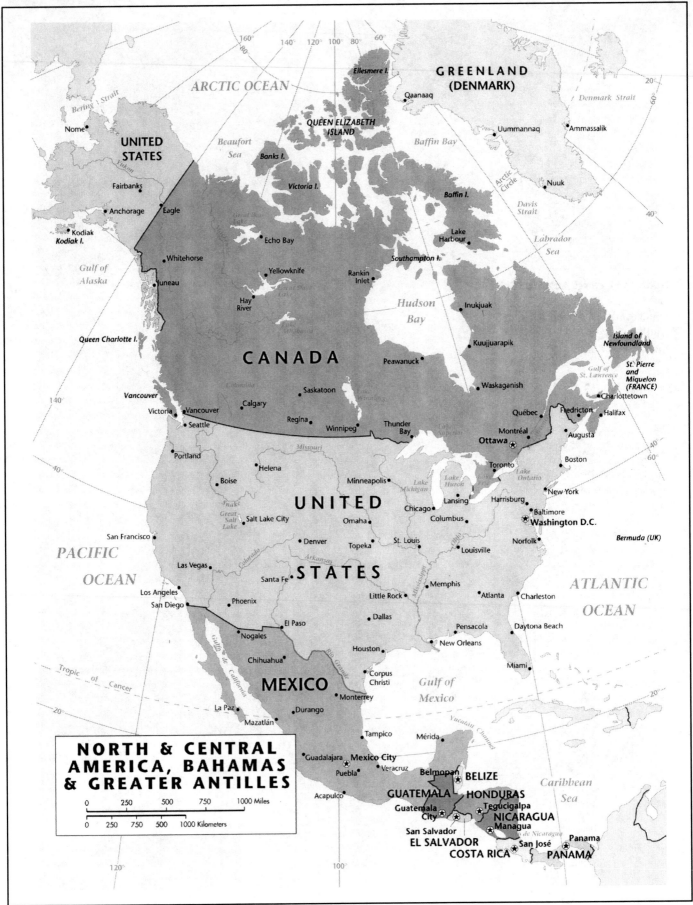

North and Central America, regional map, illustration by Maryland Cartographics. Reproduced by permission of Gale, a part of Cengage Learning.

South America, regional map, inset of the Caribbean region, illustration by Maryland Cartographics. Reproduced by permission of Gale, a part of Cengage Learning.

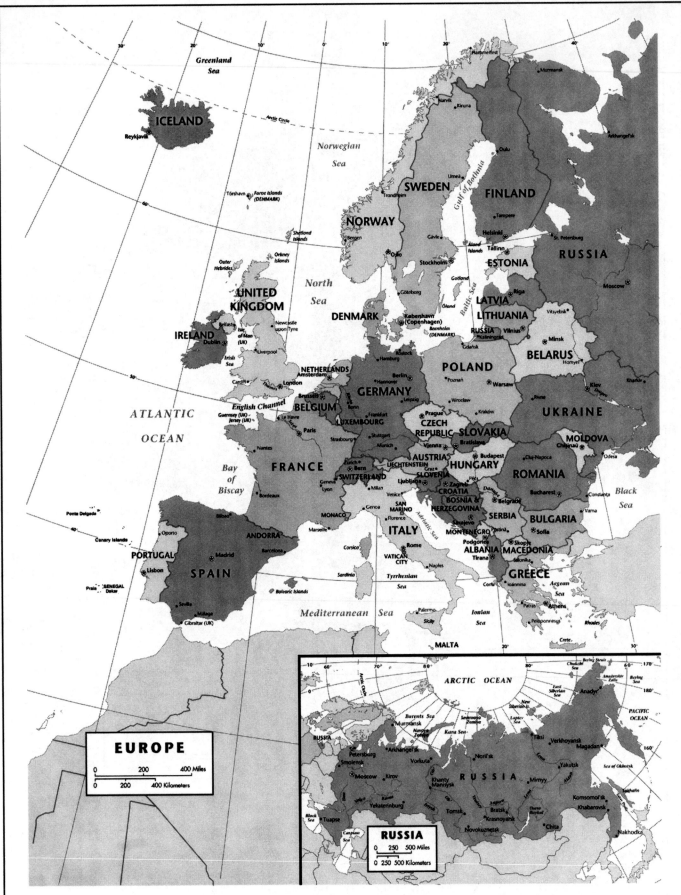

Europe, regional map with inset of Russia, illustration by Maryland Cartographics. Reproduced by permission of Gale, a part of Cengage Learning.

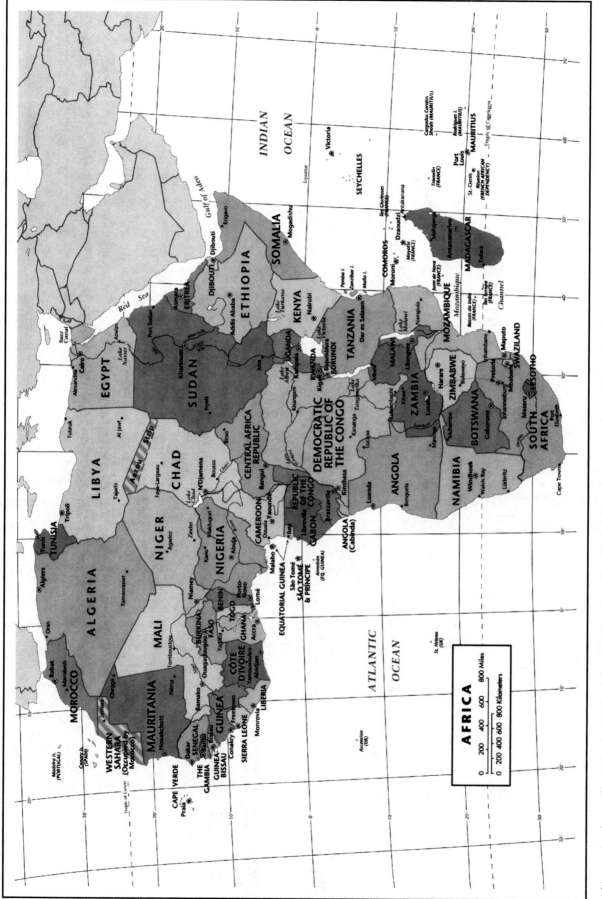

Africa, regional map, illustration by Maryland Cartographics. Reproduced by permission of Gale, a part of Cengage Learning.

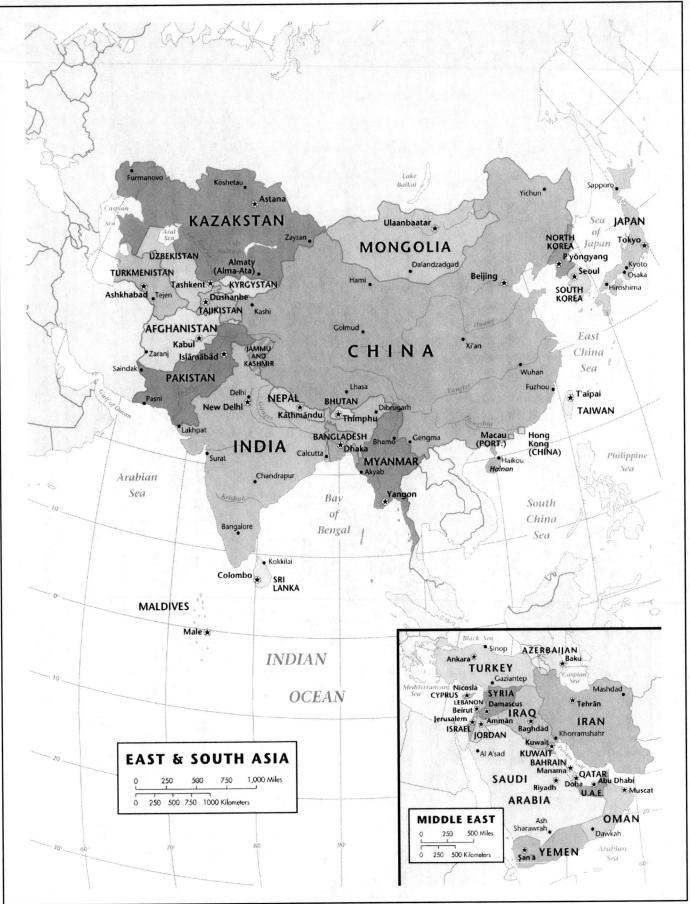

East and South Asia, regional map of inset of the Middle East, illustration by Maryland Cartographics. Reproduced by permission of Gale, a part of Cengage Learning.

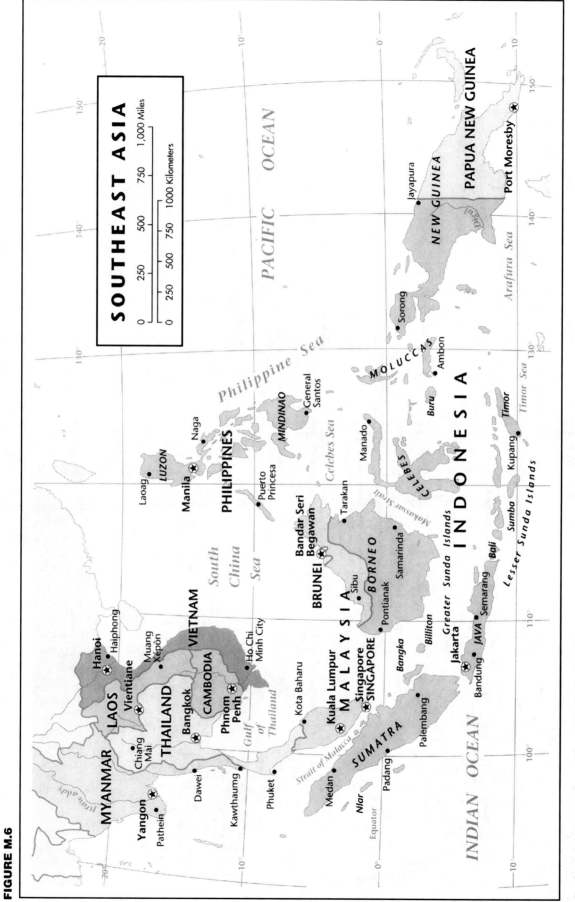

SOUTHEAST ASIA

Southeast Asia, regional map, illustration by Maryland Cartographics. Reproduced by permission of Gale, a part of Cengage Learning.

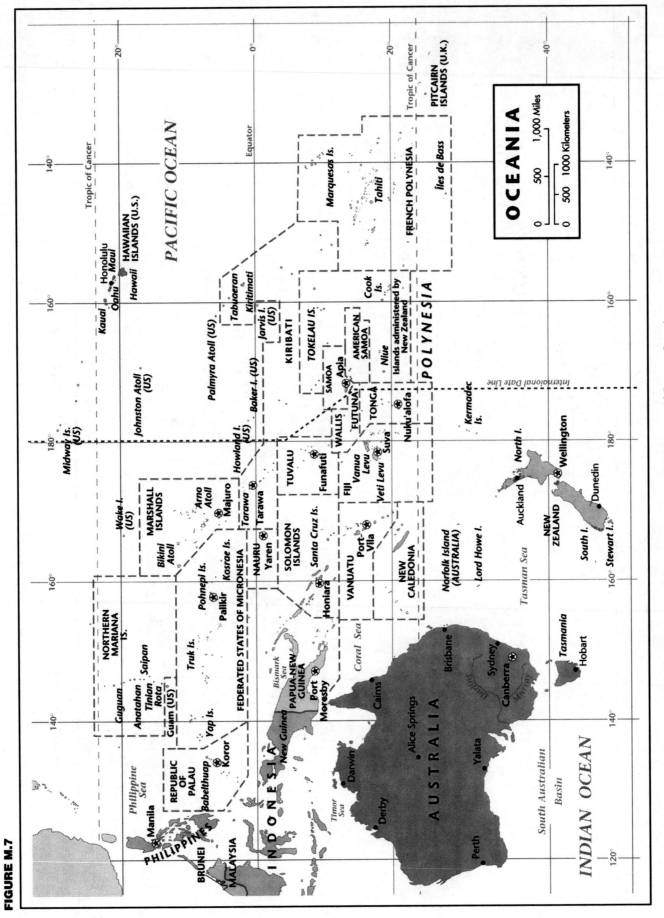

Oceania, regional map, illustration by Maryland Cartographics. Reproduced by permission of Gale, a part of Cengage Learning.

IMPORTANT NAMES
AND ADDRESSES

American Action Forum
1747 Pennsylvania Avenue NW, Fifth Floor
Washington, DC 20009
(202) 559-6420
URL: http://www.americanactionforum.org/

American Civil Liberties Union
125 Broad St., 18th Floor
New York, NY 10004
(212) 549-2500
URL: http://www.aclu.org/

American Immigration Lawyers Association
1331 G St. NW, Ste. 300
Washington, DC 20005-3142
(202) 507-7600
FAX: (202) 783-7853
URL: http://www.aila.org/

Amnesty International USA
Five Penn Plaza
New York, NY 10001
(212) 807-8400
FAX: (212) 627-1451
E-mail: aimember@aiusa.org
URL: http://www.amnestyusa.org/

The Brookings Institution
1775 Massachusetts Ave. NW
Washington, DC 20036
(202) 797-6000
E-mail: communications@brookings.edu
URL: http://www.brookings.edu/

Cato Institute
1000 Massachusetts Ave. NW
Washington, DC 20001-5403
(202) 842-0200
URL: http://www.cato.org/

Center for American Progress
1333 H St. NW, 10th Floor
Washington, DC 20005
(202) 682-1611
URL: http://www.americanprogress.org/

Center for Immigration Studies
1629 K St. NW, Ste. 600
Washington, DC 20006

(202) 466-8185
FAX: (202) 466-8076
URL: http://www.cis.org/

**Federation for American
Immigration Reform**
25 Massachusetts Ave. NW, Ste. 330
Washington, DC 20001
(202) 328-7004
1-877-627-3247
FAX: (202) 387-3447
URL: http://www.fairus.org/

**Immigration Policy Center
American Immigration Council**
1331 G St. NW, Ste. 200
Washington, DC 20005
(202) 507-7500
URL: http://www.immigrationpolicy.org/

Institute of International Education
809 United Nations Plaza
New York, NY 10017
(212) 883-8200
FAX: (212) 984-5452
URL: http://www.iie.org/

Migration Policy Institute
1400 16th St. NW, Ste. 300
Washington, DC 20036
(202) 266-1940
FAX: (202) 266-1900
E-mail: Info@MigrationPolicy.org
URL: http://www.migrationpolicy.org/

National Conference of State Legislatures
444 N. Capitol St. NW, Ste. 515
Washington, DC 20001
(202) 624-5400
FAX: (202) 737-1069
URL: http://www.ncsl.org/

National Council of La Raza
Raul Yzaguirre Bldg.
1126 16th St. NW, Ste. 600
Washington, DC 20036-4845
(202) 785-1670
FAX: (202) 776-1792

E-mail: comments@nclr.org
URL: http://www.nclr.org/

National Foundation for American Policy
2111 Wilson Blvd., Ste. 700
Arlington, VA 22201
(703) 351-5042
URL: http://www.nfap.com/

National Immigration Forum
50 F St. NW, Ste. 300
Washington, DC 20001
(202) 347-0040
FAX: (202) 347-0058
URL: http://www.immigrationforum.org/

Pew Research Center
1615 L St. NW, Ste. 700
Washington, DC 20036
(202) 419-4300
FAX: (202) 419-4349
URL: http://www.pewresearch.org/

Refugee Council USA
1628 16th St. NW
Washington, DC 20009
(202) 319-2102
FAX: (202) 319-2104
E-mail: info@rcusa.org
URL: http://www.rcusa.org/

**United Nations High Commissioner
for Refugees**
Case Postale 2500
CH-1211 Genève 2 Dépôt, Switzerland
(011-41) 22-739-8111
FAX: (011-41) 22-739-7377
URL: http://www.unhcr.org/cgi-bin/texis/
vtx/home

**U.S. Committee for Refugees and
Immigrants**
2231 Crystal Dr., Ste. 350
Arlington, VA 22202-3711
(703) 310-1130
FAX: (703) 769-4241
URL: http://www.refugees.org/

RESOURCES

The U.S. government provides a great deal of authoritative statistical information concerning immigration and naturalization. Much of the information in this book comes from branches of the U.S. Department of Homeland Security (DHS). Beyond the websites of the DHS branches, a primary source of data is the annual *Yearbook of Immigration Statistics*, an online publication of the U.S. Citizenship and Immigration Services. Other DHS reports that provide valuable data include *Estimates of the Unauthorized Immigrant Population Residing in the United States: January 2012* (Bryan Baker and Nancy Rytina, March 2013), *Refugees and Asylees: 2013* (Daniel C. Martin and James E. Yankay, August 2014), and *U.S. Lawful Permanent Residents: 2013* (Randall Monger and James Yankay, May 2014).

Another important source of government data on immigration is the U.S. Census Bureau, which collects and distributes a variety of information about the nation's foreign-born population. Helpful data sets include the regularly updated American Community Survey, the Current Population Survey, and the *National Population Projections: Summary Tables*.

The Congressional Budget Office (CBO), an independent and nonpartisan agency responsible for providing economic and budgetary analysis to Congress, has produced a number of reports and briefs that illuminate the economic and budgetary impacts of immigration as well as the projected impacts of changes to immigration law. The CBO reports that were instrumental in the preparation of this volume include *A Description of the Immigrant Population—2013 Update* (May 2013), *The Economic Impact of S.744, the Border Security, Economic Opportunity, and Immigration Modernization Act* (June 2013), and *How Changes in Immigration Policy Might Affect the Federal Budget* (January 2015).

Other government data sources that were central to the compilation of this volume include "Foreign-Born Workers: Labor Force Characteristics—2013" (May 2014) by the U.S. Department of Labor's Bureau of Labor Statistics; *Attorney General's Annual Report to Congress and Assessment of U.S. Government Activities to Combat Trafficking in Persons, Fiscal Year 2012* (July 2014) by the Office of the Attorney General; *Trafficking in Persons Report* (June 2014) by the U.S. Department of State; and *Annual Report, October 1, 2011–September 30, 2012* (July 2013) by the Department of Labor's Office of Foreign Labor Certification.

Independent nonprofit organizations that study immigration also provide useful statistics and perspective on the issue. The Institute of International Education's annually updated *Open Doors Data* (November 2014) offers recent and historical data on international student populations. Various reports and issue briefs by the American Action Forum, the Center for American Progress, the Center for Immigration Studies, the Gallup Organization, the Migration Policy Center, and the Pew Research Center, among many others, centrally informed the presentation of issues in this book.

INDEX

Statistical information

asylees, by country of nationality, 83t, 84t

budgetary effects of immigration reform, 120t, 121t

citizen and noncitizen demographics, 108t

countries of last residence, 1820–2013, 5t–8t

Deferred Action for Childhood Arrivals, 102t, 103t

denied entry, by reason, 13t

Department of Homeland Security budget, 113f

deportations, 100t

economic effects of immigration reform, 119f

employment, by occupation and sex, 49t

employment status, 47t–48t

fertility, 45f

foreign students, 72t

foreign students, by countries of origin, 73t

foreign-born population, 1850–2010, 20f

foreign-born population, by place of birth, 40t–41t

foreign-born population, by state of residence, 42t

foreign-born workers, 110f

gross domestic product effects of immigration reform, 118(f6.6)

H-1 visas approved, by occupation, 69t

H-class visas issued, 67f

household type and size, 45t, 46t

immigrants granted permanent resident status, 1820–2013, 4t

income, 51t–52t, 53t–54t

international adoption, 63(f3.4), 63t

language issues, 116f

legal permanent resident flow, by age, 62(t3.20)

legal permanent resident flow, by city, 61(t3.19)

legal permanent resident flow, by gender, 62(t3.21)

legal permanent resident flow, by marital status, 62(t3.22)

legal permanent resident flow, by region and country of birth, 60t

legal permanent resident flow, by state, 61(t3.18)

legal permanent residents, by type and major class of admission, 57t–58t

legal permanent residents, flow of, 59f

Los Angeles County immigrant population, 134t–135t

Los Angeles County school enrollment and language characteristics, 136t

marital status, by sex, nativity, and citizenship status, 43t

marital status, by sex and world region at birth, 44t

Miami-Dade County immigrant population, 137t–138t

Miami-Dade County school enrollment and language characteristics, 139t

naturalization, by region of birth, 63(f3.5)

New York City immigrant population, 131t–132t

New York City school enrollment and language characteristics, 133t

nonimmigrant admissions, by class, 65t–66t

occupations for H-2 visa recipients, 70f

population projections, 124t

population projections, by nativity, 38t

population projections, by race/ethnicity, 125t–128t

poverty status, 55t, 56t

projections of foreign-born population, by sex and age, 39t

race/ethnicity of U.S. population, 1790–1990, 2t–3t

refugee admission ceilings, 79t

refugee admissions, 1900–2013, 79f

refugee arrivals, by admission category, 80(t4.2)

refugee arrivals, by country of nationality, 80(t4.3)

returns and removals of aliens, 75f

temporary foreign workers, 68t

tier placement of countries' efforts to eliminate human trafficking, 88t

trafficking and violence victims, 87t

trafficking victims, 85t, 86t

unaccompanied children, Border Patrol apprehension of, 98t

unauthorized immigrants, 93f

unauthorized immigrants, by age and sex, 95(t5.7)

unauthorized immigrants, by country of birth, 94(t5.4)

unauthorized immigrants, by country of birth and state of residence, 95(t5.6)

unauthorized immigrants, by region of birth, 94(f5.2)

unauthorized immigrants, by state of residence, 94(t5.5)

unauthorized immigrants' periods of entry, 93t

visa application backlogs, 92t

visa denials, 74t–75t

wage estimates and immigration reform, 118(f6.7)

STEM degrees, 71

Student and Exchange Visitor Information System (SEVIS), 28

Students, foreign. See Foreign students

T

Taxes, 9, 11, 110, 118–119

Temporary Agricultural Worker Program, 68–70

Temporary protected status, 25–26

Temporary status

Immigration Act of 1907, 11

Immigration Act of 1990, 25

refugees, 15

temporary foreign workers, 64, 67–71, 67f, 68t, 69t, 70f

Terrorism, 78, 105, 153, 158

Tests, naturalization, 59

Texas, 97–98, 100

Torture victims, 89–90

Torture Victims Relief Act, 89–90

Trafficking and violence victims, 84–87, 85t, 86t, 87t

Trafficking Victims Protection Act, 84–87, 97

Trafficking Victims Protection Reauthorization Act, 84

Transactional Records Access Clearinghouse, 84

Transparency and Responsibility Using State Tools (TRUST) Acts, 35, 104

Transportation funds for refugees, 87

Truman, Harry S., 14

TRUST (Transparency and Responsibility Using State Tools) Acts, 35, 104

U

Unaccompanied children, 89, 97–98, 98t

Unauthorized immigrants

age and sex, 95(t5.7)

Canadian border, 105

by country of birth and state of residence, 95(t5.6)

Cutler, Michael W., testimony of, 152–154

deferred action programs, 29–32, 151–152

enforcement costs, 113–115

history, 16

Illegal Immigration Reform and Immigrant Responsibility Act, 26

immigrant-friendly state legislation, 34–35

immigration reform, 116–120

Immigration Reform and Control Act, 20–21

Murguía, Janet, statement of, 143–146

Obama, Barack, immigration reform address by, 142

period of entry, 93t

population estimates, 92–98, 93f, 94f, 94t

quota laws, impact of, 12

state and local immigration enforcement, 154–157

unaccompanied children, 89, 97–98, 98t

water crossings, 104–105

Undocumented immigrants. See Unauthorized immigrants

Unemployment rate, 42

CPSIA information can be obtained
at www.ICGtesting.com
Printed in the USA
FFOW05n1828170915